Abstracts of

Chester County

Pennsylvania

Land Records

Volume 2

1729-1745

Carol Bryant

HERITAGE BOOKS
2006

HERITAGE BOOKS
AN IMPRINT OF HERITAGE BOOKS, INC.

Books, CDs, and more—Worldwide

For our listing of thousands of titles see our website at
www.HeritageBooks.com

Published 2006 by
HERITAGE BOOKS, INC.
Publishing Division
65 East Main Street
Westminster, Maryland 21157-5026

Copyright © 1997 F. Edward Wright

Other books by Carol Bryant:

Abstracts of Chester County, Pennsylvania Land Records: Volume 1: 1681-1730

Abstracts of Chester County, Pennsylvania Land Records: Volume 3: 1745-1753

Abstracts of Chester County, Pennsylvania Land Records: Volume 4: 1753-1758

Abstracts of Chester County, Pennsylvania Land Records: Volume 5: 1758-1765

New Castle County, Delaware Land Records, 1673-1710

New Castle County, Delaware Land Records, 1715-1728

All rights reserved. No part of this book may be reproduced or transmitted in any form or by any means, electronic or mechanical, including photocopying, recording or by any information storage and retrieval system without written permission from the author, except for the inclusion of brief quotations in a review.

International Standard Book Number: 978-1-58549-008-3

CONTENTS

Introduction v

Excerpts from "Holme's Map of the Province of Pennsylvania, with Names of Original Purchasers":
    Chester County (now Delaware County) viii
    Chester County (Eastern present-day Chester and Western present-day Delaware counties) x

Land Records
    Book A 1
    Book B 83
    Book C 121
    Book D 174

Index 239

INTRODUCTION

When the English eventually gained control of the region which became Chester County authority was established at Upland (later named Chester). Under the Duke of Kent the Upland court as early as 1672 was concerned with the area from the mouth of Christiana Creek (Wilmington, Delaware) northward to the limits of European settlement near the falls of the Delaware River at Trenton. Among its responsibilities the Upland court was empowered to deal with land titles. See *Memoirs of the Historical Society of Pennsylvania, Vol. 7, The Record of the Court at Upland, 1676-1681*. Philadelphia, 1860. For the preceding periods see "Papers Relating to the Dutch and Swedish Settlements on the Delaware River," *Pennsylvania Archives*, Series 2, 7:485-873.

William Penn received a grant to the territory of Pennsylvania in 1681. Chester County was established as one of the original counties of Pennsylvania under William Penn in 1682. The line between Philadelphia and Chester counties began at the mouth of Bough Creek on the Delaware River, went northwest up Bough and Mill creeks and turned northeast along the west side of the liberty lands, to the Schuylkill River and then followed the Schuylkill northwest. Deeds begin in 1688. Lancaster County was formed from Chester County in 1729 and Delaware County was formed in 1789. A portion of Chester County was given up to form a part of Berks County in 1752 (along with portions from Lancaster and Philadelphia counties).

The port town of Upland was established on the Delaware River in 1660, later named Chester. Quakers began arriving in large numbers in 1677 from western England. By 1683 Upland Township had been partitioned to form Chester Township, and the town of Upland was renamed Chester. Additional Quakers from western England and northeastern Ireland rapidly expanded the population into southern Chester County and in 1789 a proposal was made before the Pennsylvania Assembly to move the county seat from Chester to a more central location. Representatives from the borough of Chester blocked the proposal, which led to a compromise that allowed the county seat to be moved to Bradford Township and the creation of Delaware County with its county seat in Chester. Today the city of Chester is the county seat of Delaware County and West Chester is the county seat of Chester County.

The first volume of this work begins after the formation of Chester County as one of the original counties. Among the first records appear to be the recording of patents issued by Penn in 1681. In some instances Penn is shown as signing the deed and in other cases they were signed by William Markham, Penn's cousin, whom he had appointed as Lieutenant Governor in April 1681. This volume concludes with the recording of records in 1730 and thus includes the entire period before Lancaster County was formed.

In this work we have included references to all persons found in the records. Our primary goal was to reveal information useful to genealogical research. We have eliminated the proforma legal requirements and also the specific descriptions of the metes and bounds of the tracts - all for reasons of economy. The reader is invited to acquire complete copies of the records through the county courthouse or by ordering microfilm through a local Family History Center (LDS library).

For a thorough discussion of the complex history of the administration of the land under William Penn see Donna Bingham Munger, *Pennsylvania Land Records. A History and Guide for Research*. Published by Scholarly Resources, Inc., Wilmington, DE. (1991).

F. Edward Wright
Westminster, Maryland
1997

CHESTER BOOK E - Volume 5

Lease & Release. On 19 & 20 May 1730 William Branson of the City of Philadelphia, joiner, & Elizabeth his wife, to Francis Ferris of Caln, weaver. William Branson & Elizabeth his wife for £47.4.5 granted to Francis Ferris a tract in Caln bounded by land of Nicholas Smith containing 122 acres, being part of 1,225 acres granted to William Branson by William Penn on 28 Oct 1700, recorded Book A, Vol 4, Page 102. Signed William Branson & Elizabeth Branson. Delivered in the presence of George Howell, John Buller, & William Parsons. Recorded 19 Nov 1730. (E5:1).

Lease & Release. On 2 Feb 1708 John Palmer & Thomas Palmer of the City of Philadelphia, yeomen, sons of George Palmer, dec., to David Lloyd of the City of Philadelphia, gentleman. Whereas by deed dated 26 & 27 Apr 1682 William Penn granted to George Palmer of Onesuch in the County of Surrey, yeoman, for £100 a tract 5,000 acres in the province. George Palmer made his will dated 4 Sep 1682 and devised to his son John Palmer 800 acres & to his son Thomas Palmer 800 acres and soon after died. Thomas Palmer was surveyed 800 acres & John Palmer was surveyed 420 acres, part of his 800 acres. Now John Palmer & Thomas Palmer for £73 granted to David Lloyd a tract for one whole year 1,220 acres. Signed John Palmer & Thomas Palmer. Delivered in the presence of Joshua Lawrence, Richard Newcomb & Richard Heath. Recorded 7 Oct 1729. (E5:3).

Release. On 7 Oct 1730 Abraham Clement of Bristol in the County of Bucks, tailor, to Jeremiah Clement of Chester, hatter, both sons of Abraham Clement. Whereas Abraham Clement the eldest son of Abraham Clement, dec., for £30 grant to Jeremiah Clement all my right in the lands devised to me by my late father. Signed Abraham Clement. Delivered in the presence of James Trego & Benjamin Yard. Recorded 9 Oct 1730. (E5:5).

Release. On 2 Feb 1708 George Palmer of the City of Philadelphia, son of George Palmer, dec., late of Nonesuch in the County of Surrey, yeoman, to David Lloyd of the City of Philadelphia, gentleman. Whereas George Palmer by Letter of Attorney dated 25 Jan 1703 appointed John Palmer his attorney, recorded in Philadelphia, Book D2, Vol 5, Page 126, on 16 Sep last past. Now John Palmer in the name of George Palmer £73 grants to David Lloyd 1220 acres, part of the 5,000 acres granted to George Palmer the father by William Penn. Signed John Palmer. Delivered in the presence of Joshua Lawerence, Richard Newcombe & Richard Heath. Recorded 17 Oct 1729. (E5:7).

Lease & Release. On 20 May 1715 William Palmer of the City of Philadelphia, wheelwright, one of the sons of George Palmer, dec., to David Lloyd of Chester County, gentleman. Whereas on 2 Feb 1708 John Palmer & Thomas Palmer, sons of George Palmer, dec., granted to David Lloyd 1220 acres & whereas by another deed dated 2 Feb 1708, then of the City of Philadelphia, mariner, son of George Palmer & his brother John Palmer, confirmed unto David Lloyd the 1,220 acres. Now William Palmer for 5 shillings confirms to David Lloyd the 1,220 acres. Signed William Palmer. Delivered in the presence of Thomas Palmer, Peter Evans & John Cadwalader. Recorded 17 Oct 1729. (E5:8).

Lease & Release. On 1 & 2 Oct 1729 Anthony Baldwin of Birmingham, yeoman, & Margery his wife, to Thomas Smith of Birmingham, yeoman. Whereas John Harnum of Concord, yeoman, & Margery his wife, by deed dated 10 Jan 1722, granted to Anthony Baldwin 70 acres in Birmingham. Anthony Baldwin & Margery his wife for £44 granted to Thomas Smith a tract in Birmingham bounded by land of Henry Gunston, Robert Harnum, late of Edmond Butcher, late of Samuel Scott, Thomas Caldry & Robert Chaldont, containing 70 acres. Signed Anthony Baldwin & Margery Baldwin. Delivered in the presence of James Trego & Joseph Parker. Recorded 27 Mar 1730. (E5:9).

Lease & Release. On 11 & 12 Mar 1730/1 Joseph Vernon of Nether Providence, yeoman, eldest son & heir of Randolph Vernon, late of Providence, dec., & Lydia his wife, to Jacob Vernon of Thornbury, yeoman, 2nd son of Randolph Vernon. Whereas John Simcock & Ralph Fishbourne & Elizabeth his wife, & Thomas England by deed dated 12 Dec 1699 did grant to Randolph Vernon a tract containing 500 acres, & whereas Randolph Vernon by deed dated 22 June 1709 did grant to Jacob Vernon the 500 acres. Joseph Vernon & Lydia his wife for 10 shillings confirm to Jacob Vernon a tract in Thornbury where Jacob now dwells bounded by land of George Pearce, Benjamin Hickman, Benjamin Mendenhall, John Cook, Richard Marsh & John Bellars containing 500 acres. Signed Joseph Vernon & Lydia Vernon. Delivered in the presence of Jacob Howell & John Chamberlin. Recorded 13 Mar 1730/1. (E5:12).

Lease & Release. On 22 June 1704 David Davies of Radnor, gentleman, to Richard Ormo of Radnor, yeoman, & Mary his wife. Whereas there is a tract in Radnor, being part of 200 acres which James Claypoole & Robert Turner, commissioners of William Penn, granted to David Davies by patent dated 30 Oct 1685. Now David Davies for & in the consideration that Richard Ormo maintain David Davies & Katherine Davies his sister with meat, drink & apparel during their natural life a tract of 100 acres, part of the 200 acres bounded by the other 100 acres now in the possession of Ann Thomas, widow, land of John Morgan, John Richards & land late of Mathias Jones now in the possession of David Harry. David Davies has made David Lloyd his attorney. Signed David Davies. Delivered in the presence of David Llewellyn & Jenkin Griffith. Recorded 26 Mar 1731. (E5:15).

Deed. On 28 Mar 1730 John Broom of Darby, yeoman, to Margret Morton of Ridley, widow of Andrew Morton. Whereas there are 2 tracts of land in Darby, one bounded by Menianipalls Creek, land of Hance Urins, Morton Mortens & Swan Boon, containing 42 acres & another tract bounded by Mucanipat Creek, Thorough Fair Creek, Darby Creek, containing 13 acres, being part of tract granted to Isreal Holme & Company by Richard Nicholas, Governor of New York, & the Isreal Holme granted to Mounce Peterson & Mounce Peterson granted same by gift to his son Peter Peterson dated 13 Mar 1695 & Peter Peterson granted to John Broom dated 8 Oct 1711. Now John Broom for £30 grants to Margret Morton the 2 tracts containing 55 acres. Signed John Broom. Delivered in the presence of John Crosby & Hance Torton. Recorded 28 Mar 1730. (E5:17).

Deed. On 10 May 1721 David Morton of Darby, yeoman, & Eleanor his wife, to Andrew Morton the son of Darby, yeoman. David Mortin & Eleanor his wife for £7.12 grant to Andrew Morton a tract on Darby Creek bounded by land of Andrew Urins, Thoroughfair Creek, a run called Caty Scaps & land of Henry Boons, containing 11 1/2 acres. David Morton protects against all claims from the heirs of his father Morton Mortonson. Signed David Morton & Eleanor Morton. Delivered in the presence of George Campinott, John Broom, Hance Boon & Andrew Urin. Recorded 20 Apr 1731. (E5:18).

Lease & Release. On 28 Dec 1730 David Morton of Darby, yeoman, & Eleanor his wife, to Margret Morton of Ridley, widow of Andrew Morton. Whereas Richard Nichols, Governor of New York, by patent dated 18

4

June 1668, granted to Isreal Holme, Hendrick Jacobson, Oele Kook & Jan Minssorman, a tract on the west side of the Delaware River, recorded in the Secretaries Office in New York, & whereas Isreal Holme by deed written in Dutch dated 29 Apr 1671 granted to Mounce Peterson of Darby his 1/3 share of the tract. Whereas Andrew Boon of the County of Philadelphia by deed dated 3 June 1690 granted to Mounce Peterson & Peter Peterson a tract in Darby containing 36 acres. Mounce Peterson by Deed of Gift dated 13 Mar 1695 granted to his son Peter Peterson all his land. Peter Peterson by deed dated 1 Aug 1711 granted to Morton Morton & Mathias Natssoilles a tract in Darby formerly belonging to his father Mounce Peterson, recorded Chester, Book C, Page 200. Morton Morton in his life & Mathias Natsellies did make a division of the said lands to the satisfaction of both parties. Morton Morton by his will dated 21 Nov 1718 bequeathed to his son David Morton his land. Mathias Netsellies by deed dated 26 May 1723 did release to David Morton the said land. Now David Morton & Eleanor his wife for £50 grant to Margret Morton a tract in Calcon Hook in the township of Darby bounded by Darby Creek, land of Hans Urins & Morton Morton, containing 64 acres & another lot lying between Morton Morton's land & Darby Creek containing 10 acres & another tract lying between Morton Morton's land & Darby Creek containing 2 3/4 acres, another tract lying between Darby Creek & Thoroughfair Creek bounded by land of Hans Urins & Calcon Hook Landing, containing 2 acres, & another piece called Hay Island adjoining Thoroughfair Creek & land of Hans Urins, containing 2 acres, & another piece of land bounded by land of Hans Urin, Darby Creek & Boons Marsh, containing 17 acres, out of which the last lot Mathias Natsellies is to have 5 acres as per agreement dated 29 May 1721 between David Morton & Mathias Natsellies, being in all 93 1/3 acres, except 1 1/2 acres sold to Conrad Nethermark. Signed David Morton & Eleanor Morton. Delivered in the presence of John Crosby & Thomas Preecos. Recorded 17 Apr 1730. (E5:20).

Bond. On 25 June 1718 Andrew Morton of Amos land in the County of Chester, yeoman, hath firmly bound to Andrew Morton, Sr., of Amos, land, yeoman, for the sum of £100 to be truly paid by Andrew Morton, Jr. The condition of this obligation is such that Andrew Morton fully & abide by the determination & judgement of John Wood of Darby, gentleman, & William Smith & John Hood of Darby, yeoman, & Joseph Harvey of Ridley, yeoman, being elected & chosen arbitrators. Signed Andrew Morton. Delivered in the presence of John Owen & John Reece. Recorded 18 Apr 1731. (E5:23).

Judgement. On 28 July 1718 John Wood, William Smith & John Hood of Darby, yeomen, & Joseph Harvey of Ridley, yeoman, send greetings. Whereas there has been differences, quarrels & contention between Andrew Morton, Sr., & Andrew Morton, Jr., both of Ridley, yeomen, chiefly concerning the division of 615 acres in Ridley. Now John Wood, William Smith, John Hood & Joseph Harvey unanimously agree that within 6 months the 615 acres shall be equally divided between Andrew Morton, Jr. & Andrew Morton, Sr., & Andrew Morton, Jr., is to pay £7 to Andrew Morton, Sr., for the maintaining of Andrew Morton's mother in her great weakness & could not help herself & young Andrews father of whose estate he is possessed of was allowed 50 acres & his father's personal estate to take care of & maintain his father & mother during their natural life. Signed John Wood, William Smith, John Hood & Joseph Harvey. Delivered in the presence of Jonathon Hood & James Jones. Recorded 18 Apr 1731. (E5:24).

Deed. On 30 Dec 1730 Hance Torton & his wife Letitia, Charles Grantum & his wife Katherine, Rebecca Morton & Lydia Morton, all of Ridley, to Adam Arther & his wife Ellin. Whereas there is a tract in Ridley bounded by land of Thomas Tatnall, Edward Smith, Andrew Morton & the Kings Road, containing 35 acres; another tract bounded by the mentioned land, the Kings Road, bounded by land of Andrew Morton, containing 31 acres; another tract bounded by Darby Creek & land of Andrew Morton, containing 6 1/2 acres, being part of land that Andrew Morton, Sr., had conveyed to him by his father Morton Morton by deed dated 23 May 1703 containing 257 acres, being part of a tract Morton Morton purchased of Andrew Johnson, late of Amosland in Ridley by deed dated 12 Mar 1694/5. Now the Andrew Morton died having possession of said tract & having no sons but 5 daughters which names are Letitia, Ellin, Katherine, Rebecca & Lydia which daughters by agreement had the said tract divided into 5 equal shares & drawing lots, and Ellins share was the described 3 tracts of land, & whereas the said Ellin has married Adam Archer. Now Hance Torton & Letitia his wife, Charles Grantum & Katherine his wife, Rebecca Morton & Lydia Morton for 5 shillings release all right to the 3 tracts containing 72 acres. Signed Hance Torton, Letitia Torton, Charles Grantum, Katherine Grantum, Rebecca Morton & Lydia Morton. Delivered in the presence of John Crosby & Daniel Brown. Recorded 1 May 1731. (E5:26).

Deed. On 16 Mar 1730 Francis Windlo of Marlborough, yeoman, to John Jackson of Marlborough, yeoman. Whereas Caleb Pussey & Ann his wife, by deed dated 20 Mar 1713, granted to John Smith & Ann his wife, the daughter of the said Caleb & Ann Pussey, 2 tracts of land in Marlborough, containing 515 acres, recorded Chester, Book D, Vol 4, Page 343, & whereas Ann, the wife of John Smith, has departed this life leaving the said John Smith to survive her who by deed dated 30 Nov 1727 granted to Francis Windlo a tract containing 115 acres. Now Francis Windlo for £112 grants to John Jackson a tract in Marlborough bounded by land of Thomas Vernon, Henry Hays, Robert Pyle & John Smith, containing 115 acres. Signed Francis Windlo. Delivered in the presence of Robert Carter, Samuel Jackson & Isaac Jackson. Recorded 3 May 1731. (E5:28).

Lease & Release. On 26 & 27 Jan 1729 Moses Coppeck of Marlborough, yeoman, to Francis Widlo of Malborough, yeoman. Whereas William Penn, lately dec., granted by patent dated 8 June 1702 to Bartholemew Coppeck, grandfather of Moses Coppeck, a tract on the south side of Brandywine Creek containing 338 acres, recorded Chester, Book A, Vol 2, Page 323. Bartholemew Coppeck made his will dated 10 July 1718 & devised to his grandson Moses Coppeck the 338 acres & and then died. Now Moses Coppeck for £130 granted to Francis Windlo a tract in Marlborough bounded by land of Thomas Wikersham containing 140 acres. Signed Moses Coppeck. Delivered in the presence of Samuel Jackson, Isaac Jackson & William Pussey. Recorded 4 May 1731. (E5:30).

Lease & Release. On 18 Nov 1730 Nicholas Newlin of Concord. yeoman, eldest son of Nathaniel Newlin late of Concord, gentleman, dec., Nathaniel Newlin of Concord, yeoman, 2nd son of Nathaniel Newlin, dec., John Newlin of Concord, yeoman, 3rd son of Nathaniel Newlin, Richard Evenson of Thornbury, yeoman, & Jemima his wife one of the daughters of Nathaniel Newlin, dec., Richard Clayton of Concord & Mary his wife, another daughter of Nathaniel Newlin, dec., & William Baily of Kennet, yeoman, & Keria his wife, the other daughter of Nathaniel Newlin, dec., to John Mendenhall, Jr., of Caln, yeoman. Whereas Abraham Musgrave eldest son of Thomas Musgrave, dec., & David Price & Hannah his wife, the widow of Thomas Musgrave, as executors of the will of Thomas Musgrave by deed dated 23 Mar 1712 granted to John Mendenhall, Jr., 2 tracts in the township of Caln, one containing 400 acres, the other 50 acres. John Mendenhall & Susannah his wife by deed dated 3 & 4 May 1728 granted to Nathaniel Newlin, the dec., 2 tracts one containing 200 acres being part of the 400 acres & the other containing 50 acres, recorded Book D, Vol 4, Page 371. Nathaniel Newlin, the dec., by deed dated 4 May 1728 for £100 to be paid in payments (final payment to be made 15 Sep 1732), granted to John Mendenhall, Jr., the 2 tracts. Now Nicholas Newlin, Nathaniel Newlin, John Newlin, Richard & Jemima Evenson, Richard & Mary Clayton & William & Keria Baily for £100 plus interest grant & confirm to John Mendenhall, Jr., 2 tracts in Caln one bounded by land of Phillip Roman containing 200 acres & the other bounded by land of Joseph Pykes, & Phillip Roman, containing 50 acres. Signed Nicholas Newlin, Nathaniel Newlin, John Newlin, Richard Evenson, Jemima Evenson, Richard Clayton, Mary Clayton, William Baily & Keria Baily. Delivered in the presence of John Brinton, Henry Pierce & John Taylor. Recorded 24 May 1731. (E5:32).

Lease & Release. On 25 Nov 1730 John Mendenhall, Jr., of Caln, yeoman, & Susannah his wife, to William Pim of Caln, yeoman. Whereas William Penn, by deed dated 15 & 16 Oct 1689, granted to James Read 500 acres to be laid out; 100 acres was laid out in Bucks county & the 400 acres was laid out in Chester county, & James Read soon after died, & since his death his widow Mary married Thomas Brintmade who sold 400 acres to Thomas Musgrave. Whereas William Penn by deed dated 17 & 18 Mar 1698 granted to Thomas Musgrave & John Brook 1,500 acres & Thomas Musgrave has since died. The tract of 400 acres & the moiety of the 1,500 acres being 500 acres was laid out in the township of Caln. The commissioners of William Penn confirmed said tracts to Hannah, the widow of Thomas Musgrave, the now wife of David Price, recorded in Philadelphia, Book A, Vol 2, Page 572. Whereas Abraham Musgrave son & heir of Thomas Musgrave, dec., and David Price & Hannah his wife, by deed dated 23 Mar 1712, granted 450 acres, part of the 500 acres, to John Mendenhall, Jr., recorded Chester, Book C, Vol 4, Page 345. Now John & Susannah Mendenhall for £450 grant to William Pim a tract in Caln bounded by land of Phillip Roman & Joseph Pykes, containing 400 acres, and the other tract bounded by land of Phillip Roman & Joseph Pykes, containing 50 acres. Signed John Mendenhall, Jr., & Susannah Mendenhall. Delivered in the presence of Thomas McChin, Joshua Box & Samuel Shaw. Recorded 3 May 1731. (E5:36).

Deed. On 30 Oct 1718 Esther Tyler of Chester, widow & sole executrix of the will of John Tyler, late of Chester, dec., & Samuel Tomlintin, late of Chester but now of Black Bird Creek in the County of New Castle, cordwainer, & Tobias Hendricks of Chester, yeoman, to David Lloyd of Chester, gentleman. Whereas John Bristow, late of Elk River in

Maryland, yeoman, by deed dated 27 May 1708, for £60 grants to John Tyler a tenement where Esther Tyler now or lately dwelt lying in Chester with 5 lots in one continuous piece, bounded by Chester Creek, David Lloyd's plantation, lot late of Urin Keen but now of Jonas Sandelands & Edgmont Road & a lot then belonging to David Roberts bounded by land of late of Urin Keen, David Lloyd's plantation & Chester Creek being the lot which David Roberts & Susanna his wife by deed dated 14 Apr 1714 granted to John Tyler. John Tyler made his will dated 23 July 1717 & empowered Samuel Tomlinson & Tobias Hendricks to sell all his land in Chester or elsewhere. The will was proved 26 Aug 1717. Now Samuel Tomlinson & Tobias Hendricks, by special request of Esther Tyler, for £60 grant to David Lloyd all 6 lots. Signed Tobias Hendricks & Esther Tyler in the presence of John Owen, Joseph Parker, & James Reece. Signed Samuel Tomlinson in the presence of Robert Barber, John Owen, & Joseph Parker. Recorded 15 Mar 1730. (E5:39).

Deed. On 27 May 1708 John Bristow of Elk River in Maryland, yeoman, to John Tyler of Chester, tailor. John Bristow for £60 grant to John Tyler 5 lots in Chester lying contiguous, bounded by land of David Lloyd, land late of John Hoskins, Charles Whitaker, & Chester Creek. Signed John Bristow. Delivered in the presence of William Clayton & Benjamin Moulder. Recorded 15 May 1731. (E5:42).

Release. On 30 July 1723 Ann Friend of Ridley, widow & sole executrix of the will of Neels Laarson, alias Friend, late of Chester, alias Upland, yeoman, dec., & Gabriel Friend of Ridley, yeoman, & Lawerence Friend of Ridley, yeoman, the younger sons of Ann by her late husband, to David Lloyd of Chester, gentleman. Whereas Neels Laarson in his lifetime was seized of a tract in Chester where David Lloyd now dwells containing 180 acres which he purchased of Justast Anderson. Neels Laarson made his will dated 20 Dec 1686, proved & recorded Philadelphia, Book A, Page 145. Whereas Ann having purchased a greater plantation where she now dwells did sell for £110 to David Lloyd, & with the £110 paid for the plantation she now dwells & disposed therof amongst her sons reserving a share for herself. Her 2 eldest sons, Andrew & Johnannes, joined with her in conveying the plantation to David Lloyd, recorded 27 May 1689, and the said Gabriel & Lawerence parties to these presents being then under age. Now Ann Friend for the consideration of £110, paid by David Lloyd & Gabriel & Lawerence, as well for & in consideration of their shares of the said plantation

purchased with the said money & 5 shillings to each paid by the David
Lloyd release & confirm unto David Lloyd the said plantation. Signed
Ann Friend in the presence of Enoch Enochson, William Davies, &
Joseph Parker. Signed Gabriel Friend in the presence of William Davies
& Joseph Parker. Signed Lawerence Friend in the presence of Joseph
Parker & Richard Hays. Recorded 27 May 1731. (E5:44).

Deed. On 3 Mar 1730/1 Joseph Royner of Chester, cordwainer, & Mary
his wife to Samuel Preston of Chester, sadler. Whereas Jonas
Sandelands, late of Chester, gentleman, & Mary his wife by their deed
dated 26 & 27 Apr 1725 granted to Joseph Royner & Mary his wife a
tract in Chester. Now Joseph Royners & Mary his wife for £8 grant to
Samuel Preston a lot in Chester being 40' x 120' bounded on the south by
a lot belonging to the Church of England, west & north by lots now or
lately belonging to Richard Bickham, & east with the Welsh Street being
part of 20 acres confirmed James Sandelands, late father of Jonas
Sandelands, by William Penn on 31 May 1686. Signed Joseph Royner &
Mary Royner. Delivered in the presence of Joseph Parker & John
Wharton. Recorded 25 Aug 1731. (E5:46).

Deed. On 29 Aug 1705 Joseph Jervis of Middletown, yeoman, to John
Worrall of Edgmont. Whereas there is a lot in Chester 80' x 120' intended
to be the Market Place bounded on the east by land of Stephen Kings,
south with James Street, west with land of William Pickles & north with
a vacant lot being part of 20 acres William Penn granted to James
Sandelands by deed dated 31 May 1686. James Sandelands died & the
said tract descended to James Sandelands, his son, who, for £17, sold
said lot to Samuel Bishop, who on 24 Apr 1705 sold the said to Joseph
Jervis of Middletown for £23. Now Joseph Jervis for £20 grant to John
Worrall the lot. Signed Joseph Jervis. Delivered in the presence of
George Simpson, Samuel Tomlinson & Paul Saunders. Recorded 25 Aug
1731. (E5:48).

Deed. On 25 Dec 1730 Thomas Hollingsworth of the County of New
Castle on the Delaware, yeoman, & Judith his wife to Joseph
Hollingsworth of Chester County, yeoman. Whereas William Penn by
deed dated 23 Oct 1701 granted to his daughter Letitia, then named
Letitia Penn, a tract of land then known as the Manor of Stening
bounded on the south by Brandywine Creek, part in Chester & part in
New Castle County containing 15,500 acres, recorded Philadelphia, Book

A, Vol 2, Page 404. Letitia Penn married William Aubrey of London, merchant, who by a Letter of Attorney dated 8 Feb 1713 made James Logan & Reece Thomas, gentlemen, their attorneys. Recorded Philadelphia, Book D3, Vol 5, Page 79. James Logan & Reece Thomas on 23 June 1726 granted a tract lying in Chester County bounded by Red Clay Creek & land of John Gregg & the line of the late William Penn, Jr.,'s manor containing 150 acres to Thomas Hollingsworth. Now Thomas Hollingsworth & Judith his wife for £100 grant to Joseph Hollingsworth the 150 acres. Signed Thomas Hollingsworth & Judith Hollingsworth. Delivered in the presence of Joseph Webb & Alexander Pentland. Recorded 30 Aug 1731. (E5:50).

Deed. On 20 Aug 1729 Ezekiel Harlan of Kennit, yeoman, & Ruth his wife to Ezekiel Harlan of Marlborough, yeoman, one of the sons of Ezekiel & Ruth. Whereas Margaret Cook, late of Philadelphia, widow, by deed dated 26 Apr 1707 granted to Richard Buffington & Ezekiel Harlan the father 1,500 acres then unsurveyed being part of 5,000 acres granted by William Penn, lately dec., to Arthur Cook, the late husband of Margaret Cook. Ezekiel Harlans part of the 1,500 acres was 1,000 acres. Whereas the commissioners of William Penn granted to Ezekiel Harlan a tract containing 237 acres, recorded Philadelphia, Book A, Vol 5, Page 248. Now Ezekiel Harlan & Ruth his wife for the natural love & 5 shillings grant to their son Ezekiel Harlan a tract in Marlborough bounded by land of John Taylor, William Harlan, land late of Gayen Stephenson, & land late of Jacob Simcock containing 320 acres being part of the 2 tracts. Signed Ezekiel Harlan & Ruth Harlan. Delivered in the presence of William Webb, William Harlan & Joseph Evans. Recorded 30 Aug 1731. (E5:52).

Deed. On 22 Mar 1714 William Penn of London, eldest son & heir apparent of William Penn, Griffith Owen, practioner of Physick, James Logan, gentleman, & Robert Ashton, gentleman, all of Philadelphia to Joseph Sharp of Chester County, yeoman. Whereas William Penn, the father, by patent under the hands of Edward Shippen, Griffith Owen, Thomas Story, & James Logan, late commissioners of property, granted to William Penn, Jr., a tract on the south side of Brandywine Creek part in the County of New Castle & part in the County of Chester containing 14,500 acres by patent dated 24 May 1706, recorded Philadelphia, Book A, Vol 3, Page 279. Whereas William Penn, Jr., by Letter of Attorney dated 7 Oct 1704 appointed Griffith Owen, James Logan & Robert Ashton his attorneys to sell said land, recorded Philadelphia, Book B, Vol

2, Page 149, on 24 Nov 1709. Now William Penn, Jr., for £80 paid to James Logan & Griffith Owen grant to Joseph Sharp 2 tracts one being bounded by land of Thomas Garnett, Michael Lightfoot, William Tanner, John Sharp & Mary Rowland containing 200 acres, and the other tract bounded by land of the London Company & Joseph Garnett containing 200 acres. Signed Griffith Owen, James Logan & Robert Ashton. Delivered in the presence of Nicholas Pyle, Gawen Miller & James Boyden. Recorded 16 Aug 1731. (E5:55).

Release. On 2 Sep 1727 Erasmus Cole of Muck Hallandbury in the County of Essex, tanner, John Mead of Sawbridgeworth in the County of Harford, wool comber, & Edmund Peacock, citizen of vintner of London, & Elizabeth Green wife of John Green, citizen & wine cooper of London & daughter of the late Richard Collett, late citizen & vintner of London, dec., to Joshua Salkeld of Chester County, malster. Whereas by deed dated 15 & 16 May 1722 Richard Collet granted to Erasmus Cole, John Mead & Edmund Peacock 1,000 acres in the province of Pennsylvania being land William Penn granted on 11 July 1681 to Richard Collett. Richard Collett is to receive rents & profits of the 1,000 acres during his natural life & after his death the rents & profits are to be paid Elizabeth Green, not to John Green as he would order but into the hands of Elizabeth for her separate & personal use exclusive of John Green & where with he was in no sort to intermediate to, nor was the same to be subject to, his debts or disposition. Upon further trust that they, the said trustees, should immediately after the death of John Green, if Elizabeth should survive him, convey all property to her for her natural life, & after her death to go to her child or children by her husband John Green or any other husband she might marry, or if there is no issue of Elizabeth to go to the heirs of Richard Collett. Also it may be lawful for the trustees to sell said 1,000 acres with the consent of Elizabeth but not jointly with her husband. And whereas Richard Collett departed this life on or about the month of Aug 1721. Erasmus Cole, John Mead & Edmund Peacock with the consent of Elizabeth Green for £100 grant to John Salkeld 1,000 acres which £100 is to be paid out in 1 yearly rent charge of £5 per annum to be issued out of lands of William Holland, citizen & mason of London situated in the Parish of St. Leonard Sharedich in the County of Middlesex. Signed Elizabeth Green, John Mead & Edmund Peacock in the presence of Ralph Lees, Robert Robertson & John Page. Signed Erasmus Cole in the presence of Thomas Kittoll & Thomas Cornelius. Recorded 18 Oct 1731. (E5:57).

12

Deed of Gift. On 22 June 1709 Randolph Vernon of Nether Providence, yeoman, to his son Jacob Vernon. Whereas William Penn granted 5,000 acres to John Simcock by deed dated 16 Mar 1681 part of the said 5,000 acres was laid out in Thornbury & John Simcock gave his daughter Elizabeth wife of Ralph Fishbourne, dec., 500 acres by deed dated 12 Dec 1699. Ralph Fishbourne in his lifetime with the consent of his wife Elizabeth granted the 500 acres to Thomas England of Philadelphia, baker. Thomas England for £130 granted the 500 acres to Randolph Vernon by the same deed dated 12 Dec 1699. The 500 acres is bounded by land of George Pearces, Richard Arnold formerly Benjamin Hickman, Benjamin Mendenhall, Joseph Baker formerly John Cook, Richard Marsh & John Bellars containing 500 acres. Now Randolph Vernon for love & affection give & grant to his loving son Jacob Vernon all 500 acres. Signed Randolph Vernon. Delivered in the presence of Richard Arnold, Joseph Baker & Joseph Edwards. Witnessed at the time of recording by Joseph Vernon, eldest son & heir-at-law of Randolph Vernon. Recorded 29 Oct 1731. (E5:61).

Mortgage. On 8 Dec 1709 William Nookes of Middletown, yeoman, & Ruth his wife to Peter Hunter of Middletown, tanner. William Nookes & Ruth his wife for £80 grant to Peter Hunter a tract in Middletown bounded by Edgmont Road, land of George Smedley, Peter Hunter & William Trego containing 119 acres being tract Peter Hunter sold to William Nookes 24 June last past. William Nookes is to pay to Peter Hunter £80.9.6 before 15 Mar 1730. Signed William Nookes & Ruth Nookes. Delivered in the presence of John Worrall, John Wogan & John Taylor. Recorded 8 June 1730. (E5:63).

Mortgage. On 30 June 1730 Josiah Harvey of Middletown, clothworker, to Benjamin Duffield of the City of Philadelphia, tanner. Josiah Harvey for £100 grant to Benjamin Duffield all his grist mills, fulling mill & 3 tracts belonging to them bounded by Ridley Creek, land of Elizabeth Cookson, Joseph Jervis & Daniel Cookson containing 52 acres, another tract in Upper Providence bounded by Ridley Creek containing 8 1/2 acres, & another tract bounded by Ridley Creek, & land of Peter Taylor containing 3 acres. The full sum of £100 plus £6 yearly interest to be paid before 30 June 1733. Signed Josiah Harvey. Delivered in the presence of Charles Brockden & Edward Bradley. Recorded 15 Nov 1731. (E5:66).

Mortgage. On 17 May 1731 Robert Brown late of the County of Orange in the govern of New York but now of Newgarden in the County of Chester, yeoman, to James Starr of Newgarden, yeoman. Robert Brown for £240 grant to James Starr a tract in New Garden bounded by land of James Miller, Michael Lightfoot, Francis Hobson & Moses Starr containing 200 acres. Robert Brown to pay £80 on 10 Nov 1731, £80 10 May 1732, & 10 Nov 1732. Signed Robert Brown. Delivered in the presence of Abraham Ayres, Benjamin Fredd & Moses Starr. Recorded 15 Nov 1731. (E5:68).

Deed. On 14 Mar 1722 Tobias Collett of London in Old England, haberdasher, Daniel Quare of London, watch maker, Henry Goldney of London, Linen draper, to John Smith of Marlborough, yeoman, Joseph Pennock of Marlborough, yeoman, Caleb Pussey, Jr., of Marlborough, yeoman, William Swain of Marlborough, yeoman, & John Cook of the London Tract in Chester County, yeoman. Whereas William Penn, Esq., late Governor, dec., on 11 & 12 Aug 1699 granted to Tobias Collett, Daniel Quare, Henry Goldney & Michael Russell a tract containing 60,000 acres, recorded Philadelphia, Book B, Vol 2, Page 336. Whereas William Penn, by 3 warrants dated 17 Aug 1699, directed Thomas Fairman, one of the surveyors of the province, to survey the 60,000 acres. One of the warrants Thomas Fairman laid out on the back side of New Castle county containing 16,506 acres, Isaac Taylor surveyor laid out in Chester County 718 acres, both part of 60,000 acres. Michael Russell is now dec. & his share is vested in Tobias Collett, Daniel Quare & Henry Goldney. Now Tobias Collett, Daniel Quare & Henry Goldney for 5 shillings grant to John Smith, Joseph Pennock, Caleb Pussey, Jr., William Swain & John Cook a tract on the northeast side of the London Tract bounded by land of Joseph Pennock containing 10 acres. Tobias Collett, Daniel Quare & Henry Goldney appoint William Pussey & John Fincher as their attorneys. Signed Tobias Collett, Daniel Quare & Henry Goldney. Delivered in the presence of Sarah Dimsdale, John Estaugh & Elizabeth Estaugh. Recorded 16 Nov 1731. (E5:69).

Deed. On 20 Feb 1713 Gaein Stevenson of Chester County, malster, to John Salkeld of Chester, yeoman. Whereas John Wade of Essex House & Frances his wife on 1 Oct last past granted to Gaien Stevenson all the tract hereafter mentioned. Now Gaien Stevenson for £150 grant to John Salkeld a tract in the township of Chester on the west side of Chester Creek bounded by land of George Simcock, Chester Creek, and lots sold by John Wade to Alexander Moses, but now in the tenure of George Simcock, Essex Street & land of Henry Hollingsworth containing 2 acres with the Mault House. Signed Gaien Stevenson. Delivered in the presence of John Blunstone, Jr., Richard Webb, Caleb Pussey, Jacob Howell & David Lloyd. Recorded 16 Nov 1731. (E5:72).

Release. On 30 Apr 1723 Isaac Few of Kennet, yeoman, to James Few of Kennet, cooper. Whereas the commissioners of property on 6 Sep 1703 granted to William Huntly of Kennet a tract in Kennet containing 200 acres. William Huntly made his will dated 1 Mar 1707/8 & Mary Huntly, widow & executrix of William Huntly, dec., by deed dated 25 Nov 1709 granted 200 acres to Isaac Few. Now Isaac Few for £25 grant to James Few a tract in Kennet bounded by land of Richard Fletcher, Thomas Hope & land formerly of Peter Dicks containing 47 acres. Signed Isaac Few. Delivered in the presence of Joseph Harlan, Stephen Harlan & William Webb. Recorded 23 Nov 1731. (E5:74).

Deed. On 13 Apr 1726 James Few & Dorcas his wife to William Harvey of Kennet, maulster. James Few & Dorcas his wife for £50 grant to William Harvey a tract containing 47 acres. Signed James Few & Dorcas Few. Delivered in the presence of Jane Elwall & Charles Osborne. Recorded 23 Nov 1731. (E5:76).

Lease & Release. On 3 & 4 Mar 1726 John Shaw of Milthrop in the County of Westmoreland, mercer, eldest surviving son & heir Rebecca Shaw, late of Kirkby Kendall in the County of Westmoreland, widow & relict of John Shaw, late of Kirkby Kendall, cordwainer, dec., which said Rebecca was only daughter & heir of Robert Barrow, late of Kirkby Kendall, yeoman, dec., to Anthony Shaw of Kirkby Kendall, clothier. Whereas William Penn by deed dated 14 & 15 June 1682 granted to Robert Barrow 300 acres in Pennsylvania. Robert Barrow died & the 300 acres descended to his daughter Rebecca Shaw, on 29 Oct 1714 the 300 acres was surveyed and laid out in Chester County bounded by Peque Creek, land of Thomas Elderidge, William Lewis, James Clemson & James Logan. Whereas Rebecca Shaw is now dec., the 300 acres descended to John Shaw. Now John Shaw for £12.10 & affection grant to his brother Anthony Shaw 300 acres. Signed John Shaw. Delivered in the presence of Isaac Halden, William Collinson, Robert Wharton & James Winn. Recorded 4 Dec 1731. (E5:77).

Articles. On 29 Nov 1731 an agreement was made between Josiah Harvey of Middletown, yeoman, to William Pennell of Middletown & Frederick Engle of Middletown, yeoman. Josiah Harvey for £130 grant to William Pennell & Frederick Engle a tract in Middletown bounded by Ridley Creek, land of Crosley & William Surman containing 52 acres, & another small tract in Middletown bounded by Ridley Creek containing 8 1/2 acres, & another small tract in Middletown bounded by Ridley Creek & land of Peter Taylor containing 3 acres with all mills & mill works. Whereas Josiah Harvey by deed of Mortgage made over to Benjamin Duffield of Philadelphia for £100 for a certain time specified, where there is 1 year 8 months to come. Now Josiah Harvey shall pay of the said mortgage at the time specified in the mortgage deed & redeem said mortgage & shall keep 1 acre of said land to build a milling house. Signed Josiah Harvey, William Pennell & Frederick Engle. Recorded 11 Dec 1731. (E5:82).

Deed. On 25 Mar 1724 Charles Read, Job Goodson, Evan Owen, George Fitzwater, Joseph Pidgeon of the City of Philadelphia, merchants, trustees of the Society of Free Traders, to David Lloyd of Chester, gentleman. Whereas William Penn by deed dated 24 Mar 1681 granted to the Society of Free Traders a tract of land containing 20,000 acres. Now the trustees for £230 grant to David Lloyd a tract containing 1,000 acres. Signed Charles Read, Job Goodson, Evan Owen, George Fitzwater & Joseph Ridgeon. Delivered in the presence of David Evans & Merick Davies. Recorded 24 Jan 1731. (E5:85).

Deed. On 22 May 1711 Richard Buffington of Chester County, yeoman, to Ezekiel Harland of Chester County, yeoman. Whereas Margaret Cook of the City of Philadelphia, widow, by deed dated 26 Apr 1707 granted to Richard Buffington & Ezekiel Harland, 1,500 acres. Whereas Ezekiel Harland obtained from the commissioners of property 2 warrants dated 26 Apr 1707 directed to Jacob Taylor, surveyor, requiring him to survey 1,000 acres of the 1,500 acres to Ezekiel Harland. Now Richard Buffington for 5 shillings release all right to the said 1,000 acres. Signed Richard Buffington. Delivered in the presence of Robert Benson, Richard Buffington, Jr., & Isaac Taylor. Recorded 26 Feb 1731. (E5:87).

Deed. On 19 Dec 1717 John Cook of Duck Creek, in the County of Kent upon Delaware, yeoman, & Mary his wife to Ezekiel Harland of Kennet, yeoman. Whereas Margaret Cook, late of Philadelphia, widow, whose son

& heir is John Cook, by her deed dated 26 Apr 1707 granted to Richard Buffington & Ezekiel Harlan 1,500 acres then unsurveyed being part of 5,000 acres which William Penn granted to Arthur Cook, dec., late husband of Margaret & father of John Cook. Whereas Ezekiel Harland had 1,000 acres surveyed unto him, 500 acres was laid out in Kennet bounded by land of Benjamin Chambers, & 500 acres was laid out in Hilltown bounded by land of John Simcock. Now John Cook for 5 shillings release & confirm to Ezekiel Harland the 2 tract containing in whole 1,000 acres. Signed John Cook & Mary Cook. Delivered in the presence of Joseph England, Ben Shurmor & Thomas Harland. Recorded 26 Feb 1731. (E5:88).

Mortgage. On 22 Nov 1731 Mary Smith of Darby, widow, to Benjamin Duffield of the City of Philadelphia, tanner. Mary Smith for £111 grant to Benjamin Duffield a plantation & tract of land in Darby bounded by land of William Smith & John Hallowell containing 50 acres which Edward Smith, late husband of Mary, by his will dated 10 Mar last past, devised to Mary the said plantation & land. Mary Smith shall pay to Benjamin Duffield £111 plus interest in one payment on or before 22 Nov 1732. Signed Mary Smith. Delivered in the presence of Charles Brockden & W. Sarsons. Recorded 28 Feb 1731. (E5:90).

Deed. On 10 Feb 1731 Henry Miller, Jr., of Upper Providence, yeoman, to his father Henry Miller of Upper Providence, yeoman. Henry Miller the son for £100 grant to Henry Miller the father a tract in Upper Providence containing 247 acres. Which John Miller, the late son of Henry, the father & brother of Henry the son, died seized of the said 247 acres & they came to Henry Miller the son. Signed Henry Miller, Jr. Delivered in the presence of Susannah Pyle, Thomas Minshall & John Taylor. Recorded 23 Mar 1731/2. (E5:92).

Deed. On 10 Nov 1731 Josiah Harvey of Middletown, clothworker, to Frederick Engle, cordwainer, & William Pennell, yeoman, both of Middletown. Josiah Harvey for £130 granted to Frederick Engle & William Pennell a tract with grist mill & fulling mill & 3 tracts, one in Middletown bounded by Ridley Creek, land of Elizabeth Cookson & Daniel Cookson containing 52 acres, another tract in Upper Providence bounded by Ridley Creek containing 8 1/2 acres, & another tract in Upper Providence bounded by Ridley Creek & land of Peter Taylor containing 3 acres. Which said tracts Job Harvey father of Josiah Harvey by deed dated 10 Apr 1729 granted to Josiah Harvey. Samuel Robinette & Mary his wife, Joseph Carter & Sarah his wife, the said Samuel & Sarah being children of Allin Robinett, dec., who was an original purchaser on 17 May last past, released & confirmed all estate rights to Josiah Harvey. Signed Josiah Harvey. Delivered in the presence of John Owen, John Wharton, Goldsmith Edward Hollwell. Recorded 9 Apr 1732. (E5:93).

Memorandum. On 10 Nov 1731 it is hereby agreed between Frederick Engle & William Pennell that no benefit shall be had or taken by survivorship of either of them. Signed Frederick Engle & William Pennell. Delivered in the presence of John Owen, John Wharton & Goldsmith Edward Hollwell. (E5:95).

Deed. On 17 May 1720 William Landor of the City of Philadelphia, merchant, to Samuel Richardson of Chester County, yeoman, one of the sons of Joseph Richardson of the County of Philadelphia, yeoman. Whereas William Landor stands seized of 1/16 part of 5,358 acres called Pickering Mines, which was lately divided and a tract containing 340 acres was allotted to William Landor on 28 Aug 1705. Now William Landor for £90 grant to Samuel Richardson a tract lying in Chester county lying between land late of Samuel Carpenter & Joseph Richards containing 340 acres. Signed William Landor. Delivered in the presence of Owen Roberts & Joshua Lawerence. Recorded 12 May 1732. (E5:95).

Deed. On 10 Mar 1724 Samuel Richardson of Charles Town in the County of Chester, yeoman, & Ann his wife to Henry Pugh of Merion in the County of Philadelphia, yeoman. Whereas William Landor of 16 & 17 May 1720 granted to Samuel Richardson of the County of Chester, yeoman, one of the sons of Joseph Richardson of the County of Philadelphia 1/16 share of 5,358 acres called Pickering Mines containing 340 acres. Now Samuel Richardson & Ann his wife for £160 grant to Henry Pugh for the term of 1 year a tract lying between land late of Samuel Carpenter & Joseph Richardson containing 340 acres. Signed Samuel Richardson in the presence of Charles Brockden & William Coleman. Signed Ann Richardson in the presence of David Evans & Isaac Rees. Recorded 12 May 1732. (E5:97).

Mortgage. On 18 Mar 1731 Minovah Carter of Chester, weaver, to Edward Horn of the Northern Liberties of the City of Philadelphia, merchant. Minovah Carter for £100 grant to Edward Horn a tract in Caln bounded by land of Thomas Moore, Jason Cloud, the north branch of Brandywine Creek & George Aston containing 225 acres. Minovah Carter to pay £100 plus interest to Edward Horn in payments £32 on or before 18 Mar 1732, £29.10 on or before 18 Mar 1733/4, £28 on or before 18 Mar 1734, & £26.10 on or before 18 Mar 1735. Signed Minovah Carter. Delivered in the presence of Robert Midwinter & Edward Co---. Recorded 22 May 1732. (E5:99).

Note. 20 Apr 1734 Edward Horn, by James Howell his attorney, acknowledged satisfaction of mortgage at the office of recording deeds. Signed Joseph Parker. (E5:100).

Lease & Release. On 19 & 20 July 1732 Richard Bickham of Greenidge in the County of Glouster in the province of West New Jersey, yeoman, & Jane his wife to William Preston of the City of Philadelphia, mariner. Whereas Jonas Sandelands & Mary his wife by deed dated 5 & 6 Jan 1721 granted to John Salkeld 2 lots in Chester, one lot 40' x 120' bounded by Welsh Street, with a lot late of Peter Dicks now of John Salkeld & lots of Jonas Sandelands, & the other lot 40' x 120' bounded by Middle Street, a lot late of Peter Dicks, lots of Jonas Sandelands, lots of John Crosby, formerly of Isaac Taylor, & lots formerly belonging to Thomas Powell. Whereas Jonas Sandelands & Mary his wife by deed dated 4 Feb 1714 granted to Sarah Powell, widow, a lot in Chester containing 40' x 120' bounded by Middle Street, Welsh Street & lots of Jonas Sandelands. Whereas Sarah Powell has since married Peter Dicks, who by their deed dated 29 Apr 1723 granted to John Salkeld the above mentioned lot, & whereas John Salkeld & Agnes his wife by deed dated 30 & 31 Mar 1724 granted to Richard Bickham the 3 lots. Now Richard Bickham & Jane his wife for £24 grant to William Preston all 3 lots, being part of 20 acres granted & confirmed to James Sandelands the late father of Jonas Sandelands by William Penn dated 31 May 1686. Signed Richard Bickham & Jane Bickham. Delivered in the presence of J. Backhouse & J. Mather & William Mather. Recorded 1 Sep 1732. (E5:101).

Deed. On 16 Oct 1705 David Lloyd of Philadelphia, gentleman, Samuel Bishop of Chester, yeoman, & George Oldfield of Chester, gentleman, to Alexander Badcock, late of Philadelphia, but now of Chester, cordwainer. Whereas there is a tract in Chester bounded by Chester Creek, the road that leads from David Lloyd's plantation to Chester Creek, land of John Hoskins & James Lowndes being tract David Lloyd sold but not conveyed to Samuel Bishop, & Samuel Bishop sold all his right to George Oldfield, & George Oldfield for £90 sold to Alexander Badcock. Now David Lloyd at the direction of Samuel Bishop & George Oldfield for 2 shillings rent yearly convey to Alexander Badcock the use of said lot. Signed Alexander Badcock. Delivered in the presence of John Willis, Humphrey Johnson & James Lowns. Recorded 1 Sep 1732. (E5:103).

Deed. On 24 Feb 1717/8 Nicholas Fairlamb, Esq., sheriff of Chester County, sends greetings, whereas John Simcock, late clerk of the said county, who in the name of William Penn presented in Court of Common Pleas, lately held before the Justices of Chester County, did recover of Mathias Mincent, Robert Thomson, Esq., & Daniel Cox, Esq., of London in Old England, the sum of £313.10 for the arrears of certain county rates made payable according to the laws of the province from 29 Sep 1687 to 29 Sep 1715 for 30,000 acres surveyed & laid out to Mathias, Robert, & Daniel on the west side of Skoolkill River in Chester County. By writ of execution dated 30 Aug last past, I was commanded to cause to be levied on the land & chattels of Mathias, Robert & Daniel for £313.10 & that I should have the money before the Court of Common Pleas on 26 Nov next. John Simcock & I, the sheriff, seized a tract of 467 acres part of the 30,000 acres being bounded by land of David Lloyd. Now Nicholas Fairlamb for £50 grant to David Lloyd of Chester the 467 acres. Signed Nicholas Fairlamb. Delivered in the presence of Jasper Yeates, Henry Pearce, Henry Nayles & Joseph Parker. Acknowledged in open court 28 Feb 1718. George Yeates, clerk. Recorded 1 Sep 1732. (E5:105).

Deed. On 30 Oct 1718 John Powell of Nether Providence, yeoman, & Elizabeth his wife, Joseph Powell of Marple, yeoman, & Mary his wife, & Joseph Powell, Jr., of Ridley, yeoman, son & heir apparent of John Powell, to Peter Dicks of Upper Providence, yeoman, Sarah his wife. Whereas William Penn by deed dated 21 & 22 Mar 1681 granted to Thomas Powell of the Lordship of Rudheath in the county Palatine of Chester, husbandman, 500 acres. Recorded Chester, Book A, Folio 10. Whereas Thomas Powell in consideration of a marriage which was solemnized between his son Thomas Powell (since dec.) & the said Sarah (now wife of Peter Dicks) granted by Deed of Gift to Thomas Powell one half of all his land & the other half to Ann his wife for her life, & after her death to go to Thomas Powell, their son, as by Deed of Gift & Thomas Powell, the father, soon after died, since his dec. the said half became vested in his son, Thomas Powell, who by his will gave to Sarah his then wife all the estate which he had in his possession, also what should fall to him at the death of his mother Ann, provided that his wife should pay his & her 2 daughters Anna & Susannah £200, and soon after died, and his mother Ann Powell is also dec., and whereas the above mentioned Deed of Gift being mislaid or lost and some doubt arising upon the words of the said will, the above named John Powell being the eldest son of Thomas Powell & his first wife, & Joseph Powell of Marple being his eldest son by Ann, the second wife, & also that Joseph Powell, Jr., agreed with Sarah, when she was widowed, to convey & assure to her all right & title to the estate of Thomas Powell, Sr., & Ann his wife at their death, & of Thomas Powell, Jr., at the time of his death, excepting 40 shillings payable to John Powell, whereas Sarah obliged herself to pay her children's portions besides £57 to John Powell, Joseph Powell, Jr., & Joseph Powell, Sr., by agreement dated 4 Jan 1714. Now in further performance of the agreement & £57 paid & the sum of 5 shillings a piece to John Powell, Joseph Powell, Sr., & Joseph Powell, Jr., the said John Powell & Elizabeth his wife, Joseph Powell, Sr., & Mary his wife & Joseph Powell, Jr., confirm unto Peter Dicks & his wife Sarah the plantation where they now dwell lying in Upper Providence bounded by Crum Creek, land of Joseph Taylor, Randle Crockson, other land of Peter Dicks, land of Peter Taylor & Thomas Jones containing 230 acres, 180 acres are part of the 500 acres. Signed John Powell, Elizabeth Powell, Joseph Powell, Mary Powell & Joseph Powell. Delivered in the presence of John Crosby, Samuel Bond & Edward Bennett. Recorded 23 Nov 1732. (E5:107).

Lease & Release. On 28 July 1732 Peter Dicks of Upper Providence, yeoman, & Sarah his wife to Joseph Swafer of Nether Providence, blacksmith. Whereas William Penn by deed dated 21 Mar 1681 granted to Thomas Powell of the Lordship of Rudheath in the county Palatine of Chester, husbandman, 500 acres, recorded 7 July 1688, Chester, Book A, Folio 10. Thomas Powell for the marriage of his youngest son Thomas Powell (who is now dec.) & Sarah (now the wife of Peter Dicks) by Deed of Gift to his son 1/2 of all his estate, the other 1/2 to his wife Ann during her life, & after her death to Thomas Powell their son, Thomas Powell the father soon after died. Thomas Powell the son made his will & bequeathed to his wife Sarah all his estate that was in his possession &

all the estate that would come to him at his mother's death provided that his wife pay to their 2 daughters Anna & Susannah £200, and soon after died, & his mother Ann Powell is since dec. Whereas the above mentioned Deed of Gift being mislaid or lost & to prevent any controversy that might arise touching the said title to the said Sarah, John Powell, eldest son of Thomas Powell, the father, by his first wife, & Elizabeth his wife, & Joseph Powell, the eldest son of Thomas Powell & Ann his 2nd wife, & Mary his wife, & Joseph Powell, Jr., by deed dated 30 Oct 1718 did grant & confirm to Peter Dicks & Sarah his wife the 230 acres where Thomas Powell, the father, & Thomas Powell, the son, lately dwelt containing 230 acres recorded Book E, Vol 5, Page 107. Whereas Peter Dicks discharges all debts & legacies of Thomas Powell, Jr., & secured the payment of £200 to Thomas Powell's 2 daughters Anna & Susannah. Now Peter Dicks & Susannah his wife for £300 grant to Joseph Swarfer a tract in Upper Providence bounded by Crum Creek, land late of Joseph Taylor & land of Thomas Jones containing 180 acres being part of 500 acres excepting about 3/4 acre which was formerly conveyed by Thomas Powell the father to certain persons in trust for a burying place for the people called Quakers. Signed Peter Dicks & Sarah Dicks. Delivered in the presence of Peter Taylor, Elizabeth Taylor & Dorothy Turner. Recorded 23 Nov 1732. (E5:109).

Deed. On 26 Mar 1726 Thomas Cheney of Chester County, yeoman, & Elizabeth his wife to John Cheney of Chester County, yeoman. Whereas John Bellars by deed dated 16 Jan 1724 granted to Thomas Cheney & John Cheney a tract in Thornbury containing 1,500 acres. Whereas John Cheney & Thomas Cheney for the mutual advantage of each other have made a division of the said tract, whereby John Cheney's tract is bounded by land of Jonathon Hunters, Daniel Hoops, Aaron James, James Gibbons, Thomas Cheney & John Taylor containing 800 acres. Now Thomas Cheney & Elizabeth his wife for 5 shillings granted & released all claim to John Cheney the tract of 800 acres. Signed Thomas Cheney & Elizabeth Cheney. Delivered in the presence of Jacob Minshall, Sarah Minshall & John Taylor. Recorded 19 Feb 1732/3. (E5:112).

Lease & Release. On 9 & 10 Aug 1730 Joseph Swaffer of Nether Providence, blacksmith, & John Sharples, Jr., of Nether Providence, shoemaker, executors of the will of Jacob Swaffer of Nether Providence, dec., to Joseph Vernon of Nether Providence, yeoman. Whereas there is a tract in Nether Providence bounded by Crum Creek, Providence Road, land of John Sharples & John Edge containing 174 1/2 acres, being part of 180 acres granted to William Swaffer, dec., & Mary his wife by William Penn by deed dated 7 May 1705, recorded Philadelphia, Book A, Vol 3, Page 164. William Swaffer with the consent of Mary his wife by his will dated 15 Apr 1719 did bequeath to his eldest son Jacob Swaffer the tract mentioned, Jacob Swaffer, after the death of his mother Mary Swaffer, became seized of the said tract & made his will dated 10 Feb 1727 & authorized his executors, his brother Joseph Swaffer & his cousin John Sharples, Jr., to dispose of his whole estate & divide amongst his brothers & sisters the money from the sale. Now Joseph Swaffer & John Sharples, Jr., for £141 did grant to Joseph Vernon the tract containing 174 1/2 acres. Signed Joseph Swaffer & John Sharples, Jr. Delivered in the presence of John Crosby & Robert McConachey. Recorded 20 Feb 1732/3. (E5:114).

Lease & Release. On 31 Aug & 1 Sep 1730 Joseph Vernon of Nether Providence, yeoman, & Lydia his wife to Joseph Swaffer of Nether Providence, blacksmith. Whereas there is a tract in Nether Providence bounded by Crum Creek, land of John Sharples, Providence Road & land formerly belonging to John Edge containing 174 1/2 acres, being part of 180 acres William Penn granted to William Swaffer & Mary his wife dated 7 May 1705, recorded Philadelphia, Book A, Vol 3, Page 164. William Swaffer with the consent of his wife Mary by his will dated 15 Apr 1719 bequeathed to his eldest son Jacob Swaffer the above mentioned tract. Jacob Swaffer by his will dated 10 Feb 1727 authorized his executors to sell all his real & personal estate. John Sharples & Joseph Swaffer for £141 granted to Joseph Vernon by deed dated 9 & 10 Aug 1730 all 174 1/2 acres. Now Joseph Vernon & Lydia his wife for £142 grant to Joseph Swaffer the tract containing 174 1/2 acres. Signed Joseph Vernon & Lydia Vernon. Delivered in the presence of John Crosby & Thomas Sill. Recorded 20 Feb 1732. (E5:117).

Lease & Release. On 28 & 29 July 1732 Joseph Swaffer of Nether Providence, blacksmith, to Peter Dicks of Upper Providence, yeoman. Whereas William Penn by deed dated 7 May 1705 granted to William Swaffer, the late father of Joseph Swaffer, a tract containing 180 acres, recorded Philadelphia, Book A, Vol 3, Page 146, on 17 Nov 1705. William Swaffer made his will dated 15 Apr 1719 & bequeathed to his wife Mary Swaffer 40 acres bounded by Providence Road, to hold to for the term of her natural life, & after her death to my son Jacob Swaffer & bequeathed to his son Jacob Swaffer the residue of the estate & soon after died. Whereas Mary Swaffer has since died & all the tract became vested to Jacob Swaffer & Jacob Swaffer made his will dated 10 Feb 1727/8 & authorized his executors Joseph Swaffer & John Sharples, Jr., to dispose of all my estate & the money to be divided between my 3 brothers & 5 sisters & soon after died. Joseph Swaffer & John Sharples, Jr., by deed dated 9 & 10 Aug 1730 granted said tract to Joseph Vernon, a tract in Nether Providence containing 174 1/2 acres, & whereas Joseph Vernon & Lydia his wife by deed dated 30 Aug & 1 Sep 1730 granted to Joseph Swaffer the tract containing 174 1/2 acres. Now Joseph Swaffer for £400 grant to Peter Dicks the tract in Nether Providence bounded by Crum Creek, land of John Sharples, Providence Road, & land formerly of John Edge, containing 174 1/2 acres being part of the 180 acres mentioned. Signed Joseph Swaffer. Delivered in the presence of Peter Taylor, Elizabeth Taylor & Dorothy Turner. Recorded 20 Feb 1732/3. (E5:120).

Lease & Release. On 19 & 20 Jan 1726/7 John Minshall of Chester, cordwainer, & Hannah his wife to Stephen Cole of Chester, butcher. Whereas Samuel Tomlinson & Mary his wife by deed dated 12 May 1718 granted to John Minshall a lot in Chester where John Minshall now dwells under the yearly rent of 9 pence paid to Jonas Sandelands. Whereas Jonas Sandelands & Mary his wife by deed dated 24 Nov 1719 granted to John Minshall a lot in Chester for the yearly rent of 1 shilling paid to Jonas Sandelands & Jonas Sandelands & Mary his wife by deed dated 1 Mar 1719/20 granted to John Minshall a lot in Chester for the yearly rent of 1 shilling. Thomas Dutton & Lucy his wife by deed dated 10 Mar 1721 granted to John Minshall a tract in Chester for a yearly rent to be paid Jonas Sandelands. James Thomas & Martha his wife by deed dated 1 & 2 Oct 1722 granted to John Minshall 2 tracts in Chester for the yearly rent of 2 shillings paid to Jonas Sandelands. Now John Minshall & Hannah his wife for £100 grant to Stephen Cole all the tenement where John Minshall now dwells in Chester containing 6 lots lying together in one bounded by James Street, lots late of Sarah Smith, lots late of Rodger Jackson & Griffith Howell, Middle Street, lots of John Baldwin, lots late of William Pickle & lots of John Worrall. Stephen Cole to pay the yearly rent to Jonas Sandelands. Signed John Minshall & Hannah Minshall. Delivered in the presence of Joseph Parker, William Weldon & Robert Park. Recorded 24 Feb 1732/3. (E5:123).

Lease & Release. On 7 Mar 1726/7 John Baker of Edgmont, yeoman, & John Minshall of Chester, cordwainer, & Hannah his wife to Stephen Cole of Chester, butcher. Whereas John Baker became seized of 2 lots formerly belonging to Rodger Jackson & sold lots to John Minshall, but did not effectively convey said lots to John Minshall. Now John Baker for 5 shillings & John Minshall for £20 grant to Stephen Cole the 2 lots lying together in Chester being 80' x 120' bounded by High Street, other lots of Stephen Cole, lots late of Richard Mardon, now of Griffith Howell, & lots late of Sarah Smith being part of 20 acres granted to James Sandelands by deed dated 31 May 1686 by William Penn. Signed John Baker, John Minshall & Hannah Minshall. Delivered in the presence of John Mather & James Mather. Recorded 24 Feb 1732/3. (E5:125).

Lease & Release. On 28 & 29 Mar 1729 Thomas Morgan of Chester, tailor, to Stephen Cole of Chester, yeoman. Whereas Jonas Sandelands late of Chester, gentleman, & Mary his wife by deed dated 14 Jan 1714 granted to Nicholas Fairlamb then of Chester, gentleman, a tract in Chester for the yearly rent of 5 shillings payable to Jonas Sandelands. Whereas Nicholas Fairlamb & Katherine his wife by deed dated 20 July 1718 granted to John Crosby of Ridley, gentleman, all the said tract with the yearly rent of 5 shillings to be paid Jonas Sandelands. Whereas John Crosby & Susannah his wife by deed dated 15 & 16 June 1726 granted to Thomas Morgan all the said tract with the yearly rent of 5 shillings to be paid Jonas. Now Thomas Morgan for £35 grant to Stephen Cole all that tract in Chester bounded by Chester Creek, a lot once of Robert Hutchison but now of Ruth Hoskins, Edgmont Road & land late of Richard Friend containing 11 1/2 acres. Signed Thomas Morgan. Delivered in the presence of John Owen & John Tomkins. Recorded 24 Feb 1732/3. (E5:127).

Lease & Release. On 30 & 31 Mar 1729/30 Thomas Smith of Salem in West New Jersey, yeoman, & Grace his wife, & Thomas Empson of Graves End upon the Duck Creek in the County of New Castle on the Delaware, yeoman, & Stephen Cole of Chester, yeoman. Whereas James Sandelands, late of Chester, by deed dated 11 Mar 1700 grant to Thomas Smith, late of Darby, dec., 2 lots in Chester. Thomas Smith made his will dated 11 Feb 1705/6 & bequeathed to his loving wife Sarah Smith the 2 lots in Chester & his other lands, goods & chattels & made Sarah Smith his sole executor & soon after died. Sarah Smith died intestate & after her death the lots descended to Thomas Smith & Thomas Empson, 2 of the eldest grandchildren of Sarah Smith by her 2 daughters, Ann Smith

& Dorothy Empson, both dec. Now Thomas Smith & Grace his wife & Thomas Empson for £20 grant to Stephen Cole the 2 lots in Chester, one fronting the market place, bounded by James Street, the other lot fronting market place & bounded by High Street being part of 20 acres William Penn granted to James Sandelands. Signed Thomas Smith, Grace Smith & Thomas Empson. Delivered in the presence of Edward Johnson, John Johnson, James Mullin, Thomas Morgan & Abraham Barton. Recorded 24 Feb 1732/3. (E5:130).

Mortgage. On 28 Apr 1732 George Simpson of Chester, tailor, & Ruth his wife to Peter Dicks of Providence & Thomas Cummings of Chester, both executors of the will of John Baldwin, late of Chester, dec., John Simpson & Ruth his wife for £30 grant to Peter Dicks & Thomas Cummings all the tenement & lot where George Simpson now dwells lying in Chester bounded by the street that leads from Grace Lloyd's plantation to Chester Creek, lot late of John Hoskins, lot late of George Woodier, & lot late of Robert Barber. George Simpson & Ruth his wife shall pay Peter Dicks & Thomas Cummings £39 in payments to be paid in full on or before 28 Apr 1737. Signed George Simpson & Ruth Simpson. Delivered in the presence of Joseph Parker & John Tomkins. Recorded 2 Mar 1732/3. (E5:133).

Deed. On 23 May 1730 Robert Barber, Esq., sheriff of Lancaster County, to Jonathon Hunter of Chester County, yeoman. Whereas Thomas Bourn & Sarah his wife, executrix of the will of Joseph Redman, dec., on 27 Feb 1728 in the Court of Common Pleas did recover against Samuel Baker, late of Chester, blacksmith, a debt of £86.92.6 for damages to be levied of the lands & goods of Samuel Baker in my baileywick. 1/8 equal undivided part in 500 acres in the County of Lancaster was seized. Now Robert Barber, sheriff, for £30 grant to Jonathon Hunter the one full equal & undivided part of the tract lying in Lancaster County bounded by Peque Creek, Susquahanah River, containing 500 acres. Signed Robert Barber, sheriff. Delivered in the presence of Joseph Taylor & John Taylor. Recorded 6 Mar 1732/3. (E5:135).

Deed. On 10 Aug 1732 Arthur Sheil of Chester, yeoman, & Mary his wife, who was the widow & admin. of the goods & chattels of Jonas Sandelands, late of Chester, dec., to Jonathon Hunter of Middletown, tanner. Whereas in Chester County Orphans Court on 10 Apr 1732 before John Crosby, Joseph Brinton, Samuel Hollingsworth & Thomas

Cummings, justices present, whereas Arthur Sheil & Mary his wife, the widow & admin. of Jonas Sandelands, her late husband, Letter of Administration granted in Chester 17 Apr 1728 & at the time of his death Jonas Sandelands was owner of several lots of land and left 8 young children begotten of Mary to survive him, one lot bounded by a lot of Jacob Howell, a lot of John Wharton & Chester Creek containing 1 1/4 acre, & another lot bounded by a lot of Jonas Sandelands, dec., & a lot of Ruth Hoskins containing 2 1/2 acres, another lot bounded by the Great Road, & a lot of Ruth Hoskins containing 1 acre, another lot bounded by High Street, land of Grace Lloyd, & a lot of John Owens containing 1 3/4 acre, & 2 lots being 80' x 120' bounded by a lot of Richard Bickham, Middle Street, & lots of Evan & Thomas Morgan. Arthur Shell & Mary his wife exhibited a true inventory of the estate of the dec., the value being £124.8, & the debts of the dec. come to £181.17, & an account of debts yet due being £210.10. The said Intestates personal estate will not be sufficient to pay his debts & maintain his children until the eldest reaches 21 years or to put them out to apprentices & to teach them to read & write. Arthur Sheil & Mary his wife be allowed to sell said lands to pay the said debts & the residue to the maintenance of the children. Now Arthur Shell & Mary his wife for £26.10 grant to Jonathon Hunter the 2 lots in Chester being 80' x 120' bounded by land of Richard Bickham, Middle Street, land of Evan & Thomas Morgan & land of the church. Signed Arthur Sheil & Mary Sheil. Delivered in the presence of Benjamin Davis, Richard Meghee & Robert Park. Recorded 7 Mar 1732/3. (E5:136).

Deed. On 30 Sep 1732 James Barber of Chester, yeoman, & Susannah his wife to Thomas Cummings of Chester, cordwainer. Whereas David Lloyd, James Lowns & Susannah his wife by deed dated 27 & 28 Nov 1712 granted to James Barber 2 lots in Chester where James Barber now dwells containing 20 acres to pay to David Lloyd 5 shillings yearly rent. Now James Barber & Susannah his wife for £73 grant to Thomas Cummings the 2 lots in Chester bounded by the street that leads from the late David Lloyd's plantation to Chester Creek, a lot of John Hoskins, a lot late of David Ogden, a lot late of Robert Hodgson the other lot bounded by lying next to the former lot bounded by a lot late of David Ogden, the street & a lot late of Robert Barber. Thomas Cummings to pay the yearly rent of 5 shillings payable to the heirs of David Lloyd. Signed James Barber & Susannah Barber. Delivered in the presence of Joseph Parker & Richard Weaver. Recorded 7 Mar 1732/3. (E5:139).

Lease & Release. On 9 & 10 Oct 1732 John Owen of Chester, gentleman, & Hannah his wife to Grace Lloyd of Chester, widow. Whereas Arthur Sheil & Mary his wife, widow & admin. of the goods & chattels of Jonas Sandelands, dec., by deed dated 28 Aug 1732 granted to John Owen a tract in Chester bounded by High Street, land of Grace Lloyd, & the lot of John Owens containing 1 3/4 acres forever under the yearly rent of 3 shillings to the heirs of Jonas Sandelands. Now John Owen for £36.5 grant to Grace Lloyd 3/4 acres part of the 1 3/4 acres under the yearly rent of £1.6 payable to the heirs of Jonas Sandelands. Signed John Owen & Hannah Owen. Delivered in the presence of Arthur Shell & Joseph Parker. Recorded 19 Mar 1732/3. (E5:141).

Release. On 20 Aug 1730 Mary Powell of New Garden in Chester County, now the wife of Evan Powell but formerly the widow of Thomas Rowland, dec., & William Miller on New Garden, Ruth his wife, & Thomas Wily of Kennet & Rachel his wife (the said Ruth Miller & Rachel Wily being daughters of Thomas Rowland, dec.) to Joshua Hadly & Mary his wife of Mill Creek Hundred in the County of New Castle on Delaware. Now Mary Powell, William Miller, Ruth Miller, Thomas Wily & Rachel Wily release to Joshua & Mary Hadly a tract in Aston containing 250 acres bounded by land of Moses Key, Chester Creek, land of John Neals & John Pennell. Signed Mary Powell, William Miller, Ruth Miller, Thomas Wily & Rachel Wily. Delivered in the presence of William Wily, Margaret Richards & Sarah Powell. Recorded 28 Mar 1733. (E5:144).

Deed. On 12 Aug 1730 Nicholas Newlin of Concord, yeoman, eldest son of Nathaniel Newlin, late of Concord, gentleman, dec., John Newlin of Concord, another son of Nathaniel, Nathaniel Newlin of Concord, the other son of Nathaniel, dec., Richard Clayton of Concord, cordwainer, & Mary his wife, one of the daughters of Nathaniel, dec., William Baily of Kennet & Kezia his wife, another daughter of Nathaniel, dec., & to Richard Eavonson of Thornbury, yeoman, & Jemima his wife, another daughter of Nathaniel, dec. Whereas William Penn, dec., by deed dated 22 & 23 Mar 1681 granted to Nicholas Moore, James Claypoole, Phillip Ford, William Shardlow, Edward Pierce, John Simcock, Thomas Brassey, Thomas Parker & Edward Brooks 20,000 acres of land to be laid out in the province in trust for the Free Society of Traders. On 1 June 1688 there was laid out to Benjamin Chambers, president of the Free Society of Traders, for the use of the Society, 7,100 acres being part in the County of Chester. The trustees of the Society of Free Traders by deed dated 10 June 1724 granted to Nathaniel Newlin the 7,100 acres, recorded Chester, Book D, Vol 4, Page 369. Whereas Nathaniel Newlin died intestate, all his lands were divided amongst his children & the eldest to receive a double share. Now the division of said lands Nicholas Newlin, John Newlin, Nathaniel Newlin, Richard Clayton & Mary his wife, William Baily & Kezia his wife grant & release to Richard Eavenson & Jemima his wife a tract bounded by land of John Newlin, Richard Clayton & Nathaniel Newlin containing 410 acres, & the other tract bounded by land of Joseph English, Richard Clayton, William Baily & John Newlin containing 503 acres. Signed Nathaniel Newlin, Nicholas Newlin, John Newlin, Richard Clayton, Mary Clayton, William Baily & Kezia Baily. Delivered in the presence of Joseph Brinton, Henry Pierce & John Taylor. Recorded 23 May 1733. (E5:145).

Deed. On 28 Aug 1732 John Owen, sheriff of Chester County, to Obidiah Johnson of Chester County, yeoman. Whereas Thomas Pearson at the Court of Common Pleas on 30 May 1732 did recover of Samuel Pritchet late of Chester, blacksmith, a debt of £6 & damages of £0.70.6. Whereas Samuel Pritchet has a 1/2 part or moiety of a blacksmith shop & a lot of ground, the goods & chattels were seized. John Owen for £7.7 grant to Obidiah Johnson a lot in Darby township with the smith's shop. Signed John Owen. Delivered in the presence of Phillip Yarnall, Jr., & Robert Love. Recorded 24 May 1733. (E5:149).

Deed. On 30 May 1731 John Owen, sheriff of Chester County, to Obidiah Johnson of Chester County, yeoman. Whereas John Crooker at the Court of Common Pleas on 25 May 1731 did recover against John Wallace of Chester, cutter, a debt of £44.60 damages. Whereas John Wallace has a moiety of a smith's shop & a lot of ground lying in Darby bounded by the foot of the bridge & the mill race, & these were seized. Now John Owen for £30.10 grant to Obidiah Johnson the above mentioned 1/2 part of the smith's shop & ground. Signed John Owen. Delivered in the presence of Thomas Giffing & John Best. Recorded 24 May 1733. (E5:149).

Deed. On 31 Aug 1732 Arthur Shiel of Chester & Mary his wife, the widow & admin. of Jonas Sandelands, late of Chester, gentleman, her

29

late husband to William Trehern of Chester, innholder. Whereas in Chester County Orphans Court on 10 Apr 1732 before John Crosby, Joseph Brinton, Samuel Hollingsworth & Thomas Cummings, justices present, whereas Arthur Sheil & Mary his wife, the widow & admin. of Jonas Sandelands, her late husband, Letter of Administration granted in Chester 17 Apr 1728, & at the time of his death Jonas Sandelands was owner of several lots of land and left 8 young children begotten of Mary to survive him, one lot bounded by a lot of Jacob Howell, a lot of John Wharton & Chester Creek containing 1 1/4 acre, & another lot bounded by a lot of Jonas Sandelands, dec., & a lot of Ruth Hoskins containing 2 1/2 acres, another lot bounded by the Great Road, & a lot of Ruth Hoskins containing 1 acre, another lot bounded by High Street, land of Grace Lloyd, & a lot of John Owens containing 1 3/4 acre, & 2 lots being 80' x 120' bounded by a lot of Richard Bickham, Middle Street, & lots of Evan & Thomas Morgan. Arthur Shell & Mary his wife exhibited a true inventory of the estate of the dec., the value being £124.8, & the debts of the dec. come to £181.17 & an account of debts yet due being £210.10. The said Intestates personal estate will not be sufficient to pay his debts & maintain his children until the eldest reaches 21 years or to put them out to apprentices & to teach them to read & write. Arthur Sheil & Mary his wife be allowed to sell said lands to pay the said debts & the residue to the maintenance of the children. Now Arthur Shell & Mary his wife £135.10 grant to William Trehorn 2 lots of land in Chester, one bounded by Free Street, a small piece of land of Jonas Sandelands, land of Ruth Hoskins & High Street containing 2 1/2 acres, & another lot bounded by land of Ruth Hoskins, & the last mentioned lot containing 1 acre. Signed Arthur Sheil & Mary Sheil. Delivered in the presence of Joseph Parker, John Wright & Robert Parke. Recorded 25 May 1733. (E5:150).

Deed. On 22 June 1723 David Mortonson of Calcoone Hooke in Darby, yeoman, to Conrad Nethermarke of Calcoone Hooke in Darby, yeoman. Whereas Peter Peterson by deed dated 1 Aug 1711 granted to Mathias Noselins & Morton Mortonson, the late father of David, a tract in Calcoone Hooke in the township of Darby containing 145 acres, recorded Chester, Book C, Page 200, on 28 Nov 1711. Now David Mortonson & Ellin his wife for £50 grant to Conrad Nethermarke 1 lot bounded by the Creek & the road containing 124 perches, another lot bounded by the road & land of Hans Urin containing 14 2/3 acres, another piece of land on Grey Island lying between land of Hans Urin & Morton Mortonson containing 2 acres, another lot on Grey Island bounded by land of Hans Urin, Darby Creek & Boobe's marsh containing 17 acres, another lot lying between Morton Mortonson's land & Darby Creek containing 2 3/4 acres, another lot being undivided bounded by Darby Creek opposite a small run called Worm Creek containing 3 acres, & another lot undivided situated by Mackupuepotes containing 1 1/2 acres which was confirmed & released to David Mortonson by Mathias Neselins. Signed David Mortonson & Ellin Mortonson. Delivered in the presence of Thomas Cook, Jonathon Smith & Thomas Pulford. Peaceable possession of land & receipt of £50 from Conrad Nethermarke. Signed David Mortonson. Delivered in the presence of Morris Howell & Thomas Mugleston. On Dec 13 1731 receipt of £5 being last payment from Conrad Nethermarke. Signed David Mortonson. Delivered in the presence of Lawerence Ross & Thomas Curry. Recorded 25 June 1733. (E5:154).

Deed. On 13 Oct 1728 David Morton & Ellin his wife & Swan Boon, all of Darby, to Conrad Nethermarke of Darby, weaver. Whereas this is a tract of land laid out for the use of the mill upon Mackerneppales Creek in the township of Darby bounded by land of Andrew Yeion & John Brown containing 12 acres which was equally divided between Andrew Yeion, Swan Boon & David Morton, the David Morton having 2 shares. Now David Morton & Ellin his wife, with Swan Boon, for £6.10 grant to Conrad Nethermarke his 2 shares of the said land. Signed David Morton, Ellin Morton & Swan Boon. Delivered in the presence of Morris Howell & Thomas Mugleston. Recorded 26 June 1733. (E5:156).

Deed. On Feb 1724 Edward Dangor of Chester, cooper, to Joseph Reyner of Chester, cordwainer, & Mary his wife. Whereas Lydia Wade by deed dated 10 Oct 1699 granted to Edward Dangor a tract in Chester bounded by the courthouse, the Delaware River & the street, recorded Chester, Book A, Vol 1, Page 187, on 23 May 1702. Now Edward Dangor for £70 grants to Joseph Reyner & Mary his wife all the said tract. Signed Edward Dangor. Delivered in the presence of Thomas Gifting & Joseph Parker. Recorded 28 June 1733. (E5:158).

Deed. On 28 Aug 1732 Arthur Shiel of Chester, yeoman, & Mary his wife, the widow & administer of Jonas Sandelands, late of Chester, gentleman, her late husband, to John Owen of Chester, gentleman. Whereas Arthur Sheil & Mary his wife, relict & admin. for the goods & chattels of Jonas Sandelands, came before the Orphans Court on 22 May

1732, whereas Jonas Sandelands died intestate & letters of admin. were granted to Mary on 17 Apr 1728. Jonas Sandelands was, at his death, owner of several lots of land lying in Chester & 8 children begotten of the body of Mary, the one lot bounded by land of Jacob Howell, John Wharton & Chester Creek containing 1 1/4 acres, another lot bounded by Free Street, land of Jonas Sandelands, dec., land of Ruth Hoskins & High Street containing 2 1/2 acres, another lot bounded by the Great Road & land of Ruth Hoskins containing 1 acres, another lot bounded by High Street, land of Grace Lloyd & John Owens containing 1 3/4 acres, & a piece being 2 lots being 80' x 120' bounded by land of Richard Bickmans, Middle Street, lots of Evan & Thomas Morgan & church land. Whereas the Jonas Sandelands estate was not enough to pay his debts & support his children until the eldest becomes 21 years, Arthur Sheil & Mary his wife are allowed to sell above mentioned lots. Now Arthur Sheil & Mary his wife for £72.10 and a yearly rent of 3 shillings to be paid the heirs of Jonas Sandelands grant to John Owen a lot described above containing 1 3/4 acres. Signed Arthur Sheil & Mary Sheil. Delivered in the presence of John Wharton & Peter Looden. Memorandum. Peaceful possession was given to John Owen in the presence of Phillip Phillip & Joseph Parker. Recorded 27 June 1733. (E5:160).

Release. On 2 June 1733 Ruth Hoskins of Chester, widow & admin. of the goods & chattels of John Hoskins, late of Chester, gentleman, dec., John Hoskins of Chester, eldest son of John Hoskins, dec., Stephen Hoskins of Chester, son of John Hoskins, dec., Joseph Hoskins of Chester, son of John Hoskins, dec., to John Mather of Chester, merchant, & Mary his wife, who was the daughter of John Hoskins, dec. Whereas the commissioners of William Penn by deed dated 20 Aug 1705 granted to Caleb Pussey 3 tracts in the township of Chester, one containing 17 acres, another containing 1 + acre, & the other containing 117 acres, recorded Philadelphia, Book A, Vol 3, Page 119. Whereas by deed dated 20 Dec 1706 Caleb Pussey granted to Henry Worley 1/4 share of the 3 tracts of land recorded 19 Sep 1707 in Chester, Book B, Page 100. Whereas Jonas Sandelands & Mary his wife by deed dated 21 June 1714 granted to Henry Worley a tract of land containing 1 1/2 acres adjoining the tract containing 17 acres. Whereas Caleb Pussey & Henry Worley did grant to Nicholas Fairlamb, John Sharples & others 1/2 acre of the 17 acres for a burying ground for the Quakers. Whereas Caleb Pussey & Ann his wife & Henry Worley & Mary his wife by deed dated 22 June 1714 granted to John Hoskins all the remaining part of 17 acres after the burying ground was conveyed & the 1 1/2 acres from Jonas

Sandelands containing 18 1/4 acres. Whereas Jonas Sandelands by lease dated 27 Feb 1711/2 did let to Robert Hodgson adjoining the 18+ acres for 551 years, recorded Chester, Book C, Page 240, on 3 Apr 1712 & Robert Hodgson & Sarah his wife by deed dated 4 Apr 1715 assigned lot to John Hoskins for the residue of 551 years. John Hoskins died intestate leaving his wife Ruth & 4 children being minors to survive him. The children have now come of age & in their own interest to prevent further differences that might arise amongst them agreed the said properties to be the share of Mary, the now wife of John Mathers & daughter of the dec. Now Ruth Hoskins, John Hoskins, Stephen Hoskins & Joseph Hoskins release to John Mather & Mary his wife the tract in Chester bounded by land of the late Jonas Sandelands, the road that leads from Chester to Edgmont, land late of Samuel Buckly, burying ground & Chester Creek containing 18 1/4 acres, & another tract conveyed by lease to John Hoskins bounded by Chester Creek, Edgmont Road, & the other tract containing 3 acres. Signed Ruth Hoskins, John Hoskins, Stephen Hoskins & Joseph Hoskins. Delivered in the presence of Joseph Parker & Robert Parke. Recorded 3 July 1733. (E5:164).

Mortgage. On 24 May 1733 Owen Thomas of Merion in the County of Philadelphia, merchant, to Benjamin Duffield of the City of Philadelphia, tanner. Owen Thomas for £100 grant to Benjamin Duffield a tract in the township of Whiteland in Duffrun Manor in the County of Chester bounded by land of William Burge & company, land of Thomas Richard, Isaac Molyn, James Davids, David Evans, Owen Owen & Richard Owen containing 550 acres. Owen Thomas to pay £6 on or before 24 May 1734 & £106 on or before 24 May 1735. Signed Owen Thomas. Delivered in the presence of Samuel Lewis, Charles Brockden & William Parsons. Recorded 4 Aug 1733. (E5:168).

Release of Right. On 5 Apr 1733 Mary Yard of Darby, widow, to Benjamin Duffield of the City of Philadelphia, tanner. Whereas Mary Yard, by the name of Mary Smith, by mortgage deed dated 22 Nov 1731 granted to Benjamin Duffield for £111 a tract containing 50 acres with the payment of £111 plus interest to be paid in one payment on or before 22 Nov 1732, recorded Chester, Book E, Vol 5, Page 90, & the sum of £111 & interest are unpaid. Now Mary Yard for the previous amount advanced & £10 paid now grant & release to Benjamin Duffield the tract in Darby bounded by land of John Hallowell containing 50 acres. Signed

Mary Yard. Delivered in the presence of Charles Brockden & Joseph Brentnall. Recorded 4 Aug 1733. (E5:170).

Lease & Release. On 15 & 16 June 1726 John Crosby of Ridley, gentleman, & Susannah his wife to Thomas Morgan of Chester, tailor. Whereas Sarah Taylor, widow of Isaac Taylor, dec., late of Springfield, & Isaac Taylor, eldest son & heir of Isaac Taylor, by deed dated 28 Nov 1721 granted to John Crosby 4 lots lying together in Chester being 160' x 120' bounded by Middle Street, land of John Owens & High Street with the rent of 6 pence payable to Jonas Sandelands & his heirs. Whereas Jonas Sandelands & Mary his wife by deed dated 14 Jan 1714 granted to Nicholas Fairlamb a tract of land in Chester containing 11 1/2 acres with the yearly rent of 5 shillings to be paid Jonas Sandelands & his heirs, & whereas Nicholas Fairlamb & Katherine his wife by deed dated 20 July 1718 granted to John Crosby the 11 1/2 acres. Now John Crosby & Susannah his wife for £50 grant to Thomas Morgan a lot in Chester being 40' x 120' bounded by land of Thomas Giffing, John Owens, & Middle Street, also a tract in Chester bounded by Chester Creek, land late of Robert Hodgson, now of Ruth Hoskins, Edgmont Road, & land late of Richard Friends containing 11 1/2 acres. Also Thomas Morgan to pay £0.5.6 yearly rent to Jonas Sandelands & his heirs. Signed John Crosby & Susannah Crosby. Delivered in the presence of Richard Bond & Joseph Reynolds. Recorded 3 Sep 1733. (E5:172).

Sheriffs Deed. On 25 Aug 1733 John Parry, sheriff of the County of Chester, to John Hopkins of the City of Philadelphia, mariner, & Joshua Maddox of the City of Philadelphia, merchant. Whereas Isaac Norris, Jr., of Philadelphia, gentleman, at the Court of Common Pleas on 23 Feb 1730/1 did recover against Thomas Pattison, late of Chester County, yeoman, a debt of £254 & £0.70.6 for damages. John Owen, Esq., late sheriff of Chester County (my predecessor), was commanded to levy against goods & chattels of Thomas Pattison for the debt being a tract of land in Darby being about 2 1/2 acres. Now John Parry by order of the Court of Common Pleas for £235 grants to John Hopkins & Joshua Maddox a tract in Darby bounded by land of Edward Williams, the road leading from Darby to Haverford, land of John Paschalls, a lot of Isaac Norris now in the possession of Thomas Pulford containing 2 1/2 acres. Signed John Parry. Delivered in the presence of Stephen Evans & John Owen. Recorded Aug 1733. (E5:175).

Deed. On 13 May 1725 John Simcock of Hilltown in the township of Marlborough, yeoman, & Martha his wife to Joseph Parker of Chester, yeoman. Whereas William Penn by deed dated 3 & 4 May 1682 granted to John Simcock of Ridley, yeoman, father of John Simcock a tract containing 2,875 acres. John Simcock, the father, by his will dated 25 July 1702 bequeathed to his son, John Simcock, a tract containing 1,000 acres being part of the 2,875 acres. Now John Simcock & Martha his wife for £120 grant to Joseph Parker 3 pieces of land in Hilltown, one bounded by land of John Bennett containing 200 acres, another bounded by land of Thomas Parsons containing 100 acres, & another bounded by land of Richard Barnard & Henry Hayes containing 159 acres. Signed John Simcock & Martha Simcock. Delivered in the presence of Robert Carter, Richard Story & Robert Jones. Recorded 6 Sep 1733. (E5:177).

Lease & Release. On 7 & 8 Apr 1730 John Salkeld of Chester, malster, & Agnes his wife to Joseph Parker of Chester, yeoman. Whereas William Penn by deed dated 3 & 4 Mar 1681 granted to Richard Collett of the Parish of St. Martin's in the County of Middlesex, vintner, a tract of 1,000 acres in the province of Pennsylvania. Whereas 1,000 acres was laid out in the township of Westtown to Richard Collett. Richard Collet by deed dated 15 & 16 May 1721 with limitations & trusts confirm to Erasmus Cole, John Mead & Edward Peacock the 1,000 acres. Whereas Erasmus Cole, John Mead & Edward Peacock with Elizabeth Green wife of John Green of London, wine cooper, the daughter of Richard Collett, by deed dated 1 & 2 Sep 1727 grant to John Salkeld the 1,000 acres. Now John Salkeld & Agnes his wife for £80 grant to Joseph Parker one full moiety of the 1,000 acres to be divided in 2 equal parts. Signed John Salkeld & Agnes Salkeld. Delivered in the presence of Joseph Salkeld & John Salkeld, Jr. Recorded 7 Sep 1733. (E5:179).

Lease & Release. On 30 Apr & 1 May 1733 John Wright of Hempfield in the County of Lancaster in the province of Pennsylvania, gentleman, to Joseph Parker of Chester, yeoman. Whereas the commissioners of William Penn by deed dated 11 May 1702 granted to Albert Hendricks a tract in Chester containing 570 acres, recorded Philadelphia, Book A, Vol 2, Page 248. Whereas Albert Hendricks did give but not effectively convey unto his son James Hendricks 100 acres, Albert Hendricks did give to his son Johannes Hindricks 50 acres and Johannes Hindricks by deed dated 1 Aug 1702 granted to his brother James Hindricks the 50 acres, and whereas Albert Hindricks did give but not effectively convey to his son Albert Hindricks the younger a tract of 70 acres, & whereas

John Childs by deed dated 10 Feb 1703 granted to James Hindricks 1+ acres, & whereas Albert Hindricks the father, James Hindricks, one of the sons of Albert & Lucy Hindricks, Albert Hindricks, Jr., another son & his wife Elizabeth by deed dated 8 Jan 1714 did grant to John Wright all those several tracts of land containing 221 acres. Now John Wright for £370 granted to Joseph Parker all the plantation where he had dwelt in Chester, bounded by the Delaware River, land of Albert Hindrickson, Thomas Bright, Jeremiah Carter & Jacob Romans containing 221 acres. Signed John Wright. Delivered in the presence of Benjamin Davis, Richard Barry & Robert Parker. Recorded 8 Sep 1733. (E5:183).

Lease & Release. On 29 & 30 Nov 1731 Jeremiah Carter of Chester, weaver, & Mary his wife to Ninevah Carter of Chester, weaver, one of the sons of Jeremiah & Mary Carter. Whereas the commissioners of William Penn by deed dated 15 Apr 1689 granted to Robert Wade of Essex House in Chester a tract containing 230 acres, recorded Chester, Book A, Vol 1, Page 21, & whereas Robert Wade & Lydia his wife by deed dated 8 Mar 1797/8 granted to Henry Worley a tract in Chester containing 180 acres being part of the 230 acres. Henry Worley & Mary his wife by deed dated 23 Nov 1702 granted to Jeremiah Carter a tract containing 180 acres. Now Jeremiah Carter & Mary his wife, for the love they bear their son & 10 shillings, grant to Ninevah Carter a tract in Chester bounded by land of Joseph Parker, the road from Chester to Bethell, land of Jacob Roman & Roger Shelly containing 88 acres. Signed Jeremiah Carter & Mary Carter. Delivered in the presence of Ann Swarfer, Joseph Parker & Michael Atkinson. Recorded 8 Sep 1733. (E5:186).

Release. On 1 Nov 1731 John Yeates, late of the City of Philadelphia, but now of the Island of Barbados, merchant, to Joseph Parker of Chester, yeoman. Whereas John Taylor, Esq., sheriff of the County of Chester, by deed dated 27 Feb 1723 granted to Samuel Carpenter a tract, whereas Jasper Yeates, the father of John Yeates, lately dwelt with a grainer, store house & several lots of parcels of land in the town of Chester. Whereas Samuel Carpenter & Mary his wife by deed dated 9 & 10 Oct 1724 grant to George McCall of Philadelphia, merchant, all the said tract of lands. Whereas George McCall & Ann his wife by deed dated 13 & 14 Jan 1729 granted to John Yeates all the brick tenement & lots of land. Now John Yeates for £200 grant & confirm to Joseph Parker all the lots in Chester, one being 2 lots with the brick house bounded by lots of John Hoskins, Joseph Reyner, George Albridge & Robert Barber, and 2 lots being 88' x 120' bounded by land late of David Lloyd, the street that runs from the land of the late David Lloyd & Chester Creek & Robert Barber, & another lot being 80' wide running to the low water mark of the Delaware River, bounded by land late of David Lloyd & the Delaware River, also one back lot being in 3 parcels one of which is bounded by the land late of David Lloyd, land late of Jonas Sandelands containing 2 1/2 acres, the other 2 parcels adjoin the 1st parcel bounded by land of Jasper Yeates, David Lloyd, Queen's Road containing 3+ acres. Signed John Yeates. Delivered in the presence of Henry Coombe, Francis Sewer & Samuel Mickle. Memorandum. On 6 Jun 1732 John Yeates received of Joseph Parker £132.10 with the £67.10 in the loan office is the full consideration. Signed George McCall. Delivered in the presence of John Ladd, Jr., & Peter Robertson. Recorded 10 Sep 1733. (E5:189).

Lease & Release. On 27 & 28 Mar 1732 Nineveh Carter of Chester, yeoman, & Mary his wife to Joseph Parker of Chester, yeoman. Whereas the commissioners of William Penn by deed dated 15 Apr 1689 granted to Robert Wade of Essex House in Chester, a tract containing 230 acres, recorded Chester, Book A, Vol 1, Page 21. Whereas Robert Wade & Lydia his wife by deed dated 8 Mar 1697/8 granted to Henry Worley of Chester 180 acres, part of the 230 acres. Whereas Henry Worley & Mary his wife by deed dated 23 Nov 1702 granted the 180 acres to Jeremiah Carter, father of Nineveh Carter. Whereas Jeremiah Carter by deed dated 29 & 30 Nov 1731 granted to Nineveh Carter, his son, 88 acres being part of the 180 acres, recorded Chester, Book E, Vol 5, Page 186. Now Nineveh Carter & Mary his wife for £110 grant to Joseph Parker a tract in Chester bounded by land Jacob Roman, land of Joseph Parker, the road that leads from Chester to Bethell & land of Rodger Shelly containing 88 acres. Signed Nineveh Carter & Mary Carter. Delivered in the presence of Jeremiah Carter, Joseph Cowpland & Timothy Morton. Recorded 1733. (E5:192).

Deed. On 26 Sep 1733 Phillip Yarnall of Edgmont, yeoman, & Dorothy his wife to John Mather of Chester, merchant. Whereas James Sandelands, late of Chester, merchant, dec., son & heir of James Sandelands, late of Chester, dec., by deed dated 10 Sep 1700 granted to Stephen Jackson all the house & land, being a corner lot in Chester, being 40' x 120'. Whereas Stephen Jackson by deed dated 17 June 1701 granted to John Worrilaw the house & lot. Whereas James Sandelands by deed dated 15 Jan 1701 granted to John Worrilaw a lot lying to the above mentioned lot being 40' x 120'. John Worrilaw by deed dated 29

Aug 1704 granted to Phillip Yarnall the 2 lots in Chester. Now Phillip
Yarnall & Dorothy his wife for £175 granted to John Mather the 2 lots.
Signed Phillip Yarnall & Dorothy Yarnall. Delivered in the presence of
James Mather, William Turner & Robert Parke. Recorded 27 Sep 1733.
(E5:195).

Lease & Release. On 29 & 30 Apr 1733 John Troke of Caln, yeoman, to
John Bullar of Chester County, yeoman. John Troke for £60 grant to
John Bullar a tract in Caln bounded by land of Nicholas Smith containing
122 acres, being land John Troke purchased of John Bullar. Signed John
Troke. Delivered in the presence of John Taylor, Jacob Taylor & Francis
Fore. Recorded 4 Oct 1733. (E5:197).

Lease & Release. On 21 Jan 1720 Jonas Sandelands of Chester, yeoman,
& Mary his wife to John Wright of Chester, yeoman. Whereas Jonas
Sandelands & Mary his wife for £24 grant to John Wright 4 lots in
Chester lying together, being 120' x 160' bounded by land of Jacob
Howell, High Street, & land of Jonas Sandelands, being part of 20 acres
William Penn granted to James Sandelands, the father of Jonas, by deed
dated 31 May 1686. Signed Jonas Sandelands & Mary Sandelands.
Delivered in the presence of John Wade & Richard Marsden. Recorded 9
Nov 1733. (E5:200).

Lease & Release. On 29 Dec 1719 John Cox of Kennet, yeoman, &
Rachel his wife to Robert Carter of Marlborough, yeoman. Whereas the
commissioners of William Penn by deed dated 7 Feb 1704 granted to
John Budd of Philadelphia, brewer, a tract in Kennet containing 500
acres, recorded Philadelphia, Book A, Vol 2, Page 228. John Budd by
deed dated 26 Oct 1706 granted to Nicholas Pyle then of Concord,
yeoman, 200 acres, part of the 500 acres, recorded Chester, Book C, Vol
3, Page 102. Nicholas Pyle by deed dated 1 Apr 1713 granted to John
Cox the 200 acres. Now John Cox & Rachel his wife for £130 grant to
Robert Carter a tract in Kennet bounded by Letetia's Manor containing
200 acres. Signed John Cox & Rachel Cox. Delivered in the presence of
Vincent Caldell, Henry Nayle, John Talkinton & Betty Caldwell.
Recorded 9 Nov 1733. (E5:202).

Lease & Release. On 1 & 2 July 1733 Richard Barry of Chester,
merchant, & Mary his wife to Richard Backhouse of Chester, clerk.
Whereas James Sandelands, late of the County of Chester, merchant,

dec., became seized of certain lots in Chester, one being 40' x 120' bounded by High Street, Delaware River, the Market Place, St. Paul's Church & a church lot, another lot being 40' x 80' bounded by land of Isaac Taylor & the Market Place, sometime after James Sandelands died. Whereas James Sandelands, son & heir of James Sandelands, dec., granted the first lot to John Evans, late of Chester, joiner, dec., the last lot granted to Isaac Tayler of Chester, yeoman, who likewise granted the said lot to John Evans. John Evans died intestate, & whereas Edward Evans of the City of Philadelphia, yeoman (son & heir of John Evans dec.), by deed dated 13 July 1715 granted to John Frogg of the City of Philadelphia & Mary his wife the 2 said lots. John Frogg died intestate & the 2 lots fell to Mary Frogg, widow of John Frogg, & whereas Mary Frogg sometime later died intestate & the 2 lots descended to her son William Battle of Cristiana Mills in the County of New Castle upon the Delaware, gentleman. William Battle by deed dated 25 & 26 Mar 1723 granted to Robert Barber the 2 lots of land. Whereas Parnella the wife of William Battle at the request of Robert Barber by release dated 13 May 1723 released all right to said 2 lots. Whereas Robert Barber by deed dated 1 & 2 Apr 1730 granted to Richard Barry the 2 lots of land. Now Richard Barry & Mary his wife for £30 grant to Richard Backhouse the said 2 lots. Signed Richard Barry & Mary Barry. Delivered in the presence of John Wade, Thomas Bracken & Arthur Shaw. Recorded 15 Nov 1733. (E5:205).

Lease & Release. On 1 & 2 Mar 1732 Thomas Wills of Middletown, cordwainer, & Ann his wife, one of the daughters of Peter Hunter, late of Middletown, tanner, dec., to Jonathon Hunter of Middletown, tanner. Whereas William Penn by deed dated 1 Aug 1684 granted to David Ogden a tract containing 200 acres. David Ogden made his will dated 16 July 1705 whereby he gave his estate to his wife Martha for her lifetime, & at her death or marriage to go to his son Jonathon Ogden. If Martha should marry, Jonathon Ogden to pay her £8 a year during her life, David Ogden soon after died & Martha married James Thomas & the 200 acres came to Jonathon Ogden as per the directions of his father's will. Whereas Caleb Pussey by deed dated 3 Feb 1710 granted to Jonathon Ogden a tract containing 134 acres adjoining the tract in Middletown. Whereas Jonathon Ogden, James Thomas & Martha his wife by deed dated 29 & 30 July 1717 granted to Peter Hunter the 134 acres & 41 acres of the 200 acres, recorded Chester, Book D, Vol 4, Page 64. Whereas Thomas Bransley, late of Middletown, blacksmith, by deed dated 30 May 1716 granted to John Baldwin then of Chester, merchant,

3 tracts in Middletown containing in whole 335 acres, one tract contains 30 acres which Thomas Bransley purchased of George Smedley being part of 295 acres confirmed to George Smedley by patent dated 18 May 1702, another tract contains 105 acres which Jonathon Ogden & others conveyed to Thomas Bransley, the other tract containing 200 acres which Henry Hollingsworth granted to Thomas Bransley. Whereas John Baldwin & Katherine his wife by deed dated 26 May 1720 granted the 3 tracts to their son John Baldwin. Whereas John Baldwin, the son, by deed dated 22 Dec 1725 granted the 3 tracts to Peter Hunter. Peter Hunter died intestate, & after his death the same descended to his children. Now Thomas Wills & Ann his wife for £70.10 grant to Jonathon Hunter the 1 full equal & undivided part of the plantation & 2 tracts in Middletown, one tract bounded by land of John Turner, William Hill, Phillip Otleys, Edgmont Road, William Nook, William Trego & John Worrals containing 221 acres, & another tract bounded by Dismall Run, land of Jacob Minshall, George Smedley & William Nooks containing 170 acres, in whole 391 acres. Signed Thomas Wills & Ann Wills. Delivered in the presence of John Taylor & William Hill. Recorded 16 Nov 1733. (E5:209).

Release. On 3 Oct 1728 Martha Taylor of Thornbury, widow & relict of Isaac Taylor, late of Thornbury, practioner of Physic, dec., & executrix of his will, & John Taylor of Thornbury, yeoman, executor of the will of Isaac Taylor, to Jacob Taylor of Thornbury, yeoman. Whereas James Widdows, Mary Edwards, Christian Pullin, Margaret Von & William Thomas having came over as servants into the province at the settlement & thereby having rights to 50 acres each. James Widdows & Mary Edwards by deed dated 30 Mar 1704, Christian Pullin by deed dated 28 Mar 1705, Margret Von by deed dated 3 Apr 1705, & William Thomas by deed dated 29 Sep 1705 granted to Isaac Taylor each of their said right to 50 acres amounting to 250 acres. Whereas John Martin, late of Chester County, who came into this province a servant in 1681 having a right to 50 acres by deed dated 10 Apr 1707 granted the 50 acres to Isaac Taylor. The said 50 acres & 250 acres being laid out in the township of Bradford lying together, & whereas James Chevers & John Sangor came over as servants thereby having rights to 50 acres each by warrant dated 29 Nov 17109. James Chevers by deed dated 26 Dec 1710 & John Sangor by deed dated 27 July 1715 conveyed their rights in 50 acres each to Isaac Taylor, whereas the 100 acres was laid out adjoining the above mentioned land. Whereas John Broomal & John Clews came as servants in the year 1682, John Broomal by deed dated 1 June 1717 & John Clew by 12 June 1717 conveyed all rights to 50 acres each to Isaac Taylor, the said 100 acres was laid out adjoining the above tract. Isaac Taylor in possession of 500 acres by his will dated 14 May 1728, whereby he gave 1 moiety of the tract to his son Jacob Taylor, & some lands & tenements to his wife & sons John & Phillip with part of his personal estate. Executrix & executor to dispose of estate and divide residue between my wife & 5 children. 1/6 part to my wife, 1/6 part to my son John, 1/6 part to my son Phillip, 1/6 part to my son Jacob, 1/6 part to my daughter Ann, & 1/6 part to my daughter Mary. Monies to be paid within 2 years of my death; if either of the daughters should die before the division, their share is to be divided amongst the surviving children, and Isaac Taylor soon after died. Now Martha Taylor, John Taylor, for £150 grant to Jacob Taylor that tract in Bradford bounded by land of Abiah Taylor, Jacob Taylor, Richard Woodward & Joseph Townsend containing 250 acres, being 1/2 of the 500 acres. Signed Martha Taylor & John Taylor. Delivered in the presence of Phillip Taylor, Reece Jones & Anne Taylor. Recorded 1 Dec 1733. (E5:214).

Release. On 3 May 1733 Jacob Taylor of Bradford, yeoman, & Grace his wife to John Taylor of Thornbury, yeoman. Whereas James Widdows, Mary Edwards, Christian Pullin, Margaret Von & William Thomas having came over as servants into the province at the settlement & thereby having rights to 50 acres each. James Widdows & Mary Edwards by deed dated 30 Mar 1704, Christian Pullin by deed dated 28 Mar 1705, Margret Von by deed dated 3 Apr 1705, & William Thomas by deed dated 29 Sep 1705 granted to Isaac Taylor each of their said right to 50 acres amounting to 250 acres. Whereas John Martin, late of Chester County, who came into this province a servant in 1681 having a right to 50 acres by deed dated 10 Apr 1707 granted the 50 acres to Isaac Taylor. The said 50 acres & 250 acres being laid out in the township of Bradford lying together & whereas James Chevers & John Sangor came over as servants thereby having rights to 50 acres each by warrant dated 29 Nov 1709. James Chevers by deed dated 26 Dec 1710 & John Sangor by deed dated 27 July 1715 conveyed their rights in 50 acres each to Isaac Taylor, whereas the 100 acres was laid out adjoining the above mentioned land. Whereas John Broomal & John Clews came as servants in the year 1682, John Broomal by deed dated 1 June 1717 & John Clews by 12 June 1717 conveyed all rights to 50 acres each to Isaac Taylor, the said 100 acres was laid out adjoining the above tract. Isaac Taylor in possession of 500 acres by his will dated 14 May 1728, whereby he gave 1 moiety of the tract to his son Jacob Taylor, & some lands & tenements to his wife &

sons John & Phillip with part of his personal estate. Executrix & executor to dispose of estate and divide residue between my wife & 5 children. 1/6 part to my wife, 1/6 part to my son John, 1/6 part to my son Phillip, 1/6 part to my son Jacob, 1/6 part to my daughter Ann, & 1/6 part to my daughter Mary. Monies to be paid with 2 years of my death if either of the daughter should die before the division their share is to be divided amongst the surviving children, and Isaac Taylor soon after died. On 2 & 3 May 1728 Martha Taylor & John Taylor conveyed to Jacob Taylor the residue of the 500 acres being 250 acres. Now Jacob Taylor & Grace his wife for £400 grant to John Taylor a tract in Bradford bounded by land of Abiah Taylor, Richard Woodward & Joseph Townsend, containing 500 acres. Signed Jacob Taylor & Grace Taylor. Delivered in the presence of Abraham Johnson & William Seymour. Recorded 1 Dec 1733. (E5:217).

Deed. On 27 May 1729 John Taylor, sheriff of Chester County, to John Welden, Jr. Whereas Anthony Morris of Philadelphia in the Court of Common Pleas recovered against Henry Hollingsworth & Paul Sanders, late of Chester, executors of the will of James Mills, tailor, for £12.14.6 debt & 56 shillings for damages levied on the land of James Mills at the time of his death being 2 lots & 4 acres of wood land in Chichester bounded by the River Delaware, land of Johannes Rolson, William Clayton, James Brown, John Hulbert & Walter Martin. Whereas John Taylor sold said land to Richard Edwards, & Richard Edwards sold to John Welden, Jr., for £12.10. Signed John Taylor, sheriff. Delivered in the presence of Peter Evans & Joseph Parker. Recorded 31 Dec 1733. (E5:220).

Deed. On 18 Apr 1719 Thomas Baldwin of Chester, blacksmith, & Mary his wife to Edward Carter of Chester, weaver. Whereas William Penn by deed dated 1 June 1684 granted to William Woodmansee a tract lying on the west side of Upland Creek. William Woodmansee by deed dated 8 Mar 1697/8 granted to Thomas Baldwin. Now Thomas Baldwin & Mary his wife for £37.10 grant to Edward Carter the tract in Chester bounded by Chester Creek, land of Edward Carter & Thomas Baldwin containing 50 acres being part of 100 acres as in the above mentioned deeds. Signed Thomas Baldwin & Mary Baldwin. Delivered in the presence of John Baldwin, Nicholas Fairlamb, William Baldwin & Joseph Parker. Recorded 13 Feb 1733/4. (E5:222).

Deed. On 15 Oct 1725 John Crosby of Ridley, gentleman, & Susannah his wife & Jonas Sandelands of Chester, gentleman, & Mary his wife to John Owen of Chester, carpenter. Whereas Sarah Taylor & Isaac Taylor by deed dated 8 Nov 1721 granted to John Crosby 4 lots in Chester. Now John Crosby & Susannah his wife for £7 & Jonas Sandelands for 5 shillings grant & confirm to John Owen a lot in Chester being 40' x 120' bounded by High Street, lot of John Crosby & church land. John Owen to pay Jonas Sandelands 6 pence yearly rent. Signed John Crosby, Susannah Crosby, Jonas Sandelands & Mary Sandelands. Delivered in the presence of William Davis, Enoch Enochson, Phillip Phillips & James Sandelands. Quiet & peaceful possession. Delivered in the presence of Robert Parke & Oliver Thomas. Recorded 13 Feb 1733/4. (E5:224).

Release. On 27 July 1719 Nicholas Fairlamb of Chester, gentleman, to Isaac Norris of Philadelphia, merchant. Whereas Nicholas Fairlamb & Katherine his wife by deed dated 31 May 1716 granted to Isaac Norris a tract in Chester bounded by a lot of John Sharples, Front Street, Bridge Street, Chester Creek, being piece of land Nicholas Fairlamb purchased of Jonas Sandelands on 28 May 1713 with the provision that Nicholas Fairlamb should pay £372, recorded Chester, Book D, Vol 4, Page 9. Whereas the said monies have not been paid. Now Nicholas Fairlamb for 5 shillings released all right to said lot to Isaac Norris. Signed Nicholas Fairlamb. Delivered in the presence of David Lloyd, Jonathon Ogden, Joseph Parker. Recorded 18 Feb 1733/4. (E5:226).

Lease & Release. On 30 & 31 Jan 1733/4 Isaac Norris of Fair Hill in the County of Philadelphia & Mary his wife to James Mather of Chester, hatter. Whereas Jonas Sandelands, late of Chester, & Mary his wife by deed dated 26 May 1713 granted to Nicholas Fairlamb a lot in Chester with the yearly rent of 5 shillings to be paid Jonas Sandelands, which the said piece was part of 4 acres of land formerly belonging to Urin Keen, the late grandfather of Jonas, who conveyed the same to James Sandelands, the late father of Jonas. Nicholas Fairlamb & Katherine his wife by deed dated 31 May 1716 mortgaged to Isaac Norris the said lot on the provision that Nicholas Fairlamb should pay a sum of money to Isaac Norris, recorded Chester, Book D, Vol 4, Page 9. Whereas Nicholas Fairlamb by deed dated 27 July 1719 released all right to said lot to Isaac Norris. Now Isaac Norris & Mary his wife for £425 grant to James Mather the stone tenement where James Mather now dwells lying in Chester known as Ship Tavern bounded by land of John Sharples, Front

Street, Bridge Street, & Chester Creek, also to pay 5 shillings yearly to the heirs of Jonas Sandelands. Signed Isaac Norris & Mary Norris. Delivered in the presence of Stephen Cole, William Robison, William Mather & Charles Norris. Recorded 19 Feb 1733/4. (E5:228).

Deed. On 31 Aug 1732 Arthur Sheel of Chester, yeoman, & Mary his wife, widow & admin. of the goods & chattels of Jonas Sandelands of Chester, gentleman, dec., to Jacob Howell of Chester, tanner. Whereas Arthur Sheil & Mary his wife, relict & admin. for the goods & chattels of Jonas Sandelands, came before the Orphans Court on 22 May 1732, whereas Jonas Sandelands died intestate & letters of admin. were granted to Mary on 17 Apr 1728. Jonas Sandelands was at his death owner of several lots of land lying in Chester & 8 children begotten of the body of Mary, the one lot bounded by land of Jacob Howell, John Wharton & Chester Creek containing 1 1/4 acres, another lot bounded by Free Street, land of Jonas Sandelands, dec., land of Ruth Hoskins & High Street containing 2 1/2 acres, another lot bounded by the Great Road & land of Ruth Hoskins containing 1 acre, another lot bounded by High Street, land of Grace Lloyd & John Owens containing 1 3/4 acres, & a piece being 2 lots being 80' x 120' bounded by land of Richard Bickmans, Middle Street, lots of Evan & Thomas Morgan & church land. Whereas the Jonas Sandelands estate was not enough to pay his debts & support his children until the eldest becomes 21 years, Arthur Sheil & Mary his wife are allowed to sell above mentioned lots. Now Arthur Sheil & Mary his wife for £65 grant to Jacob Howell a tract in Chester bounded by the lot of Jacob Howell, Front Street, John Whartons & Chester Creek containing 1 1/4 acres. Signed Arthur Shiel & Mary Shiel. Delivered in the presence of William Trehearne, Solomon Trener & Samuel Morris. Recorded 25 Feb 1733/4. (E5:231).

Deed. On 25 Aug 1722 Abraham Emmit of Chester County, yeoman, to Abraham Emmit, Jr., of Chester County, yeoman. Whereas William by deed dated 26 & 27 July 1681 granted to Nathaniel Allen, late of the City of Bristol in Old England, cooper, dec., 2,000 acres. Whereas Nehemiah Allen, eldest son & heir of Nathaniel Allen, by deed dated 19 Feb 1702 granted to John Budd of the City of Philadelphia, brewer, 626 acres being part of the 2,000 acres. Whereas William Penn by deed dated 2 Apr 1705 granted to John Budd a tract in Chester containing 620 acres being full compliment of the said 2,000 acres taken up. Whereas John Budd by deed dated 6 Apr 1705 granted to Abraham Emmit, Sr., a tract containing 125 acres. Now Abraham Emmit, Sr., for £37.10 grant to

Abraham Emmit, Jr., a tract in Chester County being part of the tract of 615 acres on the west side of Elk River containing 112 acres. Signed Abraham Emmit. Delivered in the presence of David Emmit & Elston Wallis. Recorded 4 Mar 1733/4. (E5:235).

Deed. On 15 Jan 1729 Abraham Emmit of Chester County, yeoman, to Abraham Emmit, Jr., of Chester County, yeoman. Whereas William by deed dated 26 & 27 July 1681 granted to Nathaniel Allen, late of the City of Bristol in Old England, cooper, dec., 2,000 acres. Whereas Nehemiah Allen, eldest son & heir of Nathaniel Allen, by deed dated 19 Feb 1702 granted to John Budd of the City of Philadelphia, brewer 626 acres being part of the 2,000 acres. Whereas William Penn by deed dated 2 Apr 1705 granted to John Budd a tract in Chester containing 620 acres being full compliment of the said 2,000 acres taken up. Whereas John Budd by deed dated 6 Apr 1705 granted to Abraham Emmit, Sr., a tract containing 625 acres, where he has lately erected a corn mill bounded by land of Abraham Emmit, Sr., the Elk River & land of Abraham Emmit, Jr., containing 3 acres being part of the 624 acres. Now Abraham Emmit, Sr., the father for £100 grant to Abraham Emmit, Jr., the son, 1 equal & undivided moiety of the water corn mill. Signed Abraham Emmit. Delivered in the presence of William Wallis & John Messar. Recorded 5 Mar 1733/4. (E5:237).

Deed. On 28 Nov 1733 John Parry, sheriff of Chester County, to Samuel Powell, Jr., of Philadelphia, merchant. Whereas Samuel Preston & Samuel Powell of Philadelphia, gentlemen, in the Court of Common Pleas on 30 May 1732 did recover against James Trent, late of Chester, gentleman, a debt of £178.16 & damages of £0.70.6 to be levied against the lands of James Trent being 160 acres being 4/5 of 1 equal 1/3 share of 600 acres being in Willis Town, also a tract of 77 acres being 4/5 of 1 equal 1/3 share of 289 acres in Goshen. The tract in Willis Town bounded by land of Yarnall, Michael Jobsons, Reece Thomas & Peter Jones containing 600 acres & the tract in Goshen bounded by land of Richard Jones, Henry Saunders, David Jones, Humphrey Thomas & land of Trent & company containing 289 acres. John Parry, sheriff, for a certain sum of money grant to Samuel Powell both tracts, one being 160 acres & one being 77 acres. Signed John Parry, sheriff. Delivered in the presence of John Kinsey, Jr., J. Growden & Joseph Parker. Recorded 5 Mar 1733/4. (E5:239).

Deed of Gift. On 19 Nov 1731 James Miller, Sr., of Newgarden in the County of Chester, yeoman, to James Miller, Jr., of Newgarden. James Miller, Sr., for love & affection grant to his son James Miller, Jr., a tract in Newgarden bounded by land of Michael Lightfoot, land formerly belonging to Joseph Willy, land which belonged to Nathaniel Richards & land of James Miller, Sr., containing 250 acres. Signed James Miller. Delivered in the presence of Thomas Hiett, William Cambell & Michael Lightfoot. Recorded 25 Mar 1734. (E5:241).

Release. On 2 June 1733 Ruth Hoskins of Chester, widow & admin. of the goods & chattels of John Hoskins late of Chester, gentleman, dec., John Hoskins of Chester, eldest son of John Hoskins, dec., Stephen Hoskins of Chester, son of John Hoskins, dec., John Mather of Chester, merchant, & Mary his wife who was the daughter of John Hoskins, dec., to Joseph Hoskins of Chester another son of John Hoskins, dec. Whereas Robert Wade late of Essex House, yeoman, was seized of a tract of land in Chester directly opposite of the old court house bounded by Chester Creek & the street with another piece of land sold & conveyed by Ann Friend & Andrew Friend to Robert Wade by deed dated 7 Sep 1687, recorded Philadelphia, Book E, Vol 5, Page 111. Robert Wade made his will dated 9 Mar 1698 & amongst other things devised the remaining of his estate to his wife Lydia Wade & soon after died. Lydia Wade by deed dated 10 Sep 1700 granted to Joseph Coebourn, recorded Chester, Book A, Vol 2, Page 6. Joseph Coebourn by deed dated 4 Feb 1703/4 granted to John Hoskins, dec., the above mentioned piece of ground. Whereas David Lloyd late of Chester, gentleman, by deed dated 13 Dec 1693 granted to John Hoskins a lot in Chester & 20 acres of woodland in Chester bounded by Ship Creek. Whereas James Sandelands late of Chester, gentleman, dec., by deed dated 10 Dec 1700 granted to John Hoskins a tract in Chester bounded by the market place & High Street. John Hoskins died intestate leaving his wife Ruth & 4 children (being then minors) to survive him. Now for the division of the said lands it is agreed between all the parties, Ruth Hoskins, John Hoskins, Stephen Hoskins, John Mather & Mary his wife grant to Joseph Hoskins his full share of his late father's land one piece being in Chester opposite the Old Courthouse, bounded by Chester Creek, the other piece being bounded by the street running from the late David Lloyd's plantation to Chester Creek, land of the late John Hoskins, land of James Lowns & land late of Samuel Bishops & the 20 acres of woodland bounded by the road from Chester to Edgmont & land late of John Simcock also a piece of land bounded by High Street. Signed Ruth Hoskins, John Hoskins, Stephen

Hoskins, John Mather & Mary Mather. Delivered in the presence of Joseph Parker & Robert Parke. Recorded 22 Apr 1734. (E5:242).

Mortgage. On 30 Oct 1733 Samuel Gelston, Minister of the Gospel to John Henderson of New London. Samuel Gelston for £32 grant to John Henderson a tract in New London bounded by land of Thomas McKain, & the creek containing 150 acres. Samuel Gelston to pay John Henderson £32 & interest on or before 1 Dec next. Signed Samuel Gelston. Delivered in the presence of John Ross & Robertson. Recorded 29 Apr 1734. (E5:245).

Lease & Release. On 1 & 2 Aug 1725 Robert Ashton of the City of Philadelphia, gentleman, to Robert Smith of New London, yeoman. Whereas the commissioners of William Penn by deed dated 2 July 1705 granted to Robert Ashton a tract in Chester County bounded by the line of the London Companies Land & land of John Budd containing 500 acres, recorded in Philadelphia, Book A, Vol 8, Page 89. Now Robert Ashton for £100 grant to Robert Smith the tract containing 500 acres. Signed Robert Ashton. Delivered in the presence of David Emmit, William Gelespy, Charles Brockden & Joseph Watson. Recorded 3 May 1734. (E5:247).

Letter of Attorney. On 17 Apr 1734 Edward Horne of Philadelphia, merchant, by mortgage dated 13 May 1730 did mortgage to Edward Bradly of Philadelphia, glazier a tract in Caln for the consideration of £100, recorded Chester, Book D, Vol A, Page 455. Now Edward Bradly for the full discharge of said mortgage appoint Jacob Howell of Chester, tanner, my lawful attorney to acknowledge that I have received full satisfaction of said mortgage. Signed Edward Bradly. Delivered in the presence of Jeremiah Langhorn & James Hamleton. Recorded 9 May 1734. (E5:249).

Letter of Attorney. On 17 Apr 1734. Whereas Neevah Carter of Chester, weaver, by mortgage dated 18 Mar 1731/2 mortgaged to Edward Horne of the Northern Liberties of the City of Philadelphia, merchant, a tract in Caln for the consideration of £100 plus interest, recorded Chester, Book E, Vol 5, Page 99. Now Edward Horne for the full discharge of said mortgage appoint Jacob Howell of Chester, tanner, my lawful attorney to acknowledge I have received full satisfaction of mortgage. Signed

47

Edward Horne. Delivered in the presence of John Wood & William
Clayton. Recorded 9 May 1734. (E5:250).

Release. On 16 May 1734 John Young of Chester, cooper, & Mary his
wife, the only daughter & heir of James Barber, late of Chester, yeoman,
dec., to Peter Dicks of Providence, yeoman. Whereas Robert Barber, late
of Chester, cordwainer, dec., uncle to James Barber, owned a tenement
& 5 lots of land in Ridley containing in whole 93 acres. Robert Barber
made his will dated 13 July 1708, wherein amongst other things devised
to his cousin the said James Barber & the heirs of his body all the
tenement & several lots of land & soon after died. James Barber granted
to David Lloyd, late of Chester, gentleman, & David Lloyd granted to
Peter Dicks said land. Now John Young & Mary his wife for £20 paid to
them by Grace Lloyd, executrix of the will of David Lloyd, as well as for
£20 paid to them by Peter Dicks for further insurance grant, convey &
confirm unto Peter Dicks all the tenement containing 93 acres. Signed
John Young & Mary Young. Delivered in the presence of Samuel
Lightfoot & Robert Parke. Recorded 22 May 1734. (E5:251).

Deed. On 23 Jan 1733 Thomas Linvill of Chichester, husbandman, &
Dinah his wife to John Worrall of Ridley, wheelwright. Whereas there is
a tract of land in Chichester bounded by Marcus Creek, land of Grubs,
meeting house road, land of Edward Richards & land of Daniel Brown
containing 86 acres being part of 2 tracts of land granted to William
Swaffer, one tract by Richard Buffington & Henry Hastings by deed
dated 6 June 1701, the other tract was granted to William Swaffer by
Phillip Roman, Robert Carter & John Kinsman by deed dated 24 May
1705 & James Swaffer & Elizabeth his wife by deed dated 29 May 1713
granted to Thomas Linvill the 2 tracts of land containing in whole 190
acres. Now Thomas Linvill & Dinah his wife for £61 grant to John
Worrall the said 86 acres. Signed Thomas Linvill & Dinah Linvill.
Delivered in the presence of Daniel Brown & Susanna Brown. Recorded
3 June 1734. (E5:253).

Mortgage. On 27 July 1734 James Buckley of Fallowfield in the County
of Chester, miller, & Mary his wife to Samuel Mickle of the City of
Philadelphia, merchant. Whereas James Buckley & Mary his wife for
£350 grant to Samuel Mickle a water corn mill & plantation lying in
Fallowfield bounded by Octoraro Creek & land of John Devors
containing 250 acres. James Buckley & Mary his wife to make entire

payment of £350 plus interest on or before 27 July 1735. Signed James Buckley & Mary Buckley. Delivered in the presence of Joseph Brinton, Richard Clayton & Elizabeth Clayton. Recorded 8 Aug 1734. (E5:255).

Acknowledgement. On 12 July 1734 whereas by an agreement between the children of Peter Hunter, late of Chester, dec., the lands of said Peter, who died intestate, lying in Chester County were divided amongst his 5 children on or about 6 Dec 1732. Whereas said division there was a particular part of the said lands distinct from the shares of Jonathon Hunter, Elizabeth wife of George Aston & Ann the wife of Thomas Wills allotted & laid out for Susanna Slocum one of the daughters of Peter Hunter, and for the children of Mary Dobson another of the daughters of Peter Hunter, late the wife of Thomas Dobson, which 2 shares remain yet undivided & whereas Jonathon, being since dec., and some doubt arising about the validity of the said division, we John Slocum & Susanna Slocum do hereby declare we are content with the said division & that we have no claim to make to any share allotted to Jonathon Hunter, George Aston & Elizabeth his wife, Thomas Wills & Ann his wife, but that they & their heirs may hold. Signed John Slocum & Susanna Slocum. Delivered in the presence of William Trehearn & Thomas Wills. Recorded 13 Aug 1734. (E5:257).

Lease & Release. On 15 & 16 Nov 1722 William Hudson of the City of Philadelphia, tanner, & Hannah his wife to John Collier of the County of Chester, yeoman. Whereas John Cornwell, late formerly of Powle in the County of York, but late of Philadelphia, merchant, dec., was seized of a tract in Bradford bounded by land of Richard Webb, John Davies, Robert Jeffries & Brandywine Creek containing 566 acres. John Cornwell by deed dated 7 & 8 June 1716 granted to William Hudson all 566 acres. Now William Hudson & Hannah his wife for £101.14 grant to John Collier a tract in Bradford bounded by land of Robert Jeffries, land late of John Davies, dec., land of Samuel Painter & Brandywine Creek containing 254 acres being part of the 566 acres. Signed William Hudson & Hannah Hudson. Delivered in the presence of William Pyle, Charles Turner of Birmingham, cordwainer, & Samuel Painter of Birmingham, tailor. Recorded 14 Aug 1734. (E5:257).

Deed. On 30 Nov 1731 John Owen, sheriff of Chester County, to Edward Woodward of the County of Chester, yeoman. Whereas Samuel Mickles in the Court of Common Pleas on 27 Aug 1730 recovered against William Fisher, the admin. of the goods & chattels of Jonathon Bradley, who died intestate, for the debt of £44.92.6 damages to be levied on the goods & chattels of Jonathon Bradley in the hands of William Fisher. Seized a tract containing 200 acres which had been surveyed to Jonathon Bradley 17 June 1729 situated on the branches of Brandywine Creek. Now John Owen for £60 grant to Edward Woodward the said 200 acres. Signed John Owen. Delivered in the presence of Thomas Giffing, James Mather & Jonathan Taylor. Recorded 15 Aug 1734. (E5:261).

Marriage Certificate. Richard Linnard of Chichester, cordwainer, & Rebecca Edwards of Chichester, spinster, having published their intentions of taking each other as husband & wife on 29 July last past with no objections. On 2 Sep 1734 before a number of persons at the house of Caleb Cowpland, Esq., in Chester they, the said Richard Linnard & Rebecca Edwards, openly appeared and the said Richard Linnard standing up & taking the said Rebecca Edwards by the hand declared as follows: "Be you witnesses that I take Rebecca Edwards to be my true and lawful wife promising with God's assistance to be unto her a faithful & loving husband till death separate us " & the said Rebecca Edwards did in like manner take the said Richard Linnard by the hand & declared the following: " Be you my witnesses that I take Richard Linnard to be my true & lawful husband promising with God's assistance to be unto him a faithful & loving wife till death separate us" & for further confirmation they have subscribed their names. Signed Richard Linnard & Rebecca Linnard. Witnesses Caleb Cowpland, James Cawley, Robert Dixon, William Willes, Joseph Templar, William Gillham, William Mullin, Jr., & Henry Edwards. (E5:263).

Deed of Gift. On 9 Sep 1729 Henry Lewis of New Town, farmer to Ellenor Goldsmith now of the City of Philadelphia, widow of James Goldsmith, late dec. Henry Lewis, for natural love & affection, does for his beloved daughter grant to Ellenor Goldsmith all of the plantation where I now dwell (after my death) in New Town bounded by land of Lewis Reece, Richard Hiddins, Edward David & James Cooper. Signed Henry Lewis. Delivered in the presence of George Emlen, Obidiah Eldridge & Nicholas Rogers. Recorded 16 Oct 1734. (E5:263).

Lease & Release. On 28 & 29 Jan 1733/4 Robert Stewart of East Marlborough, yeoman, & Martha his wife to John Stroud of West Marlborough. Robert Stewart & Martha his wife for £60 grant to John Stroud a tract ly ing in East Marlborough bounded by land of George

Baily, Robert Stewart & land formerly belonging to Richard Clayton containing 150 acres being part of 7,100 acres formerly belonging to the Free Society of Traders in Pennsylvania who granted 7,100 acres to Nathaniel Newlin & his heirs, recorded Chester, Book D, Vol 4, Page 396. Signed Robert Stewart & Martha Stewart. Delivered in the presence of William Hayes, Joseph Hayes & William Buffington. Recorded 30 Oct 1734. (E5:264).

Bill of Sale. On 19 Feb 1721/2 William Grimson of Sadsbury, yeoman, to Samuel Jones of Calne, wool comber. William Grimson for £31 grant to Samuel Jones a tract in Sadsbury. Signed William Grimson. Delivered in the presence of James Williams & Joseph Griffiths. Recorded 8 Nov 1734. (E5:267).

Deed. On 4 Feb 1733 Nathan Dicks of Chester County, yeoman, & Deborah his wife, Ann Gibbons, the widow & relict of James Gibbons, dec., to Samuel Jones of Lancaster County, yeoman. Whereas the Commissioners of Property on 1 Apr 1714 granted to Nathan Dicks a tract in Sadsbury bounded by land of William Grimson containing 500 acres & Nathan Dicks verbally granted said land to James Gibbons & James Gibbons sold said land to Samuel Jones. Now Nathan Dicks & Deborah his wife by the direction & appointment of Ann Gibbons for the consideration of £100 grant to Samuel Jones the tract containing 500 acres. Signed Nathan Dicks & Deborah Dicks in the presence of Stephen Cornelius, Aaron James & Richard Jones. Signed Ann Gibbons in the presence of Aaron James & Richard Jones. Recorded 8 Nov 1734. (E5:268).

Deed. On 16 Nov 1733 John Stocking of Hillborough in the County of Norfolk in Old England, blacksmith, & Clement Plumstead of the City of Philadelphia, merchant, to Richard Richardson of Whiteland in the County of Chester, yeoman. Whereas Joseph Coleman & Mary his wife by deed dated 29 & 30 Sep 1725 granted to Thomas Stocking, late of Chester County, yeoman, a tract containing 280 acres. Whereas Thomas Stocking made his will dated 3 Oct 1729 & devised 1/3 of his estate to his wife the other 2/3 to his father Francis Stocking. Whereas Francis Stocking made his will dated 27 Jan 1729 and devised all his estate to his kinsman John Stocking (the will proved in Court in Canterbury). John Stocking by letter of attorney dated 23 Aug 1732 authorized Clement Plumstead to take said lands & sell them. Now Clement Plumstead for

£70 grant to Richard Richardson a tract lying in Whiteland bounded by land of Edward Kennisons, John Sharples, William Paschall, William Crouch, Joseph Hayes & Isaac Richardson containing 280 acres. Signed Clement Plumstead, attorney to John Stocking. Delivered in the presence of William Burge & John Duraborow. Recorded 11 Nov 1734. (E5:269).

Lease & Release. On 27 Nov 1734 Arthur Sheil of Chester, yeoman, & Mary his wife, widow & admin. of the goods & chattels of Jonas Sandelands of Chester, gentleman, dec., to James Mather of Chester, hatter. Whereas Arthur Sheil & Mary his wife, relict & admin. for the goods & chattels of Jonas Sandelands, came before the Orphans Court on 22 May 1732, whereas Jonas Sandelands died intestate & letters of admin. were granted to Mary on 17 Apr 1728. Jonas Sandelands was at his death owner of several lots of land lying in Chester & was survived by his wife Mary & 8 children begotten of the body of Mary. One tract bounded by land of the widow Lloyd, Delaware River & land of David Sandelands containing 10 acres, another tract bounded by the 10 acres, land of widow Lloyd & land James Sandelands granted to James Mather containing 6 acres & another tract bounded by High Street containing 4 lots, also one lot adjoining the market place extending to the church yard. Arthur Shell & Mary his wife exhibited a true inventory of the estate of the dec., the value being £124.8, & the debts of the dec. come to £181.17, & an account of debts yet due being £210.10. The said Intestates personal estate will not be sufficient to pay his debts & maintain his children until the eldest reaches 21 years or to put them out to apprentices & to teach them to read & write. Arthur Shell & Mary his wife be allowed to sell said lands to pay the said debts & the residue to the maintenance of the children. Now Arthur Shell & Mary his wife for £103 grant to James Mather the 2 tracts of land, one containing 10 acres & the other containing 6 acres. Signed Arthur Sheil & Mary Sheil. Delivered in the presence of Joseph Parker, Benjamin Davis, T. Barton & Robert Parke. Recorded 27 Nov 1734. (E5:272).

Lease & Release. On 11 & 12 Nov 1734 James Sandelands of Chester, eldest son & heir of Jonas Sandelands, late of Chester, gentleman, dec., to James Mather of Chester, hatter. Whereas Jonas Sandelands, the late father of James Sandelands, became lawfully seized of several tracts of land & died intestate leaving a wife & 8 children. Whereas letters of administration were granted unto the widow, some of the land was sold to cover Jonas Sandelands debts. The surplus to be divided amongst the widow & children. Whereupon the request of all parties concerned the Orphans Court on 30 May last past directed John Crosby, Samuel Lightfoot, Thomas Cummings, John Mather & John Carter all of the said county, yeomen, to make an equal division of the lands of Jonas Sandelands, dec. Division was made & returned to Orphans Court on 30 Aug last past. Whereas a piece of said lands was laid out to James Sandelands & James Sandelands for £12 grant to James Mather a tract lying in Chester bounded by Chester Road containing 1 1/2 acres. Signed James Sandelands. Delivered in the presence of John Pindar, John Mather & Robert Parke. Recorded 28 Nov 1734. (E5:277).

Deed. On 28 Feb 1703 John Pearson (also Pearse) of Newtown, yeoman, to Thomas Pearson of Marple, yeoman. Whereas William Penn by deed dated 2 & 3 Mar 1681 granted to John Pearse (Pearson) of Hyall in the count of Chester, weaver, a tract containing 250 acres lying in Marple bounded by land late of Ralph Dracott, land late of Ann Broom, widow, the Great Road, land late of Joseph Selby & Crum Creek, also a lot in the City of Philadelphia. Now John Pearson for £5 grant to Thomas Pearson the 250 acres. Signed John Pearson. Delivered in the presence of Henry Hollingsworth. Recorded Sep 1734. (E5:280).

Release. On 15 Feb 1723 Thomas Pearson of Marple, yeoman, & Margery his wife to Robert Pearson of Marple, yeoman, eldest son of Thomas & Margery. Whereas William Penn on 2 & 3 Mar 1681 granted to John Pearson (Pearse) late of Newtown, weaver, a tract of 250 acres. Whereas John Pearson (Pearse) by deed dated 28 Feb 1703 granted to Thomas Pearson. Whereas the commissioners of William Penn by deed dated 22 Jan 1684 granted to George Willard a tract containing 300 acres & whereas George Willard by Deed of Gift dated 2 Dec 1689 for consideration Ralph Draycott should take Elizabeth, widow of Joseph Willard, as his wife grant a tract containing 100 acres. George Willard by deed dated 5 Nov 1690 granted to Ralph Draycott the remaining 200 acres & whereas Ralph Draycott & Elizabeth his wife & George Willard by deed dated 29 Dec 1697 granted to Thomas Pearson a tract containing 300 acres recorded Book A, Vol 1, Page 118. Whereas William Penn by deed dated 6 Oct 1683 granted to John Pearson & Mary Smith a tract of 100 acres. Whereas Mary Smith has since married Daniel Williamson of Chester County, yeoman, Daniel Williamson & Mary his wife by deed dated 30 Jan last past granted to Thomas Pearson one moiety of the 100 acres, being 50 acres. Now Thomas Pearson & Margery his wife for £500 grant to Robert Pearson all that tract in Marple bounded by Chester Road, land of Richard Maris, Enoch Pearson, Crum Creek & land of Joseph Roades containing 300 acres being 198 acres of the 250 acres tract, 62 acres of the 300 acres tract & 40 acres of the said 50 acres tract. Signed Thomas Pearson & Margery Pearson. Delivered in the presence of Mordecai Massey, Robert Penrose & Thomas Massey. Recorded 31 Dec 1734. (E5:282).

Release. On 7 Sep 1727 Joseph Wanton of Tiverton in the County of Bristol in the province of Massachusetts Bay, yeoman, one of the sons of Edward Wanton, late of Situate in the County of Plymouth in the province of Massachusetts Bay, dec., John Wanton of Newport in the colony of Rhode Island, merchant, another son of Edward Wanton, William Wanton of Rhode Island, merchant, another son of Edward Wanton to Joseph Townsend of Bradford, weaver. Whereas the commissioners of William Penn by deed dated 2 July 1686 granted to Arthur Cooke, since dec., a tract in Chester County containing 1,500 acres. Whereas Margaret Cooke, widow & executrix of Arthur Cooke & John Cooke, son & heir of Arthur Cooke, by deed dated 9 July 17?? granted to Edward Wanton 800 acres lying in Bradford bounded by land of Ruth Moore & Markus Hook Creek. Whereas Edward Wanton made his will dated 14 July 1714 & devised to his 3 sons Joseph Wanton, John Wanton & William Wanton the 800 acres. Now Joseph Wanton, John Wanton & William Wanton for £320 grant to Joseph Townsend all 800 acres. Signed Joseph Wanton, John Wanton & William Wanton. Delivered in the presence of John Casey & Thomas Marke. (Underwritten in Newport 7 Sep 1727, signed by William Anthony, assistant). Recorded 31 Dec 1734. (E5:285).

Deed. On 20 Aug 1734 John Wade of Essex House, yeoman, & Frances his wife to Joseph Rayners of Chester, cordwainer, & Mary his wife. Whereas Phillip Eilbert of Chester, merchant, & Lydia his wife granted & released to John Wade a tract called Essex House in Chester where John Wade now lives but formerly in the tenure of his Uncle Robert Wade. Now John Wade & Frances his wife for £40 grant to Joseph Rayners a tract in Chester bounded Chester Creek, land of Jacob Howell, land of John Wade & Chester Road containing 10 acres. Signed John Wade & Frances Wade. Delivered in the presence of Joseph

Parker, Samuel Lightfoot & Jacob Lightfoot. Recorded 3 Jan 1734/5. (E5:287).

Deed. On 24 Dec 1724 George Pierce of Thornbury, yeoman, to Caleb Pierce of Thornbury, yeoman, son of George Pierce. Whereas the late commissioners of William Penn by deed dated 24 May 1715 granted to George Pierce a tract containing 600 acres, recorded Philadelphia, Patent Book A, Vol 5, Page 133. Now George Pierce for 5 shillings & love grant to Caleb Pierce a tract bounded by land of Isaac Taylor, west side of Octoraroo Creek & land of Moses Musgrave containing 600 acres. George Pierce appointed William Smith his lawful attorney. Signed George Pierce. Delivered in the presence of William Pyle, Thomas Gillpin & John Griffin. Quiet & peaceful possession was witnessed by Robert Mathews & Thomas Baily. Recorded 8 Jan 1734/5. (E5:289).

Release. On 21 June 1725 Samuel Bonham, Samuel Turner, John Midford all of London, merchants, the surviving, in the trust of the Pennsylvania Land Company, to Thomas Black of London Grove in Pennsylvania, husbandman. Samuel Bonham, Samuel Turner & John Midford for £92 grant to Thomas Black a tract in Chester County bounded by land of Thomas Cook containing 400 acres being part of a larger tract containing 16,300 acres. Signed Samuel Bonham, Samuel Turner & John Midford. Delivered in the presence of John Estaugh & Thomas Annis. Recorded 9 Jan 1734/5. (E5:291).

Lease & Release. On 9 & 10 Sep 1723 John Smith of London in Old England, merchant, & Thomas Chalkley of the City of Philadelphia to Thomas Lindley of Philadelphia, blacksmith. Whereas William Penn by deed dated 15 & 16 Mar 1681 granted William Isaac of Stock Verdon in the County of Wilts, yeoman, a tract of 500 acres & whereas William Penn by deed dated 19 & 20 Aug 1681 granted to Thomas Sagar of Foxham in the Parish of Christian Malford in the County of Wilts, yeoman, Samuel Workman of Longly Burial in the County of Wilts, yeoman, & Susannah Baily of Catcomb in the Parish of Hillmartin in the County of Wilts, widow, the quantity of 500 acres, & whereas William Penn by deed dated 26 & 27 Sep 1681 granted to Henry Barnard of Goatacre in the County of Wilts a tract of 500 acres & whereas William Penn by deed dated 11 & 12 Oct 1681 granted to Thomas Hatt of Goatacres in the County of Wilts, cordwainer, a tract of 500 acres. Whereas William Isaac on 22 & 23 Mar 1685 granted to Daniel Smith of Marlborough in the County of Wilts his 500 acres, & Thomas Sagar,

Samuel Workman & Susannah Baily, the then wife of Samuel Workman, on 19 & 20 May 1696 granted to Daniel Smith the 500 acres, Henry Barnard on 28 & 29 Mar 1686 granted to Daniel Smith his 500 acres & Thomas Hatt on 16 & 17 Apr 1686 granted to Daniel Smith his 500 acres. Whereas Daniel Smith by mortgage dated 29 Sep 1687 for securing the payment of £50 with interest granted to Barbara Blagdon of the City of Bristol, widow, all the 2,000 acres except 100 acres Daniel Smith sold to George Chandler. Barbara Blagdon having received the said £50 plus interest on 18 Feb 1694 did grant & release all the 1,900 acres to Daniel Smith. Daniel Smith died & the 1,900 acres descended to Daniel Smith, late of Marlborough, cheese factor, son & only heir of Daniel Smith. Randle Spakeman, admin. of the estate of Daniel Smith, requested Isaac Taylor, surveyor in the County of Chester, to survey & lay out a quantity of 1,000 acres which was laid out in Caln in 2 tracts laying together. Whereas Daniel Smith, the son, has since died the said 100 acres descended to John Smith, eldest son of Daniel Smith. Whereas John Smith by Letter of Attorney dated 5 Jan 1719, recorded in Philadelphia, Book D, Vol 5, Page 215, on 17 Aug 1721, appointed Thomas Chalkley his attorney to sell said 1,000 acres. Now John Smith by his attorney Thomas Chalkley for £150 grant to Thomas Lindley a tract in Caln bounded by land of Lewis Lewis, George Aston & Aaron Mendenhall containing 500 acres being part of the 1,000 acres. Signed Thomas Chalkley. Delivered in the presence of George Aston, Daniel Durborow & Edward West. Recorded 9 Jan 1734/5. (E5:293).

Lease & Release. On 29 & 30 Dec 1725 Thomas Lindley of the City of Philadelphia, blacksmith, & Hannah his wife to Thomas Parke of Chester, yeoman. Whereas William Penn by deed dated 15 & 16 Mar 1681 granted William Isaac of Stock Verdon in the County of Wilts, yeoman, a tract of 500 acres & whereas William Penn by deed dated 19 & 20 Aug 1681 granted to Thomas Sagar of Foxham in the Parish of Christian Malford in the County of Wilts, yeoman, Samuel Workman of Longly Burial in the County of Wilts, yeoman, & Susannah Baily of Catcomb in the Parish of Hillmartin in the County of Wilts, widow, the quantity of 500 acres & whereas William Penn by deed dated 26 & 27 Sep 1681 granted to Henry Barnard of Goatacre in the County of Wilts a tract of 500 acres & whereas William Penn by deed dated 11 & 12 Oct 1681 granted to Thomas Hatt of Goatacres in the County of Wilts, cordwainer, a tract of 500 acres. Whereas William Isaac on 22 & 23 Mar 1685 granted to Daniel Smith of Marlborough in the County of Wilts his

500 acres, & Thomas Sagar, Samuel Workman & Susannah Baily, the then wife of Samuel Workman, on 19 & 20 May 1696 granted to Daniel Smith the 500 acres, Henry Barnard on 28 & 29 Mar 1686 granted to Daniel Smith his 500 acres & Thomas Hatt on 16 & 17 Apr 1686 granted to Daniel Smith his 500 acres. Whereas Daniel Smith by mortgage dated 29 Sep 1687 for securing the payment of £50 with interest granted to Barbara Blagdon of the City of Bristol, widow, all the 2,000 acres except 100 acres Daniel Smith sold to George Chandler. Barbara Blagdon having received the said £50 plus interest on 18 Feb 1694 did grant & release all the 1,900 acres to Daniel Smith. Daniel Smith died & the 1,900 acres descended to Daniel Smith, late of Marlborough, cheese factor, son & only heir of Daniel Smith. Randle Spakeman, admin. of the estate of Daniel Smith, requested Isaac Taylor, surveyor in the County of Chester, to survey & lay out a quantity of 1,000 acres which was laid out in Caln in 2 tracts laying together. Whereas Daniel Smith the son has since died the said 100 acres descended to John Smith eldest son of Daniel Smith. Whereas John Smith by Letter of Attorney dated 5 Jan 1719, recorded in Philadelphia, Book D, Vol 5, Page 215, on 17 Aug 1721, appointed Thomas Chalkley his attorney to sell said 1,000 acres. Thomas Chalkley for John Smith granted 500 acres to Thomas Lindley on 9 & 10 Sep 1723. Now Thomas Lindley & Hannah his wife for £350 grant to Thomas Parke a tract in Caln bounded by land of Lewis Lewis, George Aston & Aaron Mendenhall containing 500 acres. Signed Thomas Lindley & Hannah Lindley. Delivered in the presence of Thomas Watson, Cornelius Nice & Jeremiah Cowman. Recorded 10 Jan 1734/5. (E5:298).

Release. On 8 June 1716 John Cornwell, late of Epwle in the County of York in Old England, but now of Philadelphia, merchant, to William Hudson of Philadelphia, tanner. John Cornwell for £150 grant & release to William Hudson a tract on the northeast side of Brandywine Creek in the township of Bradford bounded by land of Richard Webb, John Davis, Robert Jeffery & Brandywine Creek containing 566 acres. Signed John Cornwell. Delivered in the presence of Joshua Grainger, William Lawerence & Joshua Lawerence. Recorded 20 Jan 1734/5. (E5:302).

Deed. On 14 Feb 1722 Thomas Coeburn the younger of Chester, yeoman, & Elizabeth his wife to Joseph Coeburn, the younger brother of the said Thomas of Middletown, yeoman, & Lydia his wife. Whereas Joseph Coeburn the elder & Sarah his wife on 10 Jan 1722 for £200 granted to Joseph Coeburn the eldest son of Joseph & Thomas Coeburn the 2nd son of Joseph all the corn grist mill called Coeburn Mills & tract of land with the mill lying in Chester & Middletown containing 324 acres, with a piece of land purchased to fix the west end of the mill dam containing 1/2 acre. Whereas Caleb Harrison & Hannah his wife by deed dated 16 Jan 1722 for £21 granted to Thomas Coeburn & Joseph Coeburn a tract bounded by the other tract, land of William Coeburn & Edgmont Road containing 24 1/2 acres. Thomas Coeburn & Joseph Coeburn to prevent any differences which might happen between their heirs decided lands should be divided. Thomas Coeburn the younger paid £50 to Joseph Coeburn to make his division of land equal to that of Joseph. Thomas Coeburn for 5 shillings granted to Joseph Coeburn & Lydia his wife the plantation where Joseph now dwells lying in Middletown bounded by Edgmont Road, Chester Creek, land of Thomas Martin, the Mill Dam, the Mill Race, the Mill Pond & land of Thomas Coeburn containing 172 acres & one full moiety of the Grist Mill & a piece of land on the west side of the Mill dam is fixed containing 1/2 acres & the piece of land where the mill stands lying in Chester bounded by Chester Creek, the mill pond & the mill race containing 4 acres & the profits of the said mill to be divided equally. Also Joseph Coeburn for £50 granted to Thomas Coeburn his part of the said lands being the plantation where Thomas & Elizabeth his wife dwell in Chester bounded by the Mill Pond, Edgmont Road, land of William Coeburn, land of Thomas Coeburn, Sr., & Chester Creek containing 172 acres & 1 full moiety of the Mill, the piece of land west of the Mill dam & the land that the mill stands & 1/2 of all profits. Signed Joseph Coeburn & Lydia Coeburn. Delivered in the presence of John Hurford, Thomas Martin & James Trego. Recorded 8 Feb 1734/5. (E5:304).

Deed. On 16 Jan 1722 Caleb Harrison of Chester, yeoman, & Hannah his wife to Thomas Coeburn the younger of Chester, yeoman, & his brother Joseph Coeburn, Jr., of Middletown, yeoman. Whereas Joseph Coeburn the elder & Sarah his wife on 21 May 1719 granted to Caleb Harrison a tract containing 76 acres in Chester. Now Caleb Harrison & Hannah his wife for £21 grant to Thomas Coeburn & Joseph Coeburn, Jr., a tract in Chester bounded by land of William Coeburn containing 24 1/2 acres being part of the 76 acres. Signed Caleb Harrison & Hannah Harrison. Delivered in the presence of William Hudson & William Coeburn. Recorded 10 Feb 1734/5. (E5:308).

Deed. On 21 May 1719 Joseph Coeburn of Chester, Esq., & Sarah his wife to Caleb Harrison of Chester, yeoman. Joseph Coeburn & Sarah his wife for £85 grant to Caleb Harrison a tract in Chester bounded by land of William Coeburn, Ridley Creek, land of Caleb Harrison & Edgmont Road containing 76 acres being part of land purchased of William Penn by Thomas Coeburn the father of Joseph Coeburn on 10 Mar 1695. Signed Joseph Coeburn & Sarah Coeburn. Delivered in the presence of John Crosby, Susannah Crosby, Nathaniel Newlin, Jr., & Aston. Peaceable possession delivered in the presence of Edward Woodward & Thomas Martin. Recorded 8 Feb 1734/5. (E5:309).

Release. On 3 Jan 1734/5 William Baily of Kennet, yeoman, & Kezia his wife to Robert Mills of Kennet, carpenter. William Baily & Kezia his wife for £120 grant to Robert Mills a tract in Kennet bounded by land of William Baily containing 100 acres being part of 375 acres which the late commissioners of property by deed dated 14 Jan 1708, recorded Philadelphia, Book A, Vol 4, Page 131, granted to Nathaniel Newlin & whereas Nathaniel Newlin has since died all his land were divided between his children, His children by deed dated 12 Aug 1730 granted to William Baily & Kezia his wife, recorded in Philadelphia, Book E, Vol 6, Page 83. Signed William Baily & Kezia Baily. Delivered in the presence of William Webb, Richard Clayton, James Armstrong & Thomas George. Recorded 14 Feb 1734/5. (E5:311).

Lease & Release. On 16 & 17 Dec 1734 Arthur Sheil of Chester, yeoman, & Mary his wife who was the widow & admin. of the goods & chattels of Jonas Sandelands of Chester, gentleman, dec., to James Mather of Chester, hatter, Thomas Barton of Chester, coach maker, & Stephen Cole of Chester, butcher. Whereas Arthur Sheil & Mary his wife came before the Orphans Court held at the house of Mathias Kerlin in Concord on 25 Oct 1734 before Henry Pierce, Samuel Hollingsworth, Joseph Brinton & Caleb Cowpland, justices. Whereas Jonas Sandelands died intestate & letters of admin. were granted to Mary on 17 Apr 1728. Jonas Sandelands was at his death owner of several lots of land lying in Chester & was survived by his wife Mary & 8 children begotten of the body of Mary. One tract bounded by land of the widow Lloyd, Delaware River & land of David Sandelands containing 10 acres, another tract bounded by the 10 acres, land of widow Lloyd & land James Sandelands granted to James Mather containing 6 acres & another tract bounded by High Street containing 4 lots also one lot adjoining the market place extending to the church yard. Arthur Shell & Mary his wife exhibited a true inventory of the estate of the dec. the value being £124.8 & the debts of the dec. come to £181.17 & an account of debts yet due being £210.10. The said Intestates personal estate will not be sufficient to pay his debts & maintain his children until the eldest reaches 21 years or to put them out to apprentices & to teach them to read & write. Arthur Shell & Mary his wife be allowed to sell said lands to pay the said debts & the residue to the maintenance of the children. Now Arthur Sheil & Mary his wife for £6 grant to James Mather, Thomas Barton & Stephen Cole a lot in Chester bounded by being 40' x 120' bounded by High Street, land of Richard Backhouse, church yard & lots of John Owen. Signed Arthur Sheil & Mary Sheil. Delivered in the presence of John Owen, John Backhouse & Robert Parke. Recorded 20 Feb 1734/5. (E5:312).

Declaration of Trust. On 19 Feb 1734/5 James Mather of Chester, hatter, Thomas Barton of Chester, coach maker, & Stephen Cole of Chester, butcher, send greetings. Whereas Arthur Sheil & Mary his wife by deed dated 16 & 17 Dec 1734 granted to James Mather, Thomas Barton & Stephen Cole a lot in Chester being 40' x 120' bounded by High Street, lots of Richard Backhouse, the church yard & lots of John Owen. Know ye that James Mather, Thomas Barton & Stephen Cole according to the trust in us do declare that the said lot conveyed to us by the direction & appointment of the members of the Society of St. Paul's Church of Protestant religion in Chester, intended to intrust in us that we shall continue in religious fellowship with the said society. Whereas we release the said lot to John Mather & John Sketchley the present church wardens & their successors of Protestant Church. Signed James Mather, Thomas Barton & Stephen Cole. Delivered in the presence of John Backhouse & Robert Parke. Recorded 20 Feb 1734/5. (E5:316).

Lease & Release. On 14 Jan 1734/5 Thomas Parke of East Caln, yeoman, & Rebecca his wife to Robert Parke of East Caln, eldest son to Thomas & Rebecca. Whereas Thomas Lindley of the City of Philadelphia, blacksmith, & Hannah his wife by deed dated 29 & 30 Dec 1725 granted to Thomas Parke a tract in Caln containing 500 acres, recorded in Chester, Book E, Vol 5, Page 298. Now Thomas Parke & Rebecca his wife for natural love & £40 grant to Robert Parke a tract in Caln bounded by land of Phinehas Lewis, Thomas Parke & Abel Parke containing 124 1/2 acres being part of the 500 acres, with the privilege to dig a drain or ditch from the run called Thousand Acre Run through any part of the land now in the possession of Abel Parke (also being a part of the 500 acres) to convert half of the said stream of water. Signed Thomas Parke & Rebecca Parke. Delivered in the presence of George Aston, Thomas Parke, Jr., & John Jackson. Recorded 26 Feb 1734/5. (E5:317).

Power of Attorney. On 27 Sep 1734 Elizabeth Bond of Chichester, widow & admin. of the good & chattels of Joseph Bond, late of Chichester, dec., have appointed her loving & trusty friend John Riley of Chichester, yeoman, her true & lawful attorney to recover & demand any such monies due her. Signed Elizabeth Bond. Delivered in the presence of William Haley & Mary Brownhill. Recorded 3 Mar 1734/5. (E5:320).

Deed. On 4 Mar 1734/5 Joseph Baker, Sr., of Edgmont to Jasper Yeates of Chester County, gentleman, & Joseph Jervis of Chester County, yeoman. Joseph Baker for £8 grant to Jasper Yeates & Joseph Jervis a tract near Ridley Creek & joining the tract where the corn mill now stand owned by William Pennel, yeoman, containing 8 1/2 acres with full authority to dam up Ridley Creek for the use of the mill. Signed Joseph Baker. Delivered in the presence of Nehemiah Baker, goldsmith, & Edward Follwell. Recorded 7 Mar 1734/5. (E5:321).

Deed. On 4 Mar 1734/5 Joseph Jervis being co-purchaser of the above mentioned 8 1/2 acres having afterward purchased of Jasper Yeates his full part of the said land, and then sell & convey the 8 1/2 acres to James Cooper. Signed Joseph Jervis. Delivered in the presence of Nehemiah Baker, Goldsmith, Edward Follwell. Recorded 7 Mar 1734/5. (E5:321).

Mortgage. On 4 Dec 1734 Thomas Parke, Jr., of East Caln to Joseph Parker of Chester, gentleman. Thomas Parker, Jr., for £70 grant to Joseph Parker a tract in East Caln bounded by land of Thomas Parke, Phinehas Lewis, Aaron Mendenhall, George Aston, Beaver Run & land of Robert Parke containing 276 acres. Thomas Parke, Jr., to pay Joseph Parker £82.12 on or before 4 Dec 1737. Signed Thomas Parke, Jr. Delivered in the presence of Thomas Hughs & Robert Parke. Note on side of Deed. Full payment received 4 Dec 1737. J. Parker. Recorded 26 Mar 1734/5. (E5:322).

Deed. On 10 Dec 1695 Oliver Cope now of New Castle to Robert Pyle of Bethell, yeoman. Oliver Cope for £21 grant to Robert Pyle a tract containing 250 acres lying in Birmingham bounded by the Concord line & land of John Buckley being as by a survey dated 8 Nov 1684 to Robert Pyle. Signed Oliver Coope. Delivered in the presence of Andrew Job & David Lloyd. Recorded 27 Mar 1735. (E5:323).

Deed. On 27 July 1734 the deed following was produced before Joseph Brinton, Esq., one of the Justices of the Peace for the County of Chester. Whereupon William Pyle of Chester County, yeoman, aged about 50 years & John Pyle of Chester County, yeoman, aged about 45 years being the sons of Robert Pyle the grantor in the following deed. Who on their solemn affirmations declare that from long acquaintance they had with their fathers writing, they are very positive that his name wrote against the seal of the following deed was of his own hand writing also that they have heard him say that he had executed a deed to their brother Robert Pyle for 250 acres as mentioned in the said deed.

On 23 May 1715 Robert Pyle of Bethell, yeoman, to Robert Pyle, Jr., eldest son of Robert Pyle. Whereas William Penn by deed dated 9 Sep 1681 granted to Oliver Cope then of Aubrey in the County of Wilts, tailor, a tract of 250 acres, recorded in Philadelphia, Vol 3, Folio 334, on 12 Dec 1684. Whereas Oliver Cope by deed dated 10 Dec 1695 granted to Robert Pyle the said 250 acres. Robert Pyle for love & affection grant to his eldest son Robert Pyle, Jr., a tract in Birmingham bounded by the Concord line & land of John Buckley containing 250 acres. Signed Robert Pyle. Delivered in the presence of William Lewis, Gressell Lewis & Robert Booth. Recorded 27 Mar 1735. (E5:324).

Release On 19 Mar 1716 John Lea of Concord, yeoman, & Hannah his wife to Peter Hatton of Thornbury, wheelwright. Whereas the late commissioners of William Penn by deed dated 3 Dec 1701 granted to John Lea a tract in Concord bounded land of John Mendenhall, Thomas Martin, James Hayward & Morgan Jones containing 136 acres, recorded Philadelphia, Book A, Vol 2, Page 275. Whereas John Lea on 2 Mar 1708/9 granted to Richard Hill of the City of Philadelphia, merchant, the 136 acres, recorded in Chester, Book C, Vol 3, Page 67. Whereas Richard Hill on 3 Mar 1708/9 granted to John Lea all the said land paying a yearly rent to Richard Hill the sum of £6. Whereas John Mendenhall of Concord & Esther his wife, George Mendenhall son & heir apparent of John Mendenhall, John Mendenhall, Jr., one of the sons of John & Susannah his wife, Aaron Mendenhall the 3rd son of John the elder & George Maris of Springfield, yeoman, son & heir of George Maris, dec., on 18 &

19 Aug 1710 granted to John Lea a tract in Concord bounded by land of Mary King, John Mendenhall, Jr., Thomas Martin & John Lea containing 81 acres. Now John Lea & Hannah his wife for £220 grant to Peter Hatton the plantation with a certain parcel of land being part of the 2 pieces of land bounded by Chester Road, the Concord Meeting house, land of William Hill, land of Robert Chamberlain, James Hayward & Morgan Jones containing 195 acres. Signed John Lea in the presence of Thomas Masters, Morgan Cornack & Joshua Lawerence. Signed Hannah Lea in the presence of Jacob Vernon & Ann Vernon. Recorded 14 Apr 1735. (E5:326).

Release. On 12 Sep 1722 Joseph Gillpin of Birmingham, yeoman, & Hannah his wife to Peter Hatton of Concord, wheelwright. Whereas William Penn by deed dated 27 June 1684 granted to John Mendenhall the elder a tract in Concord bounded by land of Peter Louder & street of the said town containing 300 acres, recorded in Philadelphia, 5 Jan 1696 in Book A, Page 336. John Mendenhall by deed dated 8 Mar 1691 did grant & make over to George Maris, dec., the late father of Elizabeth the first wife of John Mendenhall with the use of said land to John Mendenhall during his life & after his death to be equally divided between his 3 sons by Elizabeth & if John should be living when the said children came of age shall settle & plant on said land not disturbing John, recorded in Chester, Book A, Page 56. Whereas the said 3 sons came of age & whereby on part of land being 150 acres fell to John Mendenhall, Jr. Whereas John Mendenhall the father & Esther his wife, George Mendenhall son & heir apparent, John Mendenhall, Jr., & Susannah his wife, Aaron Mendenhall & George Maris son & heir of George Maris, dec., on 4 Nov 1713 granted to Joseph Gillpin a tract in Concord containing 150 acres part of the 300 acres, recorded in Chester, Book C, Page 420, on 20 Feb 1713. Now Joseph Gilpen & Hannah his wife for £126 grant to Peter Hatton a tract in Concord bounded by land of Peter Hatton, Robert Chamberlain, Nicholas Pyle, Birmingham Road, land of John Perkins & the meeting house yard containing 117 acres being part of the 150 acres. Signed Joseph Gillpin & Hannah Gillpin. Delivered in the presence of John Taylor, Nicholas Pyle & Samuel Gillpin. Recorded 15 Apr 1735. (E5:329).

Lease & Release. On 5 & 6 May 1735 Parrick Carrigon of Conistogoe in the County of Lancaster in the province of Pennsylvania, yeoman, & Susanna his wife to Charles Conner of Aston, yeoman. Whereas John Baldwin, late of Chester, yeoman, dec., by deed dated 2 Mar 1713/4 granted to Roger Hawking of New Bristol in the County of Bucks, brick maker, 2 tracts in Aston containing in whole 100 acres & endorsed by Katherine Baldwin the wife of John Baldwin, recorded in Chester, Book C, Page 339. Whereas Roger Hawking & Elizabeth his wife by deed dated 2 Apr 1714 granted to Abraham Darlington of Aston the 2 tracts. Whereas Abraham Darlington & Elizabeth his wife by deed dated 27 & 28 Mar 1724 granted to Andrew Miller the 2 tracts. Andrew Miller & Sarah his wife by deed dated 2 & 3 May 17(35) granted to Patrick Carrigon the said 2 tracts. Now Patrick Carrigon & Susanna his wife for £76 grant to Charles Connor a tract in Aston bounded by land of Richard Mason, William Sissell, Andrew Moor & widow Dutton containing 50 acres being one to the 2 tracts mentioned. Signed Patrick Carrigon & Susanna Carrigon. Delivered in the presence of James Mather, Stephen Cole & Robert Parke. Recorded 9 May 1735. (E5:332).

Deed. On 13 Nov 1734 John Cheney of Thornbury, yeoman, to Jacob Vernon, Jr., of Thornbury, yeoman. Whereas Thomas Cheney, late of Thornbury made his will dated 31 Aug 1728 & did appoint Elizabeth his wife & John Cheney his executors & soon after died. There is a sum of £120 to be paid to his daughter Ann Cheney when she attains the age of 25 years & the said Elizabeth at the time of her widowhood did give to her daughter Ann £50 to be paid her at the age of 21 years, Whereas Jacob Vernon & Elizabeth his wife to John Cheney they the said Jacob Vernon & Elizabeth his now wife for the better securing of the sum of £120 & the £50 an the times appointed, release & convey to John Cheney a tract in Thornbury bounded by land of John Taylor, Abraham Vernon, Anthony Arnolds, Caleb Peirce, Jacob Vernon & John Cheney containing 208 acres. Now the full intent of the said parties is hereby declared to that John Cheney is contented, agreed, promise & grant to & with Jacob Vernon, that if Jacob Vernon or his heirs shall cause to be paid Ann Cheney the sum of £50 when she attains the age of 21 years which will be 21 Feb 1748 & the full sum of £120 at the age of 25 years to which will be 21 Feb 1752, but in case of her death before the age of 21 years then the £120 shall be paid her executors at the above recited time. John Cheney to release to Jacob Vernon & his heirs the said lands when the said sums are paid. Signed John Cheney. Delivered in the presence of Thomas Smedley, John Yarnall & James Gibbons. Recorded 24 May 1735. (E5:335).

Lease & Release. On 29 & 30 May 1735 James Claxton of Chester, hosier & Mary his wife one of the daughters of Jonas Sandelands, late of Chester, gentleman, dec., to James Mather of Chester, hatter. Whereas Jonas Sandelands the late father of Mary had several tracts of land in his lifetime & died intestate leaving a wife & 8 children to survive him. After his dec., his widow was appointed admin., after the discharge of debts the surplus of the estate was to be divided amongst the widow & said children as ordered in the Orphans Court dated 30 May last past & directed John Crosby, Samuel Lightfoot, Thomas Cummings, John Mather & John Carter to make an equal division and the division was made & returned to the Orphans Court 30 Aug last past. Whereupon the tract of land herein mentioned was laid out & allotted to James Claxton & Mary his wife. Now James Claxton & Mary his wife for £105 grant to James Mather a tract lying in Chester bounded by Edgmont Road, land of Caleb Cowpland, John Sharples & Richard Magees containing 44 acres. Signed James Claxton & Mary Claxton. Delivered in the presence of John Mather, Thomas Barton & Robert Parke. Recorded 3 June 1735. (E5:337).

Release. On 25 Mar 1724 William Brinton of Birmingham, yeoman, the only surviving son & heir apparent of William Brinton, late of Birmingham, yeoman, dec., & Jane his wife, Elizabeth Harry of Kennet, widow & relict of Hugh Harry, dec., & one of the daughters of William Brinton, dec., Evan Harry of Kennet, yeoman, eldest son & heir of Hugh Harry & Elizabeth, William Harry of Kennet, yeoman, another son of Hugh & Elizabeth, John Willis of Thornbury, yeoman, & Esther his wife another daughter of William Brinton, dec., & John Bennet of Birmingham & Sarah his wife, he being the only surviving son of Ann Bennett, late of Birmingham, dec., which said Ann Bennett was the widow & relict of John Bennet & the other daughter of William Brinton, dec., to Daniel Davis of Birmingham, yeoman. Whereas the commissioners of William Penn, dec., by deed dated 28 Nov 1688 granted to William Brinton a tract of 400 acres. Whereas William Brinton by deed dated 10 Dec 1695 granted to John Willis & Esther his wife a tract of 100 acres being part of the 400 acres. John Willis by deed dated 4 Mar 1699 granted to Daniel Davis the 100 acres, recorded in Chester, Book A, Vol 1, Page 150. Whereas William Brinton by deed dated 11 June 1695 granted to Hugh Harry & Elizabeth his wife a tract of 150 acres another part of the 400 acres. Whereas Hugh Harry & Elizabeth his wife on 16 Oct 1707 granted to Daniel Davis the said 150 acres, recorded in Book B, Vol 1, Page 171. Whereas William Brinton by deed dated 11 June 1695

granted to John Bennett the late father of John Bennett & the said Ann
his wife 2 tracts of the said 400 acres, one of which containing 50 acres.
Whereas John Bennett by deed dated 1 Mar 1697 grant to Daniel Davis a
tract of 50 acres recorded Book A, Vol 1, Page 126. Now William Brinton
& Jane his wife, Elizabeth Harry, Evan Harry, William Harry, John
Willis & Esther his wife, John Bennet & Sarah his wife for 5 shillings to
each of them to better confirm to Daniel Davis the said 3 tracts of land.
One tract in Birmingham bounded by land of John Bennett but since
purchased by Daniel Davis, land of Richard Webb, Brandywine Creek,
other land of Daniel Davis, land late of John Willis & land late of William
Radley containing 100 acres being the tract John Willis conveyed to
Daniel Davis. Another tract bounded by Brandywine Creek, land of John
Bennett, William Radley, Daniel Davis containing 150 acres which Hugh
Harry granted to Daniel Davis. The other tract bounded by land of John
Willis containing 50 acres which John Bennet granted to Daniel Davis,
being in whole 300 acres. Signed William Brinton, Jane Brinton, John
Willis & John Bennett in the presence of Thomas Higgins, John Clark,
Thomas Ward & Bud Willis. Signed Elizabeth Harry, Evan Harry &
William Harry in the presence of William Whitaker & Elizabeth
Whitaker. Recorded 28 July 1735. (E5:340).

Release. On 25 Mar 1724 Daniel Davis of Birmingham, yeoman, &
Deborah his wife to Robert Pyle of Bethell, yeoman. Whereas William
Brinton & Jane his wife, Elizabeth Harry, Evan Harry, William Harry,
John Willis & John Bennet & Sarah his wife by deed granted to Daniel
Davis 2 tracts being 300 acres. Now Daniel Davis & Deborah his wife for
£116.13.4 grant to Robert Pyle all the said tract in Birmingham bounded
by Brandywine Creek, land of John Bennett, land late of William Radley,
land late of John Davis, land late of Richard Webb, containing 300 acres.
Signed Daniel Davis & Deborah Davis. Delivered in the presence of
William Pyle, Mary Taylor & John Taylor. Recorded 28 July 1735.
(E5:343).

Release. On 6 Dec 1729 Robert Pyle of Bethell, gentleman, & Susannah
his wife to William Seal & William Dean both of Birmingham, yeomen.
Whereas Daniel David & Deborah his wife by deed dated 25 & 26 Mar
1724 granted to Robert Pyle a tract containing 300 acres. Whereas
Robert Pyle by a lease dated 27 Mar 1724 for the yearly rent of £7 being
the interest of £116.13.4. Daniel Davis to pay Robert Pyle the £116.13.4.
Whereas Daniel Davis on 12 Dec 1726 for £190 granted to William Seal &

William Dean the 2 tracts containing 300 acres. Now Robert Pyle & Susannah his wife for £116.13.4 paid to them by William Seal & William Dean grant to them the said land in Birmingham bounded by Brandywine Creek, land of John Bennett, land late of William Radley, land late of John Davis & land late of Richard Webb containing 300 acres & discharging the said yearly rent of £7. Signed Robert Pyle & Susannah Pyle. Delivered in the presence of John Gibbons & John Martin. Recorded 24 June 1735. (E5:344).

Deed. On 12 Aug 1730 Nicholas Newlin of Concord, yeoman, eldest son of Nathaniel Newlin, late of Concord, gentleman, dec., Nathaniel Newlin of Concord, yeoman, 2nd son of the dec., John Newlin of Concord, yeoman, 3rd son of the dec., Richard Evanson of Thornbury, yeoman, & Jemima his wife one of the daughters of the dec., William Baily of Kennet, yeoman, & Kezia his wife, another daughter of the dec., to Richard Clayton of Concord, cordwainer, & Mary his wife, the other daughter of the dec. Whereas William Penn, dec., by deed dated 22 & 23 Mar 1681 granted to Nicholas Moore, James Claypoole, Phillip Ford, William Sharlo, Edward Pierce, John Simcock, Thomas Brassey, Edward Brooks & Thomas Barker over 20,000 acres to be laid out in the province with some lots in or near Philadelphia in trust for the Free Society of Traders, recorded in Philadelphia. Whereas virtue of a warrant dated 1 June 1688 there was laid out on 20 Sep 1688 to Benjamin Chambers, president of the Society for the use of the Society a tract of 7,100 acres since found to be in the County of Chester & whereas by an Act of Assembly the said 20,000 acres was actually vested, settled & adjudged to be in Charles Road, Job Goodson, Evan Owen, George Fitzwater & Joseph Pidgeon of the City of Philadelphia, merchants. Whereas Charles Road, Job Goodson, Evan Owen, George Fitzwater & Joseph Pidgeon by deed dated 10 June 1724 grant to Nathaniel Newlin, dec., the tract containing 7,100 acres, recorded in Chester, Book D, Vol 4, Page 369. Whereas William Penn by deed dated 27 June 1684 granted to John Mendenhall of Chester, yeoman, a tract in Concord containing 300 acres, recorded in Philadelphia, Book A, Page 336. Whereas John Mendenhall by deed dated 8 Mar 1694 granted to George Maris, late of the County of Chester, dec., father of Elizabeth the 1st wife of John Mendenhall, to be used by John Mendenhall during his life & after his death to be divided amongst his 3 sons by Elizabeth. John did live until all three of the children came of age, they could settle on said land but not disturb the said John Mendenhall & after his death to be equally divided between the sons, recorded in Chester, Book A, Page 56. Whereas John

Mendenhall of Concord & Esther his wife, George Mendenhall son & heir apparent of John Mendenhall, John Mendenhall, Jr., one of the sons of John & Susannah his wife, Aaron Mendenhall the 3rd son of John the elder & George Maris of Springfield, yeoman, son & heir of George Maris, dec., on 4 Nov 1713 granted to Joseph Gillpin a tract in Concord containing 150 acres part of the 300 acres, recorded in Chester, Book C, Page 420, on 20 Feb 1713. Whereas Joseph Gillpin & Hannah his wife by deed dated 3 May 1719 granted to Caleb Perkins a tract containing 33 acres part of the 150 acres. Caleb Perkins & Ann his wife by deed dated -----. Nathaniel Newlin died intestate & all his said lands to be divided amongst his children the eldest receiving a double share. Now Nathan Newlin, John Newlin, Nicholas Newlin, Richard Eaveson & Jemima his wife, William Baily & Kezia his wife do grant to Richard Clayton & Mary his wife the full share of said lands being 3 tracts. One tract bounded by land of William Baily, Richard Eaveson, Joseph English, Marlborough township, land of Nathan Newlin & Willis containing 410 acres being part of 7,100 acres. Another tract bounded by land of Abraham Marshall, Bradford Township, Ellis Lewis, Joel Bayly & Mordecai Cloud containing 485 acres being part of 7,100 acres. The 3rd tract bounded by land of Nicholas Pyle, the road from Birmingham & Chester Road containing 33 acres. Signed Nathaniel Newlin, Nicholas Newlin, John Newlin, Richard Eaveson, Jemima Eaveson, William Baily & Kezia Baily. Delivered in the presence of Joseph Brinton, Henry Pierce & John Taylor. Recorded 19 Aug 1735. (E5:347).

Deed. On 11 Feb 1734/5 Phillip Taylor of Thornbury, yeoman, to John Taylor of Thornbury, yeoman. Phillip Taylor for £150 grant to John Taylor a plantation in Thornbury being 2 tracts one tract is bounded by land Thomas Mercer & Caleb Pierce containing 150 acres, the other tract bounced by land of Joseph Eaveson & Caleb Pierce containing 140 acres. Signed Phillip Taylor. Delivered in the presence of Richard Barry, James Mather & Nathan Worley. Recorded 20 Aug 1735. (E5:351).

Lease & Release. On 8 & 9 Aug 1735 William Taylor of East Calne, yeoman, & Mary his wife to John Bullar of East Calne, yeoman. Whereas Peter Whitaker & Mary his wife by deed dated 21 & 22 Feb 1734 granted to William Taylor a tract in East Calne containing 170 acres. Now William Taylor & Mary his wife for £60 grant to John Bullar a tract in East Calne bounded by land of James Lockhart, John Morgan & Peter Whitaker containing 170 acres. Signed William Taylor & Mary Taylor.

Delivered in the presence of Abel Parke, Peter Whitaker & Robert Parke. Recorded 21 Aug 1735. (E5:352).

Lease & Release. On 27 & 28 June 1735 Thomas Parke of Calne, yeoman, & Rebecca his wife to Abel Parke of Calne, yeoman, one of the sons of Thomas & Rebecca. Whereas Thomas Lindley of the City of Philadelphia, blacksmith, & Hannah his wife by deed dated 29 & 30 Dec 1725 granted to Thomas Parke a tract containing 500 acres, recorded in Chester, Book E, Vol 5, page 298. Now Thomas Parke & Rebecca his wife for love & 5 shillings grant to their son Abel Parke a tract in Caln bounded by land of George Aston, Thomas Parke, Beaver Run, land of Robert Parke & Thousand Acre Run containing 100 acres being part of the 500 acres. Signed Thomas Parke & Rebecca Parke. Delivered in the presence of Thomas Parke, Jr., John Jackson & Robert Parke. Recorded 22 Aug 1735. (E5:354).

Lease & Release. On 3 & 4 Dec 1734 Thomas Parke of Calne, yeoman, & Rebecca his wife to Thomas Parke, Jr., of Calne, yeoman, one of the sons of Thomas & Rebecca. Whereas Thomas Lindley of the City of Philadelphia, blacksmith, & Hannah his wife by deed dated 29 & 30 Dec 1725 granted to Thomas Parke a tract containing 500 acres, recorded in Chester, Book E, Vol 5, Page 298. Now Thomas Parke & Rebecca his wife for love & £200 grant to their son Thomas Parke, Jr., a tract in East Calne bounded by land of Thomas Parke, Phinehas Lewis, Aaron Mendenhall, George Aston, Beaver Run & land of Robert Parke containing 276 acres. Signed Thomas Parke & Rebecca Parke. Delivered in the presence of Abel Parke & Robert Parke. Recorded 23 Aug 1735. (E5:357).

Lease & Release. On 24 & 25 Aug 1733 John Wade of Essex House in Chester, gentleman, & Frances his wife to Joseph Parke of Chester, yeoman. John Wade & Frances his wife for £151.15 grant to Joseph Parke a tract in Chester where John Wade & Frances now dwell bounded by New Castle Road, lots of John Salkeld, Jr., lot late of Jonathon Ogden, Chester Creek, Delaware River containing 50 acres excepting out of the a small lot within the bounds containing less than 1/2 acre now in the possession of John Salkeld, Jr., & a small lot less than 1 acre belonging to the late Jonathon Ogden dec., also another lot in the same bounds containing 3/4 acre late in the possession of Thomas England. Signed John Wade & Frances Wade. Delivered in the presence of J. Reyners, James Mather & Robert Parke. Recorded 8 Oct 1735. (E5:360).

Release. On 1 Mar 1710/1 Jacob Simcock of Ridley, yeoman, to his brother John Simcock, Sr., of Ridley, yeoman. Jacob Simcock for 28 shillings release to John Simcock, Sr., all right, interest or claim in to a tract in Hill Town bounded by land of Caleb Pussey in Marlborough, land of Christopher Pennock, the Governors Manor Spring Town, land of John Dutton & Joseph Pennock containing 1,015 acres. Signed Jacob Simcock. Delivered in the presence of Benjamin Simcock & John Simcock. Recorded 15 Oct 1735. (E5:362).

Release. On 4 Oct 1735 John Dutton of Chichester, yeoman, & Elizabeth his wife, the only daughter of John Kinsman & Hannah his wife, one of the daughters of John Simcock, late of Ridley, dec., to Joseph Parker of Chester, yeoman. John Dutton & Elizabeth his wife for £20 release to Joseph Parker all right, interest or claim in 3 pieces of land in Marlborough, one bounded by land of John Bennet containing 200 acres, another bounded by land of Thomas Pearson containing 100 acres, & the other bounded by land of Richard Barnard & Henry Hayes containing 100 acres. Signed John Dutton & Elizabeth Dutton. Recorded 16 Oct 1735. (E5:363).

Mortgage. On 20 June 1735 William Hill of Chester, yeoman, to Edward Burling of the City of New York, one of the executors of the will of Thomas Dobson of the City of New York, dec. William Hill for securing the debt of £144.4 owed to Edward Burling as executor to Thomas Dobson, dec., & for the use of the children of Thomas Dobson grant & confirm to Edward Burling a full 5/6 part of a plantation & land in Middletown, late the estate of Peter Hunter, dec., bounded by land of John Turner, William Hill, Phillip Otley, Edgmont Road, land of William Hooke, William Trego & John Worrall containing 221 acres, also 5 equal & undivided 6 parts of tract lying in Middletown bounded by land of William Hill, Jacob Minshall & Dismal Run containing 170 acres. William Hill to pay Edward Burling, his heirs & executors the sum of £144.4 plus interest. Signed William Hill. Delivered in the presence of John Kinsey & Thomas Jackson. Recorded 17 Oct 1735. (E5:364).

Lease & Release. On 30 & 31 May 1734 John Evans of Denbigh in the County of Denbigh, Esq., & Peter Evans of Philadelphia, gentleman, to

John Evans of Chester County, yeoman. Whereas John Evans, Esq., by Letter of Attorney dated 16 June 1732 appointed Peter Evans his lawful attorney to dispose of his lands in Pennsylvania, East or West Jersey, the lower counties upon Delaware River & the province of Maryland, recorded in Philadelphia, Book D2, Vol 2, Page 92. Now Peter Evans for John Evans, Esq., for £400 grant to John Evans, yeoman, a tract of land lying in Chester County & New Castle County bounded by land of William Miller, other land of John Evans, White Clay Creek, land of John Thomas & Daniel Worsley containing 1,000 acres being part of 14,500 acres William Penn on 24 May 1706 granted to his son William Penn, who by deed dated 20 Sep 1715 granted to John Evans, Esq. Signed John Evans by Peter Evans. Delivered in the presence of Edward Fretwell & John Ross. Recorded 17 Nov 1735. (E5:366).

Release. On 26 May 1735 William Williams, late of Uwchlan in the County of Chester, yeoman, to John Cuthbert of Whiteland, yeoman. William Williams for good causes release to John Cuthbert all right, interest or claim in one full moiety of a grist mill & 60 acres of land. Signed William Williams. Delivered in the presence of Henty Atherton, Peter Worrall & Thomas Edwards. Recorded 17 Nov 1735. (E5:369).

Mortgage. On 6 Nov 1735 Richard Richardson of Whiteland, yeoman, & Ann his wife to Jonas Langford of the Island of Antigua, gentleman. Richard Richardson & Ann his wife for £120 grant to Jonas Landford a tract in Whiteland bounded by land of Edward Kennison, John Sharples, William Crouch & Joseph Hayes containing 283 acres. Richard Richardson & Ann his wife to pay Jonas Langford £120 plus interest on or before 6 Nov 1736. Signed Richard Richardson & Ann Richardson. Delivered in the presence of Charles Brockden, John Webb & John Duncan. Recorded 25 Nov 1735. (E5:370).

Mortgage. On 4 Apr 1735 Obidiah Johnson of Darby, yeoman, & Ann his wife to Rebecca Wood of Darby, widow. Obidiah Johnson & Ann his wife for £150 grant to Rebecca Wood a tract in Darby bounded land of Rebecca Wood, Haverford Road, the meeting house, land of Samuel Bunting, Thomas Worth & Darby Creek containing 97 acres. Obidiah Johnson to pay £213 to Rebecca Wood in payments all to be paid on or before 4 Apr 1742. Signed Obidiah Johnson & Ann Johnson. Delivered in the presence of Benjamin Pearson & Samuel Bunting. Recorded 14 Jan 1735/6. (E5:372).

71

Lease & Release. On 14 Feb 1731/2 Morton Canteson of Chester, yeoman, & Mary his wife to Erasmus Morton of Chester, being one of the sons of Morton Canteson & Mary. Whereas James Instason by deed dated 10 Dec 1698 granted to Morton Canteson a tract in Chester containing 45 acres, recorded in Chester, Book A, Vol 1, Page 146, on 7 Apr 1699. Morton Canteson & Mary his wife for love & affection & £35 grant to Erasmus Morton a tract bounded by Chichester Road, land late of John Child now of Jacob Roman, land late of Robert Langham, & a run called Meadow Runn containing 45 acres. Signed Morton Canteson & Mary Morton. Delivered in the presence of Joseph Coeburn, Timothy Morton, Morton Morton & Joseph Parker. Recorded 17 Feb 1735/6. (E5:374).

Receipt. On 21 Feb 1734/5 Margery Hunter of Middletown, widow & admin. of Jonathan Hunter, yeoman, dec., had received from William Hell of Middletown the sum of £26.5 in full of all demands on account of any lands formerly belonging to my late husband. Signed Margery Hunter. Delivered in the presence James Gibbons & John Taylor. Recorded 17 Feb 1735/6. (E5:377).

Release. On 2 Oct 1717 John Worrilaw of Thornbury, yeoman, & Ann his wife, Mary Baker the elder of Edgmont, widow & relict of Joseph Baker the elder, dec., John Baker of Edgmont, yeoman, surviving son & heir & the sole executor of the will of Joseph Baker the elder, Walter Worrilaw of Thornbury, yeoman, son & heir apparent of John & Ann Worrilaw, Mary Baker the younger of Thornbury, widow & relict of Joseph Baker the younger, dec., and one of the daughters of John & Ann Worrilaw, Peter Yarnall of Willis Town, yeoman, & Alice his wife, the other daughter of John & Ann Worrilaw, Daniel Hoops of Chester County, yeoman, to Phillip Yarnall of Edgmont, yeoman. Whereas Thomas Worrilaw, the late father of John, made his will dated 23 May 1709 & devised to son John Worrilaw all my lands in Chester County upon condition he discharge the debts of son-in-law Daniel Hoops which he stands bound. Thomas Worrilaw soon after died. Whereas John Worrilaw performed the said condition discharging the debts of Daniel Hoop. John Worrilaw on deed dated 15 & 16 Nov 1714 granted to Joseph Baker the elder & Phillip Yarnall a tract containing 250 acres but to be void upon payment of £180 plus interest. Whereas the said money was not paid. Joseph Baker died & the land fell to Phillip Yarnall by right of survivorship. Phillip did permit John Worrilaw to place the land at Public

Sale & Phillip Yarnall was the highest bidder. Now John Worrilaw & Ann his wife, Mary Baker the elder, John Baker, Walter Worrilaw, Mary Baker the younger, Peter Yarnall & Alice his wife & Daniel Hoops for £224 grant, release & confirm to Phillip Yarnall a tract in Edgmont bounded by land of Richard Marsh & Phillip Yarnall containing 250 acres. Signed Mary Baker, Peter Yarnall, Alice Yarnall, Daniel Hoops, John Worrilaw, Ann Worrilaw, Mary Baker, John Baker & Walter Worrilaw. Delivered in the presence of Thomas Weston, Jacob Minshall, Richard Ellwell & Evan Edwards. Recorded 18 Feb 1735/6. (E5:377).

Lease & Release. On 25 Mar 1730 Phobe Coppeck Massy was relict of Thomas Massy, late of Marple, dec., & Henry Lewis of Haverford, yeoman, both executors of the will of Thomas Massy, dec., to Henry Camm of Upper Providence. Whereas James Sandelands of Chester, merchant, dec., by deed dated 2 Oct 1703 granted to Thomas Massey then of Marple, dec., 3 lots of land, one being 40' x 120' bounded by High Street & land of Caleb Pussey, the 2nd lot bounded by a lot of John Hoskins being 40' x 120', & the 3rd lot bounded by the back part of the other 2 lots, lot of John Hoskins, land of Caleb Pussey & James Street being 40' x 80' being part of 20 acres that came to James Sandelands from his late father. Whereas Thomas Massey made his will dated 24 Mar 1707/8 & amongst other things the 3 lots in Chester be sold by my executors & did soon after. Now Phobe Massey now Coppeck & Henry Lewis for £11 grant to Henry Camm the 2nd lot of land. Signed Phobe Coppeck & Henry Lewis. Delivered in the presence of Ephraim Jackson, William Musgrove & Batholemew Coppeck. Recorded 19 Feb 1735/6. (E5:380).

Lease & Release. On 4 Aug 1730 Moses Coppeck of Marlborough, yeoman, to Henry Camm of Upper Providence, stocking weaver. Whereas William Penn, dec., granted to Bartholemew Coppeck, the grandfather of Moses Coppeck, a tract on the south side of Brandywine Creek containing 338 acres on 8 June 1702 recorded Book A, Vol 2, Page 323. Bartholemew Coppeck made his will dated 10 July 1712 & devised to his grandson Moses Coppeck the 338 acres. Now Moses Coppeck for £50 grant to Henry Camm a tract in Marlborough bounded by land of Francis Windlo & Thomas Wickersham containing 198 acres. Signed Moses Coppeck. Delivered in the presence of Richard Barry & William Surman. Recorded 20 Feb 1735/6. (E5:383).

Deed. On 30 Sep 1735 Ralph Pyle of Concord, yeoman, to Edward Bezar of Bethell, yeoman. Whereas Edward Bezar & Margaret his wife by deed dated 29 & 30 Sep 1735 granted to Ralph Pyle a tract in Bethell bounded by land of William Eyer, Edward Bezar, Edwar Poun, Francis Mechum, Walter Martin containing 121 acres. That is to say Edward Bezar to pay £65 to Ralph Pyle in payments to be paid in full on or before 30 Sep 1740. Signed Ralph Pyle. Delivered in the presence of William Cowpland & Joseph Parker. Recorded 28 Feb 1735/6. (E5:385).

Lease & Release. On 30 & 31 Mar 1719 Ann Whitpain of the City of Philadelphia, widow & relict of John Whitpain, late of the said City, merchant, dec., & executrix of his will, to Richard Eavison of Thornbury, yeoman. Whereas Rees Thomas of Merion in the County of Philadelphia, merchant, & Martha his wife & Anthony Morris, Jr., of the City of Philadelphia, brewer, & Phobe his wife by deed dated 27 & 28 May 1718 granted to John Whitpain a 1/3 part of 2,500 acres. John Whitpain made his will dated 20 Sep 1718 and devised the residue of my estate to be divided between my wife & 2 children, Sarah & Zachariah Whitpain & all lands & other estates due me as the heir of my grandfather Richard Whitpain & John Whitpain soon after died. Now Ann Whitpain for £32 granted to Richard Eavison a tract bounded by land of Richard Eavison, Thomas Mercer, John Millison & John Yearsley containing 219 acres being part of the 2,500 acres. Signed Ann Whitpain. Delivered in the presence of John Yearsley, Phillip Taylor & John Taylor. Recorded 1 Mar 1735/6. (E5:387).

Lease & Release. On 29 & 30 Mar 1719 Rees Thomas of Merion in the County of Philadelphia, gentleman, & Martha his wife & Anthony Morris, Jr., of the City of Philadelphia, brewer, & Phebe his wife to Richard Eavenson of Thornbury, yeoman. Whereas Richard Whitpain of London, butcher, in his lifetime became seized of several tracts of land in the province of Pennsylvania containing 7,000 acres (the 1,763 acres hereafter mentioned being at the time in Chester County). Richard Whitpain made his will dated 27 Apr 1689 & made his loving wife Mary Whitpain to be executrix to dispose of said lands as needed to cover debts. Richard Whitpain sometime after died. Whereas Mary Whitpain & the creditors of Richard Whitpain being Mary Davis, spinster, Thomas Cooper, Benjamin Henshaw, James Fodey, Ann Mill & others on 30 July 1689 granted to John Edridge of the Parish of St. Mary's Hill, London, distiller, William Ingran of London, salter, John Blackall of London, draper, John Wace of London, clothworker, also being creditors of

Richard Whitpain all the said land in the province except 500 acres not yet taken up, in trust to dispose of said lands to raise money to pay said debts. Whereas John Edridge, William Ingram & John Wace afterwards dying the premises vested to John Blackall by right of survivorship. Whereas John Blackall by deed dated 27 & 28 Nov 1712 for a great sum of money for the payment of debt of Richard Whitpain granted to William Aubrey of London, merchant, the said mentioned lands recorded Philadelphia, Book E7, Vol 9, Page 143. Whereas William Aubrey by deed dated 24 & 25 Apr 1713 granted to Rees Thomas & Anthony Morris the said lands recorded Philadelphia, Book E6, Vol 7, Page 255. Whereas the commissioners of William Penn confirmed to Rees Thomas & Anthony Morris a tract in Chester County containing 1,763 acres. Now Rees Thomas & Martha his wife & Anthony Morris, Jr., & Phebe his wife for £62.10 grant to Richard Eavenson a tract bounded by land of Richard Eavenson, Thomas Mercer, John Willison & John Yearsley containing 219 acres. Signed Rees Thomas, Martha Thomas, Anthony Morris, Jr., & Phebe Morris. Delivered in the presence of John Taylor, John Yearsley & Phillip Taylor. Recorded 2 Mar 1735/6. (E5:390).

Deed. On 15 Feb 1730 Robert Benson of Uwchlan in the County of Chester, yeoman, & Katherine his wife, who was the widow of Isaac Richardson, her late husband, dec., Isaac Melin of Whiteland, yeoman, & William Paschall of Whiteland, yeoman, (Katherine, Isaac & William were the executors of the will of Isaac Richardson) to John Chadds of Birmingham, yeoman, & Elizabeth his wife, one of the daughters of Isaac Richardson, dec. Whereas William Penn by deed dated 24 & 25 July 1681 granted to Richard ap Thomas (since dec.) 5,000 acres to be laid out in the province, recorded Philadelphia, Book A, Vol 1, Page 241. On 30 Mar 1684 5,000 acres was laid out in the Great Welsh Tract to Richard Thomas son of Richard ap Thomas, dec., in several tracts, one in Whiteland containing 500 acres which Richard Thomas, the son, by deed dated 12 & 13 Oct 1713 granted to Isaac Richardson. Isaac Richardson made his will dated 14 Oct 1726 devised all his lands to his son John & daughters Elizabeth, Mary, Elinor & Martha to be equally divided between them & made Katherine his wife, Isaac Malin & William Paschall his executors & died soon after. Whereas Katharine has married Robert Benson. Now Robert Benson, Katharine his wife, Isaac Malin & William Paschall have allotted to John Chadds & Elizabeth his wife as Elizabeth's share a tract in Whiteland bounded by land of Edward Kinnison, James Thomas & William Smith containing 100 acres. Signed Robert Benson, Katharine Benson, Isaac Malin & William Paschall.

Delivered in the presence of John Lilly, Jacob Wright & Richard Jones. Recorded 3 Mar 1735/6. (E5:395).

Deed. On 15 Feb 1730 Robert Benson of Uwchlan in the County of Chester, yeoman, & Katherine his wife who was the widow of Isaac Richardson her late husband, dec., Isaac Melin of Whiteland, yeoman, & William Paschall of Whiteland, yeoman, (Katherine, Isaac & William were the executors of the will of Isaac Richardson) to Jacob Wright of Whiteland, yeoman, & Mary his wife one of the daughters of Isaac Richardson, dec. Whereas William Penn by deed dated 24 & 25 July 1681 granted to Richard ap Thomas (since dec.) 5,000 acres to be laid out in the province, recorded Philadelphia, Book A, Vol 1, Page 241. On 30 Mar 1684 5,000 acres was laid out in the Great Welsh Tract to Richard Thomas son of Richard ap Thomas, dec., in several tracts, one in Whiteland containing 500 acres which Richard Thomas the son by deed dated 12 & 13 Oct 1713 granted to Isaac Richardson. Isaac Richardson made his will dated 14 Oct 1726 devised all his lands to his son John & daughters Elizabeth, Mary, Elinor & Martha to be equally divided between them & made Katherine his wife, Isaac Malin & William Paschall his executors & died soon after. Whereas Katharine has married Robert Benson. Now Robert Benson, Katharine his wife, Isaac Malin & William Paschall have allotted to Jacob Wright & Mary his wife Mary's share being a tract in Whiteland bounded by land of Edward Kinnison & John Chadds containing 100 acres. Signed Robert Benson, Katharine Benson, Isaac Malin & William Paschall. Delivered in the presence of John Chads, John Lilly & Richard Jones. Recorded 4 Mar 1735/6. (E5:397).

Lease & Release. On 1 May 1733 John Chads of Birmingham, yeoman, & Elizabeth his wife one of the daughters of Isaac Richardson, dec., to Jacob Wright of Whiteland, blacksmith, & Mary his wife. Whereas William Penn by deed dated 24 & 25 July 1681 granted to Richard ap Thomas (since dec.) 5,000 acres to be laid out in the province, recorded Philadelphia, Book A, Vol 1, Page 241. On 30 Mar 1684 5,000 acres was laid out in the Great Welsh Tract to Richard Thomas son of Richard ap Thomas, dec., in several tracts, one in Whiteland containing 500 acres which Richard Thomas the son by deed dated 12 & 13 Oct 1713 granted to Isaac Richardson. Isaac Richardson made his will dated 14 Oct 1726 devised all his lands to his son John & daughters Elizabeth, Mary, Elinor & Martha to be equally divided between them & made Katherine his wife, Isaac Malin & William Paschall his executors & died soon after.

Whereas Katharine has married Robert Benson. Robert Benson, Katharine his wife, Isaac Malin & William Paschall allotted to John Chadds & Elizabeth his wife a share in Whiteland bounded by land of Edward Kinnison, James Thomas & William Smith containing 100 acres. Now John Chadds & Elizabeth his wife for £100 grant to Jacob Wright the 100 acres. Signed John Chadds & Elizabeth Chadds. Delivered in the presence of James Wilmer & Abraham Parker. Recorded 5 Mar 1735/6. (E5:398).

Lease & Release. On 2 Feb 1734/5 Jacob Wright of Whitelands, yeoman, & Mary his wife to Richard Eavenson of Thornbury, yeoman. Whereas William Penn by deed dated 24 & 25 July 1681 granted to Richard ap Thomas (since dec.) 5,000 acres to be laid out in the province, recorded Philadelphia, Book A, Vol 1, Page 241. On 30 Mar 1684 5,000 acres was laid out in the Great Welsh Tract to Richard Thomas son of Richard ap Thomas, dec., in several tracts, one in Whiteland containing 500 acres which Richard Thomas the son by deed dated 12 & 13 Oct 1713 granted to Isaac Richardson. Isaac Richardson made his will dated 14 Oct 1726 devised all his lands to his son John & daughters Elizabeth, Mary, Elinor & Martha to be equally divided between them & made Katherine his wife, Isaac Malin & William Paschall his executors & died soon after. Whereas Katharine has married Robert Benson. Robert Benson, Katharine his wife, Isaac Malin & William Paschall allotted to John Chadds & Elizabeth his wife a share in Whiteland bounded by land of Edward Kinnison, James Thomas & William Smith containing 100 acres. John Chads & Elizabeth his wife by deed dated 1 & 2 May 1730 granted the 100 acres to Jacob Wright & Mary his wife. Now Jacob Wright & Mary his wife for £100 grant to Richard Eavenson the above mentioned 100 acres. Signed Jacob Wright & Mary Wright. Delivered in the presence of John Chads, Elizabeth Chads & Zachariah Butcher. Recorded 6 Mar 1745/6. (E5:401).

Lease & Release. On 5 & 6 Mar 1734/5 Jacob Wright of Whitelands, yeoman, & Mary his wife to Richard Eavenson of Thornbury, yeoman. Whereas William Penn by deed dated 24 & 25 July 1681 granted to Richard ap Thomas (since dec.) 5,000 acres to be laid out in the province, recorded Philadelphia, Book A, Vol 1, Page 241. On 30 Mar 1684 5,000 acres was laid out in the Great Welsh Tract to Richard Thomas son of Richard ap Thomas, dec., in several tracts, one in Whiteland containing 500 acres which Richard Thomas the son by deed dated 12 & 13 Oct 1713 granted to Isaac Richardson. Isaac Richardson made his will dated 14 Oct

1726 devised all his lands to his son John & daughters Elizabeth, Mary, Elinor & Martha to be equally divided between them & made Katherine his wife, Isaac Malin & William Paschall his executors & died soon after. Whereas Katharine has married Robert Benson. Robert Benson, Katharine his wife, Isaac Malin & William Paschall allotted to Jacob Wright & Mary his wife a share in Whiteland bounded by land of Edward Kinnison containing 100 acres. Now Jacob Wright & Mary his wife for £200 grant to Richard Eavenson the tract of 100 acres. Signed Jacob Wright & Mary Wright. Delivered in the presence of Isaac Malin, John Chads & Zachariah Butcher. Recorded 8 Mar 1735/6. (E5:404).

Deed. On 29 Jan 1719/20 George Wood of Darby, yeoman, & Hannah his wife to William Wood of Darby, yeoman. Whereas John Wood of Darby father of George Wood by deed dated 13 Feb 1713/4 granted to George Wood a tract in Darby where George now dwells containing 184 acres provided only that neither George Wood or any of his heirs should sell the said land within 7 years without the consent of John Wood, recorded Chester, Book C, Page 456. Now George Wood for £25 grant to William Wood a tract in Darby bounded by land of William Wood containing 21 acres & a part of meadow land in Darby containing 4 acres. Signed George Wood & Hannah Wood. Delivered in the presence of Samuel Hood, Jonathon Hood. Endorsed. The within mentioned Deed of Sale is with my consent. Signed John Wood. Delivered in the presence of Samuel Hood & Jonathon Hood. Memorandum. On 16 Feb 1723/4 George Wood did give peaceable possession to William Wood. Delivered in the presence of Jacob Bonsall & John Wood. Recorded 30 Apr 1736. (E5:407).

Deed. On 10 Aug 1718 John Wood of Darby, gentleman, & Rebecca his wife to William Wood of Darby, yeoman, son of John Wood. Whereas William Penn by deed dated 4 Aug 1684 granted to George Wood, late of Darby, yeoman, father of John Wood a tract in Darby containing 655 acres, recorded Philadelphia, Book A, Page 212. George Wood made his will dated 29 July 1696 amongst other things did give all his land to John Wood & shortly after died. Now John Wood & Rebecca his wife for the natural love for their son grant to William Wood a tract in Darby bounded by land of Michael Blunston, George Wood, Darby Creek & Jacob Bonsall containing 184 acres being part of the 655 acres. Signed John Wood & Rebecca Wood. Delivered in the presence of Thomas Kendall & John Rees. On 16 Feb 1723/4 John Wood did give peaceable possession to William Wood. Delivered in the presence of Jacob Bonsall & George Wood. Recorded 1 May 1736. (E5:409).

Lease & Release. On 16 Apr 1736 Caleb Cowpland of Chester, gentleman, & Sarah his wife to Jacob Howell of Chester, tanner, Thomas Cummings of Chester, cordwainer, John Owen of Chester, gentleman, Samuel Lightfoot & John Salkeld, Jr., both of Chester, yeomen, & John Sharples, Jr., of Ridley, cordwainer. Whereas the late commissioners of William Penn by deed dated 20 Aug 1705 granted to Caleb Pussey a tract in Chester containing 1+ acre, recorded in Philadelphia, Book A, Vol 3, Page 119. Whereas Caleb Pussey by deed dated 20 Dec 1706, recorded in Chester, Book B, Page 109, granted to Henry Worley a 1/4 part of the said 1+ acres. Caleb & Henry by deed dated 31 Aug 1713 granted to Joseph Vernon that part of the 1+ acres that lies between Chester Creek & the west side of Front Street & between the lots of John Sharples & Jonas Sandelands, recorded in Chester, Book C, Vol 3, Page 431. Whereas Henry Worley & Mary his wife by deed dated 24 June 1714 granted to Caleb Pussey amongst other things all their right & interest of the 1/4 part of the remaining part of the 1+ acre. Whereas Caleb Pussey & Ann his wife by deed dated 25 & 26 Mar 1723 granted to John Wright the remaining part of the 1+ acre. Whereas John Wright by deed dated 2 & 3 Aug 1727 amongst other things granted to John Owen that part of the 1+ acre that lies on the east side of Market Street. John Wright by deed dated 18 & 19 Dec 1728 grant the residue of the said 1+ acre to Caleb Cowpland. Now Caleb Cowpland & Sarah his wife for £55 grant to Jacob Howell, Thomas Cummings, John Owen, Samuel Lightfoot, John Saldkeld, Jr., & John Sharples, Jr., that lot in Chester bounded by a lot of Caleb Cowpland, Ruth Hoskins, George Maris, High Street & lots late of Jonas Sandelands being part of the 1+ acre. Signed Caleb Cowpland & Sarah Cowpland. Delivered in the presence of James Sharp, Edward Russel & Robert Parke. Recorded 8 May 1736. (E5:411).

Defeazance. On 18 Apr 1736 Jacob Howell of Chester, tanner, Thomas Cummings of Chester, cordwainer, John Owen of Chester, gentleman, Samuel Lightfoot & John Salkeld, Jr., both of Chester, yeomen, & John Sharples, Jr., of Ridley, cordwainer, send greetings. Whereas Caleb Cowpland of Chester, gentleman, & Sarah his wife by deed dated 16 & 17 Apr 1736 granted to Jacob Howell, Thomas Cummings, John Owen, Samuel Lightfoot, John Salkeld, Jr., & John Sharples, Jr., a lot in Chester bounded by a lot of Caleb Cowpland, Ruth Hoskins, George

Maris, High Street & lots late of Jonas Sandelands. There for Jacob Howell, Thomas Cummings, John Owen, Samuel Lightfoot, John Salkeld, Jr., & John Sharples, Jr., according to the trust in us & by the direction of the members belonging to the monthly meeting of Quakers in Chester being only for the use of the poor people of the Quakers. Signed Samuel Lightfoot, John Salkeld, Jr., John Sharples, Jr., Jacob Howell, Thomas Cummings & John Owen. Recorded 10 May 1736. (E5:415).

Lease & Release. On 4 May 1736 James Sandelands of Chester, son & heir of Jonas Sandelands, late of Chester, gentleman, dec., to John Wharton of Chester, sadler. James Sandelands for £43.15 grant to John Wharton a tract in Chester by Ridley Creek, land of George Asbridge & land of James Sandelands containing 8 1/4 acres being part of James Sandelands share of the estate of Jonas Sandelands, dec. Signed James Sandelands. Delivered in the presence of William Trehearn, Thomas Coeburn & Jacob Lightfoot. Recorded 8 June 1736. (E5:416).

Deed. On 1 May 1733 Jacob Howell of Chester, tanner, & Sarah his wife to John Wharton of Chester, saddler. Whereas Arthur Sheil & Mary his wife, formerly the widow & admin. of Jonas Sandelands, dec., who died intestate who at the time of his death was seized of several pieces of land in Chester & being the debts were more than his personal estate could pay & the charge of maintaining a family of small children, the Orphans Court at the request of Arthur Sheil & Mary was allowed to sell all the said lats to pay such debts & Arthur & Mary for £65 granted to Jacob Howell a lot of land in Chester bounded by Front Street, land of John Wharton, Chester Creek & a lot of Jacob Howell containing 1 1/4 acre with the yearly rent of 1 shilling to be paid the heirs of Jonas Sandelands. Now Jacob Howell & Sarah his wife for £22.6.8 grant to John Wharton a pice of land in Chester bounded by a lot of John Worrall, Chester Creek, a lot of John Wharton & Front Street being 1/3 of the 1 1/4 acre lot before mentioned. Signed Jacob Howell & Sarah Howell. Delivered in the presence of J. Reyners & Nathan Pickles. Recorded 10 June 1736. (E5:419).

Lease & Release. On 28 & 29 Sep 1733 Mordecai Maddock of Springfield, yeoman, to Henry Maddock of Springfield son of Mordecai Maddock. Whereas there is a tract of land in Springfield bounded by Crum Creek, Kendall's land, Simcock's land, Isaac Norris' land & land of John

Maddock containing 200 acres which is part of 1,500 acres purchased by James Kenerly & Henry Maddock father of Mordecai Maddock of William Penn, dec., in 1681, Henry Maddock became heir-at-law at the death of James Kennerly & became vested in the right of all the 1,500 acres. Henry Maddock by Deed of Gift in 1701 granted to Mordecai Maddock his son the whole 1,500 acres. Now Mordecai Maddock for love he bears grants to one of his sons Henry Maddock a tract of 200 acres. Signed Mordecai Maddock. Delivered in the presence of John Crosby & Susanna Crosby. Recorded 21 June 1736. (E5:421).

Lease & Release. On 2 & 3 July 1736 John Wade of Essex House, gentleman, to Joseph Parker of Chester, yeoman. Whereas Phillip Eilbeck & Lydia his wife by deed dated 18 June 1702 granted to John Wade a tenement called Essex House & 360 acres lying in Chester, recorded Chester, Book C, Vol 3, Page 122, on the 12 Feb 1709. Now John Wade for £200 grant to Joseph Parker a tract in Chester bounded by New Castle Road, lots of John Salkeld, Jr., & a lot late of Jonathon Ogden, Chester Creek & the river Delaware containing 50 acres being part of the above recited 360 acres except out of this a small lot not exceeding 1/2 acres now in the possession of John Salkeld, Jr., & a small lot not exceeding 1 acres now in the possession of the heirs of Jonathon Ogden, & a small lot not exceeding 3/4 acre late in the possession to Thomas England. Signed John Wade. Delivered in the presence of John Owen, Nathan Worley, Dan Beeby & Robert Parke. Recorded 6 July 1736. (E5:423).

Deed. On 25 Mar 171721 John Willis of Thornbury, yeoman, & Esther his wife to Samuel Scott, Jr., of Chester County, yeoman. Whereas the late commissioners of William Penn, dec., by deed dated 13 Aug 1712 granted to John Willis (amongst others) a tract in Bradford containing 50 acres. Now John Willis & Esther his wife for £10.10 grant to Samuel Scott a tract in Bradford bounded by land of the Mill belonging to John Willis, Samuel Scott & George Carter containing 10 1/2 acres. Signed John Willis & Esther Willis. Delivered in the presence of Timothy Ward, Jonathon Hunter & Nehemiah Ogden. Recorded 29 July 1736. (E5:426).

Deed. On 16 Apr 1722 John Willis of Thornbury, yeoman, & Esther his wife to Samuel Scott, Jr., of Chester County, yeoman. Whereas the late commissioners of William Penn, dec., by deed dated 13 Aug 1712 did grant to John Willis (amongst others) a tract in Bradford bounded by land late of Nathaniel King & land of Richard Buffington containing 50 acres, recorded in Philadelphia, Book A, Vol 4, Page 297, & whereas John Willis has lately erected a water corn mill on tract of land bounded by the end of the Upper dam at the head race, land of John Willis & Samuel Scott & Tailrace containing 2 acres being part of the 50 acres conveyed to John Willis. Now John Willis & Esther his wife for £100 grant to Samuel Scott 1/4 share of the said mill & 2 acres. Signed John Willis & Esther Willis. Delivered in the presence of Thomas Buffington, J. Yearsly & J. Taylor. Recorded 29 July 1736. (E5:428).

Lease & Release. On 29 & 30 Sep 1731 John Salkeld of Chester, gentleman, & Agnes his wife to Samuel Scott of Bradford, yeoman. Whereas by deed dated 15 & 16 May 1722 Richard Collet, late of the Parish of St. Martin's in the County of Middlesex in Old England, vintner, granted to Erasmus Cole, John Mead & Edmund Peacock 1,000 acres in the province of Pennsylvania being land William Penn granted on 11 July 1681 to Richard Collett. Richard Collett is to receive rents & profits of the 1,000 acres during his natural life & after his death the rents & profits are to be paid Elizabeth Green not to John Green as he would order but into the hands of Elizabeth for her separate & personal use exclusive of John Green & where with he was in no sort to intermediate to nor was the same to be subject to his debts or disposition. Upon further trust that they the said trustees should immediately after the death of John Green if Elizabeth should survive him convey all property to her for her natural life & after her death to go to her child or children by her husband John Green or any other husband she might marry or if there is no issue of Elizabeth to go to the heirs of Richard Collett. Also it may be lawful for the trustees to sell said 1,000 acres with the consent of Elizabeth but not jointly with her husband. And whereas Richard Collett departed this life on or about the month of Aug 1721. Erasmus Cole, John Mead & Edmund Peacock with the consent of Elizabeth Green granted to John Salkeld the 1,000 acres, recorded in Chester, Book E, Vol 5, Page 55. Now John Salkeld & Agnes his wife for £71 grant to Samuel Scott a tract in West Town bounded by the land of Samuel Osburn, Joseph Parker, & Samuel Scott containing 71 acres being part of the 1,000 acres. Signed John Salkeld & Agnes Salkeld. Delivered in the presence of Joseph Parker & Caleb Cowpland. Recorded 30 July 1736. (E5:431).

Lease & Release. On 27 July 1736 John Wade of Essex House, gentleman, to Thomas Barton of Chester, coachmaker. Whereas Phillip Eilbeck & Lydia his wife by deed dated 18 June 1702 granted to John

Wade a tenement called Essex House & 360 acres lying in Chester, recorded in Chester, Book C, Vol 3, Page 122, on the 12 Feb 1709. Now John Wade for £215.5 grant to Thomas Barton a piece of land called Horse Shoe in Chester bounded by land late of Joseph Reyner, the Great Road, land of John Wade & Chester Creek containing 71 3/4 acres part of the 360 acres. Signed John Wade. Delivered in the presence of James Mather, Nathan Worley & Robert Parke. Recorded 2 Aug 1736. (E5:436).

Power of Attorney. On 26 Oct 1734 Ruth Smith & David Smith of Dartmouth in the County of Bristol in the province of Massachusetts Bay in New England daughter & son of Thomas Smith & Jane his wife of Dartmouth in the County of Bristol in the province of Massachusetts Bay make & appoint our well beloved Uncle John Smith of Marlborough, yeoman, to be our true & lawful attorney for us to ask, demand, levy, recover & receive all monies, debts, & legacies due us. Signed Ruth Smith & David Smith. Delivered in the presence of Nathaniel Coleman & Jacob Barney. Recorded 11 Aug 1736. (E5:439).

Deed. On 1 May 1736 John Broom of Calcoonhook in Darby, yeoman, & Mary his wife to Margaret Morton of Ridley, widow. Whereas there is 2 tracts in Darby which one lot bounded by land of John Broom, Muckanipat Creek, & Archer's Meadow containing 12 acres which said tract was sold to John Broom by Andrew Urin by deed dated 10 Apr 1725 being part of lands among other things devised to Andrew by his late father Hans Urin in his will dated 25 Mar 1713. The other tract bounded by Muckanipat Creek, land of Andrew Urin & John Broom containing 12 acres which land was conveyed to John Broom by David Morton by deed dated 19 Apr 1721. Now John Broom & Mary his wife for £37 grant to Margaret Morton the 2 pieces of land containing in whole 24 acres. Signed John Broom & Mary Broom. Delivered in the presence of John Crosby & Joseph Hibberd. Recorded 1 Sep 1736. (E5:440).

Deed. On 1 Mar 1688 Urin Keen of Chester for £10 grant to John Simcock, Thomas Brassey, John Bristow, Caleb Pussey, Randel Vernon, Thomas Vernon, Joshua Hastings, Mordecai Maddock, Thomas Martin, Richard Few, Walter Faucett & Edward Carter a tract in Chester bounded by Urin's lot & Chester Creek for the use of the Chester meeting of the people called Quakers. Signed Urin Keen. Delivered in the presence of Robert Eyre, Francis Littel, George Foreman & John Martin. Recorded 23 Sep 1736. (E5:443).

Lease & Release. On 1 & 2 Apr 1736 Mordecai Maddock of Springfield, yeoman, to Edward Russell of Chester, mariner. Whereas Urin Keen, late of Chester by deed dated 1 Mar 1688 granted to John Simcock, Thomas Brassey, John Bristow, Caleb Pussey, Randel Vernon, Thomas Vernon, Joshua Hastings, Mordecai Maddock, Thomas Martin, Richard Few, Walter Faucett & Edward Carter a tract in Chester bounded by a lot late of Urin Keen but now of the heirs of Jonas Sandelands & Chester Creek for the use of the Chester meeting of the people called Quakers. Whereas John Simcock, Thomas Brassey, John Bristow, Caleb Pussey, Randel Vernon, Thomas Vernon, Joshua Hastings, Thomas Martin, Richard Few, Walter Faucett & Edward Carter departed this life without appointing other persons to succeed them the trust whereby estate of inheritance is vested to Mordecai Maddock the only surviving trustee. Now at the request of the monthly meeting of the people called Quakers, Mordecai Maddock conveys the said lot to Edward Russell & his heirs, being the person nominated by the meeting to accept the said lot which said meeting with the money arising purchased a larger lot & have erected a meeting house on the said lot. Now Mordecai Maddock for £100 for the use of the meeting of the people called Quakers granted to Edward Russell the said lot. Signed Mordecai Maddock. Delivered in the presence of Thomas Cummings & Jacob Howell. Recorded 25 Sep 1736. (E5:442).

Lease & Release. On 25 & 26 Dec 1733 Jane Newlin executrix of the will of Nathaniel Newlin of Concord lately dec., Edward Woodward executor & Ellis Lewis & John Newlin trustees of the will of Nathaniel Newlin to Thomas Wilson of East Marlborough, laborer. Whereas William Penn, dec., by deed dated 22 & 23 Mar 1681 granted to Nicholas Moor, James Claypoole, William Shark, Edward Peirce, John Simcock, Thomas Brassey, Thomas Baker & Edward Brooks a tract containing 20,000 acres laid out with some lots in Philadelphia in the trust of the Free Society of Traders. Whereas virtue of a warrant dated 1 June 1688 there was laid out on 20 Sep 1688 to Benjamin Chambers, president of the Society for the use of the Society a tract of 7,100 acres since found to be in the County of Chester & whereas by an Act of Assembly the said 20,000 acres was actually vested, settled & adjudged to be in Charles Road, Job Goodson, Evan Owen, George Fitzwater & Joseph Pidgeon of the City of Philadelphia, merchants. Whereas Charles Road, Job

Goodson, Evan Owen, George Fitzwater & Joseph Pidgeon by deed dated 10 June 1724 grant to Nathaniel Newlin, dec., the tract containing 7,100 acres, recorded in Chester, Book D, Vol 4, Page 369. Whereas Nathaniel Newlin died intestate the 7,100 acres was divided amongst his children & 2 tracts one containing 835 acres the containing 785 acres fell to the share of Nathaniel Newlin the son by deed dated 12 Aug 1730. Nathaniel Newlin the son made his will dated 10 Jan 1732 & made his wife Jane & Edward Woodward his executors & Ellis Lewis & John Newlin trustees empowering them to sell the residue of the lands not devised and soon after died. Now Jane Newlin, Edward Woodward, Ellis Lewis & John Newlin for £90 grant to Thomas Wilson a tract bounded by land of William Wickersham, George Baily containing 327 acres. Signed Jane Newlin, Edward Woodward, Ellis Lewis & John Newlin. Recorded 27 Oct 1736. (E5:446).

Deed. On 12 Feb 1731 William Lewis of New Town, yeoman, & Lowry his wife to Nathaniel Lewis eldest son & heir apparent of William Lewis. Whereas Michael Blunston, late of Darby, yeoman, by deed dated 14 Dec 1697 granted to William Lewis, late of New Town, the father of William Lewis, a tract in New Town bounded by land late of Luke Hank, Thomas Rudyard & Crum Creek containing 180 acres. Whereas William Lewis the father by deed dated 4 Oct 1704 granted to William Lewis the son. Whereas Thomas Rees of New Town, yeoman, & Margaret his wife by deed dated 27 Mar 1713 granted to William Lewis the son a tract in New Town bounded by land lateof William Phillips, the above described land, Crum Creek & other land of Thomas Rees containing 100 acres. Now William Lewis for natural love grant to his son Nathan Lewis a tract in New Town bounded by Crum Creek, land of Thomas Rees, land late of William Phillips, other land of William Lewis & land of Evan Lewis formerly Luke Hanks which includes the last described 100 acres & part of the 180 acres containing 270 acres. Signed William Lewis & Lowry Lewis. Delivered in the presence of Owen Evans & Richard Jones. Recorded 3 Dec 1736. (E5:449).

Mortgage. On 21 Oct 1736 Stephen Beeks of Goshen, yeoman, to George Asbridge of Goshen, yeoman. Whereas Stephen Beeks by a certain obligation by the same date as this indenture stand bound to George Asbridge for £750 for the payment of £375 & interest according to the days of payment herein after mentioned. Now Stephen Beeks in consideration of the said debt of £375 to better secure the payment grant to George Asbridge a tract in Goshen bounded by land of George Asbridge, land late of Joseph Woodward, land of Joseph Phipps, Samuel Garret & the meeting house lot containing 424 acres. Payments to be made in full by 21 Oct 1739. Signed Stephen Beeks. Delivered in the presence of Thomas Lewis & John Todhunter. Recorded 4 Dec 1736. (E5:451).

Mortgage. On 21 Oct 1736 Griffith Hughs of East Town, clerk to Benjamin Duffield of the City of Philadelphia, tanner. Whereas Griffith Hughs stands bound to Benjamin Duffield for £300 conditioned for the payment of £150 here after mentioned. Now Griffith Hughs to better secure said payment grant to Benjamin Duffield a tract in East Town bounded by Shardlo's land, land of Evan Hughs & Edward Williams containing 236 1/2 acres. the sum of £150 plus interest to be paid on or before 21 Oct 1737. Signed Griffith Hughs. Delivered in the presence of C. Brockden & John Duncan. Recorded 14 Dec 1736. (E5:453).

Deed. On 20 July 1731 Grace Lloyd of Chester, widow & executrix of David Lloyd, late of Chester, gentleman, dec., to George Simpson & Ruth his wife of Chester, tailor. Whereas David Lloyd made his will dated 29 Mar 1724 & amongst other things mentioned bequeathed to his wife Grace the residue of his estate & made Grace his sole executrix & died soon after. David Lloyd in his lifetime sold but did not effectively convey the lot, therefore Grace Lloyd for £10 grant & confirm unto George Simpson a lot in Chester bounded by the street that runs from Chester Creek to Grace Lloyd's plantation, a lot late of John Hoskins, lot late of George Wookiars & a lot late of Robert Barber also to pay to Grace Lloyd a yearly rent of 2 shillings. Signed Grace Lloyd. Delivered in the presence of Stephen Hoskins & Abraham Barton. Recorded 18 Dec 1736. (E5:454).

Release. On 31 July 1735 Samuel Marshall of Willings Town in the County of New Castle on Delaware, yeoman, & Sarah his wife to John Yarnall of Edgmont, yeoman. Whereas Francis Rawle, late of Philadelphia, gentleman, dec., & Martha his wife & Stephen Pidgeon, late of the County of Bucks, merchant, dec., & Rebecca his wife by deed dated 25 & 26 Mar 1725 granted to Samuel Sellars, Jr., then of Darby, weaver, a tract containing 340 acres. Samuel Sellars, Jr., & Sarah his wife by deed dated 2 & 3 Dec 1734 granted to Samuel Marshall all the 340 acres. Now Samuel Marshall for £180 grant to John Yarnall a tract in

Charles Town in the County of Chester bounded by the Welsh line containing 340 acres being part of the full 16th part of 5,358 acres of land called Pickerings Mines. Signed Samuel Marshall in the presence of Richard Barry & John Taylor. Signed Sarah Marshall in the presence of John Webb & Samuel Scott. Recorded 21 Jan 1736/7. (E5:456).

Release. On 21 May 1719 Robert Ashton of the City of Philadelphia, gentleman, & Margarett his wife to Samuel Robinett of the County of Chester, yeoman. Whereas the commissioners of William Penn, dec., granted to Robert Ashton a tract in Chester County bounded by the land of Randal Janny & a creek containing 500 acres by deed dated 25 June 1705, recorded in Philadelphia, Book A, Vol 3, Page 34. Now Robert Ashton & Margarett his wife for £100 grant to Samuel Robinett all the 500 acres. Signed Robert Ashton & Margaret Ashton. Delivered in the presence of David Evans & Charles Brockden. Recorded 13 May 1737. (E5:458).

Lease & Release. On 10 May 1736 William Miller of New Garden, yeoman, & Ann his wife to John Morgan of Caln, yeoman. Whereas William Penn by deed dated 1 & 2 Mar 1681 granted to Roger Beck of Bramyard in the County of Hereford, iron manager, a tract 500 acres to be allotted in Pennsylvania. Whereas Roger Beck by deed dated 29 & 30 June 1721 granted to John Harris of the Parish of Kings Swinford in the County of Stafford, butcher, son & heir apparent of Edward Harris, late of Rodway in the County of Warwick, cordwainer, dec., a tract of 500 acres. Whereas the commissioners of Property at the request of John Harris laid out a tract of 500 acres in the township of Caln. John Harris by deed dated 10 & 11 Feb 1726 granted to William Miller of New Garden, miller, all 500 acres. Now William Miller & Ann his wife for £50 grant to John Morgan a tract in Caln bounded by land of William Branson, Thomas Green, land late of Francis Evetts containing 150 acres. Signed William Miller & Ann Miller. Delivered in the presence of Jeremy Starr, James Miller & Samuel Pennock. Recorded 14 June 1737. (E5:460).

Endorsement. On 13 June 1719 Jacob Kolluck for £154.10.7 grant to Thomas Howell of Chichester, yeoman, several tracts of land for the use of Thomas Howell never the less to the right of redemption which the within named Mordecai Howell hath or may can or ought to have of in and to the said lands. Signed Jacob Kolluck. Delivered in the presence of William Strutt & Charles Osborne. Recorded 7 June 1737. (E5:462).

Endorsement. On 2 Sep 1718 Samuel Preston hereby acknowledge that his name was used in the within mentioned mortgage by the special appointment of Jacob Kolluck of the County of Sussex upon Delaware, cooper & in trust for him £100 consideration money within mentioned was the proper money of the said Jacob in performance of which trust I do hereby assign, transfer & set over to him the said Jacob Kolluck all the several tract of land mentioned conveyed to me and my heirs situated & bound and all my estate right, interest, use of in the premises. Under the conditions & covenants within written. Signed Samuel Preston. Delivered in the presence of Thomas Clayton, John Owen & David Lloyd. Recorded 27 June 1737. (E5:463).

Endorsement. On 8 Jan 1724 Mordecai Howell for 5 shillings confirm unto Thomas Howell of Chichester, yeoman, all my right, interest & claim to several tracts of land within mentioned situated & bound as within mentioned. Signed Mordecai Howell. Delivered in the presence of William Tidmarsh, Joseph Bond & Joseph Lawrence. Recorded 27 June 1737. (E5:464).

Mortgage. On 23 Apr 1737 Joseph Parsons of Marple, mill wright & Susanna his wife to Benjamin Duffield of the City of Philadelphia, tanner. Whereas Joseph Parson & Susanna his wife for the debt of £40 & to better secure said debt grant to Benjamin Duffield a tract in Marple bounded by Derby Road, land of Joseph Rhodes, land of Robert Pearsons & other land of Joseph Parson purchased of Robert Pearsons containing 60 acres. Joseph Parsons to make one payment on or before 23 Apr 1738 to Benjamin Duffield. Signed Joseph Parsons & Susanna Parsons. Delivered in the presence of C. Brockden & Jonathon Duncan. Recorded 4 July 1737. (E5:464).

Lease & Release. On 28 & 29 Dec 1735 Joshua Bispham, late of Manchester in the County of Lancaster in Old England but now of the City of Philadelphia, sadler, & John Kinsey of the City of Philadelphia, gentleman, to Ephraim Jackson of Chester County, yeoman. Whereas William Penn by deed dated 2 & 3 Mar 1681 granted to William Bostock 500 acres to be laid out in the province. A tract of 500 acres was laid out to William Bostock in Thornbury. William Bostock died intestate without issue & the land descended to John Bostock of Nether Runstford in the

County of Chester, gentleman, the only brother & heir-at-law of the said William Bostock. Whereas the said tract was resurveyed & found to be 535 1/2 acres & confirmed to John Bostock by the commissioners of Property on 14 May 1702, recorded in Philadelphia, Book A, Vol 2, Page 243. Whereas John Bostock made his will dated 16 Sep 1707 & devised the 535 1/2 acres & other lands to his son Cheney Bostock, late of Ulverston in the County of Lancaster, gentleman. Whereas Cheney Bostock made his will dated 8 June 1722 devised all his lands to his sister May the wife of William Harington then of Chester, merchant, & Cheney Bostock soon after died. Whereas William Harington of Earnshaw in the County of Chester, Esq., & Mary his wife by deed dated 30 & 31 Jan 1734 granted to Joshua Bispham the tract of 535 1/2 acres, the last indenture was acknowledged before the mayor of the Burrough of Macclesfield. Whereas Joshua Bispham & Mary his wife on 18 Aug 1735 granted to John Kinsey the 535 1/2 acres for 99 years if the aforesaid Mary the wife of Joshua Bispham shall so long live upon special trust of John Kensy & to the intent & purpose the said John Kinsey should from time to time make & grant the said premises to person or persons is such manner as Joshua Bispham should direct. Now Joshua Bispham & John Kinsey for £140 grant to Ephraim Jackson a tract on Thornbury bounded by land of Thomas Willis, John Taylor, Abel Green & Jesse Baker containing 138 acres being part of the 535 1/2 acres. Signed Joshua Bispham & John Kinsey. Delivered in the presence of David Regester & Thomas Jackman. Recorded 22 July 1737. (E5:466).

Lease & Release. On 28 & 29 Dec 1735 Joshua Bispham, late of Manchester in the County of Lancaster in Old England but now of the City of Philadelphia, sadler, & John Kinsey of the City of Philadelphia, gentleman, to Jesse Baker of Chester County, yeoman. Whereas William Penn by deed dated 2 & 3 Mar 1681 granted to William Bostock 500 acres to be laid out in the province. A tract of 500 acres was laid out to William Bostock in Thornbury. William Bostock died intestate without issue & the land descended to John Bostock of Nether Runstford in the County of Chester, gentleman, the only brother & heir-at-law of the said William Bostock. Whereas the said tract was resurveyed & found to be 535 1/2 acres & confirmed to John Bostock by the commissioners of Property on 14 May 1702, recorded in Philadelphia, Book A, Vol 2, Page 243. Whereas John Bostock made his will dated 16 Sep 1707 & devised the 535 1/2 acres & other lands to his son Cheney Bostock, late of Ulverston in the County of Lancaster, gentleman. Whereas Cheney Bostock made his will dated 8 June 1722 devised all his lands to his sister

May the wife of William Harington then of Chester, merchant, & Cheney Bostock soon after died. Whereas William Harington of Earnshaw in the County of Chester, Esq., & Mary his wife by deed dated 30 & 31 Jan 1734 granted to Joshua Bispham the tract of 535 1/2 acres, the last indenture was acknowledged before the mayor of the Burrough of Macclesfield. Whereas Joshua Bispham & Mary his wife on 18 Aug 1735 granted to John Kinsey the 535 1/2 acres for 99 years if the aforesaid Mary the wife of Joshua Bispham shall so long live upon special trust of John Kensy & to the intent & purpose the said John Kinsey should from time to time make & grant the said premises to person or persons is such manner as Joshua Bispham should direct. Now Joshua Bispham & John Kinsey for £140 grant to Jesse Baker a tract in Thornbury bounded by land of Thomas Willis, Ephraim Jackson, Abel Green & Joseph Baker containing 138 acres being part of the 535 1/2 acres. Signed Joshua Bispham & John Kinsey. Delivered in the presence of David Regester & Thomas Jackman. Recorded 25 July 1737. (E5:469).

Lease & Release. On 28 & 29 Dec 1735 Joshua Bispham, late of Manchester in the County of Lancaster in Old England but now of the City of Philadelphia, sadler, & John Kinsey of the City of Philadelphia, gentleman, to Abel Green of Chester County, mason. Whereas William Penn by deed dated 2 & 3 Mar 1681 granted to William Bostock 500 acres to be laid out in the province. A tract of 500 acres was laid out to William Bostock in Thornbury. William Bostock died intestate without issue & the land descended to John Bostock of Nether Runstford in the County of Chester, gentleman, the only brother & heir-at-law of the said William Bostock. Whereas the said tract was resurveyed & found to be 535 1/2 acres & confirmed to John Bostock by the commissioners of Property on 14 May 1702, recorded in Philadelphia, Book A, Vol 2, Page 243. Whereas John Bostock made his will dated 16 Sep 1707 & devised the 535 1/2 acres & other lands to his son Cheney Bostock, late of Ulverston in the County of Lancaster, gentleman. Whereas Cheney Bostock made his will dated 8 June 1722 devised all his lands to his sister May the wife of William Harington then of Chester, merchant, & Cheney Bostock soon after died. Whereas William Harington of Earnshaw in the County of Chester, Esq., & Mary his wife by deed dated 30 & 31 Jan 1734 granted to Joshua Bispham the tract of 535 1/2 acres, the last indenture was acknowledged before the mayor of the Burrough of Macclesfield. Whereas Joshua Bispham & Mary his wife on 18 Aug 1735 granted to John Kinsey the 535 1/2 acres for 99 years if the aforesaid Mary the wife of Joshua Bispham shall so long live upon special trust of

John Kensy & to the intent & purpose the said John Kinsey should from time to time make & grant the said premises to person or persons is such manner as Joshua Bispham should direct. Now Joshua Bispham & John Kinsey for £280 grant to Abel Green a tract in Thornbury bounded by land of John Cheney, land late of Jonathon Hunter, late of Evan Howell, Jesse Baker, Ephraim Jackson & John Taylor containing 276 3/4 acres being part of the 535 1/2 acres. Signed Joshua Bispham & John Kinsey. Delivered in the presence of David Regester & Thomas Jackman. Recorded 26 July 1737. (E5:472).

Lease & Release. On 29 & 30 Jan 1735 Abel Green of the County of Chester, mason to Stephen Ogden of the County of Chester, yeoman. Whereas William Penn by deed dated 2 & 3 Mar 1681 granted to William Bostock 500 acres to be laid out in the province. A tract of 500 acres was laid out to William Bostock in Thornbury. William Bostock died intestate without issue & the land descended to John Bostock of Nether Runstford in the County of Chester, gentleman, the only brother & heir-at-law of the said William Bostock. Whereas the said tract was resurveyed & found to be 535 1/2 acres & confirmed to John Bostock by the commissioners of Property on 14 May 1702, recorded in Philadelphia, Book A, Vol 2, Page 243. Whereas John Bostock made his will dated 16 Sep 1707 & devised the 535 1/2 acres & other lands to his son Cheney Bostock, late of Ulverston in the County of Lancaster, gentleman. Whereas Cheney Bostock made his will dated 8 June 1722 devised all his lands to his sister May the wife of William Harington then of Chester, merchant, & Cheney Bostock soon after died. Whereas William Harington of Earnshaw in the County of Chester, Esq., & Mary his wife by deed dated 30 & 31 Jan 1734 granted to Joshua Bispham the tract of 535 1/2 acres, the last indenture was acknowledged before the mayor of the Burrough of Macclesfield. Whereas Joshua Bispham & Mary his wife on 18 Aug 1735 granted to John Kinsey the 535 1/2 acres for 99 years if the aforesaid Mary the wife of Joshua Bispham shall so long live upon special trust of John Kensy & to the intent & purpose the said John Kinsey should from time to time make & grant the said premises to person or persons is such manner as Joshua Bispham should direct. Joshua Bispham & John Kinsey by deed dated 28 & 29 Dec 1735 granted to Abel Green a tract containing 276 3/4 acres. Now Abel Green for £125 grant to Stephen Ogden a tract in Thornbury bounded by land late of Evan Howell, land late of Joseph Baker, land of Abel Green land late of Jonathon Hunter & John Yarnall containing 100 acres being part of 276

3/4 acres. Signed Abel Green. Delivered in the presence of James Benbridge & Ephraim Jackson. Recorded 28 July 1737. (E5:475).

Lease & Release. On 30 & 31 Jan 1734 William Harington of Earnshaw in the County of Chester, Esq., & Mary his wife, sister & devisee of Cheney Bostock, late of Ulverstone in the County of Lancaster, gentleman, dec., who was the eldest son & devisee of John Bostock, late of Nether Kuntford in the County of Chester, gentleman, dec., who was the only brother of William Bostock formerly of the City of London, cheese monger, to Joshua Bispham of Manchester in the County of Lancaster, saddler. William Harrington for 5 shillings in had & the sum of £200 to be paid grant to Joshua Bispham a tract in Thornbury bounded by land of Joseph Baker, Ephraim Jackson, John Beller, John Worrilaw & Evan Howell containing 535 1/2 acres. Signed William Harington & Mary Harington. Delivered in the presence of John Marshall & Samuel Widdall. Recorded 30 July 1737. (E:478).

Deed. On 18 Apr 1733 Aaron James of Westown, yeoman, & Elizabeth his wife to Thomas James of Westown, yeoman, & eldest son of Aaron James. Whereas William Penn granted to John Blunston, late of Darby, yeoman, a tract in Westown bounded by land of Benjamin Hickman & land late of John Bellow containing 276 acres. Now Aaron James & Elizabeth his wife for 5 shillings grant to Thomas James a tract in Westown bounded by land of Benjamin Hickman, Aaron James, Joshua Hoops & land late of Thomas Paschall containing 159 3/4 acres Signed Aaron James & Elizabeth James. Delivered in the presence of Aaron James, Jr., Joseph James & Richard Jones. Recorded 1 Aug 1737. (E5:481).

Deed. On 1 Sep 1737 John Davis of Plymoth township in the County of Philadelphia, admin. of the goods & chattels of Edward Mathias, late of Chester County, dec., admin., by Henry David, dec., who was the executor of the will of Edward Mathias. Whereas Griffith John, admin. of the goods & chattels of Henry David, who died intestate at the Court of Common Pleas the last Tues. in Aug 1737, recovered against John Davis admin. of the goods & chattels of Edward Mathias not administered by the Henry David in his lifetime £113.1 to be levied on the goods & chattels of Edward Mathias at the time of his death. Whereas John Davis made an application to the Orphans Court 25 June, it was allowed that John Davis should sell a tract of land bounded by land of James Atkinson, land formerly of Lewis Walker now of his son Abel Walker &

land formerly Rowland but now of Samuel Richards containing 50 acres. John Davis for £37 grant to Griffith John the tract containing 50 acres. Signed John Davis. Delivered in the presence of Richard Hayes, John Crosby, Henry Hayes & Abraham Emmett. Recorded 8 Sep 1737. (E5:482).

Lease & Release. On 6 & 7 Dec 1736 Richard Barry of Chester, merchant, & Mary his wife to Richard Woodward of East Bradford, yeoman, & Henry Pierce of Concord, gentleman, executors of the will of Henry Nagle, late of Thornbury, dec. Whereas Arthur Sheil & Mary his wife the widow & admin. of Jonas Sandelands, dec., by deed dated 31 Aug 1732 granted to William Trehearn of Chester, innholder, a tract in Chester containing 2 1/2 acres with the yearly rent of 5 shillings to be paid the heirs of Jonas Sandelands, recorded in Chester, Book E, Vol 5, Page 150. William Trehearn & Catherine his wife by deed dated 14 & 15 Nov 1733 granted to Richard Barry a lot in Chester being 40' x 120'. Now Richard Barry & Mary his wife for £100 grant to Richard Woodward & Henry Pierce all that lot in Chester bounded by Free Street, High Street, land of William Trehearn. Signed Richard Barry & Mary Barry. Delivered in the presence of Robert Wade, Joseph Parker & John Owen. Recorded 12 May 1737. (E5:483).

Deed. On 5 Mar 1732 John Devonald of the County of Chester in the township of London in Old England, yeoman, to his son Daniel Devonald of the same place, yeoman. John Devonald for love & affection grant to Daniel Devonald a tract on White Clay Creek bounded by land of John Jones, Richard Whitting, David Williams & John Devonald containing 103 acres. Signed John Devonald. Delivered in the presence of Richard Whitting & John Evans, Jr. Memorandum. Peaceful possession granted Daniel Devonald on 25 Apr 1733. Signed John Devonald. Delivered in the presence of John Evans, Jr., Richard Whitting, David William, Oliver Allison & William Graydon. Recorded 21 Oct 1737. (E5:485).

Mortgage. On 28 Nov 1737 Rees Pritchard of Whiteland, yeoman, & Hannah his wife to Richard Hayes of Haverford, gentleman. Whereas Rees Pritchard is under obligation to Richard Hayes for £200 & for Rees Pritchard to better secure the said payment of £100 grant to Richard Hayes a tract in Whiteland bounded by land late of Evan Bowen & old Welsh Line containing 254 acres. Rees Pritchard to pay £100 plus interest. Signed Rees Pritchard & Anna Pritchard. Delivered in the presence of Joseph Lewis, Abraham Lauder & Benjamin Hayes. Recorded 9 Jan 1737/8. (E5:486).

Mortgage. On 5 Oct 1737 Mordecai Taylor of Upper Providence, carpenter, to John Davis of Upper Providence, yeoman, & Margaret his wife. Mordecai Taylor for £250 grant to John & Margaret Davis a tract in Providence bounded by Crum Creek, land of Thomas Minshall, the road by the meeting house & land of Peter Dicks containing 150 acres. Mordecai Taylor to pay the sum of £500 to John Davis & Margaret his wife & their heirs in payments of £10 yearly for 50 years. Signed Mordecai Taylor. Delivered in the presence of Peter Trego, William Gorsuch & Mary Phillips. Recorded 9 Jan 1737/8. (E5:488).

Lease & Release. On 5 & 6 Dec 1737 Abel Parke of East Caln, yeoman, & Deborah his wife to Joseph Parker of Chester, yeoman. Whereas Thomas Parke & Rebecca his wife by deed dated 27 & 28 June 1735 granted to Abel Parke a tract containing 100 acres, recorded in Chester, Book E, Vol 5, Page 355. Whereas Thomas Parke, Jr., by deed dated 1 & 2 Dec 1737 granted to Abel Parke a tract containing 124 acres. Now Abel Parke & Deborah his wife for £100 grant to Joseph Parker both tracts of land one in Caln bounded by land of George Aston, Thomas Parke, Beaver Run, Robert Parke & Thousand Acre Run containing 100 acres the other tract adjoins the former tract bounded by land of Phineas Lewis & Thomas Parke containing 124 1/2 acres being part of a larger tract of 500 acres conveyed by Thomas Lindley & Hannah his wife to Thomas Parke by deed dated 29 & 30 Dec 1725. Signed Abel Parke & Deborah Parke. Delivered in the presence of John Wharton, Thomas Parke, Jr., & Dan Killing. Recorded 12 Jan 1737/8. (E5:491).

Lease & Release. On 13 & 14 Mar 1722 Tobias Collett of London in Old England, haberdasher, Daniel Quare of London, watchmaker, & Henry Gouldney of London, linen draper to John Cox of Chester County, yeoman. Whereas there is a tract of land lying on a branch of White Clay Creek below New Garden in the County of Chester, bounded by land of Moses Harland, Richard Cox, James Todd & John Cain containing 250 acres, being part of a tract of 17,218 acres the commissioners of William Penn granted to Tobias Collett, Daniel Quare, Henry Gouldney & the heirs of Michael Russell, late of London, merchant, dec., by deed dated 25 June 1718, recorded in Philadelphia, Book A, Vol 5, Page 300. Now Tobias Collett, Daniel Quare & Henry Gouldney for £46 grant to John

Cox the 250 acres. Signed Tobias Collett, D. Quare & Henry Gouldney. Delivered in the presence of Sarah Dinsdale, John Eastaugh & Elizabeth Eastaugh. Recorded 4 Feb 1737/8. (E5:494).

Lease & Release. On 2 & 3 Nov 1737 John Cox, late of the County of Chester, yeoman, & Mary his wife to Thomas Brian of New Garden, yeoman. John Cox & Mary his wife for £250 grant to Thomas Brian a tract lying on a branch of White Clay Creek in the township of London Grove bounded by land of Moses Harlan, Richard Cox, James Todd & John Cain containing 250 acres being the tract John Cox purchased of Tobias Collett, Daniel Quare & Henry Gouldney on 13 & 14 Mar 1722. John Cox & Mary Cox. Delivered in the presence of Benjamin Fred, Henry Dixon & William Cox. Recorded 8 Feb 1737/8. (E5:496).

Mortgage. On 9 Nov 1737 Thomas Brian of New Garden, yeoman, to John Cox, late of London Grove, yeoman, & Mary his wife. Thomas Brian for £210 grant to John Cox a tract lying on a branch of White Clay Creek in the township of London Grove bounded by land of Moses Harlan, Richard Cox, James Todd & John Cain containing 250 acres being the tract John Cox lately sold to Thomas Brian. Thomas Brian to make payments yearly & to be paid in full on or before 1 Nov 1744 to John Cox. Signed Thomas Bryan. Delivered in the presence of Benjamin Fred, William Cox & Henry Dixson. Recorded 9 Feb 1737/8. (E5:499).

Lease & Release. On 6 & 7 Oct 1737 Henry Maddock of Springfield, yeoman, to Peter Dicks of Providence, yeoman. Whereas Mordecai Maddock father of Henry Maddock by deed dated 28 & 29 Sep 1733 granted to Henry Maddock a tract in Springfield containing 200 acres & whereas Henry Maddock by deed dated 22 & 23 Nov 1736 grant to Joseph Parker the 200 acres & by another deed dated 23 Nov that if the sum was paid to Joseph Parker or his heirs at the days & times mentioned that Joseph Parker should release & confirm unto Henry Maddock the said tract. Whereas the monies being paid, Joseph Parker at the request of Henry Maddock by deed dated 5 Oct last, did confirm unto Henry Maddock the above mentioned tract. Now Henry Maddock for £78 grant to Peter Dicks a tract in Springfield bounded by land of Peter Dicks, Thomas Kendall, Springfield Road & land of John Maddock containing 42 1/2 acres being part of the 200 acre tract. Signed Henry Maddock. Delivered in the presence of Caleb Burchall, John Riely, Joseph Parker & Dan Killing. Recorded 17 Mar 1737/8. (E5:501).

Lease & Release. On 2 & 3 Feb 1737/8 Henry Maddock of Springfield, yeoman, to Peter Dicks of Providence, yeoman. Whereas Mordecai Maddock father of Henry Maddock by deed dated 28 & 29 Sep 1733 granted to Henry Maddock a tract in Springfield containing 200 acres, recorded Chester, Book E, Vol 5, Page 421, & whereas Henry Maddock by deed dated 9 10 Oct 1737 granted to Peter Dicks 42 1/2 acres part of the 200 acres. Now Henry Maddock for £300 grant to Peter Dicks a tract in Springfield bounded by land of Thomas Kendall, Simcock, Isaac Norris, John Maddock & the Great Road containing 157 1/2 acres being part of the 200 acres. Signed Henry Maddock. Delivered in the presence of Joseph Parker, John Kerlin & Dan Killing. Recorded 17 Mar 1737/8. (E5:504).

Mortgage. On 26 Nov 1737 Joseph Hollingsworth of Kennet, yeoman, to John Dixson of Mill Creek Hundred in the County of New Castle upon Delaware, yeoman. Joseph Hollingsworth for £60 grant to John Dixson a tract lying in Kennet bounded by Red Clay Creek, land of John Gregg, land of the late William Penn, Jr., manor & land of James Mcginly containing 150 acres. Joseph Hollingsworth to make yearly payments to John Dixson to be paid in full on or before 26 Nov 1743. Signed Joseph Hollingsworth. Delivered in the presence of William Beckingham, Deborah Fred & Benjamin Fred. Recorded 28 Mar 1738. (E5:506).

Release. On 28 Feb 1720 Robert Pearson of Marple, yeoman, & Katherine his wife to Bernhardns Vanleer of Philadelphia, merchant. Whereas Francis Chadds, & Grace his wife, William Huntley & Mary his wife, Edward Bennett & Sarah his wife, Thomas Hope & Elizabeth his wife, Isaac Few & Hannah his wife, Richard Woodward & Deborah his wife by deed dated 4 Feb 1703 granted to Thomas Pearson a tract of land formerly in the tenure of Francis Standfield, dec., lying in Marple bounded by land of Peter Worral, Marple Road, land of John Worral, Crum Creek & land of Joseph Worral containing 300 acres. Which said Grace, Mary, Sarah, Elizabeth, Hannah, Deborah were sister & heirs of James Standfield their late brother, dec., who was the only son & heir of Francis Standfield, dec. Whereas Thomas Pearson & Margery his wife by deed dated 22 June 1713 granted to Robert Pearson one of their sons all the tract recorded in Chester, Book D, Vol 4, Page 106. Now Robert Pearson & Katherine his wife for £170.16 grant to Bernhardns Vanleer a tract in Marple bounded by Chester Road, land late of Peter & Joseph Worral, land of John Pugh & land late of John & Peter Worral containing

248 acres being part of the 300 acres. Signed Robert Pearson & Katherine Pearson. Delivered in the presence of Caspar Hood & Joseph Lawrence. Recorded 29 Mar 1738. (E5:508).

Lease & Release. On 27 & 28 May 1736 Grace Lloyd of Chester, widow & executrix of the will of David Lloyd, late of Chester, gentleman, to John Smith of West Nottingham in the County of Chester, yeoman. Whereas Charles Read, Job Goodson, Evan Owen, George Fitzwater & Joseph Pidgeon (members of the Society of Free Traders) by deed dated 25 Mar 1724 granted to David Lloyd a tract of 1,000 acres, recorded in Chester, Book E, Vol 5, Page 25. Whereas 875 acres of the 1,000 acres was surveyed & laid out to David Lloyd on 25 Apr 1724 in the township of Uwehland. Whereas David Lloyd made his will dated 29 Mar 1724 & amongst other things devised to his wife Grace the residue of his estate & made her executrix & soon after died. Now Grace Lloyd for £170 grant to John Smith a tract in Uwehlan in the County of Chester, bounded by land of Joseph Phipps, David Davis, Aubrey Roberts, Phillip David & John Jerman containing 220 acres. Signed Grace Lloyd. Delivered in the presence of Joseph Parker & Robert Parke. Recorded 8 May 1738. (E5:510).

Deed. On 27 Feb 1725 Phillip Yarnall of Edgmont, yeoman, & Dorothy his wife to John Yarnall of Edgmont son of Phillip & Dorothy. Whereas the commissioners of William Penn by deed dated 31 Oct 1684 granted to John Bristow a tract containing 490 acres & John Bristow by deed dated 15 Sep 1681 granted to William Lewis a tract containing 490 acres. William Lewis by deed dated 10 Mar 1708 granted to Thomas Worrilaw the 490 acres. Whereas Thomas Worrilaw made his will dated 23 May 1709 & devised to son John Worrilaw all my lands in Chester County upon condition he discharge the debts of son-in-law Daniel Hoops which he stands bound. Thomas Worrilaw soon after died. Whereas John Worrilaw performed the said condition discharging the debts of Daniel Hoop. John Worrilaw on deed dated 15 & 16 Nov 1714 granted to Joseph Baker the elder & Phillip Yarnall a tract containing 250 acres but to be void upon payment of £180 plus interest. Whereas the said money was not paid. Joseph Baker died & the land fell to Phillip Yarnall by right of survivorship. John Worrilaw & Ann his wife, Mary Baker the elder, John Baker, Walter Worrilaw, Mary Baker the younger, Peter Yarnall & Alice his wife & Daniel Hoops by deed dated 1 & 2 Oct 1717 granted & released to Phillip Yarnall the tract. Now Phillip Yarnall & Dorothy his wife for £60 & love grant to their son John Yarnall a tract in Edgmont bounded by land of William Bostock & Evan Howell, Phillip Yarnall, Joseph Pennell, & Jonathon Hunter containing 200 acres being part of the 250 acres. Signed Phillip Yarnall & Dorothy Yarnall. Delivered in the presence of Mary Williamson, Joshua Thompson & Robert Keith. Recorded 16 May 1738. (E5:513).

Deed. On 17 Mar 1737/8 Nathan Yarnall of Chester, yeoman, & Rachel his wife to John Yarnal of Edgmont, yeoman. Whereas the commissioners of William Penn by deed dated 31 Oct 1684 granted to John Bristow a tract containing 490 acres & John Bristow by deed dated 15 Sep 1681 granted to William Lewis a tract containing 490 acres. William Lewis by deed dated 10 Mar 1708 granted to Thomas Worrilaw the 490 acres. Whereas Thomas Worrilaw made his will dated 23 May 1709 & devised to son John Worrilaw all my lands in Chester County upon condition he discharge the debts of son-in-law Daniel Hoops which he stands bound. Thomas Worrilaw soon after died. Whereas John Worrilaw performed the said condition discharging the debts of Daniel Hoop. John Worrilaw on deed dated 15 & 16 Nov 1714 granted to Joseph Baker the elder & Phillip Yarnall a tract containing 250 acres but to be void upon payment of £180 plus interest. Whereas the said money was not paid. Joseph Baker died & the land fell to Phillip Yarnall by right of survivorship. John Worrilaw & Ann his wife, Mary Baker the elder, John Baker, Walter Worrilaw, Mary Baker the younger, Peter Yarnall & Alice his wife & Daniel Hoops by deed dated 1 & 2 Oct 1717 granted & released to Phillip Yarnall the tract. Whereas John Worrilaw & Ann his wife by deed dated 5 May 1713 granted to Phillip Yarnall the tract of 240 acres being the other part of the 490 acres, recorded in Chester, Book C, Page 355. Whereas Phillip Yarnall made his will dated 16 Aug 1733 & devised the remaining of the land he purchased of John Worrilaw to his son Nathan containing the following tracts & a tract Nathan conveyed to Cadwallader Evans containing 31 acres. Now Nathan Yarnall & Rachel his wife for £79.10 grant to John Yarnall 2 tracts in Edgmont one bounded by Concord Road, other land of John Yarnall & other land of Nathan Yarnall containing 22 acres being part of the 250 acre tract the other tract bounded by land of Phillip Yarnall, Thomas Smedley, Joseph Pennell & other land of John Yarnall containing 47 1/2 acres being part of 240 acre tract. Signed Nathan Yarnall & Rachel Yarnall. Delivered in the presence of James Mark, Joseph Bishop, Abel Green & Lawrence Cox. Recorded 18 May 1738. (E5:516).

Lease & Release. On 6 & 7 Aug 1737 James Buckley of Fallowfield in the County of Chester, miller, & Mary his wife to Samuel Mickle of the City of Philadelphia, merchant. James Buckley & Mary his wife for £508.7 grant to Samuel Mickle a tract in Fallowfield with the corn mill or grist mill bounded by Octararo Creek extending to the skirts of a barren mountain & land of John Devor containing 151 1/2 acres being part of 251 1/2 acres. Signed John Buckley & Mary Buckley. Delivered in the presence of John Devor, William McKin & John Love. Recorded 15 Aug 1738. (E5:518).

Deed. On 27 Aug 1734 John Parry, High Sheriff of Chester County, I was commanded to seize land, goods & chattels in my baileywick of David Hough's of Philadelphia, carpenter, for the debt of £15 which Ruth Hughs in the Court of Common Pleas recovered of David Hough & £0.70.6 in damages. I seized a tract in Haverford containing 100 acres. Now John Parry for £49 grant to Richard Hayes of Haverford, gentleman, a tract bounded by land of Richard Hayes & Henry Lewis containing 100 acres. Signed John Parry. Delivered in the presence of George Aston & Benjamin Davis. (E5:520).

Release. On 5 Jan 1736 Rees David of Charles Town, yeoman, & Evan David of Charles Town, yeoman, to Thomas John of Tredufryn, laborer. Whereas John Budd of Hanover Township in the County of Hunterdon in the province of West New Jersey, gentleman, & Sarah his wife by deed dated 5 June 1728 granted to Rees David & Evan David a tract in Charles Town containing 242 acres. Rees & Evan agreed to divide said tract, the tract here after mentioned is Rees Davis's part. Now Rees David for £63 & Evan David for 5 shillings grant to Thomas John a tract bounded by Pikes land, land of Rees John, Evan David & Rees David containing 105 1/4 acres. Signed Rees David & Evan David. Delivered in the presence of James David, David Emanuel, Isaac David & Emanuel Jones. Recorded 2 Oct 1738. (E5:520).

Release. On 6 Feb 1733 Nicholas Newlin of Concord, yeoman, & Edith his wife to Magnus Tate of Chester County, yeoman. Whereas William Penn, dec., by deed dated 22 & 23 Mar 1681 granted to Nicholas Moor, James Claypoole, William Shark, Edward Peirce, John Simcock, Thomas Brassey, Thomas Baker & Edward Brooks a tract containing 20,000 acres laid out with some lots in Philadelphia in the trust of the Free Society of Traders. Whereas virtue of a warrant dated 1 June 1688 there was laid out on 20 Sep 1688 to Benjamin Chambers, president of the Society for the use of the Society a tract of 7,100 acres since found to be in the County of Chester & whereas by an Act of Assembly the said 20,000 acres was actually vested, settled & adjudged to be in Charles Road, Job Goodson, Evan Owen, George Fitzwater & Joseph Pidgeon of the City of Philadelphia, merchants. Whereas Charles Road, Job Goodson, Evan Owen, George Fitzwater & Joseph Pidgeon by deed dated 10 June 1724 grant to Nathaniel Newlin, dec., the tract containing 7,100 acres, recorded in Chester, Book D, Vol 4, Page 369. Whereas Nathaniel Newlin died intestate the said 7,100 acres was divided amongst his children, whereby a tract of 410 acres fell to his daughter Mary wife of Richard Clayton as by deed dated 12 Aug 1730 & whereas Mary wife of Richard Clayton died without issue the 410 acres descended to Nicholas Newlin her brother & heir-at-law. Now Nicholas Newlin & Edith his wife for £120 grant to Magnus Tate a tract lying on a branch of Brandywine Creek bounded by land of Richard Eavenson, John Bentley & William Baily containing 410 acres. Signed Nicholas Newlin & Edith Newlin. Delivered in the presence of Henry Osborn, John Taylor & Daniel Few. Recorded 11 Oct 1738. (E5:522).

Lease & Release. On 1 May 1738 Elizabeth Bond of Chichester, widow & admin. of the goods & chattels of Joseph Bond her late husband, dec., to John Kerlin of Concord, glazier. Whereas the Orphans Court at the house of Joshua Thompson in Ridley on 13 Sep 1737 before Richard Hayes, John Crosby, John Parry & Caleb Cowpland, Esq., justices present came Elizabeth Bond widow & admin. of the goods & chattels of Joseph Bond of Chichester, tailor, dec., her late husband, whereas Joseph Bond was at the time of his death owner of a tenement & 2 lots of land situated in Chichester, one where the tenement stands fronting the River Delaware being 48' x 190' the other said lot adjoins the last lot being 66' x 114' & a tract in Chichester bounded by the Great Road, land of John Reiley & Robert Moulder containing 14 acres & left a wife & 6 children to survive him. There is not enough goods & chattels to cover the debts & support the children is allowed & ordered that Elizabeth Bond to sell land. Now Elizabeth Bond at the direction of the Orphans Court & for £57 grant to John Kerlin a lot in Chichester bounded by the river, land of Walter Marin & Frances Baldwin being one of the lots before mentioned. Singed Elizabeth Bond. Delivered in the presence of Robert Moulder & John Riley. Recorded 13 Oct 1738. (E5:525).

Mortgage. On 29 June 1738 Daniel Davis of Marple, sawyer & Mary his wife to Barnard Vanleer of Marple, Doctor of Phisick. Whereas Daniel Davis by deed dated 16 & 17 June did purchase from William Owen, late of Marple, joiner, & Ann his wife a tract in Marple bounded by land of Barnard Vanleer, the Great Run, land of Peter Tompson, Peter Worral & lands late of Gersham Bembo & Richard Maris containing 126 acres. Now Daniel Davis & Mary his wife for £100 grant to Barnard Vanleer all the above mentioned 126 acres. Daniel Davis & Mary his wife to make yearly payments to Barnard Vanleer to pay in full on or before 28 June 1745. Signed Daniel Davis & Mary Davis. Delivered in the presence of Joseph Hawley, Jonathon Morris & Mordecai Morris. Recorded 19 Dec 1738. (E5:529).

Lease & Release. On 17 & 18 Feb 1737/8 Richard Barry of Chester, merchant, & Mary his wife to John Salkeld of Chester, yeoman. Whereas Thomas Baldwin, late of Chester, blacksmith, by deed dated 20 Nov 1708 granted to his son Joseph Baldwin a tract containing 25 acres, recorded Chester, Book C, Vol 3, Page 29. Whereas Joseph Baldwin died intestate leaving a wife names Elizabeth the late wife of Joseph Bond & 1 son named John Baldwin to survive him who by their deed dated 4 Dec 1735 granted to Richard Barry the 25 acres. Now Richard Barry & Mary his wife for £30 grant to John Salkeld a tract in Chester bounded by Chester Road containing 25 acres. Signed Richard Barry & Mary Barry. Delivered in the presence of Joseph Parker & Daniel Killing. Recorded 29 Dec 1738. (E5:532).

Release. On 1 Jan 1738/9 William Clayton of Chichester, yeoman, & Mary his wife to Daniel Boyle of Concord, yeoman. William Clayton & Mary his wife for £230 grant to Daniel Boyle a tract in Caln bounded by land of Thomas Moore, Jason Cloud, the north branch of Brandywine Creek & land of George Aston containing 225 acres. Whereby John Mendenhall of Caln & Susanna his wife by deed dated 27 Dec 1727 granted to Edward Horne who by his deed dated 18 Mar 1731 granted to Ninevah Carter who with Mary his wife by deed dated 15 Jan 1733 granted to William Clayton. Signed William Clayton & Mary Clayton. Delivered in the presence of Joshua Tompson & Edward Bourke. Recorded 24 Jan 1738/9. (E5:535).

Lease & Release. On 27 & 28 Sep 1738 Ruth Nooks of Middletown, widow, relict & executrix of William Nooks, late of Middletown, yeoman, dec., to George Lownes of Springfield, yeoman. Whereas Peter Hunter of Middletown by deed dated 23 & 24 June 1729 granted to William Nooks a tract containing 119 acres. William Nooks, dec., made his will dated 19 June 1733 bequeathed to his wife Ruth all his personal & real estate and soon after died. Now Ruth Nooks for £50 grant to George Lownes a tract in Middletown bounded by Edgmont Road, land of George Smedley, land late of Peter Hunter, Dismal Run & land of William Trego containing 119 acres. Signed Ruth Nooks. Delivered in the presence of Thomas Cummings & Joseph Parker. Recorded 25 Jan 1738/9. (E5:537).

Deed. On 4 Dec 1735 John Baldwin of the City of Philadelphia, joiner, son & only issue of Joseph Baldwin, late of Chester, tailor, dec., & Elizabeth Bond of Chichester, widow of Joseph Bond, dec., & formerly the wife of Joseph Baldwin, dec., & the mother of John Baldwin to Richard Barry of Chester, merchant. Whereas Thomas Baldwin, late of Chester, blacksmith, the father of Joseph Baldwin by deed dated 20 Nov 1708 granted to his son Joseph Baldwin a tract containing 25 acres, recorded in Chester, Book C, Page 29. Whereas Joseph Baldwin died intestate the said land descended to John Baldwin his only son subject to his mothers dower during her natural life. Now John Baldwin for £30 & Elizabeth Bond for 20 shillings grant to Richard Barry all that tract in Chester bounded by Chester Road containing 25 acres. Signed John Baldwin & Elizabeth Bond. Delivered in the presence of Richard Weaver, Elizabeth Weaver & John Riley. Recorded 8 Feb 1738/9. (E5:340).

Lease & Release. On 6 & 7 Feb 1738/9 Andrew Morton of Amosland in the township of Ridley, yeoman, & Jonas Morton eldest son of Andrew Morton to John Sketchley of Ridley, yeoman. Andrew Morton & Jonas Morton for £40 grant to John Sketchley a tract Ridley bounded by land of Joseph Harvey & John Hendricks containing 20 acres. Signed Andrew Morton & Jonas Morton. Delivered in the presence of Joseph Parker & Alexander Seaton. Recorded 21 Feb 1738/9. (E5:543).

Lease & Release. On 8 & 9 Feb 1738/9 Andrew Morton of Amosland in the township of Ridley, yeoman, to his eldest son Jonas Morton of Amosland. Now Andrew Morton for the natural love he bears to his son & £5 grant to Jonas Morton a tract in Ridley bounded by Darby Creek & Kings Road containing 115 acres & another tract in Ridley bounded by Darby Creek containing 10 acres. Signed Andrew Morton. Delivered in the presence of Joseph Parker & Alexander Seaton. Recorded 27 Mar 1739. (E5:545).

Release. On 16 Aug 1737 Elizabeth Bond of Chichester, widow & admin. of the goods & chattels of Joseph Bond, her late husband, dec., to John Druett of New Castle upon Delaware, yeoman. Whereas Edmund Andres, Esq., Governor of New York by deed dated 8 Mar 1676 granted to Charles Johnson, Olle Rawson, Haunce Ollison, Olle Nelson, Hance Hopman & John Henderson a tract situated on the Delaware River at a place now called Chichester containing 1,000 acres. Whereas Olle Rawson by deed dated 9 Apr 1683 granted to William Cloud a tract containing 55 acres being part of the Olle Rawson part of the 1,000 acres. William Cloud by deed dated 7 Apr 1685 granted to John Hobson of Kingston upon Hull, mariner the 55 acres, recorded in Philadelphia, Vol 5, Page 54. Whereas John Hobson since died without issue the land descended to his brother Jacob Hobson. Jacob Hobson by deed dated 5 & 6 March 1700 granted to Martha Hobson the 55 acres. Martha Hobson by Letter of Attorney dated 1 Mar 1726 acknowledged by the mayor of Hull, appointed Mathew Hobson of the City of London, iron monger, & Charles Read of Philadelphia, merchant, jointly to convey the said 55 acres to Clement Plumstead of Philadelphia, merchant. Whereas Charles Read for Martha Hobson by deed dated 5 Dec 1727 granted Clement Plumstead the 55 acres. Clement Plumstead by deed dated 19 & 20 Dec 1727 granted to Joseph Bond the said 55 acres. Joseph Bond died intestate leaving several children to survive him & since his death admin. of his goods & chattels was granted to Elizabeth. The Orphans Court allowed Elizabeth to sell & convey the said 55 acres. Now Elizabeth Bond for £146 grant to John Druett a tract in Chichester bounded by the River Delaware, land late of Andrew Rawson, land of Thomas Howell & land of Jacob Lamplugh containing 55 acres. Signed Elizabeth Bond. Delivered in the presence of Jonathon Riley & Benjamin Ford. Recorded 29 Mar 1739. (E5:448).

Obligation. On 15 Sep 1738 John Wilson of Chester County, yeoman, firmly bound to Thomas Gilpin of Concord, yeoman, in the full & just sum of £200 to be paid to Thomas Gilpin. The condition of the obligation is that whereas there is a marriage intended between John Wilson & Hannah Oborn of Chester County, widow therefore in the said marriage shall take effect & John Wilson shall then & in such case & suffer the said Hannah Oburn not with standing her coverture by any deed or by her last will signed & sealed in the presence of 2 or more witnesses to give or dispose of the sum of £100 part of the estate of the said John Wilson to such person she shall then meet or in case it shall happen that the said marriage is solemnized & the said Hannah shall survive the said John Wilson, the then the said John Wilson shall at the time of his death leave unto Hannah the sum of £100 & £6 to be paid after the dec. of John Wilson annually during the natural life of Hannah. Signed John Wilson. Delivered in the presence of Joseph Parker, John Owen & Alexander Seaton. Recorded 24 May 1739. (E5:550).

Deed. On 2 May 1733 Robert Jefferies of Bradford, yeoman, & Ann his wife to James Jefferies of Bradford, William Jefferies of Chester, yeomen, & Benjamin Jefferies of Bradford, yeoman. Robert Jefferies & Ann his wife for the natural affection they bear to their son Benjamin Jefferies & for the sum of £20 grant to James & William Jefferies a tract in Bradford bounded by Brandywine Creek, land of Langhorn containing 179 acres being part of a tract purchased by William Vestall of Thomas Powell of Upper Providence, dec. Signed Robert Jefferies & Ann Jefferies. Delivered in the presence of William Webb, James Few & William Carpenter. Note: Be it remembered that the above sum of £20 is secured to be paid to me by my sons James & William Jefferies which my son Benjamin shall never enjoy the above premises from my sons James & William Jefferies until the above sum of £20 with lawful interest for the same be fully paid & discharged as also that preserved my wife's widowhood therein. Recorded 15 June 1739. (E5:551).

Mortgage. On 13 July 1739 Daniel Worthington of the Northern Liberties of the City of Philadelphia, yeoman, to George Emlou of the City of Philadelphia, brewer. Whereas Daniel Worthington by a certain obligation stands bound to George Emlou for the sum of £150 & conditions for the payment of £75 on the 13 June which will be in the year 1740. Now Daniel Worthington to better secure the debt of £75 grant to George Emlou his equal 1/4 undivided share of a tract in Whiteland bounded by land of Daniel Howell, William Thomas, Henry Athertons & John Morgan containing 68 acres with grist mills, bolting mills & buildings & of the Mulifuro Toll. Daniel Worthington to pay £75 plus interest to George Emlou. Signed Daniel Worthington. Delivered in the presence of C. Brockden & John Ora. Recorded 31 July 1739. (E5:552).

Mortgage. On 30 May 1739 Henry Camm of Chester County, stocking weaver, & Margaret his wife to Rees Meredith of the City of Philadelphia, merchant. Henry Camm & Margaret his wife for £150 grant to Rees Meredith to better secure payment a tract in Marlborough bounded by land of Francis Windlo, Thomas Winkersham containing 198 acres. Henry Camm & Margaret his wife to pay to Rees Meredith £150 plus interest on or before 30 May 1745. Signed Henry Camm & Margaret Camm. Delivered in the presence of John Hainese & R. Hartshorne. Recorded 2 Aug 1739. (E5:554).

Lease & Release. On 2 Oct 1731 Thomas Moore of Naamans Mill Creek in the County of New Castle upon Delaware, yeoman, & Mary his wife to Joseph Parker of Chester, yeoman. Whereas Robert Cloud & Sarah his wife by deed dated 26 & 27 Dec 1727 granted to Thomas Moore a tract in Chichester containing 55 acres. Whereas Andrew Rawson & Gartrax his wife, John Rawson & Margaret his wife & John Rawson, Jr., by deed dated 1 & 2 Apr 1728 granted to Thomas Moore a tract containing 107 acres lying upon Naamans Mill Creek. Whereas John Shannon in right of his wife being one of the daughters of Robert French, late of New Castle, merchant, dec., being lawfully seized of 1/4 part of Naamans Mill by deed dated 4 Oct 1726 granted to Thomas Moore 1/4 part of the Naamans Mill. Thomas Moore & Mary his wife for £100 grant to Joseph Parker a tract in Chichester bounded by Naamans Creek containing 55 acres & a tract in the County of New Castle at the mouth of Naamans Creek bounded by the Delaware River, land of William Rawson, John Rawson & Jasper Yeates containing 107 acres being part of 1,000 acres which William Andres, Esq., Governor of New York, by deed dated 28 Mar 1676 to Charles Johnson, Olle Rawson, Hance Ollison, Olle Neilson, Hance Hopman & John Hendricks & 1/4 share of Naamans Water Mill which Joseph Parker is now in actual possession. Signed Thomas Moore & Mary Moore. Delivered in the presence of Edward Baldwin, Charles Gatlive & Samuel Gray. Recorded 10 Dec 1731. (E5:555).

CHESTER BOOK F - Volume 6

Lease & Release. On 20 & 21 June 1725 Samuel Bonham, Samuel Turner & John Midford of London, merchants, surviving trustees for the Pennsylvania Land Company in London to John Devonald of London Grove in Chester County, husbandman. Samuel Bonham, Samuel Turner & John Midford for £46 grant to John Devonald a tract bounded by John Jonas, William Penn's manor, Thomas Merry & Richard Whitting containing 200 acres being part of 16,500 acres. Signed Samuel Bonham, Samuel Turner & John Midford. Delivered in the presence of John Estaugh & Thomas .... Recorded 1 Aug 1739. (F6:1).

Release. On 25 July 1739 William Allen of the City of Philadelphia, Esq., & Margret his wife to John Parry of Haverford, gentleman. Whereas William Penn by deed dated 23 Oct 1681 granted to William Lowther & Margret Lowther 5,000 acres in the province, recorded in Philadelphia, Book B, Vol 2, Page 109. William Lowther died & John Nichols & Margot his wife the only daughter of Margret who survived the said William Lowther by deed dated 24 Sep 1731 granted 5,000 acres to Joseph Stanwix. Joseph Stanwix by deed dated 14 Jan 1731 granted 5,000 acres to John Simpson, recorded Book F, Vol 5, Page 557. Whereas William Penn by deed dated 23 Oct 1681 granted to John Lowther & Ann Sharlot Lowther 5,000 acres in the province. Whereas Ann Sharlot died intestate & without issue, John Lowther by deed dated 13 Aug 1731 granted to Joseph Turner the 5,000 acres. By virtue of a warrant 4,920 acres was laid out John Simpson called Bilton Manor & by virtue of another warrant 4,920 acres was laid out to Joseph Turner. Whereas 1/2 of the said Bilton Manor was resurveyed & was bounded by the Schuylkill River, Valley Creek, the manor called Mount Joy, land formerly of Charles Pickering & Company & land of William Moore containing 2,850 acres. Whereas John Simpson by deed dated 9 Mar 1737 granted to William Allen a half part of Bilton Manor containing 2,850 acres & whereas Joseph Turner deed dated 23 Feb 1736 granted to William Allen all the last mentioned 5,000 acres. Now William Allen & Margret his wife for £1400 grant to John Parry all the tract of 2,850 acres. Signed William Allen & Margret Allen. Delivered in the presence of William Carsons & James Bingham. Recorded 17 Sep 1739. (F6:4).

Release. On 5 Dec 1711 James Logan of the province of Pennsylvania but now of the City of London, merchant, for £14.16 grant to Richard Webb

& Elizabeth his wife a tract containing 500 acres being the tract William Penn by deed dated 2 & 3 Apr 1686 granted to Samuel Hardy of Badfly in Hamshire, clerk, since dec., who by his will bequeathed said 500 acres to his wife Elizabeth Hardy, who by her deed dated 20 & 21 Mar 1710 granted to Richard Owen of Grays Jim in the County of Middlesex, gentleman, who by deed dated 26 & 27 Nov 1711 granted to James Logan the said 500 acres. Signed James Logan. Delivered in the presence of John Askow & Constantine Cauts. Recorded 15 Oct 1739. (F6:6).

Commission for Receiver General. (F6:7).

Deed. On 2 Jan 1720/1 Thomas Evans of Green Hill in the County of Chester, yeoman, & Hannah his wife to David Evans of Treydssain, minister of the Gospel. Whereas there is a tract of land in Trodyfryn in the County of Chester bounded by land of Thomas Martin, Thomas Roberts & channel of the creek containing 85 acres which the land is part of 250 acres sold & conveyed to Rees Rhythey by deed dated 10 May 1686, recorded Philadelphia, Book A, Folio 150. Rees Rhythey by deed dated 3 Aug 1700 granted the 250 acres to John David & Thomas David. John David, Thomas David & Gwenllian his wife by deed dated 5 Nov 1707 granted 85 acres to Thomas Evans. Now Thomas Evans & Hannah his wife for £60 grant to David Evans a tract containing 85 acres. Signed Thomas Evans & Hannah Evans. Delivered in the presence of David Davies, John Parry & James Parry. Recorded 8 Nov 1739. (F6:8).

Release. On 13 Nov 1739 William Hancock of Elfingbourough in the County of Salem in the western division of New Jersey, gentleman, & Sarah his wife, only daughter & heir of Rebecca Thomson, late of Salem, dec., who was the daughter & co-heir of Thomas Brassey, late of Chester County, dec., to Francis Yarnall, John Yarnall, Moses Yarnall, James Massey, Thomas Massey, Peter Thomas, Joseph Thomas & Jacob Thomas all the Willis Town, yeomen. Whereas William Penn, dec., granted to Thomas Brassey a certain tract bounded by land late of Thomas Duckett, Crum Creek & New Town line containing 1,500 acres. Thomas Brassey shortly after died & the 1,500 acres descended to Rebecca Thomson & Mary Worley his daughters & the said Rebecca died & left issue Sarah. Whereas Thomas Thomson the late husband of Rebecca, Francis Worley & Mary his wife by deed dated 1 Mar 1694 granted to Charles Brooks a tract containing 1,500 acres. Shortly after the said purchase Charles Brooks by several grants divided the said 1,500 acres in to many parts. John, Francis & Moses Yarnall, James &

Thomas Massey, Peter, Joseph & Jacob Thomas by respective purchases became seized in the 1,500 acres. Now William Hancock & Sarah his wife for 5 shillings release all right to the said tract to John, Francis & Moses Yarnall, James & Thomas Massey, Peter, Joseph & Jacob Thomas. Signed William Hancock & Sarah Hancock. Delivered in the presence of James Bredin & John Ware. Recorded 3 Dec 1739. (F6:10).

Mortgage. On 2 Nov 1739 Charles Hohman of Kennet, yeoman, & Elleanor his wife to Edward Bradley of the City of Philadelphia, gentleman. Whereas Charles Hohman & Elleanor his wife stand bound to Edward Bradley for the sum of £50 for the condition for paying £25 on 2 Nov 1740 with interest. Now Charles Hohman & Elleanor his wife to better secure the said payment of £25 grant to Edward Bradley a tract in Kennet bounded by Red Clay Creek, land of John Gregg, William Pyle, Ellis Lewis & Edward Bennett containing 205 acres. Signed Charles Hohman & Elleanor Hohman. Delivered in the presence of Samuel Gillford & John Ord. Recorded 4 Nov 1739. (F6:12).

Deed. On 30 Nov 1717 Richard Arnold of Thornbury, yeoman, & Sarah his wife to Jacob Vernon of Thornbury, yeoman. Whereas William Penn by deed dated 16 Mar 1681 granted to John Simcock, late of Chester County, dec a tract containing 5,000 acres & 1,500 acres was laid out in Thornbury being part of the 5,000 acres. Whereas John Simcock granted 500 acres (of the 1,500 acres) to John Kinsman & John Kinsman by deed dated 14 Mar 1693 granted 200 acres (part of the 500 acres) to Elizabeth Hickman, late of Thornbury, widow. Whereas Elizabeth Hickman by her will bequeathed 137 acres (part of the 200 acres) to her 2 sons Joseph & Benjamin Hickman both of Chester County, yeomen. Joseph & Benjamin Hickman by deed dated 16 May 1702 granted 137 acres to Richard Arnold. Now Richard Arnold & Sarah his wife for £30 grant to Jacob Vernon a tract in Thornbury bounded by land of George Pierce, Joseph Edwards, the Great Road & other land of Richard Arnold containing 50 acres. Signed Richard Arnold & Sarah Arnold. Delivered in the presence of Peter Hatton & William Webster. Recorded 4 Dec 1709. (F6:14).

Deed. On 22 Feb 1718/9 John David & Elizabeth his wife, Thomas David & Gwen his wife all of Treduffrin in the County of Chester to Thomas Martin of Tredriffin, sawyer. Whereas there is a tract in Tredriffin bounded by land late of John Longworthy, Jr., dec., land of Thomas David & Thomas Hubbert containing 165 acres being part of 250 acres sold to John & Thomas David by Rees Rhythey by deed dated 3 Aug 1700. Now John David & Thomas David for £69 grant to Thomas Martin 155 acres. Signed John David, Elizabeth David, Thomas David & Gwen David. Delivered in the presence of William Martin, David Davis, Richard Evan & Mark Hoparts. Recorded 6 Dec 1739. (F6:16).

Lease & Release. On 12 & 13 Sep 1738 Grace Lloyd of Chester, widow & executrix of David Lloyd, late of Chester, gentleman, dec., to Michael Rees of Uwuchland, tailor. Whereas John Palmer & Thomas Palmer by deed dated 2 Feb 1708 granted to David Lloyd a tract 1,220 acres, recorded in Chester, Book E, Vol 5, Page 3, on 4 Jan 1730. Whereas the commissioners of William Penn by deed dated 26 Jan 1702 granted to David Lloyd a tract containing 95 acres in Uwuchland in part of the said 1220 acres. Whereas David Lloyd made his will dated 29 Mar 1724 devised to his wife Grace the residue of his estate & soon after died. Now Grace Lloyd for £35 grant to Michael Rees all that tract in Uwuchland bounded by land of Morris Rees, John Vaughn & John Morgan containing 69 acres part of the 95 acres. Signed Grace Lloyd. Delivered in the presence of George Simpson & Joseph Parker. Recorded 7 Dec 1739. (F6:18).

Deed. On 13 Dec 1739 Catherine Trehern of Chester, widow & executrix of William Trehern, late of Chester, dec., to John Rees of Chester, sadler. Whereas Arthur Sheil & Mary his wife who was the widow & admin. of Jonas Sandelands, late of Chester, gentleman, by the authority given them by the Orphans Court on 31 Aug 1732 granted to William Trehern a piece of land Chester containing 2 2/4 acres with the yearly rent of 5 shillings to be paid the heirs of Jonas Sandelands, recorded Chester, Book E, Vol 5, Page 158. William Trehern made his will dated 2 May 1736 & devised one lot of land to his God daughter Gartree Griffith, the remainder of his estate to his wife Catherine & made her is executrix. Now Catherine Trehern for 5 shillings & love & affection she has grant to John Rees all the new brick house in Chester where one Benjamin Davis now dwells all the 3 lots of land being 125' x 150' bounded by land of Richard Barry, other land of Catherine Trehern being part of the 2 2/4 acres with the land staying in the possession of Catherine until John Rees reaches the age of 22 years. Signed Catherine Trehern. Delivered in the presence of Richard Barry, Richard Backhouse & Joseph Parker. Recorded 13 Dec 1739. (F6:21).

Mortgage. On 12 Jan 1739/40 Thomas Salkeld of Chester, cordwainer, to William Turner of Chester, merchant. Thomas Salkeld for £50 grant to William Turner a lot in Chester where Joseph Faucett now dwells bounded by Bridge Street, Essex Street (or Concord Road), land of John Salkeld & lots late belonging to John Salkeld, dec. Thomas Salkeld to pay £59 in yearly payments to be paid in full on or before 12 Jan 1742/3. Signed Thomas Salkeld. Delivered in the presence of Edmond Bourke, Thomas Gilbert & Joseph Parker. Recorded 15 Jan 1739/40. (F6:23).

Deed. On 14 Mar 1737 John Owen, sheriff of Chester County to .... Whereas Joseph Parker in the Court of Common Pleas recovered against Jane Lewis executrix of the estate of Thomas Lewis, dec., a debt of £200 & damages of 60 shillings & William Lewis at the Court of Common Pleas recovered against Jane Lewis executrix of the estate of Thomas Lewis a debt of £130 & damages of 60 shillings to be levied against the land & chattels of Thomas Lewis in the hands of Jane Lewis in my bailiwick a tract in Darby containing 150 acres. John Owen for £351 grant to Jane Lewis a tract in Darby bounded by land of William Kirk, Samuel Garratt, Thomas Phillips & Adam Roads containing 150 acres. Signed John Owen, sheriff. Delivered in the presence of Thomas Cummings & Nathan Worley. Recorded 9 Feb 1739/40. (F6:25).

Release. On 10 Sep 1709 James Chevers of Concord, yeoman, to Isaac Taylor of Thornbury, surveyor. Whereas James Chevers for £27 grant or mortgaged to Isaac Taylor all his plantation in Concord bounded by Birmingham township line, land of Edward Wilbourne, Thomas Smith & Magnus Tate containing 100 acres. Whereas the sum has not been paid & James Chevers is unable to recover said mortgage. Now James Chevers for 10 shillings grant & release all right to said plantation to Isaac Taylor. Signed James Chevers. Delivered in the presence of Jacob Roman, Joseph Rineers & John Taylor. Recorded 11 Mar 1739/40. (F6:26).

Deed. On 20 Mar 1737/8 Nathan Yarnall of Edgmont, yeoman, & Rachel his wife to Cadwalder Evans of Edgmont, tanner. Whereas John Bristow, dec., by deed dated 3 Sep 1686 granted to William Lewis a tract in Edgmont containing 490 acres. William Lewis by deed dated 10 Mar 1688 granted to Thomas Worrilaw the tract containing 490 acres. Whereas Thomas Worrilaw made his will dated 23 May 1709 devised to his John Worrilaw the 490 acres upon condition that he shall discharge my son in law Daniel Hoops from debts he stands bound for my son John & Thomas Worrilaw soon after died & John Worrilaw performed the said condition. Whereas John Worrilaw by mortgage dated 15 & 16 Nov 1714 for £180 granted to Joseph Baker the elder & Phillip Yarnall a tract of 250 acres. Whereas monies remained unpaid the land came to Joseph Baker & Phillip Yarnall. Joseph Baker is since dec. & land has descended to Phillip Yarnall by survivorship. Phillip Yarnall did allow John Worrilaw to sell said lands to highest bidder which was Phillip Yarnall. Whereas John Worrilaw & Ann his wife, Mary Baker, the elder widow, of Joseph Baker the elder, John Baker the only surviving son, Walter Worrilaw son & heir apparent of John Worrilaw & Ann his wife, Mary Baker the younger widow of Joseph Baker the younger & Daniel Hoops by deed dated 1 & 2 Oct 1717 did grant & release said lands to Phillip Yarnall. Whereas Phillip Yarnall & Dorothy his wife by deed dated 27 Feb 1723 granted 200 acres to John Yarnall. Phillip Yarnall made his will dated 16 Aug 1733 amongst other things devised the remaining part of his land he purchased of John Worrilaw to his son Nathan Yarnall. Now Nathan Yarnall & Rachel his wife for £47.19 grant to Cadwalder Evans a tract in Edgmont bounded by Concord Road, land of Joseph Pennel, John Yarnall & other land of Nathan Yarnall containing 31 acres. Signed Nathan Yarnall & Rachel Yarnall. Delivered in the presence of James Mark, Joseph Bishop, Abel Green & Lawrence Cox. Recorded 12 Mar 1739/40. (F6:28).

Deed. On 2 May 1727 Jacob Vernon of Neither Providence, yeoman, & Ellenor his wife to James Ewing of Hopewell in the County of Hunterdon in West New Jersey, yeoman. Jacob Vernon & Ellenor his wife for £300 grant to James Ewing a tract in Neither Providence bounded by Ridley Creek, land of Joseph Vernon, the Kings High Road, land of Isaac Minshall & land of Randle Croxton containing 300 acres. Released against all claims of Robert Vernon the father of Jacob. Signed Jacob Vernon & Ellenor Vernon. Delivered in the presence of Jacob Shoemaker & Gabriel Hinton. Recorded 16 Mar 1739/40. (F6:32).

Mortgage. On 15 Jan 1739/40 Daniel Brown of Chichester, weaver, & Susannah his wife to Nathaniel Scarlett & John Allen both of New Garden, yeomen, & admin. of the goods & chattels of Shadrack Scarlett, late of London Grove, dec. Daniel Brown & Susannah his wife for £60 grant to Nathaniel Scarlett & John Allen a tract in Chichester bounded by Chichester Creek, land late of James Swarfer & land of James

Whittaker containing 96 acres. Daniel Brown shall pay £60 & interest on or before 15 Jan 1741. Signed Daniel Brown. Delivered in the presence of Joseph Sharp & Henry Dobson. Recorded 2 Apr 1740. (F6:34).

Lease & Release. On 8 Nov 1737 Elizabeth Bond of Chichester, widow & admin. of the goods & chattels of Joseph Bond, her late husband, dec., to William Ferguson of Chester, tailor. Whereas the Orphans Court held in Chester County at the house of Joseph Thompson in Ridley of 13 Sep 1737 before Richard Hayes, John Crosby, John Parry & Caleb Cowpland, justices, Elizabeth Bond admin. for the goods & chattels of Joseph Bond who died intestate, who at the time of his death was seized of 2 lots in Chichester & in a tract of land in Chichester on the River Delaware, bounded by Broad Street, the Great Road leading to Concord, land of John Riely & Robert Moulder containing 14 acres & left a wife & 6 children to survive him, is allowed to sell said land. Now Elizabeth Bond for £36 grant to William Ferguson the 2 lots in Chichester one bounded by Chichester Road, land late of William Flower, land late of Jonas Sandelands, the Upperfield formerly of James Brown containing 9 acres the other tract bounded by land of Peter Boss formerly belonging to James Brown containing 5 acres. Signed Elizabeth Bond. Delivered in the presence of Richard Bezar, William Hughes & John Weldon. Recorded 10 Apr 1740. (F6:36).

Deed. On 4 Mar 1731 John Broom of Calcoon Hook to Cunrad Nethermark of Calcoon Hook, weaver. Whereas Peter Peterson of Calcoon Hook, yeoman, by deed dated 29 Oct 1711 granted to Jonathon Broom 2 tracts in Darby butted & bounded containing 55 acres being part of a tract granted to Isreal Helm and Company by Richard Nichols, Esq., Governor of New York, & by Isreal Helm and sold to Mounce Peterson of Calcoon Hook who by his Deed of Gift dated 13 Mar 1695 granted to Peter Peterson. Now John Broom for £20 grant to Cunrad Nethermark a tract in Calcoon Hook bounded by John Archies, other land of John Broom & Thoroughfare Creek containing 4 acres. Signed John Broom. Delivered in the presence of Andrew Urin & Daniel Chubb. Recorded 26 Mar 1739/40. (F6:41).

Deed. On 8 Dec 1724 Phillip Yarnall the elder of Edgmont, yeoman, & Dorothy his wife to Yarnall the younger of Edgmont the second son of Phillip & Dorothy. Whereas Thomas Worrilaw, late of the City of Philadelphia, yeoman, dec., by deed dated 1 Sep 1690 granted to his son

John Worrilaw 250 acres part of 490 acres, recorded in Chester, Book A, Page 49, & Thomas Worrilaw made his will dated 23 May 1709 & bequeathed to his son John the remainder of the 490 acres being 240 acres. John Worrilaw & Ann his wife granted to Phillip Yarnall the said tract. Now Phillip Yarnall the elder & Dorothy his wife for £60 grant to Phillip Yarnall the younger a tract bounded by land of John Yarnall, Phillip Yarnall the elder & land late of Joseph Baker containing 204 3/4 acres. Signed Phillip Yarnall & Dorothy Yarnall. Delivered in the presence of David Regester, Sarah Yarnall & Anne George. Recorded 28 Mar 1740. (F6:43).

Lease & Release. On 5 & 6 July 1739 Benjamin Jeffries of Bradford, yeoman, to William Jeffries of Chester, yeoman. Benjamin Jeffries for £250 grant to William Jeffries a tract in Bradford bounded by Brandywine Creek containing 225 acres. Signed Benjamin Jeffries. Delivered in the presence of George Chandler, Joseph Parker & Thomas Cummings. Recorded 31 Mar 1739/40. (F6:45).

Deed. On 10 Apr 1722 John Willis of Thornbury, yeoman, & Esther his wife to John Willis of Thornbury eldest son of John & Esther. Whereas the commissioners of William Penn by deed dated 14 Aug 1705 granted to John Willis the father amongst others a tract in Thornbury containing 445 acres. Now John Willis the father & Esther his wife for 5 shillings grant to John Willis the son a tract in Thornbury bounded by land of William Radly, Henry Nayle, Richard Collett & Philip Taylor containing 200 acres being part of the 445 acres. Signed John Willis & Esther Willis. Delivered in the presence of Joseph Webb & Edward Willis. Recorded 10 Apr 1740. (F6:48).

Release. On 25 June 1738 Mary Moore of the County of New Castle on Delaware the widow & admin. of the goods & chattels of Thomas Moore, late of the County of Chester dec & Joseph Cloud of Chester County of Chester admin. of the goods & chattels of Thomas Moore to John Taylor of Thornbury, yeoman. Whereas William Penn by deed dated 6 & 7 Mar 1681 granted to Robert Vernon then of Stoak in the County of Chester, husbandman a tract of 625 acres to be laid out in the province. Robert Vernon had 330 acres (part of the 625 acres) surveyed & laid out in Lower Providence. Robert Vernon per warrant for the survey of the 285 acres the remainder of the 625 acres to be laid to him before the survey Robert Vernon by deed dated 14 Jan 1709 granted to his son Isaac Vernon the 285 acres, recorded Chester, Book C, Page 200. Whereas the

285 acres was laid out in Caln & Isaac Vernon & Hannah his wife by deed dated 3 & 4 Apr 1721 granted to Thomas Moore the 285 acres. Whereas William Penn on 26 & 27 Sep 1681 granted to William Bayly a tract containing 500 acres. William Bayly (having sold 125 acres to Daniel Smith) made his will dated 2 Nov 1691 & devised to his nephew Jacob Button all his lands in Pennsylvania. Jacob Button by deed dated 3 & 4 Oct 1701 granted to Jeremiah Collett the 500 acres of land. By virtue of a warrant 375 acres was laid out to Jeremiah Collett in Caln. Jeremiah Collett by deed dated 29 May 1705 granted to Joseph Hickman the tract of 375 acres. Joseph Hickman & Mary his wife by deed dated 5 May 1713 granted to Thomas Moore the 375 acres. Whereas the commissioners of William Penn by deed dated 30 Sep 1718, recorded in Philadelphia, Book A, Vol 5, Page 326, granted to John Moore a tract containing 315 acres in Caln. Whereas John Moore by deed dated 16 & 17 Nov 1721 granted to Thomas Moore the tract of 315 acres. Whereas Thomas Moore died intestate leaving several young children to survive him & Letters of Administration of the goods & chattels of Thomas Moore were granted to Mary Moore & Joseph Cloud. Whereas Mary & Joseph appeared in Orphans Court on 6 Aug 1737, Thomas Moore was possessed of several tracts of land & a water corn mill in Caln containing 1050 acres. Mary Moore & Joseph Cloud are allowed to sell all lands of Thomas Moore. Now Mary Moore & Joseph Cloud for £175 grant to John Taylor the plantation, the water corn mill & the 3 tracts all in Caln, one bounded land formerly of John Moore, land late of John Parker, Peter Taylor, John Baldwin, & one of the other tracts containing 285 acres another tract bounded by land late of Daniel Smith now of George Aston, land late of Joseph Cloud & land late of John Baldwin containing 375 acres another tract bounded by land late of Isaac Vernon, land of George Aston & land late of John Parker containing 315 acres in whole being 975 acres. Signed Mary Moore & Joseph Cloud. Delivered in the presence of Abraham Darling, John Chads & William Lowry. Recorded 1740. (F6:50).

Lease. On 30 May 1740 Anthony Tunes of Germantown, the County of Philadelphia, weaver, to John Knowles of the City of Philadelphia, inn holder. Whereas Jacob Bockholtz of Chester County, yeoman, by deed dated 9 Sep 1736 let to Anthony Tunes a tract in the County of Chester between the lands late of John Jodder & land late of Lawrence Christopher Nohr bounded by the river Schuylkill containing 200 acres being part of 750 acres which the commissioners of William Penn by deed dated 1 Apr 1708 granted to John Henry Hursten. John Henry Hursten by deed dated 14 Jan 1711 granted to John Jacob Tallywieler 275 acres.

Whereas Barbara the relict & executrix of the will of John Jacob Tallywieler & her husband Martin Mayteen by deed dated 28 June 1718 the said land to Jacob Bockholtz also a tract containing 10 acres. ... Now Anthony Tunes for £150 granted to John Knowles a tract containing 225 acres for 1,000 years. Signed Anthony Tunes. Delivered in the presence of ....: Recorded 30 May 1740. (F6:55).

Deed. On 23 Jan 1739/40 William Thomas of Darby & Sarah his wife to John Hopkins & Joshua Maddox & Mary his wife. William Thomas & Sarah his wife for £200 granted to John Hopkins & Joshua Maddox a tract in Darby bounded by land of Edward William, the road from Darby to Haverford, land of John Paschall & land late of Isaac Norris but now of Edward Waldren containing 2 1/2 acres. William Thomas & Sarah his wife to pay £239 to John Hopkins & Joshua Maddox to be made twice a year in full by 23 July 1743. Signed William Thomas & Sarah Thomas. Delivered in the presence of Joseph Bonsall & William Horne. Recorded 19 June 1740. (F6:57).

Deed. On 25 Mar 1730 Caleb Pussey of Marlborough, yeoman, surviving executor of the will of Elizabeth Fishbourne, late of Chester, widow, dec., the late wife of Ralph Fishbourne of Chester, merchant, dec., to William Fishbourne of the City of Philadelphia, merchant. Whereas Jacob Simcock son & heir of John Simcock, late of Ridley, yeoman, by deed dated 7 Sep 1703 granted to Ralph Fishbourne & Elizabeth his wife a lot in Chester bounded by Chester Creek. Whereas Francis Worley & Mary his wife the only surviving daughter of Thomas Brassey, dec., by deed dated 23 June 1708 granted to Ralph Fishbourne & Elizabeth his wife a tract in Chester bounded by Ridley Creek, land of Jonas Sandelands, Samuel Buckley, Francis Worley, William Pussey, John Linvill & Isaac Few containing 91 acres except for a 24 yard square for a burying ground as recorded in Chester, Book B, Vol 2, Page 255. Whereas Ralph Fishbourne died the said land vested to Elizabeth. Elizabeth made her will dated 25 Oct 1709 she devised to her son-in-law William Fishbourne the lot in Chester & the 91 acres & made Caleb Pussey & Gaien Stevenson her executors & soon after died. William Fishbourne agreed with the executors that the said land be sold to pay the debts. Caleb Pussey for £233 grant to William Fishbourne the said lands. Signed Caleb Pussey. Delivered in the presence of Peter Worrall, Nicholas ... & ... Coleman, Jr. Recorded 20 June 1740. (F6:60).

Mortgage. On 12 Apr 1740 James Russell of Upper Providence, merchant, to John Gilleylan of the City of Philadelphia, merchant. Whereas James Russell by a certain obligation for the sum of £60 to John Gilleylan, to insure the payment of £30 to be made on 20 June next. Now James Russell for the better securing the £30 grant to John Gilleylan a tract in Providence bounded by land of Peter Taylor, Providence Road, land of James McCullough & land of Randle Croxton containing 26 acres. Signed James Russell. Delivered in the presence of Edward Knott & John Ord. Recorded 2 July 1740. (F6:63).

To Andrew Hamilton, Esq., attorney of the Court of Common Pleas in the County of Chester, There are to authorize you to appear for me James Russell of Upper Providence in the County of Chester, merchant, in the said court action of debt there brought against me at the suit of John Gilleylan of the City of Philadelphia, merchant. Dated 12 Apr 1740. Signed James Russell. Delivered in the presence of Edward Knott & John Ord. (F6:66).

Deed. On 18 Sep 1738 John Owen, sheriff of Chester County to Andrew Hamilton of Philadelphia. Whereas John Penn, Thomas Penn & Richard Penn, Esq., in the County Court of Common Pleas recovered against Joseph Jervis, John Worrall, Nicholas Locherman & Ester his wife the sum of £219.17.6 as debt & £2.17 for damages. John Owen at the order of the court levied against the lands of Joseph Jervis, John Worrall, Nicholas Locherman & Esther his wife being a tract in Upper Providence containing 270 acres part of 570 acres William Penn by deed dated 24 Apr 1691 granted to Joseph Jervis, John Worrall, Nicholas Locherman & Esther his wife. Now John Owen for £300 grant to Andrew Hamilton a tract in Upper Providence bounded by Crum Creek, land of Thomas Jones, Peter Taylor, Edward Paver, Samuel Robinett, Richard Bond, Randle Matlin, William Matlin, & Daniel Calverts containing 270 acres. Signed John Owen. Delivered in the presence of Thomas Morgan, Thomas Powell & Joseph Parker. Recorded 29 Nov 1738. (F6:66).

Deed. On 10 May 1739 Andrew Hamilton of the City of Philadelphia, gentleman, to John Worrall of Chester County, yeoman. Andrew Hamilton for £300 grant to John Worrall a tract bounded by Crum Creek, land of Thomas Jones, Peter Taylor, Edward Paver, Samuel Robinett,, Richard Bond, Randle Matlin, William Matlin, & Daniel Calverts containing 270 acres. Signed Andrew Hamilton. Delivered in the presence of James Steel & Thomas Hatton. Recorded 18 July 1740. (F6:67).

Deed. On 28 Oct 1709 David Powell of Philadelphia, yeoman, to James Parry of the Great Valley in the County of Chester, husbandman. David Powell for £8 grant to James Parry a tract bounded by land formerly of William Powell & land of Thomas David containing 50 acres being part of 539 acres sold to David Powell by Jonathon Wynn son & heir of Thomas Wynn, dec., being part of his fathers original purchase. Signed David Powell. Delivered in the presence of Lewis Williams, Thomas Lloyd & Griffith Pritchard. Recorded 9 July 1740. (F6:68).

Acknowledgment. On 3 May 1740 Jacob Howell of Chester County, tanner, surviving executor of the will of Jonathon Ogden, late of Chester County, dec., acknowledge that Joseph Robinson, executor of the will of George Robinson, late of the county New Castle, dec., who was joint executor of the will of Jonathon Ogden with Jacob Howell. On 5 Mar 1738 Joseph Robinson after the death of George Robinson settled with me the account of all personal estate of Jonathon Ogden which came to George Robinson in his lifetime. I received the balance of £37.11.6 of what was due the estate of Jonathon Ogden from the estate of George Robinson. The house & lot devised to the said George Robinson & myself by the said Jonathon Ogden in trust to be sold for the use of his children still remaining unsold by the means & desire of George Robinson who was grandfather to the said children he being of opinion that the house & lots would rise considerably in value before the children should come of age & that the rents & profits of the house & lots would in the meantime be near equal to the interest the said money for which the said house could have been sold. Signed Jacob Howell. Delivered in the presence of Andrew Hamilton. Recorded 15 July 1740. (F6:70).

Release. On 1 Sep 1740 James Russell of Upper Providence, merchant, to John Gilleylan of the City of Philadelphia, merchant. Whereas James Russell by mortgage dated 12 Apr 1740 to John Gilleylan a tract in Upper Providence bounded by land of Peter Taylor, Providence Road & land of James McCullough containing 26 acres & James Russell was to pay £30, recorded in Chester, Book F, Vol 6, Page 63. Whereas the £30 was not paid the estate granted to John Gilleylan became absolute. Now James Russell for the foreclosing of the equity of the above mortgaged tract & the further sum of 5 shillings release to John Gilleylan the mortgaged tract. Signed James Russell. Delivered in the presence of Thomas Cummings, George Simpson & Joseph Parker. Recorded 1 Sep 1740. (F6:70).

Deed. On 1 Apr 1723 Jane Jones of East Town, widow to Humphrey Ellis of Haverford. Jane Jones for £50 grant to Humphrey Ellis a tract in East Town which was granted to Jane Jones by deed dated 1 Dec 1721 by Adam Roads & Katherine his wife bounded by land of Hugh Jones, land allotted to Adam Fraharn, land of Adam Road & Lydia Ellis containing 125 acres. Signed Jane Jones. Delivered in the presence of John Vaughan, William Ellis & Edward Williams. Recorded 1740. (F6:72).

Deed. On 30 Dec 1730 George Wilcockson of Uwchlan, weaver, to Phillip Yarnall of Edgmont, yeoman. George Wilcockson for £21 grants to Phillip Yarnall a tract in Uwchlan bounded by land of David Davis, Joseph Phipps, David Roberts, John Evans & Thomas Pugh containing 95 acres. Signed George Wilcockson. Delivered in the presence of Aubrey Roberts & Ruth Roberts. Recorded 6 Oct 1740. (F6:74).

Lease & Release. On 6 & 7 Sep 1740 Robert Wade of Chester, yeoman, eldest son & heir at law of John Wade, late of Chester dec & admin. of the goods & chattels of John Wade & Sarah his wife to John Salkeld of Chester, yeoman. Whereas Robert Wade by order of the Orphans Court by deed dated 16 Apr 1737 granted to Joseph Richards a tract in Chester containing 31 1/2 acres. Whereas Joseph Richards & Lydia his wife by deed dated 30 & 31 Aug 1737 granted to Robert Wade all the tract sold by the above order containing 31 1/2 acres. Whereas John Owen, high sheriff of Chester County by deed dated 31 Aug 1738 granted to Robert Wade a tract in Chester containing 35 acres. Now Robert Wade & Sarah his wife for £34 grants to John Salkeld a tract in Chester bounded by Chester Creek, land late of Henry Worley, land of John Salkeld, John Salkeld, Jr., & land late of Caleb Pussey containing 23 acres. Signed Robert Wade & Sarah Wade. Delivered in the presence of Zach Butcher & Joseph Parker. Recorded 22 Oct 1740. (F6:75).

Lease & Release. On 13 & 14 Oct 1740 Agnes Salkeld of Chester, widow & executrix of the will of John Salkeld, late of Chester, yeoman, dec., to William Salkeld of Chester, blacksmith, one of the sons of John & Agnes. Whereas Robert Wade & Sarah his wife by deed dated 6 & 7 Sep 1738 granted to John Salkeld, dec., a tract containing 23 acres. John Salkeld made his will dated 25 Feb 1733/4, amongst other things the remainder of the estate to go to wife Agnes & made her sole executrix. Now Agnes Salkeld for £34.10 & natural love grants to her son William Salkeld a tract in Chester bounded by land late of Henry Worley, land late of John Salkeld, land of John Salkeld, Jr., & Chester Creek containing 23 acres. Signed Agnes Salkeld. Delivered in the presence of Thomas Cummings & Joseph Parker. Recorded 28 Oct 1740. (F6:79).

Deed. On 26 Nov 1740 Benjamin David, sheriff of Chester County to Charles Crosley of Middletown. Whereas John Crosby at the Court of Common Pleas on 26 Feb 1730/40 did recover against John Edwards a debt of £106.16 & £0.70.6 for damages to be levied on the lands, tenements, goods & chattels of John Edward in my bailiwick. Benjamin Davis the sheriff of Chester County per order of the court sell to Charles Crosley a tract in Middletown bounded by land of John Edwards & land of John Lawrence containing 33 acres for £50. Signed Benjamin Davis. Delivered in the presence of Jonathon Ross, Joseph Parker & Jax Heating. Recorded 26 Nov 1740. (F6:83).

Reconveyance. On 9 Oct 1740 Richard Woodward of Bradford, yeoman, & Henry Pierce of Concord, gentleman, to Richard Barry of Chester, merchant. Whereas Richard Barry & Mary his wife by deed dated 6 & 7 Dec 1736 granted to Richard Woodward & Henry Pierce all their right & interest in a tract of land in Chester being 40' x 120' bounded by High Street, land late of William Trehern but now of John Hanly & Katherine his wife, recorded in Chester, Book E, Vol 5, Page 484, on 12 May 1737. Never the less the said parties by another indenture dated 7 Dec 1737, whereas it is covenanted that if the said Richard Barry or his heirs shall well & truly pay unto Richard Woodward & Henry Peirce the sum of £130 at the times appointed for payment, they shall discharge all the encumbrances. Richard Woodward & Henry Pierce for £124 release, confirm & transfer to Richard Barry the said lot of land. Signed Henry Pierce & Richard Woodward. Delivered in the presence of John Hanly & Amos Boake. Recorded 4 Dec 1740. (F6:85).

Lease & Release. On 28 & 29 Oct 1740 Richard Barry of Chester, merchant, & Mary his wife to John Hanly of Chester, inn holder. Whereas William Trehern & Catherine his wife by deed dated 14 & 15 Nov 1733 granted to Richard Barry a lot in Chester being 40' x 120'. Richard Barry & Mary his wife by deed dated 6 & 7 Dec 1736 granted to

Richard Woodward & Henry Pierce the said lot & Richard Woodward & Henry Pierce by deed dated 9 Oct 1740 for £124 release, confirm & transfer to Richard Barry the said lot of land. Now Richard Barry & Mary his wife for £250 granted to John Hanly the said lot in Chester bounded by High Street & other land of John Hanly. Signed Richard Barry & Mary Barry. Delivered in the presence of Benjamin Davis, Joseph Parker & David Ranken. Recorded 19 Dec 1740. (F6:87).

Lease & Release. On 30 & 31 Oct 1740 John Hanly of Chester, inn holder & Catherine his wife to William Preston of the City of Philadelphia, mariner. Whereas Richard Barry & Mary his wife by deed dated 28 & 29 Oct 1740 granted to John Hanly a lot in Chester. Now John Hanly & Catherine his wife for £200 granted to William Preston a lot in Chester being 40' x 120' bounded by Free Street, High Street & other land of John Hanly. Signed John Hanly & Catherine Hanly. Delivered in the presence of John Coeburn & Joseph Parker. Recorded 16 Jan 1740/41. (F6:91).

Deposition. On 9 Mar 1724 Amos Nichols says that on 19 Jan 1718/9 at the request & consent of Andrew Morton, John Morton & George Culin being joint purchasers of 2 tracts of land in Ridley which the said Andrew Morton, John Morton & George Culin purchased of John Bartles, on the day said he did divide one of the tracts lying between Andrew Torton's land & John Hendrickson's, between the said John Morton & Andrew Morton agreed to be their shares of the said purchase the upper part of which said tract of land was laid out or surveyed for the said John Morton by the consent of Andrew Morton & George Culin & the said John Morton to the best of his knowledge. J. Andrew Morton, John Morton & George Culin were present. Signed Amos Nichols. Delivered in the presence of John Crosby. (F6:94).

Deed. On 24 Mar 1739/40 Aaron Mendenhall of East Caln, yeoman, & Rose his wife to George Mendenhall of Caln, yeoman, son & heir apparent of Aaron & Rose. Whereas William Penn by deed dated 17 & 18 Mar 1698 granted to Thomas Musgrove, dec., & John Brook 1,500 acres in the province. Thomas Musgrove made his will dated 1 Aug 1699 & appointed Hannah his wife his executrix, & died vested with a right to one half of the 1,500 acres. Whereas on 9 Apr 1702 a tract was surveyed to Hannah in right of the purchase in Caln bounded by land of Joseph Pike, land of William Penn, land late of Randle Spakeman & lands late of

David Powell & Phillip Roman containing 500 acres & confirmed to the said Hannah by the name of Hannah Price wife of David Price on 9 Aug 1703, recorded in Philadelphia, Book A, Page 172. Whereas Abraham Musgrove the surviving son of Thomas Musgrove & David Price & Hannah his wife by deed dated 23 Mar 1712 granted to Aaron Mendenhall a tract in Caln bounded by land late of David Powell, land of Phillip Roman, Joseph Pikes, & land late of Randle Spakeman containing 450 acres. Now Aaron Mendenhall & Rose his wife for 5 shillings & the natural love & affection they bear to their son George Mendenhall & for his better maintenance, livelihood, & performance in the world have granted & confirmed to George Mendenhall all that tract in Caln bounded by land of Joseph Pike, Mill Creek, land of Roman & land of Aaron Mendenhall containing 100 acres. Signed Aaron Mendenhall & Rose Mendenhall. Delivered in the presence of Thomas Parke & Thomas Pim. Recorded 12 Feb 1740/1. (F6:94).

Deed. On 2 Mar 1724/5 Gayen Miller of Kennett, yeoman, & Margaret his wife to William Miller son of Gayen Miller, of New Garden, yeoman. Whereas William Penn, Jr., by letter of attorney appointing Griffith Owen, practitioner of Physick, James Logan & Robert Aston, gentleman, all of the City of Philadelphia as his attorneys by deed dated 29 Jan 1712/3 granted to Gayen Miller a tract containing 700 acres, recorded Chester, Book D, Vol 4, Page 78. Now Gayen Miller & Margaret his wife for 5 shillings granted to William Miller a tract in New Garden bounded by land of Nehemiah Hutton, Frances Hobson, Gayen Miller & William Rowan containing 234 acres being part of the 700 acres. Signed Gayen Miller & Margaret Miller. Delivered in the presence of Richard Naylor, Thomas White & Robert Miller. Recorded 20 Mar 1740/1. (F6:97).

Mortgage. On 5 Feb 1740 Richard Treveller of Tallowfield in the County of Chester, yeoman, to Caleb Emlen of the City of Philadelphia, joiner. Richard Treveller for £50 granted to Caleb Emlen a tract in Tallowfield bounded by land of Joseph Powell, Albert Skear & William Harlan containing 276 acres. Richard Treveller to pay Caleb Emlen £52.5 on or before 5 Nov 1741. Signed Richard Treveller. Delivered in the presence of William Scall & Joseph Brinton. Recorded 7 May 1741. (F6:99).

Deed. On 27 July 1730 Andrew Morton of Ridley, plow wright & Mary his wife to Joseph Harvey of Ridley, yeoman. Andrew Morton for £2 granted to Joseph Harvey a tract containing 1 + acres in Ridley bounded

by the Kings Road, land of John Archer, Joseph Harvey & Andrew
Morton being part of 138 acres which Mathias Morton, the father,
granted to Andrew Morton. Signed Andrew Morton & Mary Morton.
Delivered in the presence of John Modle, Ann Modle & John Iden.
Recorded 2 July 1741. (F6:102).

Bond. On 27 July 1730 Andrew Morton of Ridley, plow wright is firmly
bound to Joseph Harvey of Ridley, wheel wright, for £50. The condition
of this obligation is such that whereas Andrew Morton & Mary his wife
conveyed to Joseph Harvey the 1+ acre, & whereas the true intent of
although not comprised in the said bargain & that was the 1+ acre &
premises was designed to be laid out for a road or passage to Joseph
Harvey & Andrew Morton. Signed Andrew Morton. Delivered in the
presence of John Modle, Ann Modle & John Iden. Recorded 1741.
(F6:104).

Lease & Release. On 3 Apr 1741 Joseph Hoskins of Chester, cordwainer,
& Jane his wife to John Hanly of Chester, inn holder. Whereas John
Hoskins, eldest son & heir-at-law of John Hoskins, late of Chester,
gentleman, dec., by deed dated 4 & 5 May 1738 granted to Joseph
Hoskins a tract in Chester containing 50 acres. Whereas John Hoskins
by deed dated 18 Dec 1738 confirmed to Joseph Hoskins the 50 acres.
Now Joseph Hoskins & Jane his wife for £125 granted to John Hanly a
tract in Chester bounded by Ridley Creek containing 50 acres. Signed
Joseph Hoskins & Jane Hoskins. Delivered in the presence of Joseph
Parker & Grace Lloyd. Recorded 9 July 1741. (F6:105).

Release. On 18 Dec 1738 John Hoskins of Chester, yeoman, eldest son &
heir of John Hoskins, late of Chester, gentleman, dec., to Joseph Hoskins
of Chester, cordwainer, another of the sons of John Hoskins, dec.
Whereas John Hoskins died intestate leaving a wife & 4 children to
survive him & a division was made between the said parties. Whereas
the tenements & lots mentioned became the share of John Hoskins the
son. John Hoskins by deed dated 4 & 5 May 1730 granted to Joseph
Hoskins before particular bounds were made. John Hoskins for 5
shillings release all right & interest to Joseph Hoskins in the lot or
tenement where the late father dwelt lying in Chester bounded by
Market Street, land late of Jonas Sandelands, also another tract in
Chester bounded by Ridley Creek containing 50 acres. Signed John
Hoskins. Delivered in the presence of Joseph Parker, Thomas Cummings
& Michael Seaton. Recorded 23 July 1741. (F6:108).

Lease & Release. On 9 & 10 Apr 1741 Joseph Hoskins of Chester, cordwainer, & Jane his wife to Stephen Cole of Chester, yeoman. Whereas John Hoskins, late of Chester, gentleman, dec., the late father of Joseph Hoskins, died intestate leaving a wife & 4 children to survive him. The said estate was divided amongst the wife & said children according to law as all the said children being arrived at full age & agreed to make the division. Ruth Hoskins, widow, John Hoskins, eldest son, Stephen Hoskins, second son, & John Mather & Mary his wife, the only daughter of the dec., by deed dated 2 June 1733 granted to Joseph Hoskins amongst other things a tract containing 20 acres, recorded in Chester, Book E, Vol 5, Page 242. Now Joseph Hoskins & Jane his wife for £65 granted to Stephen Cole a tract in Chester bounded by the road leading from Chester to Edgmont & land late of John Simcock containing 20 acres. Signed Joseph Hoskins & Jane Hoskins. Delivered in the presence of Joseph Parker & Grace Lloyd. Recorded 24 July 1741. (F6:110).

Mortgage. On 6 Apr 1741 George Reece of Coventry in the County of Chester, yeoman, to Joseph Williams of Merion in the County of Philadelphia. Whereas Thomas Penn, Esq., in his own right & the powers granted to him by John & Richard Penn, Esqs., by deed dated 22 Nov 1740 granted to George Reece a tract in Coventry containing 231 acres, recorded in Philadelphia, Book A, Vol 10, Page 162. Now George Reece for £100 granted to Joseph Williams a tract in Coventry bounded by Schuykill River, land of Thomas Godfrey, David Stephen & Anthony Morris containing 230 acres. George Reece to pay Joseph Williams in yearly payments £130 to be paid on or before 6 Apr 1746. Signed George Reece. Delivered in the presence of William Horne & Joseph Bonsall. Recorded 18 June 1741. (F6:113).

Deed. On 13 Nov 1739 William Smith of Kennet, yeoman, & Eleanor his wife to John Smith of Kennet, yeoman. Whereas the commissioners of William Penn by deed dated 17 Feb 1704 granted to John Bird of Philadelphia a tract in Kennet containing 500 acres, recorded in Philadelphia, Book A, Vol 2, Page 228. John Bird by deed dated 26 Oct 1706 granted to Nicholas Pyle of Concord a tract in Kennet containing 200 acres part of the 500 acres, recorded Chester, Book C, Vol 3, Page 102. Nicholas Pyle by deed dated 1 Apr 17?? granted to John Cox the 200 acres. Whereas John Cox & Rachel his wife by deed dated 29 & 30 Dec 1719 granted to Robert Carter. Robert Carter & Lydia his wife by deed dated 18 & 19 Dec 1727 granted to William Smith the 200 acres. William Smith & Elleanor his wife for £100 granted to John Smith a tract in Kennet bounded by Smith's land, land of John Heald & John Packer containing 100 acres. Signed William Smith & Elleanor Smith. Delivered in the presence of William Webb, Archibald McNeile & Elizabeth McNeile. Recorded 5 Sep 1741. (F6:116).

Mortgage. On 16 May 1741 Caleb Evans of Radnor, yeoman, & Catherine his wife to Hugh Jones of Merion in the County of Philadelphia, yeoman. Whereas Caleb Evans by a certain obligation stands bound to Hugh Jones in the sum of £500 conditioned on the payment of £250 & lawful interest (which is £15 per annum) in the manner following, £15 yearly on 25 Oct until 1761 with £15 & £250 paid on 25 Oct 1762. Now Caleb Evans & Catherine his wife for the £250 to better secure said debt granted to Hugh Jones a tract in Radnor bounded by land of Caleb Evans, Hugh Williams & land late of John Langworthy but now of Aaron Roberts containing 201 acres. Signed Caleb Evans & Catherine Evans. Delivered in the presence of John Morgan, John Jerman, John Thomas, John Havard, Jr., & John Bowen. Recorded 22 Sep 1741. (F6:118).

Deed. On 16 June 1741 Benjamin Davis, sheriff of Chester County to John Richardson of New Castle on Delaware, Esq., & John Hannum of New Castle on Delaware, gentleman. Whereas John White & Abraham Taylor of the City of Philadelphia, merchants at the Court of Common Pleas recovered against Thomas Cox, late of Chester a debt of £601.13 & £0.70.6 as damages to be levied on the goods & chattels of Thomas Cox, in my bailiwick. Seized was a tract containing 146 acres with a water corn mill. Benjamin Davis, sheriff, for £295 granted to John Richardson & John Hannum a tract in Tallowfield bounded by land of John Taylor with a corn grist mill containing 1046 acres. Signed Benjamin Davis. Delivered in the presence of Caleb Cowpland & Robert Miller. Recorded 26 Aug 1741. (F6:120).

Mortgage. On 25 Mar 1741 John Scarlett of Robinson township in the County of Philadelphia, yeoman, & Eleanor his wife to Caleb Cowpland of Chester, gentleman. John Scarlett & Eleanor his wife for £50 granted to Caleb Cowpland a tract in Chester bounded by Chester Creek, land of Humphrey Johnson, Humphrey Scarlett, Thomas Barnard, Joseph Richards & Chester Road containing 131 1/2 acres. John Scarlett to make payments to Caleb Cowpland yearly, to be paid in full 25 Mar 1744.

Signed John Scarlett & Eleanor Scarlett. Delivered in the presence of Eleanor Phillip, Joseph Parker & David Ranken. Recorded 15 Sep 1741. (F6:122).

Lease & Release. On 19 & 20 Mar 1740/1 Jane Elwell of Wilmington in the County of New Castle on Delaware, spinster to John Bezar of Chichester, merchant. Whereas Phebe Coppeck & Henry Lewis, executors of the will of Thomas Massey, late of Marple, dec., by deed dated 15 & 16 Dec 1729 granted to Jane Elwell a lot in Chester. Jane Elwell for £24 granted to John Bezar a lot in Chester being 40' x 80' bounded by the market place, lot late of John Hoskins but now of Joseph Hoskins, & a lot late of Thomas Massey, dec., being a part of 20 acres granted to James Sandelands, late of Chester, merchant, dec. James Sandelands, dec., the eldest son of James Sandelands, conveyed the said lots to Thomas Massey by deed dated 2 Oct 1703. Thomas Massey made his will dated 24 Mar 1707/8 and directed his executors to sell said tract, which they sold to Jane Elwell. Signed Jane Elwell. Delivered in the presence of Joseph Pyle & Alexander Seaton. Recorded 20 Oct 1741. (F6:125).

Lease & Release. On 21 & 22 Apr 1741 Joseph Hoskins of Chester, cordwainer, & Jane his wife to John Bezar of Chichester, yeoman. Whereas John Hoskins, late of Chester, gentleman, dec., the late father of Joseph Hoskins died intestate leaving a wife & 4 children to survive him. The said estate was divided amongst the wife & said children according to law as all the said children being arrived at full age & agreed to make the division. Ruth Hoskins, widow, John Hoskins, eldest son, Stephen Hoskins, second son & John Mather & Mary his wife the only daughter of the dec. by deed dated 2 June 1733 granted to Joseph Hoskins amongst other things a lot in Chester. Joseph Hoskins for £35.10 granted to John Bezar a lot in Chester being 40' x 120' bounded by the market place & High Street. Signed Joseph Hoskins & Jane Hoskins. Delivered in the presence of Edward Russell & John Lea. Recorded 22 Oct 1741. (F6:128).

Deed. On 29 Sep 1713 William Penn of London, Esq., eldest son & heir apparent of William Penn, Esq., Governor of Pennsylvania, Griffith Owen, practitioner of Physick, James Logan, gentleman, & Robert Ashton, gentleman, all of the City of Philadelphia to John Wily of Chester county, yeoman. Whereas the commissioners of William Penn the father by deed dated 24 May 1706 granted to William Penn, the son, a tract on the south side of Brandywine Creek part in the County of New Castle & part in the County of Chester containing 14,500 acres, recorded in Philadelphia, Book A, Vol 3, Page 279. Whereas William Penn, Jr., by Letter of Attorney dated 7 Oct 1704 appointed Griffith Owen, James Logan & Robert Ashton to be his lawful attorneys to sell said land, recorded in Philadelphia, Book D2, Vol 5, Page 144. William Penn Jr., Griffith Owen, James Logan & Robert Ashton for £40 grant to John Wily a tract bounded by land of Francis Hobson, Michael Lightfoot & the manor containing 200 acres. Signed Griffith Owen, James Logan & Robert Ashton. Delivered in the presence of Nicholas Pyle, Gayen Miller & James Boyden. Recorded 26 Oct 1741. (F6:131).

Release. On 26 Apr 1723 John Wily of New Garden in the County of Chester, yeoman, & Martha his wife to John Houlton of Chester, yeoman. John Wily & Martha his wife for 5 shillings release & confirm to John Houlton a tract bounded by land of Francis Hobson, Michael Lightfoot & the manor containing 200 acres. Signed John Wily & Martha Wily. Delivered in the presence of Abraham Ayre, Michael Lightfoot & Samuel Lightfoot. Recorded 26 Oct 1741. (F6:134).

Lease & Release. On 12 & 13 June 1723 John Houlton of New Garden, yeoman, & Elizabeth his wife to Nehemiah Hutton of New Garden, weaver. Whereas John Houlton was seized in a tract of land in Chester County bounded by land of Francis Hobson, Michael Lightfoot & the Manor containing 200 acres & mortgaged said 200 acres for £50 to Samuel Carpenter, Jeremiah Langhorne, William Fishbourne & Nathaniel Newlin, trustees of the General Loan Office of the province of Pennsylvania. John Houlton & Elizabeth his wife for £43 granted to Nehemiah Hutton the 200 acres, & Nehemiah Hutton to pay the mortgage to the General Loan Office. Signed John Houlton in the presence of Samuel Wainwright & Joseph Watson. Signed Elizabeth Houlton in the presence of David Brooks & Nathaniel Houlton. Recorded 27 Oct 1741. (F6:135).

Lease & Release. On 6 & 7 Nov 1730 Nehemiah Hutton of New Garden, weaver, & Sarah his wife to John Black of Mill Creek Hundred, in the County of New Castle on Delaware. Nehemiah Hutton & Sarah his wife for £105.14 granted to John Black a tract in Chester County bounded by land of Francis Hobson, Michael Lightfoot & the Manor containing 200 acres being the tract the commissioners of William Penn the father by deed dated 24 May 1706 granted to William Penn, the son, a tract on the south side of Brandywine Creek part in the County of New Castle & part in the County of Chester containing 14,500 acres, recorded in Philadelphia, Book A, Vol 3, Page 279. Whereas William Penn, Jr., by Letter of Attorney dated 7 Oct 1704 appointed Griffith Owen, James Logan & Robert Ashton to be his lawful attorneys to sell said land, recorded in Philadelphia, Book D2, Vol 5, Page 144. William Penn Jr., Griffith Owen, James Logan & Robert Ashton by deed dated 25 June 1722 granted to John Wily. John Wily & Martha his wife by deed dated 25 Apr 1723 granted to John Houlton the 200 acres. Which John Houlton by deed dated 13 June 1723 granted the 200 acres to Nehemiah Hutton. Signed Nehemiah Hutton & Sarah Hutton. Delivered in the presence of William McDowell, John Toe & William McGaughy. Recorded 28 Oct 1741. (F6:138).

Deed. On 10 Apr 1741 John Black of Mill Creek Hundred on Delaware, fuller & Jennet his wife to Nathaniel Jenkins of New Garden, store keeper. Whereas John Black by virtue of a deed of release from Nehemiah Hutton & Sarah his wife was lawfully seized of 200 acres. John Black & Jennet his wife for £200 granted to Nathaniel Jenkins a tract in New Garden bounded by land of Francis Hobson, Michael Lightfoot, Nathaniel Jenkins, William Rowens & William Millers containing 200 acres. Signed John Black & Jennet Black. Delivered in the presence of Joseph Parker, Mary Walker & Thomas Brackden. Recorded 29 Oct 1741. (F6:141).

Release. On 10 June 1734 Charles Grantum & Katherine his wife, Lydia Morton all of Ridley & Andrew Boon of King Cess in the County of Philadelphia, yeoman, & Rebecca his wife to Hance Torton of Ridley, yeoman, & Latitia his wife. Whereas there are 3 tracts of land in Ridley, one tract bounded by the King's Road, Lydia's land & land of Andrew Morton containing 15 1/2 acres, the 2nd tract bounded by land of Plough Andrew Morton containing 64 acres & the 3rd tract bounded by land of Andrew Boon & Plough Andrew Morton containing 8 acres & a half a quarter. The said 3 tracts are part of a tract that Andrew Morton had conveyed to him by his father Morton Morton by deed dated 23 May 1705 containing 257 acres, the last tract was land Morton Morton purchased of Andrew Johnson, late of Amos, land in Ridley by deed dated 12 Mar 1694/5. Now Andrew Morton died having no sons but 5 daughters which were Latitia, Ellin, Elizabeth, Katherine, Rebecca & Lydia but Ellin died before the division of said land. The said land was divided amongst the daughters & their husbands, & the 3 tracts described fell to Hance Torton & Latitia his wife. Charles Grantum & Katherine his wife, Andrew Boon & Rebecca his wife, Lydia Morton, for 5 shillings release all right & interest to Hance Torton & Latitia his wife in the said 3 tracts. Signed Charles Grantum, Katherine Grantum, Andrew Boon, Rebecca Boon & Lydia Morton. Delivered in the presence of John Crosby, John Leetes & Salem Miller. Recorded 8 June 1741. (F6:144).

Lease & Release. On 9 & 10 June 1741 Andrew Morton, Sr of Ridley, yeoman, & Anne his wife, Morton Morton of Ridley, yeoman, eldest son of Andrew Morton & Lydia his wife to Hance Torton of Ridley. Whereas John Bartleson by deed dated 23 Feb 1704 granted to Andrew Morton, John Morton & George Vanculin a tract in Ridley containing 300 acres, recorded in Book A, Vol 1, Page 213. Whereas there was a division of said land & George Vanculin obtained his share separately & the tract containing 158 acres in Ridley fell to the shares of Andrew & John Morton to be equally divided between them, share & share alike but the land was never divided by metes & bounds, yet the said parties by mutual consent having been divided they have built & improved on their shares & are well satisfied. Whereas Andrew Morton is lawfully seized in 10 1/2 acres & the Morton Morton was seized in 15 1/4 acres & the Andrew being seized of an acre planted in orchard. Andrew Morton & Ann his wife & Morton Morton & Lydia his wife for £200 granted to Hance Torton one moiety of a tract in Ridley bounded by Darby Creek, land of John Hendricks, land late of Jacob Simcock, land late of Henry Torton containing 158 acres & all the tract in Ridley containing 15 1/4 acres, and a tract in Ridley bounded by George Culins & land formerly John Morton containing 10 1/2 acres & a tract in Ridley containing 1 acre planted in Orchard which Andrew Morton lately purchased of Andrew Torton. Signed Andrew Morton, Morton Morton & Lydia Morton. Delivered in the presence of Benjamin Kendall, Joseph Parker & David Ranken. Recorded 4 Nov 1741. (F6:146).

Lease & Release. On 9 & 10 June 1741 Hance Torton of Ridley, yeoman, & Latitia his wife to Andrew Morton, Sr., of Ridley, yeoman. Whereas Charles Grant & Katherine his wife, Andrew Boon & Rebecca his wife & Lydia Morton by deed dated 10 June 1724 granted to Hance Torton & Latitia his wife 3 tracts of land in Ridley. Hance Torton & Latitia his wife for £200 granted to Andrew Morton 3 tracts of land in Ridley the 1st tract bounded by the King's Road, land of Andrew Morton containing 15

1/2 acres, the 2nd tract bounded by land of Plow Andrew Morton containing 64 acres & the 3rd tract bounded land late of Andrew Boon but now of Morton Morton, land of Plow Andrew Morton containing 8 acres & one half quarter of an acre & also an interest in one half acre, & one half quarter of an acre. Signed Hance Torton & Latitia Torton. Delivered in the presence of Joseph Parker & David Ranken. Recorded 5 Nov 1741. (F6:149).

Deed. On 12 June 1741 Andrew Morton of Ridley, yeoman, & Anne his wife to Morton Morton of Ridley, eldest son of Andrew Morton. Whereas Andrew Morton is seized of land in Ridley, Darby & in the township of Greenwich in the province of West New Jersey & for the advancement of his son Andrew Morton & Anne his wife for love & £5 granted to Morton Morton 3 tracts of land the 1st bounded by the King's Road, Lydia's land & land of Andrew Morton containing 15 1/2 acres, another tract bounded by land of Plow Andrew Morton containing 64 acres, another tract bound by land late of Andrew Boon but now of Morton Morton & land of Plow Andrew Morton containing 8 acres & a half of a quarter acre & all right & title in 18 acres in Darby Creek, called May Island which Andrew Morton lately purchased of his brother David Morton & also the meadow situated at the mouth of Darby Creek & all that land containing 130 acres in Greenwich in the County of Gloucester in the province of West New Jersey adjoining to Andrew Matson's land from the River Delaware and is part of 211 acres which Andrew Morton purchased of John Friend & also the one half of the meadow ground (excepting 2 acres) in Greenwich between the lower line of the land which Andrew Morton purchased of Edward Nicholas & a creek call Burch Creek, beginning at Horse Neck out to Burch Creek adjoining the dry meadow & to the River Delaware & 10 acres of drained meadow in the forks of the branch of Burch Creek. Signed Andrew Morton. Delivered in the presence of Benjamin Kendall, Joseph Parker & David Ranken. Recorded 6 Nov 1741. (F6:153).

Deed. On 3 Sep 1723 Michael Harlan of Bradford, yeoman, & Dinah his wife to Stephen Harlan son of Michael & Dinah. Whereas Abiah Taylor, late of Harwell in the County of Berks in Old England, mercer did purchase from John Tovey of Henly upon Thames in the County of Oxen, citizen & Gorser of London 1250 acres in the province of Pennsylvania. Whereas Abiah Taylor by deed dated 6 & 7 Apr 1702 conveyed 250 acres to Richard Lewin since dec. Whereas Richard Lewin, son & heir of Richard Lewin, dec., by deed dated 26 Mar 1707 conveyed the 250 acres to Walter Pumphrey of Pennsylvania. Whereas Walter Pumphrey by deed dated 5 May 1707 conveyed the 250 acres to Henry Hollingsworth & Henry Hollingsworth by deed dated 16 July 1707 conveyed said 250 acres to George Robinson intending the same in trust for the use of Henry Hollingsworth. On 2 Apr 1714 the 250 acres was laid out to George Robinson in Bradford. Henry Hollingsworth by deed dated 1 Dec 1716 granted to Michael Harlan the 250 acres. George Robinson by deed dated 19 Mar 1717 for further insurance confirmed to Michael Harlan the said 250 acres. Michael Harlan & Dinah his wife for £25 granted to Stephen Harlan a tract in Bradford bounded by Society land, land of John Buffington, Richard Woodward & land late of William Buffington containing 250 acres. Signed Michael Harlan & Dinah Harlan. Delivered in the presence of Rebecca Webb, Michael Harlan, Jr., & Hannah Maris. Recorded 13 Nov 1741. (F6:156).

Deed. On 2 June 1690 Joseph Wood of Darby to John Wood his brother of Darby. Joseph Wood, son & heir of William Wood, dec., by letter of admin. granted to him to admin. his said dec. father's estate, granted to his brother, John Wood, as part of his portion a tract in Chester County on the upper end of New Town township bounded by land of Joseph Wood & William Shardlow containing 500 acres. Joseph Wood appointed John Ferne to be his attorney. Signed Joseph Wood. Delivered in the presence of George Simcock, R. Scothorn & George Forman Clarke. (F6:158).

Deed. On 19 Nov 1703 Howell James, late of Radnor but now of the County of Philadelphia, yeoman, to Edward Hughes of East Town, yeoman. Whereas there is a tract of land called Travelgwyn in East Town bounded by land of Joseph Wood & William Sharlow containing 500 acres which having descended to Joseph Wood as son & heir of William Wood, dec., who was the first purchaser & Joseph Wood by deed dated 2 June 1690 granted to his brother John Wood all 500 acres. Whereas John Wood by deed dated 10 Mar 1690/1 granted to Howell James the 500 acres, recorded in Chester, Book A, Folio 2. Howell James for £100 granted to Edward Hughes the 500 acres. Signed Howell James. Delivered in the presence of James James, Phillip Howell & Richard Heath. Recorded 1741. (F6:159).

Lease & Release. On 10 & 11 June 1741 John Plain of Coventry in the County of Chester, fuller & Mary his wife to Christian Mary of Charles Town in the County of Chester, yeoman. Whereas Thomas Penn, Esq., in his own right & with the power granted to him by Richard & John Penn, Esqs., granted to John Plain a tract in Coventry bounded by land of William Adams, John Nuter & David Hopkins containing 100 acres, recorded in Philadelphia, Book A, Vol 10, Page 102. John Plain & Mary his wife for £30 granted to Christian Mary the tract of 100 acres. Signed John Plain & Mary Plain. Delivered in the presence of James Starr & Rachel Starr, Jr. Recorded 25 Nov 1741. (F6:162).

Mortgage. On 12 Oct 1741 Edward Waldron of Darby, scythe smith, to John Nickinson of Darby, yeoman. Edward Waldron for £50 granted to John Nickinson a tract in Darby bounded by Darby Bridge, Springfield Road, Chester Road containing 3/4 of an acre. Edward Waldron to pay £53 to John Nickinson on or before 12 Oct 1742. Signed Edward Waldron. Delivered in the presence of William Parker & Benjamin Pearson. Recorded 5 Dec 1741. (F6:165).

Deed. On 19 Oct 1741 Mary Norris, widow & relict of Isaac Norris, late of Fair Hill in the City Liberties of Philadelphia, merchant, dec. Charles Norris, Samuel Norris, the son of Isaac Norris, dec. (Mary, Charles & Samuel being the executors of the will of Isaac Norris dec.) & James Logan of Kenton in the County of Philadelphia, Esq., Isreal Pemberton of the City of Philadelphia, merchant, & Richard Harrison of Merion in the County of Philadelphia, Esq., (the trustees of the will), to Joshua Thompson of Springfield, yeoman. Whereas Mordecai Maddock of Chester County, yeoman, by deed dated 4 Mar 1702/3 granted to Isaac Norris the father a tract in Springfield containing 521 acres. Isaac Norris made his will dated 17 Jan 1731 & made his wife Mary & his sons Isaac, Charles & Samuel executors. Mary Norris, Isaac Norris, Samuel Norris & Charles Norris for £160 with the advice of James Logan, Isreal Pemberton & Richard Harrison granted & confirmed to Joshua Thompson a tract bounded by land of John Gleaves & other land of Isaac Norris containing 100 acres. Signed Mary Norris, Isaac Norris, Charles Norris, Samuel Norris, Isreal Pemberton, & Richard Harrison. Delivered in the presence of Ann Lloyd & David Irwin. Recorded 14 Dec 1741. (F6:166).

Mortgage. On 26 Oct 1741 Joshua Thompson of Springfield, yeoman, & Margaret his wife to Isaac Norris of the City of Philadelphia, merchant. Joshua Thompson & Margaret his wife for £91.13.4 granted to Isaac Norris a tract in Springfield bounded by land of John Gleaves & other

131

land of Isaac Norris containing 100 acres. Joshua Thompson & Margaret his wife to pay Isaac Norris the sum of £91.13.4 plus interest on or before 26 Oct 1742. Signed Joshua Thompson & Margaret Thompson. Delivered in the presence of Charles Lloyd & Christopher Hoare. Recorded 21 Dec 1741. (F6:169).

Mortgage. On 5 Nov 1741 Oliver Thomas of Chester, carpenter, & Sarah his wife who was one of the daughters of Jonas Sandelands, late of Chester, gentleman, dec., to Caleb Cowpland of Chester, gentleman. Oliver Thomas & Sarah his wife for £80 granted to Caleb Cowpland a tract in Chester which descended & was laid out to Sarah as her share of her late fathers estate bounded by land laid out to David Sandelands, Edgmont Road & land of Buckley containing 44 1/2 acres also a tract bounded by land late of Richard Magee, & Anne his wife, Ridley Creek & the lot late of Rebecca Sandelands containing 5 acres. Oliver Thomas & Sarah his wife to pay Caleb Cowpland the £80 plus interest in yearly payments to be paid in full on 5 Nov 1744. Signed Oliver Thomas & Sarah Thomas. Delivered in the presence of James Claxton, William Smith & Joseph Parker. Recorded 24 Dec 1741. (F6:171).

Lease & Release. On 15 & 16 May 1741 John Bezar of Chichester, merchant, & Esther his wife to Joseph Pyle of Bethel, yeoman. Whereas Jacob Roman by deed dated 18 May 1719 granted to Richard Bezar of Chichester, yeoman, a tenement & 3 tracts of land. Richard Bezar by deed dated 21 & 22 Apr 1724 granted John Bezar a tract in Chichester containing 47 acres, & John Bezar has built a tenement & a corn mill on said land. John Bezar & Esther his wife for £400 granted to Joseph Pyle the tenement, corn mill & the land in Chichester bounded by land of John Cloud & Chichester Creek containing 47 acres. Signed John Bezar & Esther Bezar. Delivered in the presence of George Simpson, Joseph Parker & David Ranken. Recorded 5 Jan 1741. (F6:174).

Lease & Release. On 24 & 25 Sep 1733 Edward Woodward of Chester County, yeoman, & Alice his wife late Alice Allen, relict of John Allen of Chester County, dec., to John Williamson of Chester County, yeoman. Whereas John Allen was seized in a tract of land in New Town bounded by land of Rees Kent, Lawrence Peirson, Morgan James, William Bevan, Anne Welch & Daniel Williamson containing 128 1/2 acres, another tract bounded by land of William Bevan, Anne Welch, & Daniel Williamson containing 45 1/2 acres & on about 8 Apr 1720 made his will & amongst other things mentioned devised unto his wife Alice the remainder of his personal & real estate. After the death of John Allen, Alice married Edward Woodward. Now Edward Woodward & Alice his wife for 5 shillings granted to John Williamson the 174 acres in trust. Signed Edward Woodward & Alice Woodward. Delivered in the presence of Richard Fawkes & William Hunter. Recorded 11 Jan 1741. (F6:177).

Release. On 25 Sep 1733 John Williamson of Chester County, yeoman, to Edward Woodward of Chester County, yeoman, & Alice his wife. Whereas Edward Woodward & Alice his wife by deed dated 24 & 25 Sep 1733 granted to John Williamson land in New Town bounded by land of Rees Kent, Lawrence Peirson, Morgan James, William Bevan, Anne Welch & Daniel Williamson containing 128 1/2 acres, another tract bounded by land of William Bevan, Anne Welch, & Daniel Williamson containing 45 1/2 acres. John Williamson in trust & for 5 shillings granted to Edward Woodward & Alice his wife the 174 acres. Signed John Williamson. Delivered in the presence of William Hunter & Richard Fawkes. Recorded 12 Jan 1741. (F6:179).

Lease & Release. On 17 & 18 Mar 1739 John Pennell of Aston, yeoman, & Mary his wife to John Pennell of Aston, yeoman (son of John & Mary). John Pennell the father & Mary his wife for Whereas by warrant deed dated 17 Nov 1684 there was laid out to Thomas Brassey a tract containing 1,000 acres situated in the fork of Chester Creek, part of 5,000 acres Thomas Brassey purchased. Whereas Thomas Brassey by deed dated 27 Aug 1689 granted 119 acres to Thomas Martin, who by deed dated 7 Sep 1698 granted to William Rattew 100 acres. Whereas Thomas Brassey having sold 119 acres soon after died, seized of 881 acres which descended to his 2 daughters, Mary, who married Francis Worley & Rebecca, who married Thomas Thompson. Rebecca died before the division of said lands & by right of survivorship the lands fell to Mary wife of Francis Worley. Never the less, they did agree that Thomas Thompson should enjoy the his wife's share of the estate. Which Thomas Thompson by deed dated 22 Sep 1697 granted to Caleb Pussey the said share, recorded in Chester, Book A, Vol 1, Page 119. Whereas Caleb Pussey, Francis Worley & Mary his wife by deed dated 16 Feb 1704 granted 50 acres (part of the 881 acres) to William Rattew. William Rattew deed dated 19 Feb 1704 granted the 2 tracts of land containing 150 acres to John Pennell. Whereas Caleb Pussey & Francis Worley & Mary his wife by deed dated 3 Dec 1700 granted to John Pennell the father a tract containing 105 acres. Whereas John Simcock, John

Bristow & Randle Vernon executors of the will of Thomas Brassey by deed dated 10 Mar 1691 granted to Thomas England 100 acres, who by his deed dated 9 June 1694 granted the 100 acres to John Pennell the father. Whereas William Penn, Esq., dec., by deed dated 26 July 1684 granted to William Obourn (since dec.) a tract in Concord containing 200 acres. Whereas Henry Obourn son & heir of William Obourn by deed dated 7 Dec 1700 granted to John Pennell the 200 acres. Now John Pennell, the father & Mary his wife for £200 granted to John Pennell, the son a tract in Aston bounded by the line of Concord township, land late of Thomas Rowlan, land of James Bennett & land late of John Chamberlain containing 229 acres being part of the 3 tracts, also a tract in Concord bounded by Chester Creek & land formerly of John Palmer containing 6 acres. Signed John Pennell & Mary Pennell. Delivered in the presence of Joseph Pyle & Sarah Pyle. Recorded 20 Jan 1741. (F6:181).

Lease & Release. On 28 & 29 Jan 1741 Daniel Carrell of Concord, yeoman, & Margery his wife, late Margery Gore, widow to William Trimble of Concord, miller. Whereas William Penn, Esq., dec., by deed dated 15 July 1684 granted to Nathaniel Park a tract in Concord containing 200 acres, & the said Nathaniel Park (as it is said) granted 150 acres of the 200 acres to William Clayton who granted said land to William Rowe. William Rowe granted said land to Thomas Moore & William Vestall, who granted said land to Morgan Jones, who granted said land to Joseph Nicklin, who by deed dated 26 July 1715 granted to Daniel Evans, who by deed dated 20 Oct 1720 granted said land to Nathaniel Newlin. Nathaniel Newlin by deed dated 26 Jan 1724 granted to Joshua Pennel, who with his wife Hannah by deed dated 14 & 15 Aug 1733 granted the 73 acres to Margery Gore. Whereas Margery Gore having married Daniel Carrell. Daniel Carrell & Margery his wife for £140 granted to William Trimble a tract in Concord bounded by land of Thomas Wilcox, John Chamberlain, William Farr & Chester Creek containing 73 acres. Signed Daniel Carrell & Margery Carrell. Delivered in the presence of John Anderson & Joseph Parker. Recorded 2 Feb 1741. (F6:187).

Lease & Release. On 26 & 27 Jan 1741/2 Thomas Salkeld of Chester, cordwainer, & the sons of John Salkeld, late of Chester, maulster, dec., to William Turner of Chester, merchant. Whereas John Salkeld made his will dated 25 Feb 1733/4 & amongst other things bequeathed to his son Thomas the house & lot where his son-in-law Anthony Shaw dwells in

Chester bounded by Bridge Street, the road leading from Chester to New Castle, Essex Street or Concord Road & with other lots lately of John Salkeld. Thomas Salkeld for £122 granted to William Turner the said house & lot in Chester. Signed Thomas Salkeld. Delivered in the presence of Phillip Taylor & William Lowery. Recorded 5 Feb 1741/2. (F6:190).

Deed. On 25 Mar 1709 Frances Garratt of Bethel, widow to Thomas Gale of Chester, husbandman. Whereas Frances Garratt by virtue of a deed made to her father John Hurlbat, dec., made by William Fleming dated 13 June 1699 & by virtue of Letters of Administration granted to her husband, John Garratt, dec., & to Frances Garratt as co-admin., Frances Garratt for valuable consideration granted to Thomas Gale a tract in Bethel bounded by Naamans Creek, land of Henry Reynolds, & William Flemings containing 100 acres. Signed Frances Garratt. Delivered in the presence of John Powell, Joseph Powell & Jacob Chandler. Recorded 12 Feb 1741/2. (F6:194).

Memorandum. This is written on the back of the prior deed. On 30 May 1711 Thomas Gale for £41 granted to Mordecai Howell the described tract. Signed Mordecai Howell. Delivered in the presence of T. Clarke & George Chandler. Recorded 1741/2. (F6:195).

Mortgage. On 31 Oct 17 41 David Kennedy of Chester County to James Steel, Richard Peters & Lynford Lardner all of the City of Philadelphia, gentlemen. David Kennedy for £91 due to Thomas Penn, John Penn & Richard Penn, Esq., & 5 shillings paid to him by James Steel, Richard Peters & Lynford Lardner granted to James Steel, Richard Peters & Lynford Lardner a tract in Chester County bounded by land of John Tagg's Manor containing 475 acres. David Kennedy to pay James Steel, Richard Peters & Lynford Lardner for the use of Thomas Penn, John Penn & Richard Penn the sum of £91 plus interest to be paid in yearly payments & to be paid in full 31 Oct 1748. Signed David Kennedy. Delivered in the presence of Edward Shippen & John Callahan. Recorded 17 Feb 1741/2. (F6:195).

Mortgage. On 13 Feb 1741 Robert Mckee of Chester County to James Steel, Richard Peters & Lynford Lardner all of the City of Philadelphia, gentlemen. Robert McKee for £63 due to Thomas Penn, John Penn & Richard Penn, Esq., & 5 shillings paid to him by James Steel, Richard

Peters & Lynford Lardner granted to James Steel, Richard Peters & Lynford Lardner a tract in Chester County bounded by land of John McClenagon, Samuel Steel & James Logan containing 231 acres. Robert McKee to pay James Steel, Richard Peters & Lynford Lardner for the use of Thomas Penn, John Penn & Richard Penn the sum of £63 plus interest to be paid in yearly payments & to be paid in full on or before 13 Feb 1748. Signed Robert McKee. Delivered in the presence of William Peters & John Callahan. Recorded 11 Mar 1741. (F6:197).

Commission. On 1 Oct 1741 James Steel, Receiver General of the province appoint John Wharton of Chester County, to be collector & receiver of debts & quit rents. Signed James Steel. (F6:200).

Deed. On 20 June 1723 David Morton of Calcoon Hook in Darby, yeoman, & Ellin his wife to Andrew Morton, Sr., of Ridley, yeoman. David Morton & Ellin his wife for £5 granted to Andrew Morton a lot in Darby on a island commonly called Hay Island bounded by land of John Orchard, Lawrence Morton, an island of Isreal Taylor commonly called Great Island, Millkill, a creek known as Thoroughfare containing 18 1/2 acres being part of a tract of land granted to Isreal Helms, Hendrich Jacobs & Oele Hicock by patent from Richard Nichols, Esq., Governor of New York by deed dated 18 June 1668 which tract contains about one English mile and is situated on the west side of the River Delaware, which said tract was assigned over by Isreal Helms with the consent of Hendrich Jacobs & Oele Hicock to Peter Peterson, who sold said tract to Mathew Marcellus, who sold the tract to David Morton. Signed David Morton & Ellin Morton. Delivered in the presence of John Bethel, John Smith, James Doose, Conrad Needermardt & Mathias Morton. Recorded 22 Apr 1742. (F6:201).

Mortgage. On 20 Jan 1741 Caleb Evans of Radnor, yeoman, & Catherine his wife to Hugh Jones of Merion in the County of Philadelphia, yeoman. Whereas Caleb Evans & Catherine his wife stand bound to Hugh Jones for £100, conditioned for the payment of £50, Caleb Evans & Catherine his wife to better secure said debt grants to Hugh Jones a tract in Radnor bounded by land of Evan Evans & land late of John Meredith containing 60 acres. Caleb Evans & Catherine his wife to pay yearly payments to be paid in full on or before 20 Jan 1762. Signed Caleb Evans & Catherine Evans. Delivered in the presence of John Morgan, John Jerman & John Peter. Recorded 1 May 1742. (F6:205).

Mortgage. On 27 Feb 1741/2 Lewis Davis, Jr., of Haverford, weaver, to Jacob Jones of Merion in the County of Philadelphia, weaver. Lewis Davis for £50 granted to Jacob Jones a tract in Haverford bounded by Samuel Lewis, Lewis Davis, Sr., & Joseph Hayes containing 50 acres. Lewis Davis to pay £50 plus interest in payments on or before 27 Aug 1744. Signed Lewis Davis. Delivered in the presence of Benjamin Hayes & Jonathon Jones, Jr. Recorded 25 May 1742. (F6:205).

Deed. On 4 Apr 1737 James Hayward of Concord, yeoman, to John Palmer, Abraham Barnett & Zachary Butcher all of Chester County & Mary Hayward, wife of James Hayward. James Hayward (being now blind & impotent) as well as for & in consideration of the great care & trouble undertaken by Mary his well beloved wife to her great support & comfort as a compensation for her care grants to John Palmer, Abraham Barnett & Zachary Butcher all the tenement & tract of land lying in Concord bounded by land of Peter Hatton, Thomas Marshall, John Palmer & by land commonly called Newlin's Land containing 100 acres being where James Hayward now dwells to be held in trust .... Recorded 14 July 1742. (F6:207).

Mortgage. On 27 Mar 1741 George Aston of Whiteland, yeoman, & Esther his wife late called Esther Thomas, spinster, the only surviving daughter of Owen Thomas, late of Merion in the County of Philadelphia, merchant, dec., by Ann his wife, dec., to William Plumstead of the City of Philadelphia, merchant. Whereas Esther at her marriage with George Aston was seized in a tract of land & that George Aston had issue by Esther, now living will be entitled to said premises for his life as tenant, in case he shall happen to survive his wife. Now George Aston & Esther his wife for £211.2.8 granted to William Plumstead a tract in Whiteland bounded by land of William Burge & Company, Thomas Richard, Isaac Molyn, James David, David Evans, Owen Owen & Richard Owen containing 250 acres. George Aston & Esther his wife to pay one moiety of the £211.2.8 plus interest to William Plumstead on or before 17 Sep 1741 & to pay the other moiety on of before 17 Mar 1742. Signed George Aston & Esther Aston. Delivered in the presence of William Harrison & William Peters. Recorded 20 Aug 1742. (F6:210).

Deed. On John Palmer, Abraham Barnett & Zachary Butcher all of Chester County for a competent sum of money paid to us by Mary Hayward, widow & relict of James Hayward of Concord, lately dec., hereby grants & surrender to Mary Hayward all right they have in the tenement in Concord bounded by land of Peter Hatton, Thomas Marshall, John Palmer & by land commonly called Newlin's Land now or late in the occupation of Abraham Barnett containing 100 acres. By virtue of a deed in trust to us for the use of the said Mary Hayward, made between the dec. James Hayward, us John Palmer, Abraham Barnett & Zachary Butcher & Mary Hayward on 4 Apr 1737 recorded Book E, Vol 6, Page 207, it being 2 tracts of land formerly transferred to James Hayward in his lifetime by 2 deeds, one dated 20 Jan 1706 executed by Richard Farr for 50 acres & the other dated 30 Jan 1706 executed by Morgan Jones for 50 acres. Now John Palmer, Abraham Barnett & Zachary Butcher release all right to said tract to Mary Barnett (I think this should say Mary Hayward but this is what is written in the deed) & May Hayward should have quiet & peaceful possession of said tract. Signed John Palmer, Abraham Barnett & Zachary Butcher. Delivered in the presence of John Taylor & Michael Higgin. Recorded 4 Sep 1742. (F6:213).

Lease & Release. On 29 & 30 June 1741 William Clayton of Upper Chichester, yeoman, & Mary his wife to George Chapman of Lower Chichester, weaver. Whereas William Clayton, dec., late father of William Clayton by deed dated 3 May 1709 granted to William Clayton a tract of woodland in Chichester containing 5 1/2 acres, recorded in Chester, Book C, Vol 3, Page 91, on 10 July 1709. Whereas Thomas Howell & Rachell his wife by deed dated 15 July 1733 granted to William Clayton a tract in Chichester being of 2 1/4 acres of woodland. Now William Clayton & Mary his wife for £40 grants to George Chapman all the tract in Lower Chichester bounded by the King's Road leading from Chichester to Concord, Chichester Road, a lots late of Walter Martin & land of Thomas Clayton containing 3+ acres being part of both tracts. Signed William Clayton & Mary Clayton. Delivered in the presence of Allen Robinett, & Samson Archer. Recorded 27 Sep 1742. (F6:215).

Lease & Release. On 27 & 28 July 1739 Caleb Cowpland of Chester, gentleman, & Sarah his wife to John Lea of Chester, waterman. Whereas David Lloyd, late of Chester, gentleman, by deed dated 29 Nov 1703 granted to George Simpson of Chester, tailor, a lot in Chester paying David Lloyd the rent of 2 shillings yearly. Whereas George Simpson & Ruth his wife by deed dated 20 Dec 1711 granted the lot to William Tidmarsh, also paying 2 shillings yearly rent, recorded in Chester, Book A, Page 215. William Tidmarsh & Hannah his wife bu deed dated 29 May

1721 granted said lot to Caleb Cowpland also paying the said yearly rent 2 shillings to David Lloyd & his heirs. Now Caleb Cowpland & Sarah his wife for £140 granted to John Lea the lot in Chester bounded by lots late of Robert Barber, land late of David Lloyd, the street fronting Chester Creek & a lot late of William Pickle but now of John Baldwin being 40' x 58'. Signed Caleb Cowpland & Sarah Cowpland. Delivered in the presence of Eleanor Phillips & Joseph Parker. Recorded 29 July 1742. (F6:218).

Lease & Release. On 7 & 8 Aug 1739 Grace Lloyd of Chester, widow & executrix of the will of David Lloyd, late of Chester, gentleman, dec., to John Lea of Chester, waterman. Whereas William Penn, Esq., dec., by deed dated 24 Oct 1701 granted to David Lloyd 2 tracts of land containing 7 acres, in Chester. David Lloyd made his will dated 29 Mar 1724 & amongst other things devised to his wife, Grace Lloyd all the residue of his estate, real & personal & made Grace his executrix & soon after died. Now Grace Lloyd for £10 granted to John Lea all the land of water lot in Chester opposite the lot where John Lea now dwells lying of the west side of the street fronting Chester Creek being 40' x running to the low water mark of the creek bounded by the said street, land of John Baldwin, Chester Creek & other land of Grace Lloyd being part of the mentioned original deed & commonly called the Green. Signed Grace Lloyd. Delivered in the presence of Nathan Worley & Joseph Parker. Recorded 12 Oct 1742. (F6:221).

Deed. On 19 Jan 1742 Edward Russell of Chester, waterman & Dinah his wife to John Lea of Chester, waterman. Whereas Samuel Bell & Mary his wife by deed dated 26 & 27 June 1741 granted to Edward Russell all that tract of 5 acres on the west side of Chester Creek, in Chester with the yearly rent of 2 shillings paid to the heirs of John Wade, lately dec. Now Edward Russell & Dinah his wife for £12 granted to John Lea the tract in Chester bounded by Concord Road, other land of Russell, Chester Creek & land of John Wharton containing 2 1/2 acres with the yearly rent of 1 shilling payable to the heirs of the late John Wade, dec. Signed Edward Russell & Dinah Russell. Delivered in the presence of Aubrey Bevan, William Askill & Caleb Cowpland. Recorded 14 Oct 1742. (F6:224).

Mortgage. On 30 Aug 1742 Richard Treville of Newlin in the County of Chester, yeoman, to Joseph Paker of Chester, yeoman. Richard Treville

for £106 granted to Joseph Parker a tract in Newlin bounded by land of
Thomas Kicklins, land late of Richard Evenson but now of Ezekiel &
James Harlan, land of Nathaniel Newlin containing 313 acres. Richard
Treville to pay Joseph Parker £106 to Joseph Parker on or before 30 Aug
1743. Signed Richard Treville. Delivered in the presence of Nathan
Worley, James Treville & David Ranken. Recorded 7 Oct 1742. (F6:226).

Lease & Release. On 13 Mar 1722 Tobias Collet of London, in Old
England, haberdasher, Daniel Quare of London, watchmaker & Henry
Gouldney of London, linen draper to Richard Whitting of Chester
County, yeoman. Whereas there is a tract of land lying on a branch of
White Clay Creek in the County of Chester bounded by land of John
Devonald, Thomas Morris & Thomas Black containing 200 acres part of
17,218 acres that the Commissioners of William Penn by deed dated 25
June 1718 granted to Tobias Collet, Daniel Quare, Henry Gouldney &
the heirs of Michael Russel of London, merchant, recorded in
Philadelphia, Book A, Vol 5, Page 306. Now Tobias Collet, Daniel Quare
& Henry Gouldney for £41 grants to Richard Whitting the tract
described containing 200 acres. Signed Tobias Collet, Daniel Quare &
Henry Gouldney. Delivered in the presence of Sarah Dimsdale, John
Estaugh & Elizabeth Estaugh. Recorded 23 Nov 1742. (F6:229).

Mortgage. On 27 July 1742 David Evans of Radnor, inn holder to Samuel
Harry & John Thomas of Radnor, yeomen. Whereas David Evans was
seized in a tract of land in Radnor commonly called & known as the Sign
of the Plow, bounded by land of John Jerman & land of John Davis
containing 21 acres, which was all the tenement & land confirmed to
David Evans by deed dated 23 & 26 Mar 1733/4 from Mary Evans, widow
of David Evans, dec., Caleb Evans, son & heir of David Evans, dec., &
Catherine his wife, & Joshua Evans & Ann his wife. Now David Evans
for £38 granted to Samuel Harry & John Thomas the tract of 21 acres.
David Evans & Mary his wife shall pay Samuel Harry & John Thomas
the £38 plus interest on or before 29 July 1744. Signed David Evans &
Mary Evans. Delivered in the presence of Richard Thomas, John Moore
& John Bowen. Recorded 25 Nov 1742. (F6:232).

Release. On 20 May 1741 Thomas Howell of Chichester, yeoman, &
Rachel his wife to John Marshall of Chichester, saddler. Whereas
Edmund Andres, Esq., Governor of New York by deed dated 28 Mar
1676 granted to Charles Johnson, Olle Rawson, Hans Olleson, Olle

Nulson, Hans Hopman & John Hendrichson a tract situated on the Delaware River at a place now called Chichester containing 1,000 acres. Whereas Hans Olleson by deed dated 12 Mar 1678 granted 1/6 part of the 1,000 acres to William Clayton. Whereas William Clayton died intestate, the same 1/6 part descended to his son William Clayton. William Clayton by deed dated 8 Sep 1693 granted to Timothy Atkinson a lot & 2 acres & a quarter of woodland lying in Chichester being part of the 1/6 part of the 1,000 acres. Whereas Timothy Atkinson by deed dated 5 Oct 1706 granted the said lot, 2 acres & the quarter of woodland to John Howell, who by deed dated 30 July 1707 granted said lot, 2 acres & quarter woodland to Mordecai Howell, who by deed dated 1 Dec 1733 granted the lot, 2 acres & woodland to his son Thomas Howell. Whereas William Clayton by deed dated 8 Dec 1699 granted to Thomas Chaldrey a lot & 2 acres of woodland. Thomas Chaldrey sold said lot & 2 acres to Humphrey Johnson, who then by deed dated 3 Mar 1704 granted the lot & 2 acres to Mordecai Howell. Mordecai Howell by deed dated 19 Feb 1735 granted the lot & 2 acres to his son Thomas Howell. Now Thomas Howell & Rachel his wife for £40 grants to John Marshall 2 parcels of land in Chichester one bounded by Chichester Road, land of William Clayton & the other parcel containing 1+ acres being part of 2 acres & a quarter of land which Mordecai Howell granted to Thomas Howell, the other parcel of land bounded by Chichester Road & the other described parcel containing 2 acres, being the 2 acres that Mordecai Howell granted to Thomas Howell. Signed Thomas Howell & Rachel Howell. Delivered in the presence of John Kerlin & Thomas Giffing. Recorded 20 Dec 1742. (F6:234).

Lease & Release. On 25 & 26 Aug 1741 Benjamin Maddock of Marple, cordwainer, & Elizabeth his wife to John Fyance of the City of Philadelphia, merchant. Whereas Edward Daws by deed dated 29 Dec 1708 granted to Richard Maris a tract in Marple containing 100 acres. Whereas Richard Maris & Elizabeth his wife by deed dated 24 & 25 Aug 1741 granted to Benjamin Maddock a parcel of land containing 2 acres being part of the 100 acres. Now Benjamin Maddock & Elizabeth his wife for £130 granted to John Fyance a tract in Marple bounded by the meeting house land in Springfield, the road leading through Marple & land of Richard Maris containing 2 acres. Signed Benjamin Maddock & Elizabeth Maddock. Delivered in the presence of Abraham Lincoln & Joshua Thomson. Recorded 29 Dec 1742. (F6:237).

Power of Attorney. On 27 Dec 1742 John Fyance of Marple appoint his trusty & well beloved friends Robert Pearson of Marple, yeoman, & James Hutchison of Marple, merchant, his true & lawful attorneys. Signed John Fyance. Delivered in the presence of Isaac Gleaves, William Fyance, goldsmith, & Edward Folwell. Recorded 29 Dec 1742. (F6:241).

Lease & Release. On 15 & 16 Apr 1737 Silvester Gouldney, now or late of Chippenham in the County of Wilkes in Old England, relict of Adam Gouldney, late of Chippenham, gentleman, dec., Adam Gouldney & Henry Gouldney both of Chippenham, gentlemen, sons of Adam Gouldney, dec., & Mary Gouldney, Jane Gouldney, Sarah Gouldney & Anna Gouldney, daughters of Adam Gouldney, dec., to Jane Fenn of the County of Chester, in Pennsylvania, seamstress. Whereas William Penn, Esq., in his lifetime by deed dated 3 & 4 Apr 1695 granted to Henry Gouldney, late of London, linendraper a tract of 1,500 acres. Whereas William Penn afterwards by his deed dated 12 Apr 1695 release all quit rents unto Henry Gouldney, the elder. Whereas Henry Gouldney, the elder made his will dated 20 Aug 1724 & amongst other things devised the residue of the 1,500 acres to Adam Gouldney, Sr. Adam Gouldney, Sr., by 3 warrants dated 22 Mar 1733/4 was laid out & surveyed the 1,500 acres in 3 tracts as follows, all that tract on a branch of Tulpchawkin Creek, in the County of Lancaster bounded by land of Christopher Shimp, Hans Seller & George Grast containing 900 acres, also another tract lying on a branch of Conestogoe Creek in the County of Lancaster containing 200 acres & also a tract on a branch of Brandywine Creek, in Caln bounded by land of William Harris, John Adams, William Tregoes, Jeremiah Persels & Henry Betterton containing 400 acres. Whereas Adam Gouldney, Sr., made his will dated 24 July 1728 but did not dispose of said lands but in respect died intestate & by the laws of Pennsylvania the land descended to Silvester, his widow, Adam Gouldney & Henry Gouldney, his sons, Mary, Jane, Sarah & Anna Gouldney his daughters. Now Silvester, his widow, Adam Gouldney & Henry Gouldney, his sons, Mary, Jane, Sarah & Anna Gouldney his daughters for £300 granted to Jane Fenn all 3 tracts of land containing 1,500 acres. Signed Silvester Gouldney, Henry Gouldney & Mary Gouldney in the presence of R. Holland & Thomas Eastland. Signed Adam Gouldney & Jane Gouldney in the presence of John Richmond & Rebecca Minshall. Recorded 20 Jan 1742/3. (F6:242).

Mortgage. On 1 Oct 1742 Thomas Dennis of Radnor, tailor, & Mary his wife to Peter Jones of Merion in the County of Philadelphia, yeoman.

Whereas Thomas Dennis & Mary his wife stand bound to Edward Jones for the sum of £200 conditioned for the payment of £100, & to better secure the said debt granted to Peter Jones a tract in Radnor bounded by land of John Jerman, John Morgan, Samuel Harry & Joshua Evans containing 56 acres. Thomas Dennis & Mary his wife to make yearly payments to be paid in full on or before 1 Oct 1747. Signed Thomas Dennis & Mary Dennis. Delivered in the presence of Joseph Bonsall, Evan Evans & Lewis Reece. Recorded 15 Feb 1742/3. (F6:249).

Deed. On 13 Jan 1742 James Gibbons of West Town, yeoman, & Jane his wife to Arthur Graham of Nantmel, husbandman. Whereas James Gibbons for £164.6 granted to Arthur Graham a tract in Nantmel bounded by land of Robert Mackey, land of Robert Guttrie. Thomas Green & Richard Parker containing 431 acres. Signed James Gibbons in the presence of William Patew & John Callahan. Signed Jane Gibbons in the presence of Michael Lightfoot & Thomas Parke. Recorded 22 Feb 1742/3. (F6:251).

Mortgage. On 3 Nov 1742 Everard Ellis of Darby, yeoman, & Bridget his wife to Abraham Lewis of Darby, yeoman, & Mary his wife. Everard Ellis & Bridget his wife for £70 granted to Abraham Lewis & Mary his wife a tract in Darby bounded by the Mill Creek commonly called Cobs Creek, land of Everard Ellis, John Griffiths (formerly John Blunstons) & land of Benjamin Bonsall & Moses Hibberd (formerly belonging to John Blunston & Samuel Bradshaw) containing 50 acres. Everard Ellis & Bridget his wife to pay £82.11.10 to Abraham Lewis & Mary his wife in payments to be paid in full on or before 3 Mar 1746. Signed Everard Ellis & Bridget Ellis. Delivered in the presence of Jonathon Paschall & Isaac Pearson. Recorded 29 Mar 1743. (F6:253).

Deed. On 1 May 1742 Grace Lloyd of Chester, widow of David Lloyd, late of Chester, gentleman, dec., to Joseph Hoskins of Chester, cordwainer, & Jane his wife. Whereas Francis Lovelace, Esq., Governor General under the late Duke of York & Albany by deed dated 9 Apr 1669 granted to Neels Lansa alias Friend a tract situated in Chester on the Delaware River (late in the tenure of David Lloyd) containing 150 acres but on resurvey found to contain 183 acres bounded on the east by land formerly of Jurian Reens, recorded in the records of Upland County. Neels Lansa made his will dated 20 Dec 1686 & gave his wife authority to dispose of said lands (will recorded in Philadelphia, Book A, Page 145), &

soon after died. Whereas Ann Friend, widow of Neels Lansa, alias Friend, Andrew Friend, son & heir of Neels & Ann, & Johannes Friend their second son by deed dated 27 May 1689 granted said lands to David Lloyd. Whereas Ann Friend with Gabriel Friend & Lawrence Friend, the younger sons of Newls Lansa, her husband, dec., by deed dated 30 July 1723 confirmed unto David Lloyd 183 acres. David Lloyd by deed dated 8 Sep 1693 granted to Joseph Rockards, who by deed dated 16 Jan 1702 granted to John Bristow, who by his deed dated 29 Dec 1705 granted to Jasper Yeats & Jasper Yeates by deed dated 3 Apr 1708 granted to David Lloyd 3 acres. Whereas David Lloyd sold 2 acres to Roger Jackson, who by deed dated 7 July 1700 reconveyed to David Lloyd. Whereas Jonas Sandelands, late of Chester, dec., by deed of exchange dated 29 Dec 1714 granted to David Lloyd 3 pieces of land, a small piece of land lying between the eastern most Street in the town of Chester & David Lloyd's plantation, another piece lying between the road that leads from Philadelphia to Chester & New Castle & the plantation & another piece of land lying between the road that leads to Edgmont & the western side of the plantation containing in all about 20 acres. Whereas Jonas Sandelands & Mary his wife by deed dated 16 Dec 1720 granted to David Lloyd a tract in Chester bounded by the road from Chester to Philadelphia, David Lloyd's plantation, land of Ruth Hoskins, Springfield Road & the King's Road containing 27 acres. Whereas David Lloyd became seized of the several tracts of land he erected a mansion house. David Lloyd made his will dated 24 Mar 1724 & devised all his estate to his wife Grace Lloyd & soon after died. Now Grace Lloyd for £1,100 granted to Joseph Hoskins & Jane his wife all the plantation & mansion house containing 222 acres bounded by the road leading to Providence, the road leading to Philadelphia & the River Delaware, Back Street, Welch Street, land of Joseph Parker, other land of Grace Lloyd & land of James Mather. Reserving out of said plantation about 2 acres situated between the orchards, & the room in the southwest corner of the mansion called the dining room, the room in the northeast corner of the house called the parlor with the closet & milk house joining, the chamber over the dining room, the chamber over the parlor, half of the garret, the front part of the cellar, the old kitchen & the chamber over it, the use of the pump cider mill & cider press for making her own cider & part of the garden for the term of her natural life, also the copper now fixed in the furnace as her own property & to be removed at her pleasure. Signed Grace Lloyd. Delivered in the presence of John Bezar, Jacob Howell & Joseph Parker. Recorded 5 Apr 1743. (F6:256).

Mortgage. On 3 May 1742 Joseph Hoskins of Chester, cordwainer, & Jane his wife to Grace Lloyd, the widow of David Lloyd, late of Chester, dec., Joseph Hoskins & Jane his wife stand bound to Grace Lloyd for £1,000 & to pay £500. Joseph Hoskins & Jane his wife to better secure said debt have granted to Grace Lloyd a tract in Chester bounded by the road leading to Providence, the road leading to Philadelphia & the River Delaware, Back Street, Welch Street, land of Joseph Parker, other land of Grace Lloyd & land of James Mather containing 222 acres. Joseph Hoskins & Jane his wife to pay in annual payments in the space of 4 years. Signed Joseph Hoskins & Jane Hoskins. Delivered in the presence of John Bezar, Jacob Howell & Joseph Parker. Recorded 8 Apr 1743. (F6:262).

Mortgage. On 24 Feb 1742/3 Abraham Musgrove of Haverford, weaver, to William Allen of the City of Philadelphia, merchant. Abraham Musgrove for £50 granted to William Allen a tract in Haverford bounded by Darby Creek, land of David Lewis & John Reece containing 250 acres. Abraham Musgrove to make annual payments to William Allen & to be paid in full on or before 24 Feb 1746/7. Signed Abraham Musgrove. Delivered in the presence of Joseph Brientnall & James Bingham. Recorded 11 Apr 1743. (F6:265).

Lease & Release. On 17 & 18 Feb 1742/3 Hannah Parry of Haverford, widow, Jacob Hall of the County of Philadelphia, yeoman, John Parry of Trydrustorn in the County of Chester, yeoman, & William Lewis of Haverford, yeoman, executors of the will of John Parry, late of Haverford, dec., to George Martin of Charlestown in the County of Chester, yeoman. Whereas William Penn by release dated 23 Oct 1681 granted to William Lowther & Margaret Lowther the full 5,000 acres, recorded in Philadelphia, Book C, Vol 2, Page 109. Whereas William Lowther died, John Nicol & Margaret his wife, the only daughter & heir of Margaret who survived William Lowther, by deed dated 24 Sep 1731 granted the 5,000 acres to Joseph Stamvix. Joseph Stamvis by deed dated 18 Jan 1731 granted the 5,000 acres to John Simpson. Whereas William Penn by deed dated 23 Oct 1681 granted to John Lowther & Anne Sharlot Lowther 5,000 acres. Whereas Ann Sharlot Lowther died an infant without issue, John Lowther by deed dated 13 Aug 1731 granted the 5,000 acres to Joseph Turner. By virtue of a warrant a tract was laid out to John Simpson for the quantity of 4,920 acres in right of the original purchase by William & Margaret Lowther & to include within the same 1/2 of the tract of land called Manor of Bilton. By same warrant another tract was laid out to Joseph Turner for 4,920 acres in right of the original purchase of John & Anne Sharlot Lowther & to include into the same 1/2 of the tract called Manor of Bilton. Whereas there was a resurvey & found to be as follows bounded by Schuylkill River, Valley Creek, the Manor of Mount Joy, the Welch Tract, land formerly of Charles Pickrin, Pickerin Creek & land of William Moore containing 2,850 acres. Whereas John Simpson by deed dated 9 Mar 1737 granted to William Allen of Philadelphia, Esq., the one full equal undivided moiety or 1/2 part of all the land described tract called Manor of Bilton containing 2,850 acres. Whereas Joseph Turner by deed dated 23 Feb 1736/7 granted to William Allen all the last mentioned 5,000 acres including the other moiety of the Manor of Bilton. Whereas William Allen & Margaret his wife by deed dated 25 July 39 granted to John Parry, Esq., dec., all the tract described called the Manor of Bilton containing 2,850 acres. Whereas John Parry having sold & conveyed several tract or parcels of land part of the Manor of Bilton, made his will dated 14 July 1739 & amongst other things, devised to his wife Hannah Parry & to my son-in-law Jacob Hall & kinsman John Parry & friend William Lewis all the remainder of theat tract of land situated in Charlestown called by the name Manor of Bilton upon condition that the persons mentioned or the major part of them will sell & convey said land & the money to be used to pay just debts & legacies, and soon after died. Now Hannah Parry, Jacob Hall, John Parry & William Lewis at direction of the will & for the sum of £146 granted to George Martin all that tract situated in Charlestown bounded by the river Schuykill, other land of John Parry, dec., land late of William Griffith, & land of David Mathew containing 140 acres. Signed Hannah Parry, Jacob Hall, John Parry & William Lewis. Delivered in the presence of Andrew Buchanan, Samuel Kibby & John Martin. Recorded 26 Apr 1743. (F6:267).

Letter of Attorney. On 25 Sep 1742 the following was produced before Clement Plumstead, the Mayor of the City of Philadelphia. On 8 July 1742 before Samuel Martyn, Notary & Tabellion Public dwelling in London, Richard Pike of London, merchant, appoint Michael Lightfoot of Chester County his true & lawful attorney. Signed Richard Pike. Delivered in the presence of Edmund Peckover & John Haslam. Recorded 29 Apr 1743. (F6:273).

Deed. On 24 Mar 1743 Elizabeth McNeile of Kennett, widow & admin. of the goods & chattels of Archibald McNeile her late husband, dec., to William Webb of Kennett, gentleman. Whereas the Orphans Court held at the house of Archibald Kennett on 11 June 1737 before Henry Hayes, Joseph Brinton & Abraham Emmit, Esqs., justices present. Whereas Elizabeth McNeile who was the widow & admin. of the goods & chattels of Richard Clayton of Kennett, yeoman, her late husband has appeared in the court that the said Richard died intestate & Letters of Administration were granted to Elizabeth on 12 Mar 1735/6. Richard Clayton at the time of his death amongst other things was possessed of a tenement & 5 acres lying in Kennett bounded by land of Joshua Pierce, William Webb & Betty Caldwell containing 5 acres & left a wife & 1 child to survive him. Whereas Archibald McNeile & Elizabeth his wife hath exhibited an account of debts yet due by the said dec. more than the personal estate will extend to pay. Elizabeth McNeile is allowed to sell said 5 acres. Archibald McNeile being since dec., whereby Letters of Administration were granted to Elizabeth. Now Elizabeth McNeile for £155 granted to William Webb the tenement & 5 acres described before. Signed Elizabeth McNeile. Delivered in the presence of Thomas Harlan, William Hamilton, Jr., David Powell & Joseph Parker. Recorded 16 May 1743. (F6:275).

Lease & Release. On 22 & 23 Apr 1743 William Webb of Kennett, gentleman, & Rebecca his wife to Elizabeth McNeile of Kennett, widow. Whereas Elizabeth McNeile by deed dated 24 Mar last past granted to William Webb all that tenement & 5 acres. Now William Webb & Rebecca his wife for £155 granted to Elizabeth NcNeile a tenement & tract of land in Kennett bounded by land of Joshua Pierce, land of William Webb & land of Betty Caldwell containing 5 acres. Signed William Webb & Rebecca Webb. Delivered in the presence of Thomas Harlan, William Hamilton, Jr., & Thomas Worrall. Recorded 20 May 1743. (F6:279).

Deed. On 28 Aug 1705 Ralph Lewis of Darby, yeoman, to Evan Lewis the 3rd son of Ralph Lewis. Ralph Lewis for love & affection for his son granted to Evan Lewis a tract lying in Edgmont bounded by land of Francis Cooke & Thomas Brassey containing 300 acres being the tract Hester Freeland, John Rhodes & Hannah his wife granted to Ralph Lewis by deed dated 5 June 1701, recorded in Chester, Book A, Vol 1, Page 177. Signed Ralph Lewis. Delivered in the presence of David Lewis & David Hughs. Note: Ralph Lewis do hereby authorize & appoint William Davies of Radnor, gentleman, my true & lawful attorney to deliver possession of said land to Evan Lewis. Dated 6 May 1712. Signed Ralph Lewis. Delivered in the presence of Gabriel Davies & Mirick

Davies. Peaceable possession of said land was given to Evan Lewis. Delivered in the presence of Daniel Williamson, William Iddings, Thomas Evans, Richard Iddings & Thomas Folknor. Recorded 8 June 1743. (F6:282).

Release. On 5 Apr 1720 Evan Lewis of the western part of Brandywine in the County of Chester, yeoman, & Ann his wife to Samuel Lewis of Edgmont, yeoman. Whereas the commissioners of the late William Penn by deed dated 9 Dec 1686 granted to Thomas Duckett a tract in Edgmont containing 300 acres & whereas Thomas Duckett by deed dated 26 Feb 1686 granted to Barnabas Wilcox the 300 acres. Whereas Barnabas Wilcox died intestate, division of said land was made to his surviving children & by virtue of said division Esther Freeland (one of the daughters of Barnabas Wilcox) & John Rhodes & Hannah his wife (another of the daughters of Barnabas) became lawfully seized in said 300 acres. Whereas Joseph Wilcox, ropemaker,(only surviving son of Barnabas & brother to Esther & Hannah) released to Esther, John & Hannah all right & interest in said 300 acres, recorded in Chester, Book A, Vol 1, Page 1, on 4 June 1688. Whereas Ester Freeland, John Rhodes & Hannah his wife by deed dated 5 June 1701 granted to Ralph Lewis (the father) the 300 acres, recorded in Chester, Book A, Vol 1, Page 177. Whereas Ralph Lewis by deed dated 28 Aug 1705 granted the 300 acres to Evan Lewis. Now Evan Lewis & Ann his wife for £80 granted to Samuel Lewis a tract bounded by land of Edward Thompson, & Nathan Evans containing 80 acres part of the 300 acres. Signed Evan Lewis & Ann Lewis. Delivered in the presence of Thomas Dawson & James Swafer. Recorded. 9 June 1743. (F6:285).

Release. On 24 May 1720 Samuel Lewis of Edgmont, yeoman, & Phebe his wife to Joseph Pratt of Middletown, cordwainer. Whereas the commissioners of the late William Penn by deed dated 9 Dec 1686 granted to Thomas Duckett a tract in Edgmont containing 300 acres & whereas Thomas Duckett by deed dated 26 Feb 1686 granted to Barnabas Wilcox the 300 acres. Whereas Barnabas Wilcox died intestate, division of said land was made to his surviving children & by virtue of said division Esther Freeland (one of the daughters of Barnabas Wilcox) & John Rhodes & Hannah his wife (another of the daughters of Barnabas) became lawfully seized in said 300 acres. Whereas Joseph Wilcox, ropemaker,(only surviving son of Barnabas & brother to Esther & Hannah) released to Esther, John & Hannah all right & interest in said 300 acres, recorded in Chester, Book A, Vol 1, Page 1, on 4 June

1688. Whereas Ester Freeland, John Rhodes & Hannah his wife by deed dated 5 June 1701 granted to Ralph Lewis (the father) the 300 acres, recorded in Chester, Book A, Vol 1, Page 177. Whereas Ralph Lewis by deed dated 28 Aug 1705 granted the 300 acres to Evan Lewis. Evan Lewis by deed dated 5 Apr 1720 granted to Samuel Lewis 80 acres, being part of the 300 acres. Now Samuel Lewis & Phebe his wife for £91 granted to Joseph Pratt a tract bounded by land of Edward Thompson & Nathan Evans containing 80 acres. Signed Samuel Lewis & Phebe Lewis. Delivered in the presence of Ephraim Jackson, Joseph Jackson & Nathaniel Jackson. Recorded 14 June 1743. (F6:288).

Patent. Thomas Lloyd, James Claypoole & Robert Turner, commissioners of William Penn granted a tract of land lying in the County of Chester bounded by land of Francis Cook & Thomas Brassey containing 300 acres by deed dated 26 May 1685 & laid out by the surveyor general on 29 May 1685 granted to Thomas Duckett. Thomas Duckett asking the commissioners to confirm said patent, they have confirmed unto Thomas Duckett the said 300 acres on 9 Dec 1686. Signed James Claypoole & Robert Turner. Recorded 21 June 1743. (F6:293).

Deed. On 10 Feb 1709 Joseph Baker of Edgmont, to his son Robert Baker. Whereas Roger Jackson of Edgmont purchased of George Williard 220 acres by deed dated 6 Mar 1687 & Roger Jackson by deed dated 12 Mar 1699 granted to Joseph Baker 150 acres being part of the 220 acres. Whereas William Penn by deed dated 1 Aug 1684 granted to David Ogden 200 acres & David Ogden by deed dated 24 Nov 1685 granted 50 acres to John Bowater. John Bowater by deed dated 9 Aug 1704 granted to Joseph Baker the tract of 50 acres bounded by land of John Worrall, John Gaulden, Peter Tregoe, Jonathon Ogden, John Turner & John Musgrove containing 200 acres. Now Joseph Baker for his fatherly love granted to his son Robert Baker the above described 200 acres. Signed Joseph Baker. Delivered in the presence of Joseph Edwards, Jacob Vernon & Ann Vernon. Recorded 23 June 1743. (F6:293).

Mortgage. On 26 Nov 1742 Lewis Jerman of London Britain in the County of Chester, Pennsylvania, yeoman, & Margaret his wife to Mordecai Lewis of Newtown, yeoman. Lewis Jerman & Margaret his wife for £50.2.6 granted to Mordecai Lewis a tract in London Britain bounded by land of John Jones, Richard Whitting, David Williams & land late of John Devonald containing 103 acres. Which Daniel Devonald of London Britain, yeoman, & Mary his wife by deed dated 6 & 7 Nov 1737 granted to Lewis Jerman. Lewis Jerman & Margaret his wife to pay Mordecai Lewis £52 on or before 21 Nov 1743 Signed Lewis Jerman & Margaret Jerman. Recorded 20 May 1743. (F6:296).

Mortgage. On 15 Dec 1742 David Crawford of Ridley, yeoman, & Dorothy his wife to Isaac Norris of Fairhill with in the City Liberties of Philadelphia, merchant. David Crawford & Dorothy his wife for £30 granted to Isaac Norris his plantation in Ridley bounded by other land of David Crawford, land of John Gleaves & other land of Isaac Norris under an agreement with John Crosby containing 100 acres. David Crawford & Dorothy to pay Isaac Norris £30 plus lawful interest on or before 15 Dec 1743. Signed David Crawford & Dorothy Crawford. Delivered in the presence of Susannah Crosby & Richard Crosby. Recorded 3 June 1743. (F6:298).

Mortgage. On 22 Mar 1742 George Pumfrey of Chester County to Richard Peters & Lynford Lardner both of the City of Philadelphia, gentlemen. George Pumfrey for securing the payment of £35, granted to Richard Peters & Lynford Lardner a tract bounded by land of George Churchman, Thomas Oldham, John Ruddel, Thomas Scott & David Griggs containing 170 acres. George Pumfrey to pay £35 plus interest to Richard Peters & Lynford Lardner for John Penn, Thomas Penn & Richard Penn, Esqs., in yearly payments to be paid in full on or before 22 Mar 1747. Signed George Pumfrey. Delivered in the presence of William Peters & John Callahan. Recorded 25 June 1743. (F6:301).

Mortgage. On 25 May 1743 Peter Babb of Chester County to Richard Peters & Lynford Lardner both of the City of Philadelphia, gentlemen. Peter Babb for securing the payment of £68.14.6 granted to Richard Peters & Lynford Lardner a tract bounded by land late of George Claypoole, land of James Love, John Whites, James Taylor, John Love & John Salkeld containing 487 acres. Peter Babb to pay £68.14.6 plus interest to Richard Peters & Lynford Lardner for John Penn, Thomas Penn & Richard Penn, Esqs., in yearly payments to be paid in full on or before 25 May 1748. Signed Peter Babb. Delivered in the presence of Phineas Lewis & Jonah Remax. Recorded 27 June 1743. (F6:304).

Mortgage. On 27 May 1743 Moses Dicky of Chester County to Richard Peters & Lynford Lardner both of the City of Philadelphia, gentlemen. Moses Dicky for better securing the payment of £25 granted to Richard Peters & Lynford Lardner a tract bounded by land of William Pyles, Ralph Thompson, Andrew Kirkpatrick & Michael Cloyd containing 220 acres. Moses Dicky to pay £25 plus interest to Richard Peters & Lynford Lardner for John Penn, Thomas Penn & Richard Penn, Esqs., in yearly payments to be paid in full on or before 27 May 1748. Signed Moses Dicky. Delivered in the presence of Sam Smith & John Callahan. Recorded 29 June 1743. (F6:307).

Deed. On 27 May 1743 John Cloud, Jr., of Chichester, yeoman, & Margaret his wife to Joseph Pyle of Chichester, yeoman. Whereas John Cloud, the father, by deed dated 1 June 1741 granted to John Cloud, Jr., 2 tracts of land containing 150 acres. Now John Cloud, Jr., & Margaret his wife for £3 granted to Joseph Pyle a tract in Chichester bounded by land of Joseph Pyle & Marcus Creek containing 1 1/4 acre. Signed John Cloud & Margaret Cloud. Delivered in the presence of Thomas Cummings, Joseph Parker & David Ranken. Peaceful possession of said land in the presence of John Marshall & William Adams. Recorded 6 July 1743. (F6:311).

Lease & Release. On 23 & 24 Mar 1741/2 James House of Kennett, carpenter, & Mary his wife, John Chadds of Birmingham, yeoman, & Elizabeth his wife, Abraham Parker of Kennett, yeoman, & Eleanor his wife & Robert Stuart of Whiteland, yeoman, & Martha his wife to John Hunter of Whiteland, tanner. Whereas William Penn by deed dated 24 & 25 July 1681 granted to Richard ap Thomas (since deceased) 5,000 acres, recorded in Philadelphia, Book A, Vol 1, Page 241. The said 5,000 acres was laid out to Richard Thomas, son & heir of Richard ap Thomas, dec., in several parcels. One parcel contains 500 acres situated in Whiteland. Richard Thomas by deed dated 12 & 13 Oct 1713 granted to Isaac Richardson the said 500 acres. Isaac Richardson made his will dated 14 Oct 1726 & devised the said 500 acres to his son John & his daughters Mary, Elizabeth, Eleanor & Martha, to be equally divided between them, but if either of them shall die under age & unmarried the said tester gave the share of him or them, to his surviving children, equally divided between them, & made Catherine his wife & friends Isaac Malin & William Paschall his executors & soon after died. Whereas the said land was divided amongst the children & John Richardson was allotted a tract containing 100 acres, & John Richardson died before the age of 21 & unmarried the said 100 acres came to May, Elizabeth, Eleanor & Martha. Now James House & Mary his wife, John Chadds & Elizabeth his wife, Abraham Parker & Eleanor his wife & Robert Stuart & Martha his wife for £170 granted to John Hunter a tract in Whiteland bounded by land of Richard Evenson, land late of William Smith & land of Robert Stuart containing 100 acres. Signed James House, Mary House, John Chadds, Elizabeth Chadds, Abraham Parker & Eleanor Parker, Robert Stuart & Martha Stuart. Delivered in the presence of Joseph Brinton, Josiah Taylor & Samuel Allen. Recorded 8 July 1743. (F6:313).

Release of Right of Dower. Memorandum. ON 2 July 1743 Stephen Hoskins & Joseph Warner by the consent of Sarah Hoskins that the said Joseph Warner doth agree to pay Stephen Hoskins £20 for his part of the plantation on the mouth of Sassafras River & that Stephen Hoskins to hold his part of the plantation until 10 Nov next after which time Joseph Warner is to enter upon the part the said Stephen provided the money is paid according to agreement. Signed Stephen Hoskins. Delivered in the presence of Samuel Webster & Benjamin Kendall. Recorded 8 July 1743. (F6:319).

Deed. On 11 Dec 1740 James Anderson of Charlestown, yeoman, to Patrick Anderson, eldest son of James. Whereas James Anderson granted to the Trustees of the General Loan Office of the Province of Pennsylvania all his plantation in Charlestown containing 340 acres. James Anderson to pay the trustees £50 & bills of credit with interest. Now James Anderson (to the end that the said mortgaged premises may be redeemed his son Patrick having assumed on himself the payment of the said mortgage) granted to his son Patrick Anderson all the plantation containing 340 acres. Signed James Anderson. Delivered in the presence of Mary Davies, Merick Davies, Jr. Peaceable possession granted to Patrick Anderson in the presence of Pricilla Davis, Thomas Seleson & David Davies. Recorded 13 Aug 1743. (F6:319).

Release. On 2 July 1743 William Bradford, Jr., of the City of New York in the government of New York, pewterer, & Sytie his wife to Alexander Montgomery & William Neven, both of the County of New Castle on Delaware, yeomen. William Bradford, Jr., & Sytie his wife for £400 granted to Alexander Montgomery & William Neven a tract on a branch of White Clay Creek bounded by the land of The London Company &

land of John Tagg containing 500 acres being part of 1,000 acres granted by William Penn by deed dated 23 Aug 1682 to Andrew Lowle, who by his will dated 9 Dec 1695 devised to his wife Jane Lowle & his daughter Tacy Lowle, equally. Jane by her deed dated 22 Feb 1702 granted to Tacy Lowle, who by the name of Tacy Baylton by deed dated 28 Mar 1730 granted the 1,000 acres to Andrew Bradford & William Bradford, Jr., in common tenancy, recorded in Philadelphia, Book F, Vol 3, Page 529. Andrew Bradford by deed dated 6 & 7 Dec 1732 granted to William Bradford all the 500 acres. Signed William Bradford, Jr., & Sytie Bradford. Delivered in the presence of John Howell & Sam Nease. Recorded 24 Aug 1743. (F6:322).

Deed. On 16 Dec 1742 John Jones of Charlestown, yeoman, & Jane his wife to Stephen Evans of Trydugrin in the County of Chester, Daniel Waler of Trydugrin, yeoman, & Joseph Williams of Lower Merion in the County of Philadelphia, miller. Whereas William Penn by deed dated 22 & 23 Oct 1681 granted to William Lowther & Margaret Lowther his wife a tract of 5,000 acres, recorded in Philadelphia, Book C, Vol 2, Page 109. Whereas William Lowther died, John Nicol & Margaret his wife, the only daughter & heir of Margaret who survived William Lowther, by deed dated 24 Sep 1731 granted the 5,000 acres to Joseph Stamvix. Joseph Stamvix by deed dated 18 Jan 1731 granted the 5,000 acres to John Simpson. Whereas William Penn by deed dated 23 Oct 1681 granted to John Lowther & Anne Sharlot Lowther 5,000 acres. Whereas Ann Sharlot Lowther died an infant without issue, John Lowther by deed dated 13 Aug 1731 granted the 5,000 acres to Joseph Turner. By virtue of a warrant a tract was laid out to John Simpson for the quantity of 4920 acres in right of the original purchase by William & Margaret Lowther & to include within the same 1/2 of the tract of land called Manor of Bilton. By same warrant another tract was laid out to Joseph Turner for 4920 acres in right of the original purchase of John & Anne Sharlot Lowther & to include into the same 1/2 of the tract called Manor of Bilton. Whereas there was a resurvey & found to be as follows bounded by Schuylkill River, Valley Creek, the Manor of Mount Joy, the Welch Tract, land formerly of Charles Pickrin, Pickerin Creek & land of William Moore containing 2,850 acres. Whereas John Simpson by deed dated 9 Mar 1737 granted to William Allen of Philadelphia, Esq., the one full equal undivided moiety or 1/2 part of all the land described tract called Manor of Bilton containing 2,850 acres. Whereas Joseph Turner by deed dated 23 Feb 1736/7 granted to William Allen all the last mentioned 5,000 acres including the other moiety of the Manor of Bilton. Whereas

William Allen & Margaret his wife by deed dated 25 July 1739 granted to John Parry, Esq., dec., all the tract described called the Manor of Bilton containing 2,850 acres. Whereas John Parry by deed dated 14 & 15 Nov 1739 granted to John Jones a tract containing 526 acres. Now John Jones & Jane his wife for £35 granted to Stephen Evans, Daniel Walker & Joseph Williams a tract in Charlestown bounded by Valley Creek & Philadelphia Road containing 100 acres being part of the 526 acres. Signed John Jones & Jane Jones. Delivered in the presence of John Jordan, Daniel Williams & Mary Walker. Recorded 13 Sep 1743. (F6:326).

Release. On 28 Sep 1742 John James of East Nantmell in the County of Chester, blacksmith, & Anne his wife to Owen Givin of Nantmell, collier. Whereas John Penn, Thomas Penn & Richard Penn, Esqs., by deed dated 10 Nov 1741 granted to Simon Woodrow, Jr., a tract in East Nantmell bounded by land of David Stephen, William Branson, Nicholas Reed & Simon Meredith containing 134 3/4 acres, recorded in Philadelphia, Book A, Vol 10, Page 348. Whereas Simon Woodrow & Jane his wife by deed dated 4 & 5 Jan 1741 granted to John James all the 134 3/4 acres. Now John James & Anne his wife for £130 granted to Owen Givins the tract of 134 3/4 acres. Signed John James & Anne James. Delivered in the presence of Henry Hockley & Richard Jones. Recorded 27 Sep 1743. (F6:330).

Deed. On 18 Dec 1742 John Jones of Charlestown, yeoman, & Jane his wife to Stephen Evans & Daniel Walker of Tredyffrin, yeomen & Joseph Williams of Lower Merion, miller. Whereas William Penn by deed dated 22 & 23 Oct 1681 granted to William Lowther & Margret Lowther his wife a tract of 5,000 acres, recorded in Philadelphia, Book C, Vol 2, Page 109. Whereas William Lowther died, John Nicol & Margaret his wife, the only daughter & heir of Margaret who survived William Lowther, by deed dated 24 Sep 1731 granted the 5,000 acres to Joseph Stamvix. Joseph Stamvis by deed dated 18 Jan 1731 granted the 5,000 acres to John Simpson. Whereas William Penn by deed dated 23 Oct 1681 granted to John Lowther & Anne Sharlot Lowther 5,000 acres. Whereas Ann Sharlot Lowther died an infant without issue, John Lowther by deed dated 13 Aug 1731 granted the 5,000 acres to Joseph Turner. By virtue of a warrant a tract was laid out to John Simpson for the quantity of 4920 acres in right of the original purchase by William & Margaret Lowther & to include within the same 1/2 of the tract of land called Manor of Bilton. By same warrant another tract was laid out to Joseph

Turner for 4920 acres in right of the original purchase of John & Anne Sharlot Lowther & to include into the same 1/2 of the tract called Manor of Bilton. Whereas there was a resurvey & found to be as follows bounded by Schuylkill River, Valley Creek, the Manor of Mount Joy, the Welch Tract, land formerly of Charles Pickrin, Pickerin Creek & land of William Moore containing 2,850 acres. Whereas John Simpson by deed dated 9 Mar 1737 granted to William Allen of Philadelphia, Esq., the one full equal undivided moiety or 1/2 part of all the land described tract called Manor of Bilton containing 2,850 acres. Whereas Joseph Turner by deed dated 23 Feb 1736/7 granted to William Allen all the last mentioned 5,000 acres including the other moiety of the Manor of Bilton. Whereas William Allen & Margaret his wife by deed dated 25 July 1739 granted to John Parry, Esq., dec., all the tract described called the Manor of Bilton containing 2,850 acres. Whereas John Parry by deed dated 14 & 15 Nov 1739 granted to John Jones a tract containing 526 acres. Now John Jones & Jane his wife for £41 granted to Stephen Evans, Daniel Walker & Joseph Williams a tract in Charlestown bounded by land of David Mathias, Nathaniel Davis, John Thomas & Jenkin Thomas, Griffith John & other land of John Jones containing 101 acres being part of the 526 acres. Signed John Jones & Jane Jones. Delivered in the presence of John Jordan, Daniel Williams & Mary Walker. Recorded 29 Sep 1743. (F6:332).

Mortgage. On 15 Apr 1743 Benjamin Harvey of Darby, clothworker, to Job Harvey of Darby, clothworker. Benjamin Harvey for £117.1.6 granted to Job Harvey one full undivided fourth part a fulling mill & a piece land where Benjamin Harvey now dwells lying in Darby, one of which said pieces is bounded by Darby Mill Race, another lot of land or Tanyard belonging to Job Harvey & Mill Road, & another piece of land where the Fulling Mill stands, Darby Mill, Darby Creek & the Mill race containing 154 square perches, also one full equal fourth part of one full equal fifth part of the said Mill Dam & Race. Benjamin Harvey to pay £138.2.7 to Job Harvey in yearly payments in full on or before 15 Apr 1746. Signed Benjamin Harvey. Delivered in the presence of William Fleur & Samuel Bunting. Recorded 10 Oct 1743. (F6:336).

Deed. On 18 Aug 1726 Caleb Evans of Radnor, yeoman, & Catherine his wife to John Jerman of Radnor, yeoman. Whereas William Penn by deed dated 14 & 15 Sep 1681 granted to Richard David 5,000 acres. Richard Davis by deed dated 18 & 19 June 1682 granted to John Lloyd a tract of

100 acres part of the 5,000 acre tract, recorded in Philadelphia, Folio 126. Whereas John Lloyd, eldest son of John Lloyd, dec., by deed dated 26 & 27 Aug 1719 granted to Thomas Lloyd the 100 acres & Thomas Lloyd by deed dated 9 Feb 1722 granted to Caleb Evans the 100 acres. Now Caleb Evans & Catherine his wife, for £27 granted to John Jerman, a tract in Radnor bounded by other land of John Jerman, land late of Richard Cook & land of Hugh Williams containing 27 acres. Signed Caleb Evans & Catherine Evans. Delivered in the presence of Benjamin Humphrey & Thomas David & Richard Jones. Recorded 13 Oct 1743. (F6:340).

Lease & Release. On 11 & 12 Dec 1726 Samuel Powell of Bristow in the County of Philadelphia, yeoman, to John Jerman of Radnor, yeoman. Whereas William Penn by deed dated 14 & 15 Sep 1681 granted to Richard Davis of Welch Tool in the County of Montgomery, gentleman, 5,000 acres. Richard Davis by deed dated 19 & 20 June 1682 granted to Richard Cook of the Parish of Langgulls in the County of Radnor, glover, a tract containing 100 acres & the 100 acres was laid out in Radnor to Richard Cook. Richard Cook died & the 100 acres descended to Elizabeth Cook the daughter & sole heir of Richard Cook. Elizabeth Cook by deed dated 13 & 14 June last past granted 100 acres to Samuel Powell. Now Samuel Powell & Agnes his wife for £26.5 grant to John Jerman a tract in Radnor bounded by other land of John Jerman & land of John Davis containing 26+ acres. Signed Samuel Powell & Agnes Powell. Delivered in the presence of Thomas Thomas, Mary Davis & Richard Jones. Recorded 15 Oct 1743. (F6:342).

Lease & Release. On 7 & 8 Nov 1743 Thomas West of Concord, yeoman, & William West of Wilmington in the County of New Castle upon Delaware, yeoman, & Thomas Canby of Wilmington, admin.s of the goods & chattels of Thomas West, late of Wilmington, dec., & Thomas West, being the eldest son & heir-at-law of the said dec., & William West, another son, Joseph West, another son, Rachel West one of the daughters, James Robinson & Eleanor his wife another of the daughters, Elizabeth West, the other daughter of the dec., to William Moore & James Moore both of Fallowfield, yeomen. Whereas John Penn, Thomas Penn & Richard Penn, Esqs., by deed dated 15 July 1734 granted to James Buckley a tract part in the County of Chester & part in the County of Lancaster containing 251 1/2 acres, recorded in Philadelphia, Book A, Vol 6, Page 362. James Buckley erected a grist mill upon the land & James Buckley & Mary his wife by deed dated 6 & 7 Apr 1737 granted to Samuel Mickle of Philadelphia all the above tract, recorded in Chester, Book E, Vol 5, Page 519. Whereas Samuel Buckley & Thomasin his wife by deed dated 13 Apr & 1 May 1741 granted to Thomas West all the above tract. Thomas West by agreement dated 19 Mar 1741/2 did sell to James Moore & William Moore the said tract & grist mill. Thomas West died intestate, leaving 6 children, 3 sons & 3 daughters, whereby his estate was to be divided amongst them. Now Thomas West, William West, Joseph West, Rachel West, James Robinson, Eleanor Robinson & Elizabeth West for £850 granted & confirmed unto James Moore & William Moore the land & grist mill lying part in Fallowfield in the County of Chester & part in the township of Sadsbury in the County of Lancaster bounded by Octoraro Creek, & land of John Devor containing 251 1/2 acres with houses & mills. Signed Thomas West, William West, Thomas Canby, Rachel West & James Robinson. Delivered in the presence of Samuel Mickle & Joseph Parker. Recorded 14 Nov 1743. (F6:346).

Mortgage. On 8 Nov 1743 James Moore & William Moore both of Fallowfield, yeomen to Samuel Mickle of the City of Philadelphia, merchant. James Moore & William Moore for £575 granted to Samuel Mickle all the tenement & water grist mill part lying in Fallowfield in the County of Chester & part in Sadsbury in the County of Lancaster bounded by Octoraro Creek, & land of John Devor containing 251 1/2 acres with houses & mills. James Moore & William Moore to pay £575 plus interest to Samuel Mickle in yearly payments to be paid in full on or before 8 Nov 1746. Signed James Moore & William Moore. Delivered in the presence of Eleanor Phillips, Joseph Parker & David Ranken. Recorded 18 Nov 1743. (F6:352).

Articles of Agreement. On 8 Apr 1721 Jeremiah Collett of Chichester, yeoman, to William Clayton, Jr., of Chichester, cordwainer, & Francis Reynolds of Chichester, joiner. Jeremiah Collett shall allow a road 20 foot wide for to go to the meeting house of Wishing God & to the mill or market the said road to begin at the fence of William Clayton & run between the land of Jeremiah Collett & William Clayton & across Collett's land to Marcus Creek butting at the creek against Thomas Linvill's land a little above the line of Withers land. William Clayton & Francis Reynolds shall pay Jeremiah Collett 30 shillings & cut of all timber or saplings in 12 foot lengths for the use of Collett. Signed Jeremiah Collett. Delivered in the presence of Adam Buckley, John

Georten, Robert Booth & Edward Whitacre. Recorded 18 Nov 1743. (F6:356).

Mortgage. On 19 Nov 1743 William Jones of East Nantmell, collier to Samuel Jones of Bethlehem in the County of Hunterdon in West New Jersey. William Jones stands bound to Samuel Jones for £230, conditioned for the payment of £115. William Jones to better secure said £115 granted to Samuel Jones a tract in Nantmell bounded by land of Hugh Roberts & William Davies containing 184 acres. William Jones to pay Samuel Jones £115 plus interest on or before 19 Nov 1744. Signed William Jones. Delivered in the presence of Charles Brockden & John Keily. Recorded 22 Nov 1743. (F6:357).

Sheriff's Deed. On 1 Sep 1743 Benjamin Davis, sheriff of Chester County to David Reese of Haverford. Whereas Caleb Evans at the Court of Common Pleas recovered against David Evans a debt of £38.14.7 & 70 shillings damages to be levied against the lands & chattels of David Evans in my bailiwick. Whereas David Evans possesses a tract of land in Radnor containing 21 acres & known as the Plough Tavern. Now Benjamin Davis, sheriff, for £100 granted to David Rees all the tenement in Radnor, commonly known as the Plough Tavern bounded by land of John Jerman & John Davis containing 21 acres. Signed Benjamin Davis, sheriff. Delivered in the presence of Joseph Parker & David Ranken. Recorded 24 Nov 1743. (F6:359).

Sheriff's Deed. On 30 Sep 1743 Benjamin Davis, sheriff of Chester County to William Vaughn of Chichester. Whereas William Vaughn at the Court of Common Pleas recovered against Edward Brogdon & Elizabeth his wife, late Elizabeth Weldon, admin. of the goods & chattels of John Weldon, late dec., for a debt of £150.70.6 in damages to be levied against the goods & chattels of John Weldon, dec. Benjamin Davis, sheriff, for £150 granted to William Vaughn the tenement & lots of land in Chichester bounded by river, a lot of Johannes Rawson, Back Street & a lot of William Clayton. Signed Benjamin Davis, sheriff. Delivered in the presence of Joseph Parker & David Ranken. Recorded 13 Dec 1743. (F6:361).

Deed. On 8 Aug 1705 James Sandelands of Chester, son & heir of James Sandelands, late of Chester, merchant, dec., to John Baldwin of Aston, yeoman. James Sandelands for £22 granted to John Baldwin a lot in

Chester bounded by James Street, Chester Bridge, Chester Creek & land of Paul Saunders being part of 20 granted to James Sandelands the father by the commissioners of William Penn on 1 May 1681. Signed James Sandelands. Delivered in the presence of John Martin & Paul Saunders. Recorded 13 Dec 1743. (F6:363).

Mortgage. On 12 Dec 1743 David Crawford of Ridley, woolcomber, to Isaac Norris of the northern liberties of the City of Philadelphia, merchant. Whereas David Crawford is bound to Isaac Norris for £154 & to secure the payment of £77 granted to Isaac Norris a tract in Springfield bounded by Maddock's land, land of John Gleaves, other land of David Crawford & land of John Crosby containing 51 acres. David Crawford to pay £77 plus interest to Isaac Norris in yearly payments to be paid in full on or before 1 May 1748. Signed David Crawford. Delivered in the presence of Leyson Price & Harper Mullin. Recorded 15 Dec 1743. (F6:364).

Mortgage. On 24 Aug 1743 William Betty of Chester County to Richard Peters, Lynford Lardner both of the City of Philadelphia, gentlemen. William Betty for securing the payment of £40 to be paid to John Penn, Thomas Penn & Richard Penn, Esqs., grant to Richard Peters & Lynford Lardner a tract bounded by land of John Moore, Robert Cooper, meeting house land, land of Adam Boyd, Samuel Patters, John Dicky & William Marsh containing 188 1/2 acres. William Betty to pay Richard Peters & Lynford Lardner £44 plus interest for the use of John Penn, Thomas Penn & Richard Penn, Esqs., in yearly payments to be paid in full on or before 24 Aug 1748. William Betty appointed William Peters his lawful attorney. Signed William Betty. Delivered in the presence of Joseph Crell & John Callahan. Recorded 17 Dec 1743. (F6:366).

Agreement. On 2 Mar 1718/9 Nicholas Pyle of Concord, yeoman, to John Perkins of Concord, cordwainer. Nicholas Pyle shall at the receipt of £8 to paid on or before 25 Feb 1719/20 grant to John Perkins a tract in Concord bounded by the Great Road, the Mill Road & other land of Nicholas Pyle containing 8 acres. For the true performance of this agreement bind themselves in the penal sum of £30. Signed Nicholas Pyle & John Perkins. Delivered in the presence of John Taylor, Mary Taylor, Walter Worrilaw. Recorded 10 Jan 1743. (F6:369).

Mortgage. On 1 Dec 1743 William Noblett of Middletown, carpenter, & Mary his wife to Caleb Cowpland of Chester, gentleman. William Noblett & Mary his wife for £100 granted to Caleb Cowpland 2 tracts in Middletown one bounded by land of Joseph Jervis, Charles Croxley, land late of Henry Hollingsworth & land of William Pennell containing 50 acres & the other tract bounded by Ridley Creek containing 100 acres. William Noblett & Mary his wife to pay £100 plus interest to Caleb Cowpland in yearly payments to be paid in full on or before 1 Dec 1747. Signed William Noblett & Mary Noblett. Delivered in the presence of Joseph Parker & David Ranken. Note: Jonathon Cowpland, administrator of Caleb Cowpland, acknowledged full satisfaction of said mortgage. Signed Jonathon Cowpland - 17 Aug 1758. Recorded 16 Jan 1743/4. (F6:370).

Mortgage. On 18 Nov 1743 Jonathon Vernon of Middletown, yeoman, to Edward Woodward of Middletown, yeoman. Jonathon Vernon for £50 granted to Edward Woodward a tenement in Nether Providence bounded by land of Joseph Vernon, James Ewing & Providence Road containing 50 acres. Jonathon Vernon to pay Edward Woodward £50 plus interest in yearly payments, to be paid in full on or before 18 Nov 1748. Signed Jonathon Vernon. Delivered in the presence of Joseph Parker & David Ranken. Recorded 17 Jan 1743/4. (F6:373).

Deed. On 15 Sep 1725 Thomas Howell of Chichester, yeoman, to Thomas Clayton of Chichester, yeoman. Whereas William Clayton by deed dated 20 Aug 1724 granted to Thomas Howell a tract in Chichester. Now Thomas Howell for £100 granted to Thomas Clayton a tract in Chichester bounded by Market Street, the River Delaware & a lot of William Clayton, Jr. Signed Thomas Howell. Delivered in the presence of Joseph Parker, Joseph Bond & John Weldon. Recorded 18 Jan 1743/4. (F6:376).

Lease & Release. On 5 & 6 Jan 1743/4 Thomas Hayward of Chester, yeoman, & Sarah his wife to Edmund Bourk of Chester, barber. Whereas Jacob Simcock son & heir of John Simcock, late of Ridley, dec., by deed dated 7 Sep 1703 granted to Ralph Fishbourne, the late father of William Fishbourne & to Elizabeth his wife all that brick tenement & lot in Chester bounded by Chester Creek. Ralph Fishbourne died in Elizabeth's lifetime, & the said lat descended to Elizabeth. Elizabeth made her will dated 25 Oct 1709 & bequeathed to her son-in-law William

Fishbourne all that tenement where she lived & the adjoining tenement & a tract of land Francis Worley & Mary his wife granted to her late husband containing 91 acres on condition that he pay the debts due in Great Britain from her late husband, but in case William Fishbourne does not perform this condition then the executors of this will shall sell & convey the said lands & monies to be used to pay said debts to Daniel Wharley & John Taylor & made Caleb Pussey & Gayon Stephenson executors & soon after died. Whereas William Fishbourne agreed that the executors should sell said lands & the executors by deed dated 30 May 1710 sold said lands to William Fishbourne for £233 but before any conveyance was made, Gayon Stevenson departed this life & Caleb Pussey, the surviving executor by deed dated 25 Mar 1720 granted to William Fishbourne the said lands. Whereas William Fishbourne & Jane his wife by deed dated 8 & 9 Apr 1730 granted to John Wharton all that tenement called by the name Now Messuage, adjoining the said Brick messuage with a parcel of land containing 20' in breadth bounded by Front Street & Chester Creek. William Fishbourne & Jane his wife by deed dated 26 & 27 May 1730 granted to Thomas Hayward all the brick messuage or tenement. Now Thomas Hayward & Sarah his wife for £100 granted to Edmund Bourk all the brick messuage or tenement bounded by Front Street, Chester Creek & the lot sold to John Wharton & land of John Buckley. Signed Thomas Hayward & Sarah Hayward. Delivered in the presence of Joseph Parker, David Shaghnessy, John Hanly & William Lowry. Recorded 19 Jan 1743/4. (F6:379).

Deed. On 8 Oct 1743 Joseph Hoskins of Chester, gentleman, & Jane his wife to Edward Russell of Chester, waterman. Whereas John Hoskins, late of Chester, gentleman, dec., the late father of Joseph Hoskins became seized in a tenement in Chester & died intestate, leaving a wife & 4 children to survive him. Whereas all the children of the intestate being arrived to full age & agreed amongst themselves to make the division of said lands. Ruth Hoskins, widow of the dec., John Hoskins, eldest son of the dec., Stephen Hoskins the 2nd son of the dec., John Mather & Mary his wife, the daughter of the dec., by deed dated 2 June 1733 granted to Joseph Hoskins, amongst other things, piece of land, recorded in Chester, Book E, Vol 5, Page 242. Now Joseph Hoskins & Jane his wife for £20 granted to Edward Russell all that lot lying in Chester bounded by land belonging to the heirs of James Creagor, land of Joseph Parker, other lots of Joseph Hoskins & the street leading from Chester Creek to Market Street. Signed Joseph Hoskins & Jane

Hoskins. Delivered in the presence of George Simpson & John Lea.
Recorded 20 Jan 1743/4. (F6:384).

Mortgage. On 12 Jan 1743/4 Edmund Bourk of Chester, barber & Rachel his wife to Joseph Parker of Chester, yeoman. Edmund Bourk & Rachell his wife for £100 granted to Joseph Parker all that brick tenement in Chester joining the New Messuage sold to John Wharton, being on the west side of Front Street, bounded by Chester Creek & land of Samuel Buckley. Edmund Bourk & Rachell his wife to pay £100 plus interest to Joseph Parker in yearly payments to be paid in full on or before 12 Jan 1746/7. Signed Edmund Bourk. Delivered in the presence of David Shaghnessy, John Hanly & William Lowry. Recorded 21 Jan 1743/4. (F6:386).

Release. On 12 Aug 1743 Joseph Sharples of West Caln, yeoman, & Lydia his wife to John Taylor of Thornbury, gentleman. Whereas John Penn, Thomas Penn & Richard Penn, Esqs., by deed dated 18 June 1734 granted to Samuel Lewis a tract in Caln containing 387 acres. Whereas Samuel Lewis by deed dated 5 & 6 Aug 1734 granted to Benjamin Sharples the 387 acres. Benjamin Sharples by deed dated 24 & 25 July 1736 granted the 387 acres to Joseph Sharples. Now Joseph Sharples & Lydia his wife for £212 granted to John Taylor a tract in West Caln bounded by land of Evan Lewis, land late of Richard Trantor, land of Nathan Sharples & Thomas Dawson containing 193 acres. Signed Joseph Sharples & Lydia Sharples. Delivered in the presence of William Empson & Abraham Sharples. Recorded 2 Feb 1743/4. (F6:389).

Lease & Release. On 2 & 3 May 1743 William Riley of New Town, yeoman, to Phillip Dunn of New Town, yeoman. Whereas William Penn by deed dated 18 & 19 Jan 1681 granted to Robert Drinton, since dec., 500 acres. Whereas John Knight, William Bolt & Hannah his wife & Ruth Knight, (the said Hannah & Ruth the daughters & only children of John Knight by Elizabeth his late wife, dec., late Elizabeth Drinton, only daughter & heir of Thomas Drinton, dec., who was the only brother & heir of Robert Drinton) by deed dated 6 & 7 Apr 1733 granted the 500 acres to Robert Tipping formerly of the City of London but late of New Town, merchant, dec. Whereas there was surveyed unto Robert Tipping 264 acres in New Town, recorded in Philadelphia, Book A, Vol 8, Page 262. Whereas Robert Tipping made his will 20 Jan last past & devised all his lands to William Riley & made William Riley his executor & soon after died. Now William Riley for £135.1 granted to Phillip Dunn a tract in New Town bounded by land of William Hunter, Crum Creek, land of Mathias Aspin & Joshua Pennell containing 100 acres being part of 264 acres. Signed William Riley & Susanna Riley. Delivered in the presence of John Taylor, Methuselah Davis & Elizabeth Taylor. Recorded 6 Mar 1743/4. (F6:391).

Deed. On 29 Feb 1743 Samuel Norris of the City of Philadelphia, merchant, to Robert Rigg of Uwchlan, yeoman. Whereas David Lloyd of Chester, gentleman, & Grace his wife by deed dated 2 June 1715 granted to Thomas John of Uwchlan a tract containing 125 acres. Whereas Andrew Hamilton & other trustees of the General Loan Office, having obtained a judgement for £91, a debt due them by Thomas John, against John Elleman & Gwen John, admin. of the goods & chattels of Thomas John, John Parry, the sheriff caused the debt to be levied on land of Thomas John. John Parry, sheriff granted the said land to Isaac Norris of the City of Philadelphia, merchant, the father of Samuel Norris. Isaac Norris is since dec., whereas Isaac Norris & other children of the first Isaac Norris by deed dated 10 Dec 1741 (with concurrence of James Logan & Isreal Pemberton, trustees of the will of Isaac Norris, dec.) granted & released to Samuel Norris the tract of 125 acres which was devised to him in his father's will, recorded in Philadelphia, Book G, Vol 4, Page 334. Now Samuel Norris for £160 granted to Robert Rigg the tract of land in Uwchlan bounded by the Welsh Line, land of Robert Williams, John Cadwalder, David Loyd & Griffith John containing 125 acres. Signed Samuel Norris. Delivered in the presence of Peter Aston & Joseph Parker. Recorded 5 Apr 1744. (F6:394).

Mortgage. On 26 Mar 1744 Robert Rigg of Uwchlan, yeoman, & Elizabeth his wife to Deborah Norris of the City of Philadelphia. Robert Rigg & Elizabeth his wife for £100 granted to Deborah Norris a tract in Uwchlan bounded by the Welsh Line, land of Robert Williams, John Cadwalder, David Loyd & Griffith John containing 125 acres. Robert Riggs & Elizabeth his wife to pay £100 plus interest to Deborah Norris. Signed Robert Rigg & Elizabeth Rigg. Delivered in the presence of Joseph Parker & Peter Aston. Recorded 6 Apr 1744. (F6:397).

Mortgage. On 2 Feb 1743 William Ferguson of Chester County to Richard Peters, Lynford Lardner both of the City of Philadelphia, gentlemen. William Ferguson for better securing £35 due John Penn,

Thomas Penn & Richard Penn, Esqs., granted to Richard Peters & Lynford Lardner a tract bounded by land of Walter Gilkey, John McFarren, Doe Run & land of Adam Leach containing 164 acres. William Ferguson to pay Richard Peters & Lynford Lardner for the use of John Penn, Thomas Penn & Richard Penn, Esqs., £35 plus interest in yearly payments to be paid in full on or before 2 Feb 1750. Signed William Ferguson. Delivered in the presence of William Peters & John Callahan. Recorded 7 Apr 1744. (F6:400).

Mortgage. On 14 Mar 1743 David Thomas of Chester County to Richard Peters, Lynford Lardner both of the City of Philadelphia, gentlemen. David Thomas for better securing £115.11.4 due John Penn, Thomas Penn & Richard Penn, Esqs., granted to Richard Peters & Lynford Lardner a tract in Nantmell bounded by other land of David Thomas & land of John Moore containing 400 acres. David Thomas to pay Richard Peters & Lynford Lardner for the use of John Penn, Thomas Penn & Richard Penn, Esqs., £115.11.4 plus interest in yearly payments to be paid in full on or before 14 Mar 1750. Signed David Thomas. Delivered in the presence of Edward Reily & John Callahan. Recorded 11 Apr 1744. (F6:403).

Mortgage. On 4 Apr 1744 Catherine White of Chester County to Richard Peters, Lynford Lardner both of the City of Philadelphia, gentlemen. Catherine White for better securing £29.4 due John Penn, Thomas Penn & Richard Penn, Esqs., granted to Richard Peters & Lynford Lardner a tract in West Nottingham bounded by an old line of Nottingham containing 113 1/2 acres. Catherine White to pay Richard Peters & Lynford Lardner for the use of John Penn, Thomas Penn & Richard Penn, Esqs., £29.4 plus interest in yearly payments to be paid in full on or before 4 Apr 1748. Signed Catherine White. Delivered in the presence of John Callahan. Recorded 12 Apr 1744. (F6:407).

Deed. On 1 Oct 1742 Mordecai Lewis of Mew Town, yeoman, & Ellen his wife to Howell Howell of Radnor, yeoman. Whereas Stephen David of East Town, carpenter, & Hannah his wife by deed dated 1 & 2 Dec 1734 granted to Griffith Hughes, late of East Town, clerk a tract in East Town containing 236 acres. Whereas John Parry, late sheriff by deed dated 29 May 1740 amongst other things it contained, whereas Hugh John at the Court of Common Pleas on 27 Nov last past, recovered against Griffith Hughes a debt of £40 & £0.72.6 damages, to be levied on the lands, tenements, goods & chattels of Griffith Hughes. John Parry for £280 granted to Mordecai Lewis the tenement & land in East Town bounded by land formerly belonging to Phillip David, land of William Shardlo & Edward Williams containing 200 + acres. Now Mordecai Lewis & Ellen his wife for £320 granted to Howell Howell a tract in East Town bounded by land of Richard Harrison formerly of William Shardlo & land of Edward Williams containing 236 acres (resurveyed). Signed Mordecai Lewis & Ellen Lewis. Delivered in the presence of Rees Howell, William Lewis, Thomas James & Thomas Thomas. Recorded 13 Apr 1744. (F6:410).

Deed. On 14 July 1735 William Clayton of Chichester, yeoman, & Mary his wife to Thomas Howell of Chichester, yeoman. Whereas William Clayton, dec., the father of William Clayton by deed dated 3 May 1709 granted to William Clayton a piece or lot of land in Chichester bounded by Broad Street, a little log house belonging to William Clayton, dec., & land of William Clayton, dec., recorded in Chester, Book C, Vol 3, Page 97. Now William Clayton & Mary his wife for £20 granted to Thomas Howell the above described lot. Signed William Clayton & Mary Clayton. Delivered in the presence of John Weldon, Caleb Perkins & John Isacks. Note: peaceable possession delivered to Thomas Howell 15 July 1734. Delivered in the presence of John Riley & John Weldon. Recorded 17 Apr 1744. (F6:414).

Mortgage. On 27 Feb 1743/4 Joseph Hayes of Haverford, yeoman, & Hannah his wife to John Davis of Darby & James Jones of Bleckley in Philadelphia County, yeomen. Joseph Hayes & Hannah his wife for £200 granted to John Davis & James Jones a tract which was devised to Joseph Hayes by the will of Richard Hayes, late of Haverford, dec., on 29 Nov 1738, lying in Haverford bounded by land of Joseph Lewis & Darby Creek containing 160 acres excepting 2 1/2 acres now in the possession of the owners of the Grist Mill erected by Darby Creek. Joseph Hayes & Hannah his wife to pay £200 plus interest on or before 27 Feb 1745. Signed Joseph Hayes & Hannah Hayes. Delivered in the presence of Benjamin Hayes & Henry Tremble. Recorded 20 Apr 1744. (F6:417).

Note: On 27 Feb 1743/4, on the back of the above mentioned mortgage. That the intent to sever the joint tenancy of John Davis & James Jones, in the within described tract of land. Whereas John David & James Jones may become or stand seized in the said land as tenants in common not as joint tenancy, thereby to prevent the title & advantage of survivorship. Signed John David & James Jones. Delivered in the presence of Samuel Sharp & David Brooks. (F6:420).

Mortgage. On 10 Jan 1743/4 Joseph Lewis of Haverford, yeoman, & Margaret his wife to Bernhard Vanleer of Marple, gentleman. Joseph Lewis & Margaret his wife for £80 granted to Bernhard Vanleer all the plantation & tract of land in Haverford containing 100 acres. Joseph Lewis & Margaret his wife to pay Bernhard Vanleer £80 plus interest in yearly payments to be paid in full on or before 10 Jan 1747/8. Signed Joseph Lewis & Margaret Lewis. Delivered in the presence of Samuel Lewis & George Saunders. Recorded 23 Apr 1744. (F6:421).

Deed. On 14 Apr 1744 Amos Lewis of the City of Philadelphia, shopkeeper & Hannah his wife to Claas Johnson of Bensalem in the County of Bucks, weaver. Amos Lewis & Hannah his wife for £348.10 granted to Claas Johnson a plantation in Haverford bounded by the Mill Brook, land of James Batton, Rice Price, William Lewis & David Llewelyn containing 208 acres. Which Rice Price of Merion in the County of Philadelphia by deed dated 20 May 1736, recorded in Philadelphia, Book G, Vol 3, Page 90, granted to Amos Lewis. Signed Amos Lewis & Hannah Lewis. Delivered in the presence of William Crosthwaite & Paul Isaac. Recorded 2 May 1744. (F6:424).

Mortgage On 24 Apr 1744 Claas Johnson of Bensalem in Bucks County, weaver, & Rebecca his wife to Amos Lewis of the City of Philadelphia, shopkeeper. Whereas Claas Johnson stands bound to Amos Lewis for £200 upon the condition of paying £100 & to better secure said payment of £100 granted to Amos Lewis a tract in Haverford bounded by the Mill Brook, land of James Batton, Rice Price, William Lewis & David Llewelyn containing 208 acres. Claas Johnson & Rebecca his wife to pay £100 plus interest in yearly payments to be paid in full on or before 24 Apr 1751. Signed Claas Johnson & Rebecca Johnson. Delivered in the presence of William Crosthwaite, Paul Isaac, & Evan Jones. Recorded 3 May 1744. (F6:427).

Deed. On 15 Jan 1717 James Whitacre of Chichester, yeoman, to his son Edward Whitacre. James Whitacre of 5 shillings granted to Edward Whitacre a tract of land in Chichester bounded by Chichester Creek, land of Richard Weaver, James Whitacre & land of Edward Whitacre containing 58 1/2 acres. Signed James Whitacre. Delivered in the presence of John Kingsman, John Bezar & James Buckley. Recorded 7 May 1744. (F6:429).

Lease & Release. On 13 Mar 1722 Tobias Collet of London, in Old England, haberdasher, Daniel Quare of London, watchmaker & Henry Gouldney of London, linen draper to John Jones of Chester County, yeoman. Whereas there is a tract of land lying on a branch of White Clay Creek in the County of Chester bounded by William Penn's manor, land of John Evans & John Devonald containing 150 acres part of 17,218 acres that the Commissioners of William Penn by deed dated 25 June 1718 granted to Tobias Collet, Daniel Quare, Henry Gouldney & the heirs of Michael Russel of London, merchant, recorded in Philadelphia, Book A, Vol 5, Page 306. Now Tobias Collet, Daniel Quare & Henry Gouldney for £34.10 granted to John Jones the tract containing 150 acres. Signed Daniel Quare, Tobias Collett & Henry Gouldney. Delivered in the presence of Sarah Dimsdale, John Estaugh & Elizabeth Estaugh. Recorded 12 May 1744. (F6:431).

Lease & Release. On 5 Oct 1733 Lancelot Fallowfield of Grayrigg in the Parish of Kirby Kendall in the County of Westmoreland in Old England, yeoman, to Joseph Parker of Chester County, yeoman. Whereas William Penn, Esq., by deed dated 24 & 25 May 1683 granted to Lancelot Fallowfield then of Great Strickland in the County of Westmoreland, yeoman, the quantity of 250 acres. Whereas Lancelot Fallowfield died & the land descended to his only son & heir John Fallowfield & John Fallowfield by deed dated 29 & 30 Dec 1726 granted the said land to Lancelot Fallowfield the said son of John Fallowfield. Now Lancelot Fallowfield for £100 grant to Joseph Parker the 250 acres. Signed Lancelot Fallowfield. Delivered in the presence of John Cadwalder & Robert Jordan. Recorded 22 May 1744. (F6:435).

Deed. On 24 Dec 1719 Henry Reynolds of Chichester, yeoman, & Prudence his wife to John Reynolds of Chichester one of the sons of Henry & Prudence). Whereas William Penn, Esq., by deed dated 12 Nov 1683 granted to Henry Reynolds a tract in Chichester containing 200 acres. Whereas William Penn, Esq., by deed dated 5 & 6 Sep 1681 granted to George Andrews a tract of 250 acres. Whereas George Andrews by deed dated 16 & 17 Sep 1681 granted to John Hickman 125 acres being part of the 250 acres. John Hickman by deed dated 30 & 31 Jan 1682 granted to Henry Reynolds the 125 acres. Whereas William

Penn, Esq., by deed dated 12 & 13 July 1682 granted to George Stroud a tract containing 500 acres. George Stroud by deed dated 21 & 22 Mar 1686/7 granted to Henry Reynolds the 200 acres of the 500 acres. Now Henry Reynolds & Prudence his wife for natural love & £20 granted to their son John Reynolds a tract in Chichester being part of the 3 tracts bounded by the Middle branch of Naamans Creek, land of Henry Reynolds, William Cloud & John Cloud containing 210 acres. Signed Henry Reynolds & Prudence Reynolds. Delivered in the presence of William Clayton, William Hanby & William Reynolds. Recorded 7 June 1744. (F6:440).

Patent. On 26 Mar 1684 Whereas there is a tract of land on the Delaware River in Marcus Hook containing 100 acres which was granted by Governor Lovelace to Jan Hendricks, who then granted it to William Orian & William Orian granted the 100 acres to Michael Izard. Now Michael Izard has requested that William Penn confirm said land to him. Now William Penn confirm to Michael Izard the 100 acres. Signed William Penn. Endorsed. Charles Croswith, Jr., of the County of Glouster in West New Jersey, yeoman, by Letter of Attorney from Michael Izard only son & heir of Michael Izard, dec., dated 26 Aug 1704 from the County of Salem empowered Charles Croswith to grant said tract to Phillip Roman of Chester County, yeoman. Charles Croswith appointed his trusty friend John Child of Chester County to be his attorney to pass said deed in Open Court. Signed Charles Croswith. Delivered in the presence of John Child, Jonah Roman & Sarah Englington. Recorded 11 June 1744. (F6:444).

Deed. On 2 May 1719 Robert Pyle of Bethel, yeoman, Jonah Roman of Chichester, yeoman, & Ruth his wife to Phillip Roman of Chichester, yeoman. Whereas by a deed made in triplicate on 3 Feb 1713 between Phillip Roman & Nicholas Pyle of one part, Robert Pyle of the second part & Jonah Roman of the third part, the said Phillip Roman & Nicholas Pyle granted & conveyed to Robert Pyle all the plantation where Phillip Roman dwelt lying in Chichester containing 205 acres for the use of Phillip Roman for the term of his natural life & after his death to go to Jonah Roman, recorded in Chester County on 27 Sep 1716. Now Robert Pyle at the request of Jonah Roman & Ruth his wife for £160 paid to Jonah Roman by Phillip Roman granted to Phillip Roman a tract in Chichester bounded by the Delaware River, land of Jeremiah Collett, Stony Run, land of John Chambers, Chichester Creek, the bridge & a private road containing 205 acres. Signed Robert Pyle, Jonah Roman &

Ruth Roman. Delivered in the presence of John Dutton & Elizabeth Dutton. On 16 May 1719 Jonah Roman received of his father Phillip Roman £160. Signed Jonah Roman. Delivered in the presence of Robert Pyle & James Broome. Recorded 11 June 1744. (F6:445).

Deed. On 1 June 1741 John Cloud, Sr., of Rockland Manor in the County of New Castle upon Delaware to John Cloud, Jr. John Cloud, Sr., for £6 per annum during his natural life & for natural love granted to his son John Cloud, Jr., all the tract of land he bought from Enoch & John Flower & all the tracts of land adjoining to it that he bought of Joseph Grist lying in Chichester bounded by Marcus Creek, land of John Bezar, Roger Shelly & Robert Moulder containing 150 acres. Signed John Cloud. Delivered in the presence of Jemima Edwards & John Riley. Recorded 13 June 1744. (F6:449).

Mortgage. On 16 Apr 1744 Obidiah Wildy of Haverford, husbandman & Elizabeth his wife to Joseph Williams of Merion in the County of Philadelphia, tanner. Whereas Obidiah Wildy stands bound to Joseph Williams for a debt of £170 upon the condition of paying £85 & to better secure said payment of £85 granted to Joseph Williams a tract in Haverford bounded by land of John Humphrey, land late of Samuel Reese & Radnor line containing 85 acres. Obidiah Wildy & Elizabeth his wife to pay £85 & interest to Joseph Williams in yearly payments to be paid in full on or before 16 Apr 1747. Signed Obidiah Wildy & Elizabeth Wildy. Delivered in the presence of Rees Thomas & Daniel Humphrey. Recorded 21 June 1744. (F6:450).

Deed. On 1 June 1686 Robert Moulder of Chester County to Peter Baynton. Robert Moulder for £6 granted to Peter Baynton a tract of land lying in Chichester bounded by the River Delaware, land formerly of George Andrews, land of George Foreman being the land Robert Moulder purchased of Olle Rawson by deed dated 1 Sep 1683. Signed Robert Moulder. Delivered in the presence of Isaac Warner & Richard Crosby. Recorded 25 June 1744. (F6:452).

Assignment. On 10 Dec 1789 Peter Baynton of the County of New Castle, merchant, assign the within mentioned deed to Samuel Rowland. Signed Peter Baynton. Delivered in the presence of John Test & Edward Boothby. Recorded 1744. (F6:453).

Assignment. Know all men by these presents that I the subscriber, (married the daughter of Samuel Rowland, Esq., late of the County of Sussex, dec., whose name was Mary Rowland) do assign and make over all my right and title to the within deed, which was by will left unto me by my said wife's father, Samuel Rowland unto Thomas Howell of Chichester in Pennsylvania, to the said Howell his heirs and assigns forever from the claim of me, my heirs, executors, admins. Witness my hand & seal this 17 Feb 1728. Signed Joseph Eldridge & Mary Eldridge. Delivered in the presence of Thomas Stockley & Christopher Topham. Recorded 25 June 1744. (F6:454).

Release. On 17 Mar 1728/9 Benjamin Moulder of Chichester, mariner to Thomas Howell of Chichester, yeoman. Whereas Olle Rawson by deed dated 8 Dec 1684 granted to Robert Moulder, father of Benjamin Moulder a lot of land in Chichester bounded by the Delaware River, land formerly of George Andross & the King's Highway. Whereas Benjamin Moulder being the only son & heir of Robert Moulder & in as much as the said Robert or some claiming under him sold to Thomas Howell the said lot but did not effectively convey said lot. Now Benjamin Moulder for 10 shillings release to Thomas Howell all right to said lot. Signed Benjamin Moulder. Delivered in the presence of Joseph Bond & Richard Bezar. Recorded 25 June 1744. (F6:454).

Assignment. On 11 Apr 1744. Rees Meredith for £129.11.7 granted to Jane Fishbourne of the City of Philadelphia, widow the within mentioned Mortgage. Signed Rees Meredith. Delivered in the presence of William Fishbourne & Paul Isaac. Recorded 1 Aug 1744. (F6:456).

Lease & Release. On 8 & 9 Nov 1741 John Jones of London Britain township in the County of Chester, yeoman, & Elizabeth his wife to Jane Evans of London Britain in the County of Chester, widow. Whereas Tobias Collett, Daniel Quare & Henry Gouldney all of London in Great Britain, merchants by deed dated 14 Mar 1722 granted to John Jones a parcel of land lying on the western branch of White Clay Creek, within the township of London Britain bounded by William Penn's manor, land of John Evans & John Devonald containing 150 acres being part of 17218 acres the commissioners of William Penn granted to Tobias Collett, Daniel Quare, Henry Gouldney & others, recorded in Philadelphia, Book A, Vol 5, Page 306. Now John Jones & Elizabeth his wife for £500 granted to Jane Evans the said 150 acres. Signed John Jones &

Elizabeth Jones. Delivered in the presence of Reynold Howell, John Evans & William Sweeting. Recorded 4 Sep 1744. (F6:458).

Release. On 29 Oct 1740 Humphrey Ellis of Eastown, yeoman, to Nathan Lewis of Newtown, yeoman. Whereas Adam Rhodes of Darby, yeoman, & Catherine his wife by deed dated 1 Dec 1724 granted to Jane Jones (by her then name Jane Jones relict of John Jones, late of Radnor, yeoman, dec.) but since the wife of Humphrey Ellis a tract in Eastown where the said Humphrey Ellis now dwells containing 125 acres. Whereas by another deed dated 1 Apr 1723, Jane Jones (before her marriage to Humphrey Ellis) granted to Humphrey Ellis the 125 acres, recorded in Chester, Book F, Vol 6, Page 72. Now Humphrey Ellis for & in consideration of the marriage between Humphrey Ellis & Jane, now his wife & for settling a competent maintenance on the said Jane during her natural life, in case she shall survive Humphrey Ellis & for the natural love & affection Humphrey Ellis has for Thomas Ellis his son & Margaret Ellis his daughter & to the intent that the said piece of land may be established in the family and blood of the said Humphrey Ellis, so long as it shall please Almighty God to continue, & for 10 shillings granted & confirmed to Nathan Lewis all the plantation in Eastown bounded by land of James Lea, Adam Trehern, Adam Rhodes & Evan Ellis containing 125 acres for the uses & in trust. To the use & behoof of Humphrey Ellis & Jane his wife for & during their natural lives & after their death to the use of Nathan Lewis. Nathan Lewis to pay all rents & profits to Humphrey Ellis & his wife for their natural lives & after their deaths the said Humphrey & Jane to Thomas Ellis & or Margaret Ellis for the full term of 99 years. Signed Humphrey Ellis. Delivered in the presence of Lewis Lewis, Thomas Thomas & Mordecai Lewis. Recorded 10 Sep 1744. (F6:562).

Mortgage. On 2 Nov 1743 James Hamilton of Fallowfield, yeoman, to Richard Peters of the City of Philadelphia, gentleman. James Hamilton for £47 granted to Richard Peters a tract in Fallowfield bounded by land of John Wilson containing 136 acres. Which said tract was granted & confirmed to Edward Shippen of the City of Philadelphia, merchant, by the proprietors of the province by deed dated 30 Aug 1743, recorded in Philadelphia, Book A, Vol 11, Page 219. Edward Shippen by deed dated 1 Nov 1743 granted to James Hamilton the said tract of land. James Hamilton to pay £47 plus interest to Richard Peters on or before 1 Nov 1744. Signed James Hamilton. Delivered in the presence of Hugh Parke & John Callahan. Recorded 10 Apr 1744. (F6:567).

Release. On 4 Apr 1744 Abel Parke of East Caln, yeoman, & Deborah his wife to Thomas Parke of East Caln, yeoman. Whereas Thomas Parke & Rebecca by deed dated 27 & 28 June 1735 granted to Abel Parke a tract of land in East Caln containing 100 acres, recorded in Chester, Book E, Vol 5, Page 355. Whereas Thomas Parke, Jr., by deed dated 1 & 2 Dec 1737 granted to Abel Parke another tract of land in East Caln containing 124 1/2 acres. Now Abel Parke & Deborah his wife for £316.14 granted to Thomas Parke a tract in East Caln bounded by land of George Aston, Thomas Parke, & Robert Parke containing 100 acres, the other tract bounded by land of Phineas Lewis & Thomas Parke containing 124 1/2 acres, both being part of a larger tract of 500 acres conveyed by Thomas Linley & Hannah his wife to Thomas Parke by deed dated 29 & 30 Dec 1725. Signed Abel Parke & Deborah Parke. Delivered in the presence of Roger Hunt & John Jackson. Recorded 26 Sep 1744. (F6:570).

Deed. On 17 July 1744 Humphrey Bate of Concord, weaver, to John Bate the eldest son & heir apparent of Humphrey Bate. Whereas Humphrey Bate for some good conveyance granted to John Bate a tract mortgaged on 3 Apr 1740 to the trustees of the General Loan Office for £28 plus interest. Whereas Humphrey Bate has paid some of the said mortgage & the said John Bate has undertaken to pay the residue of the mortgage. Now Humphrey Bate for £40 paid to him granted to John Bate a tract in Concord bounded by land of Mary Cloud, Thomas Broom & land late of Jacob Pyle containing 50 acres. Signed Humphrey Bate. Delivered in the presence of C. Brockden & J. Oakley. Recorded 17 Oct 1744. (F6:473).

Deed. On 8 Oct 1740 James Logan of Stenton in the County of Philadelphia, Esq., agent & attorney of William Penn of the City of London in Old England, Esq., grandson of William Penn, late Governor of the province of Pennsylvania to Richard Halleb of Newtown in the County of Queens in Long Island in the province of New York, farmer & Anne his wife. Whereas by several deeds dated 19 & 20 Sep 1715 made between William Penn, Esq., now dec. (the late father of William Penn of the aforesaid William Penn & the son & heir apparent of William Penn, Governor), to John Evans of the County of Denbigh in Great Britain. William Penn the father granted to John Evans all that tract called Steining in the County of Chester containing 14,500 acres, except 500 acres William Penn the father granted to Evan Evans. Whereas John Evans reconveyed all the said manor to William Penn the father in his lifetime, excepting 2,000 acres reserving unto himself, John Evans, since laid out & surveyed & then in the occupation of William Miller & John Evans & the deed of Reconveyance was lost or mislaid. Upon application made by James Logan, agent of the said William Penn, the father & Springett Penn, Esq., the eldest son & to the first William Penn to make good the title of the land (part of the Penn Manor) did by deed dated 23 & 24 June 1736 confirmed to John Evans the said tract. Now James Logan for £25.7.6 for the use of William Penn, granted to Richard Halleb & Anne his wife a tract being part of the Manor of Steining bounded by land of Nathaniel Richards, Nathaniel Pope, James Linley & William Carpenter containing 40 1/2 acres. Signed James Logan. Delivered in the presence of Edward Shippen & Christopher Lehman. Recorded 17 Oct 1744. (F6:476).

Deed. On 13 Dec 1699 David Lloyd of Philadelphia, gentleman, to John Hoskins of Chester. David Lloyd for £22 granted to John Hoskins a lot in Chester bounded by a street, Chester Creek, David Lloyd's plantation, Hoskins lot, land of James Lownes, Samuel Bishops lot with 20 acres of woodland bounded by the road leading from Chester to Edgmont & land of John Simcock which part of land Charles Pickering sold to David Lloyd, recorded in Chester, Book A, Folio ?, on 2 Oct 1688. Signed David Lloyd. Delivered in the presence of Robert Barber & Henry Hollingsworth. Recorded 22 Oct 1744. (F6:479).

Mortgage. On 6 Nov 1744 George Rees of Coventry, yeoman, to Joseph Williams of Merion in the County of Philadelphia, yeoman. Whereas Thomas Penn, John Penn & Richard Penn granted to George Rees a tract containing 230 acres by deed dated 22 Nov 1740, recorded in Philadelphia, Book A, Vol 10, Page 161. Now George Rees for £200 granted Joseph Williams a tenement lying on the west side of a river called Schuylkill bounded by the said river, land of Thomas Godfrey, David Stephen & Anthony Morris containing 230 acres. George Rees to pay £248 to Joseph Williams in yearly payments to be paid in full on or before 6 Nov 1748. Signed George Rees. Delivered in the presence of Sarah Bonsall & Joseph Bonsall. Recorded 10 Nov 1744. (F6:480).

Lease & Release. On 23 & 24 Mar 1743/4 Peter Dicks of Providence, yeoman, & Sarah his wife to Jonas Culin of Ridley, yeoman. Whereas Francis Lovelace, Governor of the province of New York by deed dated 10 Mar 1690 granted to Neal Matson a parcel of land on the Delaware

River bounded by the said river, Crum Creek, & land then of Claus Andrews, but since the widow Neals, alias Friend, now dec., containing 100 acres. Neals Matson & his son Anthony Nealson by deed dated 18 Feb 1683 for £120 granted to Edward Pritchard. William Penn confirmed said land to Neals Matson by deed dated 26 Mar 1684 & Neals Matson for better assurance confirmed said tract to Edward Pritchard by deed dated 5 Aug 1684. Edward Pritchard became seized in said land, never the less one Henry Jacobson by coleur of a deed from Neals Matson dated 19 June 1689 pretended a right to one moiety of the said land & sold said tract to Reyner Peterson, who sold the said tract to Walter Fawcett. Walter Fawcett procured a resurvey with the over plus being 93 acres being granted to him & afterwards sold the 93 acres to Robert Barber, who made his will & devised said 93 acres to his nephew James Barber, paying to the testators wife Hannah a yearly rent of £5 during her life but the said Edward Pritchard having purchased of Neal Matson & his son all right & title to said land interrupted the said Jacobson, Peterson, Fawcett & Barber in their possession & so did his son & heir Edward Pritchard until he with his mother Elizabeth & brother Phillip for £160 granted to David Lloyd the said land by deed dated 20 May 1708, recorded in Chester, Book A, Vol 1, Page 202. David Lloyd not willing to contest said title of said land as Pritchard had done but for peace proposed to buy the Barber's right or sell his own. Whereupon James Barber (after the death of his Uncle) for £80 granted to David Lloyd & forever paying the said Hannah now married to William Hudson as by the deed between James Barber & Susannah his wife & his cousin Robert Barber to David Lloyd, recorded in Chester, Book C, Page 234. Whereas David Lloyd & Grace his wife by deed dated 7 & 8 Apr 1718 granted to Benjamin Head & Sarah his wife the said tract containing 186 acres. Benjamin Head & Sarah his wife to pay the yearly £5 to William & Hannah Hudson. William Hudson of Philadelphia, tanner, & Hannah his wife, who was the widow of Robert Barber, late of Chester, cordwainer, dec., by deed dated 30 Dec 1720 granted to David Lloyd all right & title to said land. Whereas Benjamin Head is since deceased & the tract was vested to Sarah Head, & Sarah Head, David Lloyd & Grace his wife by deed dated 17 & 18 Nov 1724 granted to Peter Dicks all the said tract of land lying in Ridley containing 186 acres, recorded in Chester, Book D, Vol 4, Page 262. Now Peter Dicks & Sarah his wife for £700 granted to Jonas Culin all that tract in Ridley bounded by the King's Road, land of Peter Dicks and formerly Walter Fawcett's, the river Delaware & Crum Creek containing 132 acres, being part of the 186 acres. Signed Peter

Dicks & Sarah Dicks. Delivered in the presence of Joseph Parker, David Ranken & Andrew Culin. Recorded 15 Nov 1744. (F6:484).

Mortgage. On 30 Oct 1744 John Moore of Fallowfield, miller, to John Richardson of the County of New Castle & Christian Hundred, merchant. John Moore by virtue of a Deed of Sale from James Moore & Hannah his wife dated 1743 as also by a deed from Caleb Pussey & Anne his wife by deed dated 20 Jan 1723 being granted to Caleb Pussey by the commissioners of William Penn in the year 1715. Now John Moore for £120 granted to John Richardson a tract in Sadsbury bounded by land of Samuel Miller, Andrew Moore containing 177 acres in the whole, be it remembered that there is sold of the said land 53 acres at the end joining to land of William Boyd, William Betty & Andrew Moore which is sold to James Bold making the remainder 124 acres. John Moore to pay John Richardson £120 plus interest on or before 10 Oct 1745. Signed John Moore. Delivered in the presence of Anna Richardson & Mary Richardson. Recorded 16 Nov 1744. (F6:493).

Deed. On 30 Aug 1744 John Owen, sheriff of Chester County to Joseph Parker Whereas Joseph Parker in the Court of Common Pleas recovered against Richard Treville a debt of £106 plus £0.70.6 in damages, to be levied against the land, goods & chattels of Richard Treville. Whereas John Hannum in the Court of Common Pleas recovered against Richard Treville a debt of £16.12.8 plus £0.70.6 for damages to be levied against the land, goods & chattels of Richard Treville. Whereas John Bently in the Court of Common Pleas recovered against Richard Treville a debt of £7 plus £0.70.6 in damages to be levied against the land, goods & chattels of Richard Treville. Whereas Daniel Few in the Court of Common Pleas recovered against Richard Treville a debt of £4.3.4 plus £0.70.6 in damages to be levied against the land, goods & chattels of Richard Treville. John Owen, sheriff seized a tract of land in Newlin containing 313 acres to sell to the highest bidder. John Owen, sheriff for £140 granted to Joseph Parker all that tract in Newtown bounded by land of Thomas Hicklins, land late of Richard Evenson but now of Ezekiel & James Harlan & land of Nathaniel Newlin containing 313 acres. Signed John Owen, sheriff. Delivered in the presence of John Ross & Benjamin Price. Recorded 20 Nov 1744. (F6:496).

Deed. On 9 Oct 1744 Elisha Gatchell of East Nottingham in the County of Chester, gentleman, of the 1st part, Elisha Gatchell, Jr., & Joshua

Brown of East Nottingham, yeoman, of the 2nd part John Price of East
Nottingham, blacksmith, & Abigail his wife the daughter Elisha Gatchell
the elder of the 3rd part. Whereas the Honorable Proprietors by deed
dated 20 Oct 1733 granted to Amigail (then Abigail Job) a tract in East
Nottingham bounded by land of Robert McTheys containing 200 acres,
recorded in Philadelphia, Book A, Vol 6, Page 198. Whereas John Price
& Abigail his wife by deed dated 22 Aug 1743 granted 200 acres to Elisha
Gatchell. Now Elisha Gatchell for the natural love he has for Abigail his
daughter & her children & 5 shillings paid by Elisha Gatchell, Jr. Joshua
Brown granted & confirmed to Elisha Gatchell, Jr., & Joshua Brown in
trust & during the life of Abigail Price. Signed Elisha Gatchell, Joshua
Brown & Elisha Gatchell, Jr. Delivered in the presence of John Coppeck
& William Miles. Recorded 27 Nov 1744. (F6:499).

Lease & Release. On 4 & 5 Feb 1739 Joseph Pennock of Marlborough,
yeoman, & Mary his wife to Nathaniel Pennock of Marlborough, yeoman
(son of Joseph & Mary). Whereas George Collett, late of Ireland, dec.,
did in his lifetime purchase from Francis Rogers & George Rogers of
Cork in Ireland, merchants 5,000 acres in the province of Pennsylvania
(that is to say 2500 acres from Francis Rogers & 2500 acres from George
Rogers, that each purchased of William Penn by deed dated 23 Mar 1681.
Whereas George Collett did by his will dated 28 Nov 1696 devised the
said 5,000 acres of land to his 2 grandsons, Nathaniel Pennock & Joseph
Pennock to be equally divided between them. Whereas Nathaniel
Pennock since died without issue & his half of the said 5,000 acres
descended to Joseph Pennock. Whereas by virtue of a warrant there was
late surveyed & laid out to Joseph Pennock a part of the said purchase a
tract containing 492 1/2 acres. Now Joseph Pennock & Mary his wife for
5 shillings, natural love & affection & for his better presentment in this
world granted to Nathaniel Pennock that tract in Marlborough bounded
by land of Caleb Pussey, the late William Penn's Manor, land of the
London Company & land of James Treveller containing 494 1/2 acres.
Signed Joseph Pennock & Mary Pennock. Delivered in the presence of
Joseph Pennock & James Morris. Recorded 12 Dec 1744. (F6:501).

Lease & Release. On 1 & 2 Jan 1744/5 John Hanly of Chester,
gentleman, & Catherine his wife to William Preston of the City of
Philadelphia, merchant. Whereas Arthur Sheil & Mary his wife the late
widow & admin. of the goods & chattels of Jonas Sandelands, late of
Chester, dec., by virtue of an order from the Orphans Court to them
dated 10 Apr 1732 granted to William Trehearn by deed dated 31 Aug

1732, 2 parcels of land in Chester both pieces containing 3 2/4 + acres, recorded in Chester, Book E, Vol 5, Page 150. Whereas William Trehearn & Catherine his wife by deed dated 14 & 15 Nov 1733 granted to Richard Barry, late of Chester, merchant, a lot in Chester part of the 2 parcels containing in breadth 40 feet & in length 120 feet. Richard Barry erected a brick tenement & Richard Barry & Mary his wife by deed dated 28 & 29 Oct 1740 granted to John Hanly the said lot, recorded in Chester, Book F, Vol 6, Page 88. Whereas William Trehearn made his will dated 22 May 1736 & amongst other things devised to his wife Catherine all the remainder of the parcels of land. Whereas John Hanly has since married the said Catherine. Now John Hanly & Catherine his wife for £350 grant to William Preston all those parcels of land situated in Chester, the 1st being 40' x 120' bounded by Free Street, High Street, & other land of John Hanly, the other parcel bounded by the other lot, High Street, land of John Mathews, & other land of John Hanly, both said lots being part of the first mentioned 2 tracts. Signed John Hanly & Catherine Hanly. Delivered in the presence of Joseph Parker & David Ranken. Recorded 3 Jan 1744/5. (F6:505).

Release. On 10 Nov 1741 John Bennet of Birmingham, yeoman, & Sarah his wife to William Pyle of Birmingham, yeoman. Whereas the commissioners of William Penn by deed dated 29 Aug 1706 granted to Abiah Taylor amongst other lands a tract in Bensalem, but is since found to be in the township of Marlborough bounded by land of Henry Hayes & land late of Henry Hayes but now in the possession of William Hayes containing 350 acres. Abiah Taylor by deed dated 10 July 1708 granted said tract to John Bennet the father of the above John Bennet, recorded in Chester, Book B, Page 270. John Bennet the father made his will dated 14 Apr 1709 & devised to his beloved son John Bennet all the 350 acres in Bensalem. Now John Bennet & Sarah his wife for £200 granted to William Pyle the 350 acres. Signed John Bennet & Sarah Bennet. Delivered in the presence of James Dickey & Zachariah Butcher. Recorded 14 Jan 1744/5. (F6:511).

Mortgage. On 28 Jan 1742 Joseph Wood of Chichester, yeoman, to Israel Pemberton, Jr., of the City of Philadelphia, merchant. Joseph Wood for better securing £41 granted to Isreal Pemberton a tract in Chichester bounded by Chichester Creek, land of Francis Routh, land of Nathan Wood & Chester Road containing 45 acres. Joseph Wood to pay Isreal Pemberton, Jr., £41 plus interest in 2 payments made 25 Dec 1743 & 25

Dec 1744. Signed Joseph Wood. Delivered in the presence of Charles Edgar & Charles Lloyd. Recorded 28 June 1743. (F6:514).

Mortgage. On 10 Jan 1744/5 James Edwards of Nether Providence, carpenter, & Mercy his wife to Moses Vernon of Nether Providence, yeoman. Whereas James Edwards & Mercy his wife for £35 granted to Moses Vernon a tract in Nether Providence bounded by Providence Road, land of James Sharples containing 28 3/4 acres. James Edwards & Mercy his wife to pay Moses Vernon £35 plus interest in yearly payments to be paid in full on or before 10 Jan 1748/9. Signed James Edwards & Mercy Edwards. Delivered in the presence of Joseph Parker, John Salkeld & David Ranken. Recorded 16 Jan 1744/5. (F6:516).

Lease & Release. On 2 & 3 Oct 1740 Richard Woodward of East Bradford, yeoman, & Mary his wife to Thomas Woodward of East Bradford, yeoman, son of Richard & Mary. Whereas the commissioners of William Penn by deed dated 2 July 1686 granted to Arthur Cook a tract of land containing 1,500 acres, recorded in Bucks Book A, Vol 1, Page 34. Whereas Margaret Cook, widow & executrix of the will of Arthur Cook by deed dated 11 & 12 Sep 110 granted to Nathaniel Ring & Elizabeth his wife a tract of 386 acres, part of the 1,500 acres. Nathaniel Ring & Elizabeth his wife by deed dated 25 Mar 1711 granted to Richard Woodward a tract of land in East Bradford bounded by land of John Willis, land late of Edward Wanton & other land of Nathaniel Ring containing 150 acres, part of the 386 acres, recorded in Chester, Book C, Page 259. Now Richard Woodward & Mary his wife for £200 granted to Thomas Woodward the said tract. Signed Richard Woodward & Mary Woodward. Delivered in the presence of William Smith & Jeremy Sulivan. Recorded 5 Feb 1744/5. (F6:520).

Deed. On 1 Sep 1736 Thomas Howell of Chichester, yeoman, & Rachel his wife to William Vaughn of Chichester, yeoman. Whereas Edmund Andres, Esq., Governor of New York by deed dated 28 Mar 1676 granted to Charles Johnson, Olle Rawson, Hans Olleson, Olle Nulson, Hans Hopman & John Hendrichson a tract situated on the Delaware River at a place now called Chichester containing 1,000 acres. Whereas Hans Olleson by deed dated 12 Mar 1678 granted 1/6 part of the 1,000 acres to William Clayton. Whereas William Clayton died intestate, the same 1/6 part descended to his son William Clayton. William Clayton by deed dated 8 Sep 1699 granted to Thomas Canthy a lot in Chichester bounded by the river, land of William Thomas, Back Street & a lot formerly of Isaac Taylor. Thomas Canthy bargained away the said lot to Humphrey Johnson by virtue of said bargain Humphrey Johnson with Thomas Canthy granted said lot to Mordecai Howell by deed dated 3 Mar 1704/5. Mordecai Howell by deed dated 10 Feb 1734/5 granted to Thomas Howell the said lot. Now Thomas Howell & Rachel his wife for £15 granted to William Vaughn the said lot. Signed Thomas Howell & Rachel Howell. Delivered in the presence of John Kerlin, John Price & Jacob Worrall. Recorded 6 Mar 1744/5. (F6:524).

Release. On 5 Feb 1744/5 Thomas Parsons of the County of Salem in West New Jersey, hatter & Esther his wife to William Vaughn of Chichester, ship carpenter. Whereas Edmund Andres, Esq., Governor of New York by deed dated 28 Mar 1676 granted to Charles Johnson, Olle Rawson, Hans Olleson, Olle Nulson, Hans Hopman & John Hendrichson a tract situated on the Delaware River at a place now called Chichester containing 1,000 acres. Whereas Hans Olleson by deed dated 12 Mar 1678 granted 1/6 part of the 1,000 acres to William Clayton. Whereas William Clayton died intestate, the same 1/6 part descended to his son William Clayton. William Clayton granted the lot & 2 acres (hereafter described) to William Thomas. Whereas William Thomas was indebted to William Flower of Chichester, weaver, for £18.0.5, made his will & appointed Honor the wife of James Brown his executrix & soon after died. William Flower did taker action against James Brown & Honor his wife for £18.0.5 & the court of Common Pleas on 26 Nov 1712 did recover the debt & £0.63.9 in damages to be levied on the lot & 2 acres of woodland. John Hoskins, sheriff sold said lands to Sarah Nosseter, recorded in Chester, Book D, Vol 4, Page 122. Sarah Nosseter since died & the lot & 2 acres descended to Sarah (her daughter & only issue) who is since married Benjamin Peters. Whereas Benjamin Peters & Sarah his wife by deed dated 9 & 10 Apr 1744 granted to Thomas Parsons & Esther his wife. Now Thomas Parsons & Esther his wife for £20 granted to William Vaughn all the lot in Chichester bounded by the Delaware River & a lot late of William Clayton. Signed Thomas Parson & Esther Parsons. Delivered in the presence of John Riley, Thomas Howell. Recorded 7 Mar 1744/5. (F6:527).

Release. On 24 Feb 1743 Henry Camm of Upper Providence, stocking weaver, & Margaret his wife to William Attwood & Samuel Mickle of the City of Philadelphia, merchants & Cadwalder Evans of Edgemont, yeoman. Whereas Henry Camm is seized in a tract of land in Upper Providence bounded by Ridley Creek, land of Randal Malin & land of Edward Parsons containing 100 acres & by mortgage dated 11 Oct 1739 mortgaged the said tract to the Trustees of the General Loan Office in the sum of £68 & whereas the principal is unpaid. William Attwood, Samuel Mickle & Cadwalder Evans have undertaken to pay the residue of the principal & interest. Whereas Henry Camm is possessed of other lands which are to be hereby made over & conveyed to William Attwood, Samuel Mickle & Cadwalder Evans, together with the described tract, a small piece of land bounded by the first tract, land of William Pennell & Charles Lewis containing 2+ acres & a lot lying in Chester 40' x 120' bounded by lots of John Hoskins, Caleb Pussey & James Steel & a lot in Wilmington, in New Castle bounded by land of Elias Buckingham & Market Street. Now Henry Camm & Margaret his wife for a further sum of £120 granted, released & conveyed to William Attwood, Samuel Mickle & Cadwalder Evans all the described lands. Signed Henry Camm & Margaret Camm. Delivered in the presence of Harry Travers & Joseph Brientnall. Recorded 15 mar 1744/5. (F6:531).

Lease & Release. On 22 & 23 Nov 1732 John Hutton of New Garden in the County of Chester, tailor, & Sarah his wife to Nathaniel Jenkins of New Garden, cordwainer. John Hutton & Sarah his wife for £150 granted to Nathaniel Jenkins the plantation in New Garden bounded by land of Michael Lightfoot, John Wiley, James Hobson & James Starr containing 100 acres being part of 300 acres which William Penn, Jr., granted to Michael Lightfoot, recorded in Chester, Book D, Vol 4, Page 29. Michael Lightfoot by deed dated 28 Oct 1729 granted 100 acres to John Hutton. Signed John Hutton & Sarah Hutton. Delivered in the presence of Michael Lightfoot, Giles Brumble & John Williams. Recorded 18 Mar 1744/5. (F6:534).

Declaration of Trust. On 3 Oct 1744 Thomas Howell of Chichester, yeoman, to John Moore & Elizabeth his wife. Whereas John Moore & Elizabeth his wife by deed dated 2 Oct 1744 granted to Thomas Howell the seventh part of the tract of land which was formerly Charles Rawson's, also 1/4 part of the plantation which Andrew Rawson died seized of. also all their right & interest in any lands belonging to her land husband John Driut, dec., with all the moveable or personal estate which belonged to Elizabeth before her marriage to John Moore intended to only be in trust for Elizabeth Moore for her natural life & after her death to be equally divided between the 2 children of her the said Elizabeth Moore by her former husband John Druit dec., to wit John Druit & Mary Druit. Thomas Howell do hereby acknowledge & declare he has no interest in said land. Signed Thomas Howell. Delivered in the presence of Joseph Parker & David Ranken. Recorded 3 Jan 1744/5. (F6:537).

Lease & Release. On 26 & 27 Oct 1719 Thomas Howell of Chichester, yeoman, to Thomas Clayton of Chichester, yeoman. Whereas Mordecai Howell of Chichester, gentleman, by deed dated 21 May 1708 granted to Samuel Preston of the City of Philadelphia, merchant, several pieces of land as described in said deed, subject to a condition the Mordecai Howell, his heirs & executors should pay to Samuel Preston the sum of £100 plus interest on or before 19 Sep 1710, recorded in Chester, Book B, Vol 2, Page 239. Whereas the £100 plus interest was not paid at the appointed time, Samuel Preston by deed dated 2 Sep 1718 did declare that his name was only used in the said deed by the special appointment of Jacob Hollock of the County of Sussex upon Delaware, cooker & in trust for him & in the same deed transferred over to Jacob Hollock all his right & interest in the said pieces of land. Whereas Jacob Hollock by deed dated 13 June 1719 granted to Thomas Howell all his right & interest in the pieces of land. Now Thomas Howell for £100 granted to Thomas Clayton 3 pieces of land lying in Chichester, part of the lands mentioned conveyed one piece at the west end of Chichester bounded by the River Delaware, the old King's Road, another piece of land joining the west side of the previous piece & the river Delaware & the other piece bounded by the last piece, the old King's Road, land late of Robert Moulder & Walter Martins containing in whole 31 acres. Signed Thomas Howell. Delivered in the presence of Joseph Bond, Jonathon Ottley, John Grubb & John Riley. Recorded 9 May 1745. (F6:538).

Mortgage. On 8 May 1745 Joseph Helmes of Ridley, yeoman, to Thomas Tatnall of Ridley, gentleman. Joseph Helmes for £20 granted to Thomas Tatnall all the piece of land in Ridley bounded by King's Road, land of Joseph Harvey & land of Jonas Morton containing 8 acres. Joseph Helmes to pay £20 plus interest to Thomas Tatnall in 2 payments to be paid in full on or before 8 May 1747. Signed Joseph Helmes. Delivered in the presence of Joseph Parker & David Ranken. Recorded 9 May 1745. (F6:543).

Release. On 2 Oct 1744 John Moore of Naamans Creek in the County of New Castle upon Delaware, yeoman, & Elizabeth his wife, who was one of the daughters of Charles Rawson, late of Brandywine Hundred in the County of New Castle upon Delaware, dec., to Thomas Howell of Chichester, yeoman. John Moore & Elizabeth his wife to for £5 granted Thomas Howell one seventh part of all that tract of land which Charles Rawson, her late father died seized of situated in Brandywine Hundred, also 1/4 part of the plantation which Andrew Rawson died seized of & which descended to her the Elizabeth Rawson as one of the heirs of Andrew Rawson & all right to lands belonging to her husband John Druit, dec., with all personal estate which belonged to her before her marriage to John Moore. Signed John Moore & Elizabeth Moore. Delivered in the presence of Joseph Parker & David Ranken. Recorded 10 May 1745. (F6:545).

Deed. On 18 June 1720 Samuel Preston of the County of Philadelphia, merchant, & Clement Plumstead of the City of Philadelphia, merchant, to David Jones of Chester County, mason. Whereas John Jones, late of the City of Philadelphia, merchant, dec., was seized in his lifetime a full 16th share of a tract of land containing 5,358 acres commonly called by the name Pickering Mines which was lately divided. Whereupon a certain parcel bounded by land of William Saunders, Samuel Carpenter, Henry Flowers containing 340 acres was allotted to John Jones. Whereas John Jones by a codicil to his last will 2 May 1708, duly proved & recorded in Philadelphia & bequeathed the said land to Samuel Preston & Clement Plumstead containing 340 acres & sometime after John Jones died. Now Samuel Preston & Clement Plumstead for £90 granted to David Jones all the 340 acres. Signed Samuel Preston & Clement Plumstead. Delivered in the presence of Edward Roberts & John Cadwalder. Recorded 17 May 1745. (F6:546).

Deed. On 12 Feb 1732/3 David Jones of Charlestown, yeoman, to Daniel Jones, eldest son & heir apparent of David Jones. Whereas John Jones, late of the City of Philadelphia, merchant, dec., was seized in his lifetime a full 16th share of a tract of land containing 5,358 acres commonly called by the name Pickering Mines which was lately divided. Whereupon a certain parcel bounded by land of William Saunders, Samuel Carpenter, Henry Flowers containing 340 acres was allotted to John Jones. Whereas John Jones by a codicil to his last will 2 May 1708, duly proved & recorded in Philadelphia & bequeathed the said land to Samuel Preston & Clement Plumstead containing 340 acres & sometime after John Jones died. Samuel Preston & Clement Plumstead by deed dated 18 June 1720 granted said land to David Jones. Now David Jones for £20 & natural love & affection granted to Daniel Jones a tract of land bounded by land of David Jones, George Lewis, land late of Samuel Carpenter & land of Mathew Marckus containing 107 acres. Signed David Jones. Delivered in the presence of William Reynolds, Thomas Owen & Richard Jones. Recorded 17 May 1745. (F6:549).

Deed. On 25 Feb 1741 David Jones, Sr., of Charlestown, carpenter, to John Jones, of Charlestown, carpenter. Whereas John Jones, late of the City of Philadelphia, merchant, dec., was seized in his lifetime a full 16th share of a tract of land containing 5,358 acres commonly called by the name Pickering Mines which was lately divided. Whereupon a certain parcel bounded by land of William Saunders, Samuel Carpenter, Henry Flowers containing 340 acres was allotted to John Jones. Whereas John Jones by a codicil to his last will 2 May 1708, duly proved & recorded in Philadelphia & bequeathed the said land to Samuel Preston & Clement Plumstead containing 340 acres & sometime after John Jones died. Samuel Preston & Clement Plumstead by deed dated 18 June 1720 granted said land to David Jones. Now David Jones for £100 granted to John Jones a tract of land bounded by land of Peter Gardners, Daniel Jones, Job Harvey & James John containing 233 acres. Signed David Jones. Delivered in the presence of Daniel John, David Rees & Timothy Griffith. Recorded 17 May 1745. (F6:551).

Release. On 6 May 1745 John Jones of Charlestown, carpenter, to David Jones of Charlestown, blacksmith. John Jones for £150 granted to David Jones a tract in Charlestown bounded by land of Peter Gardners, Daniel Jones, Job Harvey & James John containing 233 acres being part of 340 acres which Samuel Preston & Clement Plumstead by deed dated 18 June 1720 granted to David Jones the father of John & David parties to this. David Jones (the father) sold said 233 acres to John Jones. Signed John Jones. Delivered in the presence of John Parry & Enoch Walker. Recorded 17 May 1745. (F6:553).

Deed of Gift. On 30 Apr 1745 Samuel Robinett of Nottingham, husbandman for love & good will grant to my eldest son Allen Robinett, £31.5, to my 5 sons Stephen, Samuel, Joseph, James & Nathan Robinett each of them 1 shilling & likewise my son-in-law, John Bently, 1 shilling, likewise my son-in-law Thomas Kelly 1 shilling, likewise I give to my youngest son George Robinett the plantation which I now live on containing 175 acres forever, but not to dispose of while my wife lives without her consent, likewise my bible, my carpenter tools, reserving unto my loved wife, Mary Robinett the best room in the manor house during her natural life, 20 bushels of wheat, 6 bushels of Indian corn, 100 weight of pork & 20 shillings yearly during her natural life & other things & 77 acres bounded by land of William Crurni & William Boggs with the remainder of my personal estate, likewise I give & bequeath to my grandson George Rentfro £10 to be paid by my son George in 2 payments, the 1st one year after my death & a horse or mare within 6 months of my death. Signed Samuel Robinett. Delivered in the presence of William Maffit & Hugh Boyd. Recorded 23 May 1745. (F6:555).

Mortgage. On 13 Dec 1744 John Williams of Charlestown, weaver, & Mary his wife to Peter Gardner of Bleckley in the County of Philadelphia, yeoman. John Williams & Mary his wife for £70 granted to Peter Gardner a tract in Charlestown bounded by land of Mathias Martyn, John Evans, Rees John, Stephen Lewis & David John containing 290 acres. John Williams & Mary his wife to pay £70 plus interest to Peter Gardner in one payment due on or before 13 Dec 1747. Signed John Williams & Mary Williams. Delivered in the presence of John Davies, John Jones & William Parsons. Recorded 8 June 1745. (F6:556).

Deed. On 6 May 1745 Methusalot Davis of Trydriffrin, yeoman, to William Moore of Charlestown, Esq., Thomas James of Trydriffrin, yeoman, Morris Griffith of Willistown, yeoman, & Richard Richardson & John Cuthbert of Whiteland, yeomen. Methusalot Davis for 5 shillings grant to William Moore, Thomas James, Morris Griffith, Richard Richardson & John Cuthbert a tract in Trydriffrin bounded by a road called Rees Pritchard's Road & land of the Methusalot Davis containing 1 acres being part of 200 acres which John Penn, Thomas Penn & Richard Penn by their commissioner George Thomas, Esq., by deed dated 12 Apr last past, recorded in Philadelphia, Book A, Vol 11, Page 400, granted to Methusalot Davis. Signed Methusalot Davis. Delivered in the presence of William Hartley, George Aston & George Jarman. Recorded 24 June 1745. (F6:558).

Mortgage. On 5 Dec 1744 John Dickey of Chester County to Richard Peters & Lynford Lardner both of the City of Philadelphia, gentlemen. John Dickey for £46.4 grant to Richard Peters & Lynford Lardner a tract in Sadsbury bounded by land of William Betty & William Marsh containing 195 acres. John Dickey to pay £46.4 plus interest to Richard Peters & Lynford Lardner for the use of John Penn, Thomas Penn & Richard Penn, Esq., in yearly payments to be paid in full on or before 5 Dec 1751. Signed John Dickey. Delivered in the presence of David Wilson & John Callahan. Recorded 1 June 1745. (F6:561).

Mortgage. On 15 June 1745 Henry Feagan of Marple, yeoman, & Elizabeth his wife to Thomas Pennell of Middletown, yeoman. Henry Feagon & Elizabeth his wife for £50 granted to Thomas Pennell a tract in Marple bounded by land of Bernhard Vanleer, the Great Run, land of Peter Thompson, Peter Worral & land late of Goushen Benbow & Richard Man containing 126 acres. Henry Feagan & Elizabeth his wife to pay £25 plus interest on 16 Nov 1745 & £25 plus interest on 16 Nov 1746. Signed Henry Feagan & Elizabeth Feagan. Delivered in the presence of Eleanor Phillips & Joseph Parker. Recorded 26 June 1745. (F6:564).

Mortgage. On 22 May 1745 Thomas Lloyd of Chester County to Richard Peters & Lynford Lardner both of the City of Philadelphia, gentlemen. Thomas Lloyd for £42.5.8 grant to Richard Peters & Lynford Lardner a tract in East Nantmell bounded by land of Thomas Jones & John Williams containing 160 acres. Thomas Lloyd to pay £42.5.8 plus interest to Richard Peters & Lynford Lardner for the use of John Penn, Thomas Penn & Richard Penn, Esq., in yearly payments to be paid in full on or before 22 May 1749. Signed Thomas Lloyd. Delivered in the presence of George Duffel of Lancaster County & John Callahan. Recorded 25 July 1745. (F6:566).

Deed. On 24 Apr 1745 Samuel Levis of Springfield, yeoman, & Hannah his wife to their son Joseph Levis of Springfield, yeoman. Whereas Michael Blunston made his will dated 22 Dec 1731 & amongst other things, appointed his cousins, Samuel Levis of Springfield & Samuel Bunting of Darby, executors to sell said land in Darby within 5 years of his death & soon after died. Samuel Levis & Samuel Bunting by deed dated 25 & 26 Mar 1736/7 for £480 granted to John Davis the tract of land. John Davis & Rebecca his wife by deed dated 1 & 2 May 1737 granted to Samuel Levis the 2 tracts of land. Now Samuel Levis & Hannah his wife for natural love granted to Joseph Levis a tract in Darby bounded by land of Lewis Thomas, land formerly purchased of George Wood being part of the tracts mentioned & the old line of Michael

Blunston containing 311 acres. Signed Samuel Levis & Hannah Levis. Delivered in the presence of Samuel Bunting & Isaac Pearson. Recorded 10 June 1745. (F6:569).

Mortgage. On 18 May 1745 Joseph Levis of Darby, yeoman, & Susannah his wife to George Thomas of the City of Philadelphia, Esq. Whereas Samuel Levis & Hannah his wife by deed dated 24 Apr 1745 granted to their son Joseph Levis all that tract in Darby bounded by land of Lewis Thomas, land formerly purchased of George Wood & the old line of Michael Blunston containing 311 acres. Now Joseph Levis & Susannah his wife for £500 granted to George Thomas all the tract of 311 acres. Joseph Levis & Susannah his wife to pay £500 plus interest in full to George Thomas on or before 18 May 1746. Signed Joseph Levis & Susannah Levis. Delivered in the presence of William Peters & Richard Peters. Recorded 10 June 1745. (F6:573).

Mortgage. On 5 July 1745 Jonathan Paschall of Darby, maulster,, & Mary his wife to Moses Forster of the City of Philadelphia, wheelwright. Jonathan Paschall & Mary his wife for £50 granted to Moses Forster a tract in Calcoon Hook in the township of Darby bounded by land of Isaac Pearson, land of Otto Natzeilles & Andrew Boone containing 34+ acres. Jonathan Paschall & Mary his wife to pay £50 plus interest on or before 5 July 1746. Signed Jonathon Paschall & Mary Paschall. Delivered in the presence of George Bullock & John Reily. Recorded 12 July 1745. (F6:577).

Deed. On 16 Oct 1736 Thomas Martin of Middletown, yeoman, Mary his wife to his son John Martin. Whereas there is a tract of land in Middletown bounded by land of Caleb Hamson, Edgmont Road, Ridley Creek & land of Catherine Fairlamb containing 140 acres being part of 500 acres granted by William Penn to John Martin the father of Thomas Martin by deed dated 1 & 2 Dec 1681. 300 acres was laid out to John Martin on 10 Dec 1682 in Middletown, which the 140 acres is part & also a tract in Middletown bounded Edgmont Road, land formerly belonging to William Coebourn & land of Thomas Coebourn containing 6 acres which was purchased of Isaac Few by John Martin by deed dated 26 Feb 1705. Both parcels descended to Thomas Martin from John Martin being his sole heir. Now Thomas Martin & Mary his wife for £50 & natural love grant to one of their sons, John Martin both tracts containing in whole 146 acres. Signed Thomas Martin & Mary Martin. Delivered in the presence of John Stinson, Caleb Harrison, Jr., & Joseph Martin. Recorded 13 Aug 1745. (F6:579).

Mortgage. On 1 July 1745 Robert Turner of Fallowfield, miller, to Evan Morgan of the City of Philadelphia, merchant. Whereas Robert Turner is bound to Evan Morgan for £120 on the condition he pay £60 plus interest to Evan Morgan. Now to better secure the said payment Robert Turner granted to Evan Morgan a tract of land in Fallowfield bounded by land late of John Salkeld containing 101 acres. Robert Turner to pay £63.12 to Evan Morgan on 1 July 1747. Signed Robert Turner. Delivered in the presence of Charles Brocken & Paul Isaac. Recorded 14 Aug 1745. (F6:582).

Mortgage. On 13 June 1745 John Flemming of Londonderry township in the County of Chester to Richard Peters of the City of Philadelphia, Esq. John Flemming for £50 granted to Richard Peters a tract lying in the branches of Octararo Creek in Londonderry bounded by land of Thomas White, John Black, John Dougherty, John Griswell & William Miller containing 148 acres. John Flemming to pay £50 plus interest to Richard Peters on or before 13 June 1746. Signed John Flemming. Delivered in the presence of James Coughron & John Callahan. Recorded 15 Aug 1745. (F6:584).

Mortgage. On 6 Aug 1745 Walter Gilkey of Chester County to Richard Peters & Lynford Lardner both of the City of Philadelphia, gentlemen. Walter Gilkey for £30 grant to Richard Peters & Lynford Lardner a tract in Sadsbury bounded by Doe Run, land of William Ferguson & Hugh Divings containing 225 acres. Walter Gilkey to pay £30 plus interest to Richard Peters & Lynford Lardner for the use of John Penn, Thomas Penn & Richard Penn, Esq., in yearly payments to be paid in full on or before 6 Aug 1751. Signed Walter Gilkey. Delivered in the presence of Lewis Gordon & John Callahan. Recorded 15 Aug 1745. (F6:586).

Declaration of Intent. On 10 May 1745 William Moore, Esq., Thomas James, Morris Griffith, Richard Richardson & John Cuthbert all of Chester County, yeomen send greetings whereas Methusalot Davis by deed dated 6 May 1745 granted to William Moore, Thomas James, Morris Griffith, Richard Richardson & John Cuthbert a piece of land in Trydriffrin bounded by the road called Rees Pritchard's Road & land of Methusalot Davis containing 1 acre to be held in trust of the members of

Saint Peter's Church for a church & burying ground. Signed William Moore, Thomas James, Morris Griffith, Richard Richardson & John Cuthbert. Delivered in the presence of William Harkey, George Aston & George James. Recorded 13 Sep 1745. (F6:589).

Mortgage. On 9 Aug 1745 Joseph Talbot of Middletown, yeoman, & Hannah his wife to Edward Russell of Chester, waterman. Joseph Talbot & Hannah his wife for £50 granted to Edward Russell a tract in Middletown bounded by land late of John Worrall, land of Edward Grizell, William Hill & other land of Joseph Talbot containing 43 acres being part of a tract of 134 acres which John Talbot the late father of Joseph Talbot by his will dated 12 June 1726 devised to his children to be equally divided between them & all the children conveyed their shares to Joseph Talbot. Joseph Talbot to pay £50 plus interest to Edward Russell in yearly payments to be paid in full on or before 9 Aug 1750. Signed Joseph Talbot & Hannah Talbot. Delivered in the presence of Daniel Calvert, John Lea & David Ranken. Recorded 24 Sep 1745. (F6:591).

Deed. On 29 Aug 1745 John Owen, sheriff to William Downard of New London. Whereas John Cam in the Court of Common Pleas recovered against John Ross, executor of Alex Thompson a debt of £66 & £0.70.6 in damages to be levied on the lands, goods & chattels of Alexander Thompson. Whereas Alexander Thompson was seized in a tract of land in New London containing 100 acres bounded land of Thomas Cook, Robert McDowell, Robert Gilmore & George Curry. John Owen for £65 grant to William Downard the said tract containing 100 acres. Signed John Owen. Delivered in the presence of William Reynolds, Thomas Webster & Dan Calvert. Recorded 25 Sep 1745. (F6:594).

Lease & Release. On 25 & 26 Mar 1741 Abiah Taylor of East Bradford, yeoman, & Deborah his wife to Samuel Taylor the son & heir apparent of Abiah. Whereas the commissioners of William Penn by deed dated 19 & 20 Aug 1706 granted to Abiah Taylor a tract in Bradford bounded by land late of Isaac Taylor, land late of Edward Wanton, land late of Thomas Buffington & land late of John Buradal containing 430 acres, recorded in Book A, Vol 3, Page 328. Now Abiah Taylor the father & Deborah his wife for £150 & love & affection granted to Samuel Taylor a tract in East Bradford bounded by land late of Edward Wanton, land late of Thomas Buffington, land late of John Buradal & Randle Speakman, branch of Brandywine Creek & land of Henry Woodward containing 399 acres. Signed Abiah Taylor & Deborah Taylor. Delivered in the presence of Robert Brown & Richard Jones. Recorded 3 Oct 1745. (F6:596).

Agreement. On 26 Mar 1741. Memorandum of an agreement made between Abiah Taylor of East Bradford, yeoman, to Samuel Taylor of East Bradford, son & heir apparent of Abiah Taylor. Whereas Abiah Taylor & Deborah his wife granted to Samuel Taylor a tract of land containing 399 acres, reserving the privilege of the woods now growing on the hill adjacent Abiah's hill to take away all the wood or timber they might need. Signed Abiah Taylor. Delivered in the presence of Robert Brown & Richard Jones. Recorded 3 Oct 1745. (F6:600).

Lease & Release. On 5 & 6 Aug 1745 Swan Boon of Calcon Hook, yeoman, & Rebecca his wife to Thomas Tatnall of Ridley, gentleman. Whereas Hans Boon made his will dated 26 Nov 1724 & amongst other things devised to his son Swan Boon the house & land in Calcon Hook. Now Swan Boon & Rebecca his wife for £152 granted to Thomas Tatnall a tract in Darby bounded by other land of Thomas Tatnall, Park, Job Harvey, Charles Justices & the King's Road containing 76 2/4 acres. Signed Swan Boon & Rebecca Boon. Delivered in the presence of Peter Dicks, John Mendenhall, Joseph Parker, Simon Batten & John Crozier. Recorded 15 Oct 1745. (F6:601).

Deed. On 12 Aug 1730 Nicholas Newlin of Concord, yeoman, eldest son & heir of Nathaniel Newlin, late of Concord, gentleman, dec., Nathaniel Newlin of Concord, yeoman, the 2nd son of Nathaniel Newlin, dec., John Newlin of Concord, yeoman, the 3rd son of Nathaniel Newlin, dec., Richard Evenson of Thornbury, yeoman, & Jemima his wife, one of the daughters of Nathaniel Newlin, dec., Richard Clayton of Concord, cordwainer, & Mary his wife, another daughter of Nathaniel Newlin, dec., & William Baily of Kennet, yeoman, & Kezia his wife the other daughter of Nathaniel Newlin, dec., to Robert Lewis, Mary Lewis, Nathaniel Lewis & Ellis Lewis the children of Ellis Lewis of Kennet, yeoman, & Elizabeth his first wife, who was one of the daughters of Nathaniel Newlin, dec. Whereas William Penn by deed dated 22 & 23 Mar 1681 granted to Nicholas Moore James Claypoole, Phillip Ford, William Shardlow, Edward Pierce, John Simcock, Thomas Brassey, Thomas Parker & Edward Brooks 20,000 acres of land to be laid out in the province in trust for the Free Society of Traders. On 1 June 1688 there was laid out to Benjamin Chambers, president of the Free Society of Traders for the use of the society 7,100 acres being part in the County of Chester. The trustees of the Society of Free Traders by deed dated 10 June 1724 granted to Nathaniel Newlin the 7,100 acres, recorded Chester, Book D, Vol 4, Page 369. Whereas Nathaniel Newlin died intestate all his lands were divided amongst his children & the eldest to receive a double share & the said grandchildren to have an equal share. Whereas Nicholas Newlin, Nathaniel Newlin, John Newlin, Richard Evenson, Jemima Evenson, Richard Clayton, Mary Clayton, William Baily & Kezia Baily & the said children of Ellis Lewis in behalf of his said children who are yet under age, have agreed & consented to make a division of all the lands of the said Nathaniel Newlin, at the time of his death. Now for a division of the said land, Nicholas Newlin, Nathaniel Newlin, John Newlin, Richard Evenson, Jemima Evenson, Richard Clayton, Mary Clayton, William Baily & Kezia Baily granted to Robert Lewis, Mary Lewis, Nathaniel Lewis & Ellis Lewis their share of their late grandfather's land, all the 3 pieces of land lying in the County of Chester, one bounded by land of William Baily, Joel Baily & Richard Clayton containing 411 acres another piece of land bounded by land of Joel Baily, William Baily, Nathaniel Newlin & Marlborough township containing 546 acres & the other piece of land bounded by land of Joel Baily, William Dean, Mordecai Cloud & Richard Clayton containing 176 acres, all being part of the 7,100 acres. Signed Nicholas Newlin, Nathaniel Newlin, John Newlin, Richard Evenson, Jemima Evenson, Richard Clayton, Mary Clayton, William Baily & Kezia Baily. Delivered in the presence of Joseph Brinton, Henry Peirce & John Taylor. Recorded 21 Oct 1745. (F6:605).

Release. On 26 May 1723 Mathias Necelius of Calcon Hook in Darby township, yeoman, to David Mortonson of Darby, yeoman. Whereas Peter Peterson by deed dated 1 Aug 1711 granted to Mathias Necelius & Morton Mortonson, the father of David Mortonson a tract in Calcon Hook in the township of Darby containing 145 acres, recorded in Chester, Book C, Page 200. Whereas by a certain agreement made between Mathias Necelius & Morton Mortonson a division was made of said tract. Whereas Morton Mortonson is since dec. & no effectual release between the parties was made & David Morton being the sole executor of the Morton Mortonson. Now Mathias Necelius for £50 granted & released to David Mortonson a tract in Calcon Hook in the township of Darby bounded by the Creek, land of Hans Urins & Morton Mortonson containing 64 acres & another piece bounded by the Creek & land of Morton Mortonson containing 10 acres & another piece lying between Morton Mortonson's land & Darby Creek containing 2 3/4 acres

& another piece of land bounded by Thoroughfare Creek, land of Hans Urin, Calcon Hook landing & Darby Creek containing 2 acres & another piece of land on the island called Hay Island bounded by Thoroughfare Creek, land of Hans Urin & Morton Mortonson containing 2 acres & another piece of land on the said island bounded by land of Hans Urin, Darby Creek & Boon's Marsh containing 17 acres out of which Mathis Necelius is to have 5 acres & another piece of land bounded by land of Morton Mortonson, Thoroughfare Creek & Darby Creek containing 15 acres being in all 113 1/3 acres. Signed Mathias Necelius. Delivered in the presence of John Bethel & Benjamin Clift. Recorded 29 Oct 1745. (F6:610).

Deed. On 26 Aug 1745 John Parker of Darby, yeoman, to Thomas Tatnall of Ridley, gentleman. Whereas Joseph Wood, late of Darby, gentleman, by deed dated 4 Dec 1688 granted to Richard Parker, dec., the grandfather of John Parker a tract in Darby containing 148 acres. Richard Parker made his will dated 6 Apr 1726 & amongst other things devised to his son Richard Parker (the father of John Parker) the plantation & all other lands in Darby or elsewhere. Richard Darby (the father) made his will dated 22 Apr 1736 & amongst other things bequeathed to his son John all the southwest part of his land in Darby to be divided from the other part by a line drawn from Job Harvey's land to John Barham. Now John Parker for £70 granted to Thomas Tatnall a tract in Darby bounded by land of Swan Boon, Thomas Tatnall & Mary Smith containing 31+ acres. Signed John Parker. Delivered in the presence of Francis Harding, Jr., & Elizabeth Houlton. Memorandum. Peaceable possession given to Thomas Tatnall in the presence of Francis Harding, Jr., & John Crozier. Recorded 31 Oct 1745. (F6:513).

Mortgage. On 15 May 1745 Joseph Jackson of London Grove in the County of Chester, yeoman, to Clement Plumstead of the City of Philadelphia, Esq. Whereas Joseph Jackson is bounded to Clement Plumstead for £300 upon condition of payment of £150. Joseph Jackson for better securing said debt granted to Clement Plumstead a tract in London Grove bounded by land of Samuel Underwood & Moses Harlan containing 150 acres. Joseph Jackson to pay £150 plus interest to Clement Plumstead in one payment on or before 15 May 1746. Signed Joseph Jackson. Delivered in the presence of Joseph Shippen & John Reily. Recorded 8 Nov 1745. (F6:616).

Lease & Release. On 22 & 23 Feb 1738 John Boss of Chichester, yeoman, & Elizabeth his wife to Nathaniel Grubb of Willistown, yeoman. Whereas Edmund Andres, Esq., Governor of New York by deed dated 28 Mar 1676 granted to Charles Johnson, Woole Rawson, Hans Olleson, Woole Neilson, Hans Hopman & John Hendrichson a tract situated on the Delaware River at a place now called Chichester containing 1,000 acres. Whereas Woole Rawson by deed dated 1 Mar 1685 granted to James Brown the lot of ground being part of the 1,000 acres, recorded in Chester, Book A, Vol 1, Page 81. James Brown by deed dated 15 Sep 1699 granted to Peter Boss the late father of John Boss a lot in Chichester bounded by the river Delaware, a lot of Jeremiah Collett & land then of Samuel Brown. Peter Boss died intestate the said lot of land descended to John Boss, his son & only issue. Now John Boss & Elizabeth his wife for £100 granted to Nathaniel Grubb the lot described before. Signed John Boss & Elizabeth Ross. Delivered in the presence of Adam Buckley, William Hewes & John Taylor. Recorded 16 Nov 1745. (F6:618).

Mortgage. On 6 Dec 1745 Samuel Ogden of Springfield, sadler, to Jonathon Maris of Marple, yeoman. Samuel Ogden for £25 granted to Jonathon Maris a tract in Springfield bounded by land of George Lownes, land formerly of Isaac Norris & land now of Joshua Thompson containing 41 1/4 acres. Samuel Ogden to pay £25 plus interest to Jonathon Maris on or before 6 Dec 1749. Signed Jonathon Maris. Recorded 14 Dec 1745. (F6:622).

Deed. On 9 Mar 1742 Peter Worral of Marple, yeoman, & Elizabeth his wife to Benjamin Worral of Marple, one of the sons of Peter & Elizabeth. Whereas Peter Worral of Marple, tanner, father of Peter Worral by deed dated 11 Dec 1699 granted to his son Peter Worral a tract in Marple bounded by land of Jonathon Worral containing 150 acres taken out of 300 acres belonging to Peter Worral the father of Peter Worral. Whereas Peter Worral by deed dated 19 & 20 Apr 1734 purchased from William Winton of the County of Glouster in the province of West New Jersey & Mary his wife a plantation in Marple bounded by land of Peter Worral, land late of Jonathon Hayes & land late of William Owen containing 44 acres. Now Peter Worral & Elizabeth his wife for natural love for their son granted to Benjamin Worral all of the 2 tracts. Signed Peter Worral & Elizabeth Worral. Delivered in the presence of Joseph Hawley & Jonathon Worral. Recorded 16 Dec 1745. (F6:624).

Declaration. John Rowan, Sr., of Gray Abby in the County of Down, gentleman, eldest son & heir of Cornelius Rowan of New London in the County of Chester, gentleman, dec., & George Cochran of Kirkcubbin in the County of Down, in Ireland, gentleman, & Anne Cochran alias Anne Rowan his wife & daughter of Cornelius Rowan the only surviving legatees of Cornelius Rowan. Whereas Cornelius Rowan died in Pennsylvania seized & possessed of 2 plantations with water grist mills in the township of New London & Sadsbury both in the County of Chester. John Rowan, Sr., George Cochran & Anne his wife appoint John Rowan, Jr., of Old Harbour in Jamaica, surgeon their lawful attorney to settle the estate of Cornelius Rowan. John Rowan, Sr., George Cochran & Ann his wife must approve all actions of the said attorney. Signed John Rowan, George Cochran & Anne Cochran. Delivered in the presence of John Patton, George Cochran & John Rowan. Recorded 1745. (F6:626).

County of Interim & City of Belfast. On 26 May 1742 John Duff, Esq., sovereign of Belfast & one of his majesties Justices of the Peace, certify the said Letter of Attorney & affixed the seal of the town. Signed John Duff. Recorded 1745. (F6:627).

County of Interim & City of Belfast. On 26 May 1742 John Patten & William Willson both of Gray Abbey in the County of Downs & made an oath that Anne Rowan, Sr., alias Patten, the late wife of Cornelius Rowan, formerly of Ireland & lately of New London in the County of Chester, dec., died in Ireland in the year 1739 & further that Abraham Rowan, son of Cornelius Rowan, died in the Kingdom of Ireland about 1733, intestate, unmarried & without lawful issue & also David Rowan, grandson of Cornelius Rowan has been absent from the kingdom of Ireland for 12 years & believed to be dead, being intestate without lawful issue to their knowledge. Anne Rowan, Sr., Abraham Rowan & David Rowan are mentioned in a paper dated 18 Aug 1724 & importing the will of Cornelius Rowan. Signed John Duff. The town seal to be affixed. Recorded 1745. (F6:627).

Lease & Release. On 3 & 4 May 1742, John Rowan, Sr., of Gray Abby in the County of Down, gentleman, eldest son & heir of Cornelius Rowan of New London in the County of Chester, gentleman, dec., & George Cochran of Kirkcubbin in the County of Down, in Ireland, gentleman, & Anne Cochran alias Anne Rowan his wife to James Cochran of Sadsbury, yeoman. John Rowan, Sr., George Cochran & Anne Cochran for £5 granted to James Cochran a tract in Sadsbury being part of the estate of Cornelius Rowan containing 135 acres. Signed John Rowan, George Cochran & Anne Cochran. Delivered in the presence of John Patton, George Cochran & John Rowan. (to be sent to John Rowan, Jr., of Old Harbour, Jamaica, surgeon for the use & behoof of James Cochran. John Duff affixed the seal of Belfast. Recorded 1745. (F6:628).

Deed. On 16 Feb 1733 John Newlin of Concord, yeoman, & Mary his wife to Thomas Carrel of Chester County, yeoman. Whereas William Penn by deed dated 22 & 23 Mar 1681 granted to Nicholas Moore James Claypoole, Phillip Ford, William Shardlow, Edward Pierce, John Simcock, Thomas Brassey, Thomas Parker & Edward Brooks 20,000 acres of land to be laid out in the province in trust for the Free Society of Traders. On 1 June 1688 there was laid out to Benjamin Chambers, president of the Free Society of Traders for the use of the society 7,100 acres being part in the County of Chester. The trustees of the Society of Free Traders by deed dated 10 June 1724 granted to Nathaniel Newlin the 7,100 acres, recorded Chester, Book D, Vol 4, Page 369. Whereas Nathaniel Newlin died intestate all his lands were divided amongst his children & the eldest to receive a double share. Whereas 443 acres fell to the share of John Newlin as in deed dated 12 Aug 1730. Now John Newlin & Mary his wife for £90 granted to Thomas Carrel a tract on a branch of Brandywine Creek, bounded by land of Richard Evenson & Nathaniel Newlin containing 443 acres. Signed John Newlin & Mary Newlin. Delivered in the presence of Henry Pierce, Jr., & Abraham Barnet. Recorded 18 Jan 1745/6. (F6:631).

Deed. On 30 June 1741 Thomas Carrel, late of Chester County but now of the City of Philadelphia, mason & Ann his wife to Richard Treville of Fallowfield, yeoman. Thomas Carrel & Ann his wife for £520 granted to Richard Treville a tract in the township of Newlin bounded by land of Thomas Hicklin, land late of Richard Evenson but now of Ezekiel & James Harland & land of Nathaniel Newlin containing 313 acres. Signed Thomas Carrel & Ann Carrel. Delivered in the presence of James Hamilton, James Treviller & William Allen. Recorded 27 Jan 1745/6. (F6:634).

Mortgage. On 1 Aug 1745 Everard Ellis of Darby, yeoman, & Bridget his wife to John Thomas of Wiccacoe in the County of Philadelphia, yeoman. Whereas Abraham Lewis, of Darby, yeoman, & Mary his wife deed dated 1 & 2 Mar 1745 granted to Everard Ellis a tract in Darby bounded by the

Mill Creek commonly called Cobbs Creek, land of John Griffith formerly John Blunstons, land of Benjamin Bonsall & Moses Hibberd containing 50 acres being part of tract of 500 acres granted to William Smith & laid out to the heirs of William Smith. Now Everard Ellis & Bridget his wife for £60 granted to John Thomas the described 50 acres. Everard Ellis & Bridget his wife to pay £60 plus interest to John Thomas in yearly payments to be paid in full on or before 1 Aug 1749. Signed Everard Ellis & Bridget Ellis. Delivered in the presence of William Moses & David Parry. Recorded 9 Jan 1745/6. (F6:636).

Deed. On 28 Dec 1745 Patrick McCamish of the City of Philadelphia, mason & Ann his wife to James Rhoads of Marple, tanner. Whereas Robert Pearson of Marple, yeoman, admin. of the goods & chattels of Joseph Parsons, late of Chester, mill wright, dec., by deed dated 2 Dec 1745 granted to Patrick McCamish 2 tracts of land, one in Marple bounded by Darby Road, land of James Rhoads, land of Robert Pearson & land of Joseph Parson which he had purchased of Robert Pearson containing 80 acres, which Robert Pearson & Catherine his wife by deed dated 24 Jan 1735 granted to Joseph Parsons. Now Patrick McCamish & Ann his wife for £115 granted to James Rhoads the said 80 acres. Signed Patrick McCamish & Ann McCamish. Delivered in the presence of John Owen, Arthur Forster & George Owen. Recorded 18 Feb 1745/6. (F6:638).

Mortgage. On 2 Nov 1745 John Jones of East Caln, wheel wright & Sarah his wife to Robert Skettell & Amos Skettell both of the City of Philadelphia, merchants. Whereas John Jones is bound to Robert Skettell & Amos Skettell for £182 on the condition of the payment of £91. John Jones & Sarah his wife to better secure the said payment granted to Robert Skettell & Amos Skettell a tract in East Caln bounded by land of William Lawson, Andrew Cock, Peter Bazalian & Edward Smout containing 234 acres. John Jones to pay Robert Skettell & Amos Skettell £91 plus interest to be paid on or before 2 Nov 1746. Signed John Jones & Sarah Jones. Delivered in the presence of Joseph Brinton & William Littler. Recorded 10 Mar 1745/6. (F6:640).

Deed. On 27 Feb 1745/6 John Owen, sheriff to William Wiley of .... Whereas Sarah Prew & Mary Prew at the Court of Common Pleas recovered against William Wiley & Susannah his wife, late Susanna Prew, devisee in the will of Caleb Prew, late of Chester County, dec., a

debt of £300 & £0.70.6 in damages to be levied on the land & goods of
William Wiley & Susannah Wiley being a tract in Kennet bounded by
land of George Harlan & John Cloud containing 200 acres. Now John
Owens for £302.4 granted to William Wiley the said tract. Signed John
Owen, sheriff. Delivered in the presence of Samuel Evans & David
Ranken. Recorded 11 Mar 1745/6. (F6:642).

Deed. On 5 Dec 1718 Richard Thomas of Great Valley in the County of
Chester, carpenter, & Grace his wife to John Morgan, Sr., of Radnor,
yeoman. Richard Thomas has 2 tracts of land in the County of Chester,
one being in the Great Welsh Tract & bounded by lands lately reputed to
be Thomas Lloyd's, dec., containing 1,869 acres which was confirmed to
him by deed dated 17 May 1704 by the commissioners of William Penn
recorded Book A, Vol 2, Page 685, & the other tract joining the previous
tract containing 243 acres confirmed to him by deed dated 8 Mar 1726 by
the commissioners of William Penn. Now Richard Thomas & Grace his
wife for £39.7.6 granted to John Morgan a tract bounded by land of
Adam Baker containing 150 acres. Signed Richard Thomas & Grace
Thomas. Delivered in the presence of Thomas Edwards & Jonathon
Holland. Recorded 11 Mar 1745/6. (F6:644).

Lease & Release. On 28 & 29 Feb 1734/5 John Morgan of Radnor,
yeoman, to William Owen of Marple, joiner. Whereas Richard Thomas of
Whiteland had 2 tracts of land one bounded by the Great Welsh Tract &
land formerly Thomas Lloyd's, dec., containing 1,869 acres confirmed to
Richard Thomas by the commissioners of William Penn by deed dated 17
May 1704, recorded in Philadelphia, Book A, Vol 2, Page 685, also
another tract joining the previous tract confirmed by deed dated 8 Mar
1716, recorded in Philadelphia, Book A, Vol 5, Page 195. Richard Thomas
& Grace his wife by deed dated 5 Dec 1718 granted to John Morgan a
tract of 150 acres being part of the 2 tracts. Now John Morgan for
£152.10 granted to William Owen a tract in Whiteland bounded by land
of John Earles & Adam Bakers containing 150 acres. Signed John
Morgan. Delivered in the presence of John David, Thomas David &
Francis Wayner. Recorded 13 Mar 1745/6. (F6:646).

INDEX

-A-
ADAMS, John, 141; William, 130, 150
ALBRIDGE, George, 35
ALLEN, Alice, 131, 132; John, 110, 131, 132; Margaret, 105, 145, 153, 154; Nathaniel, 43, 44; Nehemiah, 43, 44; Samuel, 151; William, 105, 144, 145, 152, 153, 154, 193
ALLISON, Oliver, 92
ANDERSON, James, 151; John, 133; Justast, 8; Patrick, 151
ANDRES, Edmund, 102, 139, 177, 178, 191; William, 104
ANDREWS, Claus, 173; George, 166, 168
ANDROSS, George, 169
ANNIS, Thomas, 54
ANTHONY, William, 53
ARCHER, Adam, 5; Ellin, 5; John, 121; Samson, 137
ARCHIES, John, 111
ARMSTRONG, James, 58
ARNOLD, Richard, 12, 107; Samuel, 107
ARNOLDS, Anthony, 63
ARTHER, Adam, 5; Ellin, 5
ASBRIDGE, George, 79, 84, 85
ASHTON, Margarett, 86; Robert, 10, 11, 46, 86, 124, 125, 126
ASKILL, William, 138
ASKOW, John, 106
ASPIN, Mathias, 162
ASTON, Elizabeth, 48; Esther, 136; George, 18, 48, 55, 56, 60, 68, 93, 98, 100, 113, 136, 171, 183, 187; Peter, 162; Robert, 120
ATHERTON, Henty, 70
ATHERTONS, Henry, 103
ATKINSON, James, 91; Michael, 35; Timothy, 140
ATTWOOD, William, 178, 179
AUBREY, Leitita, 10; William, 10, 74
AYRE, Abraham, 125
AYRES, Abraham, 13

-B-
BABB, Peter, 149
BACKHOUSE, J., 18; Richard, 37, 59, 108
BADCOCK, Alexander, 18, 19
BAILY, George, 50, 84; Jemima, 66; Joel, 189; Keria, 6, 7; Kezia, 27, 28, 58, 66, 67, 188, 189; Mary, 66; Susannah, 54, 55, 56; Thomas, 54; William, 6, 7, 27, 28, 58, 66, 67, 99, 188, 189
BAKER, Adam, 195; Jesse, 88, 89, 90; John, 24, 71, 72, 96, 110; Joseph, 12, 60, 71, 89, 90, 91, 96, 97, 110, 112, 148; Mary, 71, 72, 96, 97, 110; Nehemiah, 60; Robert, 148; Samuel, 25; Thomas, 84, 98
BALDWIN, Anthony, 2; Edward, 104; Elizabeth, 100, 101; Frances, 99; John, 23, 25, 38, 39, 41, 62, 63, 100, 101, 113, 138, 157; Joseph, 100, 101; Katherine, 39, 63; Margery, 2; Mary, 41; Thomas, 41, 100, 101; William, 41
BARBER, Hannah, 173; James, 26, 47, 173; Richard, 34; Robert, 8, 25, 35, 36, 38, 47, 85, 138, 172, 173; Susannah, 26, 173
BARHAM, John, 190
BARKER, Thomas, 66
BARNARD, Henry, 54, 55, 56; Richard, 69; Thomas, 123
BARNET, Abraham, 193
BARNETT, Abraham, 136, 137; Mary, 137
BARNEY, Jacob, 82
BARROW, Rebecca, 14; Robert, 14
BARRY, Mary, 37, 38, 92, 100, 118, 119, 176; Richard, 35, 37, 38, 67, 72, 86, 92, 100, 101, 108, 118, 119, 176
BARTLESON, John, 127
BARTON, Abraham, 25, 85; T., 51; Thomas, 58, 59, 64, 81, 82
BATE, Humphrey, 171; John, 171
BATTEN, Simon, 188
BATTLE, Parnella, 38; William, 38
BATTON, James, 165
BAYLTON, Tacy, 152
BAYLY, Joel, 67; William, 113
BAYNTON, Peter, 168
BAZALIAN, Peter, 194
BECK, Roger, 86
BECKINGHAM, William, 95
BEEBY, Dan, 80
BEEKS, Stephen, 84, 85
BELL, Mary, 138; Samuel, 138
BELLARS, John, 2, 12, 21
BELLER, John, 91
BELLOW, John, 91
BEMBO, Gersham, 100
BENBOW, Goushen, 184

BENBRIDGE, James, 91
BENNET, John, 64, 65, 176;
  Samuel, 64
BENNETT, Ann, 64, 65; Edward,
  20, 95, 107; James, 133; John,
  34, 65, 66; Sarah, 65, 95
BENSON, Katherine, 74, 75, 76,
  77; Robert, 15, 74, 75, 76, 77
BENTLEY, John, 99
BENTLY, John, 174, 182
BEST, John, 28
BETHEL, John, 135, 190
BETTERTON, Henry, 141
BETTY, William, 158, 174, 184
BEVAN, Aubrey, 138; William,
  131, 132
BEZAR, Edward, 73; Esther, 131;
  John, 124, 131, 143, 144, 166;
  Joseph, 168; Margaret, 73;
  Richard, 111, 169
BICKHAM, Jane, 18; Richard, 9,
  18, 26, 29
BICKMANS, Richard, 31
BINGHAM, James, 105, 144
BIRD, John, 122
BISHOP, Joseph, 97, 110;
  Samuel, 9, 18, 19
BISHOPS, Samuel, 45, 172
BISPHAM, Joshua, 87, 88, 89,
  90, 91; Mary, 88, 89, 90
BLACK, Jennet, 126; John, 125,
  126, 186; Thomas, 54, 139
BLACKALL, John, 73, 74
BLAGDON, Barbara, 55, 56
BLUNSTON, John, 91, 142, 194;
  Michael, 77, 84, 184, 185
BLUNSTONE, John, 14
BOAKE, Amos, 118
BOCKHOLTZ, Jacob, 113
BOGGS, William, 183
BOLD, James, 174
BOLT, Hannah, 161; William, 161
BOND, Elizabeth, 60, 99, 100,
  101, 102, 111; John, 60;
  Joseph, 87, 99, 100, 101, 102,
  111, 159, 169, 180; Richard,
  33, 115; Samuel, 20
BONHAM, Samuel, 54, 105
BONSALL, Benjamin, 142, 194;
  Jacob, 77, 78; Joseph, 114,
  122, 142, 172; Sarah, 172
BOON, Andrew, 126, 127, 128;
  Hance, 3; Hans, 188; Rebecca,
  126, 127, 188; Swan, 3, 30,
  188, 190
BOONE, Andrw, 185
BOONS, Henry, 3
BOOTH, Robert, 61, 157
BOOTHBY, Edward, 168
BOSS, Elizabeth, 191; John,
  191; Peter, 111, 191

BOSTOCK, Cheney, 88, 89, 90,
  91; John, 87, 88, 89, 90, 91;
  May, 88, 90; William, 87, 88,
  89, 90, 91, 97
BOURK, Edmund, 159, 160, 161;
  Rachel, 161
BOURKE, Edmond, 109; Edward,
  100
BOURN, Sarah, 25; Thomas, 25
BOWATER, John, 148
BOWEN, John, 123, 139
BOX, Joshua, 7
BOYD, Adam, 158; Hugh, 183;
  William, 174
BOYDEN, James, 11, 125
BOYLE, Daniel, 100
BRACKDEN, Thomas, 126
BRACKEN, Thomas, 38
BRADFORD, Andrew, 152; Sytie,
  151; William, 151, 152
BRADLEY, Edward, 12, 46, 107;
  Jonathon, 48, 49
BRADSHAW, Samuel, 142
BRANSLEY, Thomas, 38, 39
BRANSON, Elizabeth, 1; William,
  1, 86, 153
BRASSEY, Francis, 132; Mary,
  114, 132; Rebecca, 106, 132;
  Thomas, 27, 66, 82, 84, 98,
  106, 114, 132, 133, 146, 148,
  188, 193
BREDIN, James, 107
BRENTNALL, Joseph, 33
BRIAN, Thomas, 94
BRIENTNALL, Joseph, 144, 179
BRIGHT, Thomas, 35
BRINTMADE, Mary, 7; Thomas, 7
BRINTON, Elizabeth, 64; Esther,
  64; Jane, 64, 65; John, 7;
  Joseph, 25, 28, 29, 48, 58,
  61, 67, 120, 146, 151, 189,
  194; Samuel, 64; William, 64,
  65
BRISTOW, John, 7, 8, 82, 84,
  96, 97, 109, 133, 143
BROCKDEN, C., 85, 87, 103;
  Charles, 12, 16, 17, 32, 33,
  46, 70, 86, 157, 171
BROCKEN, Charles, 186
BROGDON, Edward, 157;
  Elizabeth, 157
BROOK, John, 7
BROOKS, Charles, 106; David,
  125, 165; Edward, 27, 66, 84,
  98, 188, 193
BROOM, Ann, 52; John, 3, 82,
  111; Jonathon, 111; Mary, 82;
  Thomas, 171
BROOMAL, John, 39, 40
BROOME, James, 168

BROWN, Daniel, 5, 47, 110, 111; Honor, 178; James, 41, 178, 191; John, 30; Joshua, 175; Robert, 13, 188; Samuel, 191; Susanna, 47; Susannah, 110
BROWNHILL, Mary, 60
BRUMBLE, Giles, 179
BRYAN, Thomas, 94
BUCHANAN, Andrew, 145
BUCKINGHAM, Elias, 179
BUCKLEY, Adam, 156, 191; James, 47, 48, 98, 155, 166; John, 61, 160; Mary, 47, 48, 98, 155; Samuel, 114, 156, 161; Thomasin, 156
BUCKLY, Samuel, 32
BUDD, John, 37, 43, 44, 98; Sarah, 98
BUFFINGTON, John, 129; Richard, 10, 15, 16, 47, 80; Thomas, 81, 187; William, 50
BULLAR, John, 37, 67
BULLER, John, 1
BULLOCK, George, 185
BUNTING, Samuel, 70, 154, 184, 185
BURADAL, John, 187
BURCHALL, Caleb, 94
BURGE, William, 32, 51
BURLING, Edward, 69
BUTCHER, Edmond, 2; Zach, 117; Zachariah, 76, 77, 176; Zachary, 136, 137
BUTTON, Jacob, 113

-C-

CADWALDER, John, 2, 162, 166, 181
CAIN, John, 93, 94
CALDELL, Vincent, 37
CALDRY, Thomas, 2
CALDWELL, Betty, 37, 146
CALLAHAN, John, 134, 135, 142, 149, 150, 158, 163, 170, 184, 186
CALVERT, Dan, 187; Daniel, 187
CALVERTS, Daniel, 115
CAM, John, 187
CAMBELL, William, 45
CAMM, Henry, 72, 104, 178, 179; Margaret, 104, 178, 179
CAMPINOTT, George, 3
CANBY, Thomas, 155, 156
CANTESON, Erasmus, 71; Mary, 71; Morton, 71
CANTHY, Thomas, 177, 178
CARPENTER, Mary, 35; Samuel, 17, 35, 125, 181, 182; William, 103, 172
CARREL, Ann, 193; Thomas, 193

CARRELL, Daniel, 133; Margery, 133
CARRIGON, Parrick, 62; Susanna, 62, 63
CARSONS, William, 105
CARTER, Edward, 41, 82, 84; George, 80; Jeremiah, 35, 36; John, 52, 64; Joseph, 17; Lydia, 122; Mary, 35, 36, 100; Minovah, 17, 18; Neevah, 46; Ninevah, 35, 100; Nineveh, 36; Robert, 6, 34, 37, 47, 122; Sarah, 17
CASEY, John, 53
CAUTS, Constantine, 106
CAWLEY, James, 49
CHADDS, Elizabeth, 74, 76, 150, 151; Francis, 95; Grace, 95; John, 74, 76, 150, 151
CHADS, Elizabeth, 75; John, 75, 77, 113
CHALDONT, Robert, 2
CHALDREY, Thomas, 140
CHALKLEY, Thomas, 54, 55, 56
CHAMBELAIN, John, 133
CHAMBERLAIN, John, 133; Robert, 62
CHAMBERLIN, John, 2
CHAMBERS, Benjamin, 16, 28, 66, 84, 99, 188, 193; John, 167
CHANDLER, George, 55, 56, 112, 134; Jacob, 134
CHAPMAN, George, 137
CHENEY, Ann, 63; Elizabeth, 21, 63; John, 21, 63, 90; Thomas, 21, 63
CHEVERS, James, 39, 40, 109
CHILD, John, 71, 167
CHILDS, John, 35
CHUBB, Daniel, 111
CHURCHMAN, George, 149
CLARK, John, 65
CLARKE, George Forman, 129; Thomas, 134
CLAXTON, James, 64, 131; Mary, 64
CLAYPOOLE, George, 149; James, 3, 27, 66, 84, 98, 148, 188, 193
CLAYTON, Elizabeth, 48, 146; Mary, 6, 7, 27, 28, 66, 67, 99, 100, 137, 164, 188, 189; Richard, 6, 7, 27, 28, 48, 50, 58, 66, 67, 99, 146, 188, 189; Thomas, 87, 159, 180; William, 8, 41, 47, 100, 133, 137, 140, 156, 157, 159, 164, 167, 177, 178
CLEMENT, Abraham, 1; Jeremiah, 1
CLEMSON, James, 14

CLEWS, John, 39, 40
CLIFT, Benjamin, 190
CLOUD, Jason, 18, 100; John, 150, 167, 168, 195; Joseph, 112; Margaret, 150; Mary, 171; Mordecai, 67, 189; William, 102, 167
CLOYD, Michael, 150
COCHRAN, Anne, 192, 193; George, 192, 193; James, 192, 193
COCK, Andrew, 194
COEBOURN, Elizabeth, 57; Joseph, 45; Lydia, 57; Thomas, 57, 185; William, 57, 185
COEBURN, Elizabeth, 56; John, 119; Joseph, 56, 57, 58; Lydia, 56; Sarah, 56, 58; Thomas, 56, 79; William, 58
COLE, Erasmus, 11, 34, 81; Stephen, 23, 24, 25, 43, 59, 63, 122
COLEMAN, --, 114; Joseph, 50; Mary, 50; Nathaniel, 82; William, 17
COLLET, Richard, 81; Tobias, 166
COLLETT, Elizabeth, 11, 34; George, 175; Jeremiah, 113, 156, 167, 191; Richard, 11, 34, 112; Tobias, 13, 93, 94, 139, 169
COLLIER, John, 48
COLLINSON, William, 14
CONNER, Charles, 63
COOK, Arthur, 10, 16, 177; Elizabeth, 155; Francis, 148; John, 2, 12, 13, 15, 16; Margaret, 10, 15, 16, 177; Mary, 15; Richard, 155; Thomas, 30, 54, 187
COOKE, Arthur, 53; Francis, 146; John, 53; Margaret, 53
COOKSON, Daniel, 12, 16; Elizabeth, 12, 16
COOMBE, Henry, 36
COOPER, James, 49; Robert, 158; Thomas, 73
COPE, Oliver, 60, 61
COPPECK, Batholemew, 6, 72; John, 175; Moses, 6, 72; Phebe, 124; Phobe, 72
CORNACK, Morgan, 62
CORNELIUS, Thomas, 11
CORNWELL, John, 48, 56
COUGHRON, James, 186
COWMAN, Jeremiah, 56
COWPLAND, Caleb, 49, 58, 64, 78, 81, 99, 111, 123, 137, 138, 159; Jonathon, 159;
Joseph, 36; Sarah, 78, 137, 138; William, 73
COX, Daniel, 19; John, 37, 93, 94, 122; Lawrence, 97, 110; Mary, 94; Rachel, 37, 122; Richard, 93, 94; Thomas, 123; William, 94
CRAWFORD, David, 149, 158; Dorothy, 149
CREAGOR, James, 160
CRELL, Joseph, 158
CROCKSON, Randle, 20
CROOKER, John, 28
CROSBY, John, 3, 4, 5, 18, 20, 22, 24, 25, 29, 33, 42, 52, 58, 64, 80, 82, 92, 99, 111, 118, 127, 149; Richard, 149, 168; Susanna, 80; Susannah, 24, 33, 42, 58, 149
CROSLEY, Charles, 118
CROSTHWAITE, William, 165
CROSWITH, Charles, 167
CROUCH, William, 51, 70
CROXLEY, Charles, 159
CROXTON, Randle, 110, 115
CROZIER, John, 188, 190
CRURNI, William, 183
CULIN, Andrew, 174; George, 119; Jonas, 172, 173
CULINS, George, 127
CUMMINGS, Thomas, 25, 26, 29, 52, 64, 78, 79, 84, 101, 109, 112, 117, 118, 121, 150
CURRY, George, 187; Thomas, 30
CUTHBERT, John, 70, 183, 186, 187

-D-

DANGOR, Edward, 30
DARLING, Abraham, 113
DARLINGTON, Abraham, 63; Elizabeth, 63
DAVID, Benjamin, 118; Edward, 49; Elizabeth, 107, 108; Evan, 98; Gwen, 107, 108; Gwenllian, 106; Hannah, 163; Henry, 91; Isaac, 98; James, 136; John, 56, 106, 107, 108, 164, 165, 184, 195; Phillip, 96, 164; Rebecca, 184; Rees, 98; Richard, 154; Stephen, 163; Thomas, 106, 107, 108, 116, 155, 195
DAVIDS, James, 32
DAVIES, David, 3, 106, 151; Gabriel, 146; John, 48, 183; Katherine, 3; Mary, 151; Merick, 15, 151; Mirick, 147; William, 9, 146, 157
DAVIS, Benjamin, 26, 35, 51, 98, 108, 118, 119, 123, 157;

Daniel, 64, 65, 100; David,
96, 108, 117; Deborah, 65;
John, 66, 91, 92, 93, 139,
157, 164; Lewis, 136;
Margaret, 93; Mary, 73, 100,
155; Methusalot, 183, 186;
Methuselah, 162; Nathaniel,
154; Priscilla, 151; Richard,
154, 155; William, 42
DAWS, Edward, 140
DAWSON, Thomas, 147, 161
DEAN, William, 65, 66, 189
DENNIS, Mary, 141, 142; Thomas,
141, 142
DEVONALD, Daniel, 92, 149;
John, 92, 105, 139, 149, 166,
169; Mary, 149
DEVOR, John, 98, 156
DEVORS, John, 47
DICKEY, James, 176; John, 183,
184; Moses, 150
DICKS, Deborah, 50; Nathan, 50;
Peter, 14, 18, 19, 20, 21, 22,
23, 25, 47, 93, 94, 95, 172,
173, 174, 188; Samuel, 19, 21;
Sarah, 18, 20, 172, 173, 174
DICKY, John, 158
DIMSDALE, Sarah, 139, 166
DINSDALE, Sarah, 94
DIVINGS, Hugh, 186
DIXON, Henry, 94; Robert, 49
DIXSON, Henry, 94; John, 95
DOBSON, Henry, 111; Mary, 48;
Thomas, 48, 69
DOOSE, James, 135
DOUGHERTY, John, 186
DOWNARD, William, 187
DRACOTT, Ralph, 52
DRAYCOTT, Elizabeth, 52; Ralph,
52
DRINTON, Elizabeth, 161;
Robert, 161; Thomas, 161
DRUETT, John, 102
DRUIT, Elizabeth, 180; John,
179, 180, 181; Mary, 180
DUCKETT, Thomas, 106, 147, 148
DUFF, John, 192, 193
DUFFEL, Geoerge, 184
DUFFIELD, Benjamin, 12, 16, 32,
85, 87; Mary, 32
DUNCAN, John, 70, 85; Jonathon,
87
DUNN, Phillip, 161, 162
DURABOROW, John, 51
DURBOROW, Daniel, 55
DUTTON, Elizabeth, 69, 168;
John, 69, 168; Lucy, 23;
Thomas, 23; Widow, 63

—E—
EARLES, John, 195

EASTAUGH, Elizabeth, 94; John,
94
EASTLAND, Thomas, 141
EAVENSON, Davis, 73; Jemima,
28; Richard, 28, 73, 74, 76;
Richrd, 99
EAVESON, Jemima, 67; Joseph,
67; Richard, 67
EAVISON, Richard, 73
EDGAR, Charles, 177
EDGE, John, 22, 23
EDRIDGE, John, 73, 74
EDWARDS, Evan, 72; Henry, 49;
James, 177; Jemima, 168; John,
118; Joseph, 12, 107, 148;
Mary, 39, 40; Mercy, 177;
Rebecca, 49; Richard, 41;
Thomas, 70, 195
EILBECK, Lydia, 80, 81;
Phillip, 80, 81
ELDERIDGE, Thomas, 14
ELDRIDGE, Joseph, 169; Mary,
169; Obidiah, 49
ELIBERT, Phillip, 53
ELLEMAN, Thomas, 162
ELLIS, Bridget, 142, 193, 194;
Evan, 170; Everard, 142, 193,
194; Humphrey, 117, 170; Jane,
117, 170; Lydia, 117;
Margaret, 170; Thomas, 170;
William, 117
ELLWELL, Richard, 72
ELWALL, Jane, 14
ELWELL, Jane, 124
EMANUEL, David, 98
EMLEN, Caleb, 120; George, 49
EMLOU, George, 103
EMMETT, Abraham, 92
EMMIT, Abraham, 43, 44, 146;
David, 44, 46
EMPSON, Dorothy, 25; Thomas,
24, 25; William, 161
ENDLAND, Thomas, 12
ENGLAND, Joseph, 16; Thomas, 2,
68, 80, 133
ENGLE, Frederick, 15, 16;
Fredrick, 17
ENGLINGTON, Sarah, 167
ENGLISH, Joseph, 67
ENOCHSON, Enoch, 9, 42
ESTAUGH, Elizabeth, 13, 139,
166; John, 13, 54, 105, 139,
166
EVAN, Richard, 108
EVANS, Ann, 139; Cadwalder,
109, 178, 179; Caleb, 123,
135, 139, 154, 155, 157;
Catherine, 123, 135, 139, 154,
155; Daniel, 133; David, 15,
17, 32, 86, 106, 136, 139,
157; Edward, 38; Evan, 135,

142; Hannah, 106; Jane, 169;
John, 38, 69, 70, 92, 117,
166, 169, 170, 171, 172, 183;
Joseph, 10; Joshua, 139, 142;
Mary, 139; Nathan, 147, 148;
Owen, 84; Peter, 2, 41, 69,
70; Samuel, 195; Stephen, 33,
152, 153, 154; Thomas, 106,
147
EVANSON, Jemima, 66; Richard,
66
EVENSON, Jemima, 6, 7, 188,
189; Richard, 6, 7, 139, 151,
174, 188, 189, 193
EVETTS, Francis, 86
EWING, James, 110, 159
EYER, William, 73
EYRE, Robert, 83

—F—
FAIRLAMB, Catherine, 185;
Katherine, 24, 33, 42;
Nicholas, 19, 24, 31, 33, 41,
42
FAIRMAN, Thomas, 13
FALLOWFIELD, John, 166;
Lancelot, 166
FARR, Richard, 137; William,
133
FAUCETT, Joseph, 109; Walter,
82, 84
FAWCETT, Walter, 173
FAWKES, Richard, 132
FEAGAN, Elizabeth, 184; Henry,
184
FENN, Jane, 141
FERGONSON, William, 162, 163
FERGUSON, William, 111, 186
FERRIS, Francis, 1
FEW, Daniel, 99, 174; Dorcas,
14; Hannah, 95; Isaac, 14, 95,
114, 185; James, 14, 103;
Richard, 82, 84
FISHBOURNE, Elizabeth, 2, 12,
114, 159; Jane, 160, 169;
Ralph, 2, 12, 114, 159;
William, 114, 125, 160, 169
FISHER, William, 48, 49
FITZWATER, George, 15, 66, 84,
96, 99
FLEMING, William, 134
FLEMINGS, William, 134
FLEMMING, John, 186
FLETCHER, Richard, 14
FLEUR, William, 154
FLOWER, Enoch, 168; John, 168;
William, 111, 178
FLOWERS, Henry, 181, 182
FODEY, James, 73
FOLKNOR, Thomas, 147
FOLLWELL, Edward, 60

FOLWELL, Edward, 141
FORD, Benjamin, 102; Phillip,
27, 66, 188, 193
FORE, Francis, 37
FOREMAN, George, 83, 168
FORSTER, Arthur, 194; Moses,
185
FRAHARN, Adam, 117
FRED, Benjamin, 94, 95;
Deborah, 95
FREDD, Benjamin, 13
FREELAND, Esther, 147, 148;
Hester, 146
FRENCH, Robert, 104
FRETWELL, Edward, 70
FRIEND, Andrew, 8, 45, 143;
Ann, 8, 9, 45, 143; Gabriel,
8; Johannes, 8, 143; John,
128; Lawrence, 8; Lawrence,
143; Neels, 8; Richard, 24, 33
FROGG, John, 38; Mary, 38
FYANCE, John, 140, 141;
William, 141

—G—
GALE, Thomas, 134
GARDNER, Peter, 183
GARDNERS, Peter, 182
GARNETT, Thomas, 11
GARRATT, Frances, 134; Samuel,
109
GARRET, Samuel, 85
GATCHELL, Elisha, 174, 175
GATLIVE, Charles, 104
GAULDEN, John, 148
GELSTON, Samuel, 46
GEORGE, Ann, 112; Thomas, 58
GEORTEN, John, 157
GIBBONS, Ann, 50; James, 21,
50, 63, 71, 142; Jane, 142;
John, 66
GIFTING, Thomas, 30
GILBERT, Thomas, 109
GILHAM, William, 49
GILKEY, Walter, 163; William,
186
GILLEYLAN, John, 115, 116
GILLFORD, Samuel, 107
GILLPIN, Hannah, 62, 67;
Joseph, 62, 67; Samuel, 62;
Thomas, 54
GILMORE, Robert, 187
GILPIN, Thomas, 102
GIVIN, Owen, 153
GLEAVES, Isaac, 141; John, 149,
158
GODFREY, Thomas, 122, 172
GOLDNEY, Henry, 13
GOLDSMITH, Ellenor, 49; James,
49

GOODSON, Job, 15, 66, 84, 96, 99
GORDON, Lewis, 186
GORE, Margery, 133
GORSUCH, William, 93
GOULDNEY, Adam, 141; Anne, 141; Henry, 93, 94, 139, 141, 166, 169; Jane, 141; Mary, 141; Sarah, 141; Silvester, 141
GRAHAM, Arthur, 142
GRAINGER, Joshua, 56
GRANTUM, Charles, 5, 126, 127; Katherine, 5, 126, 127
GRAST, George, 141
GRAY, Samuel, 104
GRAYDON, William, 92
GREEN, Abel, 88, 89, 90, 91, 97, 110; Elizabeth, 11, 34, 81; John, 11, 34, 81; Thomas, 86, 142
GREGG, John, 10, 95, 107
GRIFFIN, John, 54
GRIFFING, Thomas, 28, 49, 140
GRIFFITH, Gartree, 108; Jenkin, 3; John, 194; Morris, 183, 186, 187; Timothy, 182
GRIFFITHS, John, 142; Joseph, 50
GRIGGS, David, 149
GRIMSON, William, 50
GRIST, Joseph, 168
GRISWELL, John, 186
GRIZELL, Edward, 187
GROWDEN, J., 44
GRUBB, John, 180; Nathaniel, 191
GUNSTON, Henry, 2

-H-
HADLY, Joshua, 27; Mary, 27
HAINESE, John, 104
HALDEN, Isaac, 14
HALEY, William, 60
HALL, Jacob, 144, 145
HALLEB, Anne, 171, 172; Richard, 171, 172
HALLOWELL, John, 16, 32
HAMILTON, Andrew, 115, 116, 162; James, 170, 193; William, 146
HAMLETON, James, 46
HAMSON, Caleb, 185
HANBY, William, 167
HANCOCK, Sarah, 106, 107; William, 106, 107
HANK, Luke, 84
HANKS, Luke, 84
HANLY, Catherine, 119, 175; John, 118, 119, 121, 160, 161, 175, 176; Katherine, 118
HANNUM, John, 123, 174.

HARDING, Francis, 190
HARDLAND, Thomas, 16
HARDY, Elizabeth, 106; Samuel, 106
HARINGTON, Mary, 88, 91; May, 88, 89, 90; William, 88, 89, 90, 91
HARKEY, William, 187
HARLAN, Dinah, 128, 129; Ezekiel, 10, 16, 174; George, 195; James, 139, 174; Joseph, 14; Michael, 128, 129; Moses, 94, 190; Ruth, 10; Stephen, 14, 128; Thomas, 146; William, 10, 120
HARLAND, Ezekiel, 15, 193; James, 193; Moses, 93
HARLEY, William, 183
HARNUM, John, 2; Margery, 2; Robert, 2
HARRIS, Edward, 86; John, 86; William, 141
HARRISON, Caleb, 57, 58, 186; Hannah, 57; Richard, 130, 164; William, 136
HARRY, Elizabeth, 64, 65; Evan, 64, 65; Hugh, 64, 65; Samuel, 139, 142; William, 64, 65
HARTSHORNE, R., 104
HARVEY, Benjamin, 154; Job, 16, 154, 182, 188; John, 5; Joseph, 4, 101, 120, 121, 180; Josiah, 12, 15, 16, 17; William, 14
HASLAM, John, 145
HASTINGS, Henry, 47; Joshua, 82, 84
HATT, Thomas, 54, 55, 56
HATTON, Peter, 61, 62, 107, 136, 137; Thomas, 116
HAVARD, John, 123
HAWKING, Elizabeth, 63; Roger, 63
HAWLEY, Joseph, 100, 191
HAYES, Benjamin, 93, 136, 164; Hannah, 164; Henry, 34, 69, 92, 146, 176; Jonathon, 191; Joseph, 50, 51, 70, 136, 164; Richard, 92, 98, 99, 111, 164; William, 50, 176
HAYS, Henry, 6; Richard, 9
HAYWARD, James, 61, 62, 136, 137; Mary, 136, 137; Sarah, 159, 160; Thomas, 159, 160
HEAD, Benjamin, 173; Sarah, 173
HEALD, John, 123
HEATH, Richard, 1, 2, 129
HEATING, Jax, 118
HELL, William, 71
HELM, Isreal, 111
HELMES, Joseph, 180

HELMS, Isreal, 135
HENDERSON, John, 46, 102
HENDRICHSON, John, 140, 177, 178, 191
HENDRICKS, Albert, 34; James, 34; Jan, 167; Johannes, 34; John, 101, 104, 127; Tobias, 7, 8
HENSHAW, Benjamin, 73
HEWES, William, 191
HIBBERD, Joseph, 82; Moses, 142, 194
HICKLIN, Thomas, 193
HICKLINS, Thomas, 174
HICKMAN, Benjamin, 2, 12, 91, 107; Elizabeth, 107; John, 166; Joseph, 107, 113; Mary, 113
HICOCK, Oele, 135
HIDDINS, Richard, 49
HIETT, Thomas, 45
HIGGIN, Michael, 137
HIGGINS, Thomas, 65
HILL, Richard, 61; William, 39, 62, 69, 187
HINDRICKS, Albert, 35; Elizabeth, 35; James, 35; Lucy, 35
HINTON, Gabriel, 110
HOARE, Christopher, 131
HOBSON, Frances, 120; Francis, 13, 125, 126; Jacob, 102; James, 179; John, 102; Martha, 102; Mathew, 102
HOCKLEY, Henry, 153
HODGSON, Robert, 26, 32, 33; Sarah, 32
HOHMAN, Charles, 107; Elleanor, 107
HOLLAND, Jonathon, 195; R., 141; William, 11
HOLLINGSWORTH, Henry, 14, 41, 52, 129, 159, 172; Joseph, 9, 10, 95; Judith, 9, 10; Samuel, 25, 29, 58; Thomas, 9, 10
HOLLOCK, Jacob, 180
HOLLWELL, Goldsmith Edward, 17
HOLME, Isreal, 4
HOOD, Caspar, 96; John, 5; Jonathon, 5, 77; Samuel, 77
HOOKE, William, 69
HOOP, Daniel, 71
HOOPS, Daniel, 21, 71, 72, 96, 97, 110; Joshua, 91
HOPARTS, Mark, 108
HOPE, Elizabeth, 95; Thomas, 14, 95
HOPKINS, David, 130; John, 33, 114
HOPMAN, Hance, 102, 104; Hans, 140, 177, 178, 191

HORN, Edward, 17, 18
HORNE, Edward, 46, 47, 100; William, 114, 122
HOSKINS, Jane, 121, 122, 124, 142, 143, 144, 160, 161; John, 8, 19, 25, 31, 32, 35, 45, 72, 85, 122, 124, 160, 172, 178, 179; Joseph, 32, 45, 121, 122, 124, 142, 143, 144, 160; Mary, 31, 32, 45, 46, 124, 160; Ruth, 24, 26, 29, 31, 32, 33, 43, 45, 78, 122, 124, 143, 160; Samuel, 46; Sarah, 151; Stephen, 31, 45, 85, 122, 124, 151, 160
HOUGH, David, 98
HOULTON, Elizabeth, 125, 190; John, 125; Nathaniel, 125
HOUSE, James, 150, 151; Mary, 150, 151
HOWELL, Daniel, 103; Evan, 90, 91, 97; George, 1; Griffith, 23, 24; Howell, 163; Jacob, 2, 14, 26, 29, 31, 43, 46, 78, 79, 84, 116, 143, 144; James, 18; John, 140, 152; Mordecai, 86, 87, 134, 140, 178, 180; Morris, 30; Phillip, 129; Rachel, 139, 140, 177, 178; Rachell, 137; Rees, 164; Reynold, 170; Samuel, 79; Sarah, 79; Thomas, 86, 87, 102, 137, 139, 159, 164, 169, 177, 178, 179, 180, 181
HUBBERT, Thomas, 107
HUDSON, Hannah, 48, 173; William, 48, 56, 57, 173
HUGHES, Edward, 129; Griffith, 163, 164; William, 111
HUGHS, Evan, 85; Griffith, 85; Ruth, 98
HULBERT, John, 41
HUMPHREY, Benjamin, 155; Daniel, 168; John, 168
HUNT, Roger, 171
HUNTER, Ann, 48; Elizabeth, 48; John, 150, 151; Jonathan, 71; Jonathon, 25, 26, 38, 48, 80, 90, 97; Margery, 71; Martha, 150; Peter, 12, 38, 39, 48, 101; Susanna, 48; William, 132, 162
HUNTERS, Jonathon, 21
HUNTLEY, Mary, 14, 95; William, 14, 95
HURFORD, John, 57
HURLBAT, Frances, 134; John, 134
HURSTEN, John Henry, 113
HUTCHISON, James, 141; Robert, 24

HUTTON, John, 179; Nehemiah, 120, 125, 126; Sarah, 125, 126, 179

-I-
IDDINGS, Richard, 147; William, 147
IDEN, John, 121
INGRAM, William, 74
INGRAN, William, 73
INSTASON, James, 71
IRWIN, David, 130
ISAAC, Paul, 165, 169, 186; William, 54, 55
ISACKS, John, 164
IZARD, Michael, 167

-J-
J, Thomas, 98
JACKMAN, Thomas, 88, 89, 90
JACKSON, Ephraim, 87, 88, 89, 90, 91, 148; Isaac, 6; John, 5, 6, 60, 68, 171; Joseph, 148, 190; Nathaniel, 148; Rodger, 23, 24; Roger, 143, 148; Samuel, 6; Stephen, 36; Thomas, 69
JACOBS, Hendrich, 135
JACOBSON, Hendrick, 4; Henry, 173
JAMES, Aaron, 21, 50, 91; Anne, 153; Elizabeth, 91; George, 187; Howell, 129; James, 129; John, 153; Joseph, 91; Morgan, 131, 132; Thomas, 91, 164, 183, 186, 187
JANNY, Randal, 86
JARMAN, George, 183
JEFFERIES, Ann, 103; Benjamin, 103; James, 103; Robert, 103
JEFFERY, Robert, 56
JEFFRIES, Benjamin, 112; Robert, 48; William, 112
JENKIN, Nathaniel, 179
JENKINS, Nathaniel, 126
JERMAN, John, 96, 123, 135, 139, 142, 154, 155, 157; Lewis, 148, 149; Margaret, 148, 149
JERVIS, Joseph, 9, 12, 60, 115, 159
JOB, Amigail(Abigail), 175; Andrew, 61
JOBSONS, Michael, 44
JODDER, John, 113
JOHN, Daniel, 182; David, 183; Griffith, 91, 92, 154, 162; Gwen, 162; Hugh, 163; James, 182; Thomas, 98, 162
JOHNSON, Abraham, 41; Andrew, 5, 126; Ann, 70; Charles, 102, 104, 139, 177, 178, 191; Claas, 165; Edward, 25; Humphrey, 19, 123, 140, 178; John, 25; Obidiah, 28, 70; Rebecca, 165
JONAS, John, 105
JONES, Daniel, 181, 182; David, 44, 181, 182; Edward, 142; Elizabeth, 169, 170; Emanuel, 98; Evan, 165; Hugh, 123, 135; Jacob, 136; James, 5, 164, 165; Jane, 117, 152, 153, 154, 170; John, 92, 148, 152, 153, 154, 166, 169, 170, 181, 182, 183, 194; Jonathon, 136; Mathias, 3; Morgan, 61, 62, 137; Peter, 44, 141, 142; Reece, 40; Richard, 50, 75, 84, 91, 153, 155, 182, 188; Robert, 34; Samuel, 50, 157, 194; Thomas, 20, 21, 115, 184; William, 157
JORDAN, John, 153, 154; Robert, 166
JUSTICES, Charles, 188

-K-
KEEN, Urin, 8, 42, 84
KEILY, John, 157
KEITH, Robert, 97
KELLY, Thomas, 182
KENDALL, Benjamin, 127, 128, 151; Thomas, 77, 94, 95
KENERLY, James, 80
KENNEDY, David, 134
KENNETT, Archibald, 146
KENNISON, Edward, 70
KENNISONS, Edward, 51
KENSEY, John, 90
KENT, Rees, 131, 132
KERLIN, John, 95, 99, 140, 178; Mathias, 58
KEY, Moses, 27
KIBBY, Samuel, 145
KICKLINS, Thomas, 139
KILLING, Dan, 93, 94, 95; Daniel, 100
KING, Mary, 62; Nathaniel, 80
KINGSMAN, John, 166
KINNISON, Edward, 74, 76, 77
KINSEY, John, 44, 69, 87, 88, 89, 90
KINSMAN, Hannah, 69; John, 47, 69, 107
KIRK, William, 109
KIRKPATRICK, Andrew, 150
KITTOLL, Thomas, 11
KNIGHT, Elizabeth, 161; Hannah, 161; John, 161; Ruth, 161
KNOTT, Edward, 115
KNOWLES, John, 113, 114

KOLLUCK, Jacob, 86, 87
KOOK, Oele, 4

-L-
LAARSON, Neels, 8
LADD, John, 36
LAMPLUGH, Jacob, 102
LANDFORD, Jonas, 70
LANDOR, William, 17
LANGFORD, Jonas, 70
LANGHAM, Robert, 71
LANGHORN, Jeremiah, 46
LANGHORNE, Jeremiah, 125
LANGWORTHY, John, 123
LANSA, Newls, 143
LANSA (FRIEND), Neels, 142, 143
LARDNER, Lynford, 134, 135,
  149, 150, 158, 162, 163, 183,
  184, 186
LAUDER, Abraham, 93
LAWERENCE, Joshua, 2, 17, 56,
  62; William, 56
LAWRENCE, Joseph, 87, 96;
  Joshua, 1
LAWSON, William, 194
LEA, Hannah, 61, 62; James,
  170; John, 61, 62, 124, 137,
  138, 161, 187
LEACH, Adam, 163
LEES, Ralph, 11
LEETES, John, 127
LEHMAN, Christopher, 172
LEVIS, Hannah, 184, 185;
  Joseph, 184, 185; Samuel, 184,
  185; Susannah, 185
LEWIN, Richard, 128
LEWIS, Abraham, 142, 193; Amos,
  165; Ann, 147; Charles, 179;
  David, 144; Elizabeth, 188;
  Ellen, 163, 164; Ellis, 67,
  84, 107, 188, 189; Evan, 84,
  146, 147, 148, 161; George,
  182; Gressell, 61; Hannah,
  165; Henry, 49, 72, 98, 124;
  Jane, 109; Joseph, 93, 165;
  Lewis, 55, 56, 144, 170;
  Lowry, 84; Margaret, 165;
  Mary, 142, 188, 189, 193;
  Mordecai, 148, 149, 163, 164,
  170; Nathan, 170; Nathaniel,
  84, 188, 189; Phebe, 147, 148;
  Phineas, 93, 149, 171;
  Phinehas, 60, 68; Ralph, 146,
  147, 148; Robert, 188, 189;
  Samuel, 32, 147, 148, 161,
  165; Stephen, 183; Thomas, 85,
  109; William, 14, 61, 84, 96,
  97, 109, 145, 164, 165
LIGHTFOOT, Jacob, 54, 79;
  Michael, 11, 13, 45, 125, 126,
  142, 145, 179; Samuel, 47, 52,
  54, 64, 78, 79, 125
LILLY, John, 75
LINCOLN, Abraham, 140
LINDLEY, Hannah, 55, 56, 59,
  68, 93; Rebecca, 59; Thomas,
  54, 55, 56, 68, 93
LINLEY, Hannah, 171; James,
  172; Thomas, 171
LINNARD, Richard, 49
LINVILL, Dinah, 47; John, 114;
  Thomas, 47
LITTEL, Francis, 83
LITTLER, William, 194
LLEWELLYN, David, 3
LLEWELYN, David, 165
LLOYD, Ann, 130; Charles, 131,
  177; David, 1, 2, 3, 7, 8, 9,
  14, 15, 18, 19, 26, 36, 42,
  45, 47, 61, 85, 87, 96, 108,
  137, 138, 142, 143, 144, 162,
  172, 173; Grace, 25, 27, 29,
  43, 47, 85, 96, 108, 121, 122,
  138, 142, 144, 162, 173; John,
  154, 155; Thomas, 116, 148,
  155, 184, 195; Widow, 51, 58
LOCHERMAN, Ester, 115;
  Nicholas, 115
LOCKHART, James, 67
LOGAN, James, 10, 11, 14, 105,
  106, 120, 124, 125, 126, 130,
  135, 162, 171, 172
LONGWORTHY, John, 107
LOODEN, Peter, 31
LOUDER, Peter, 62
LOVE, James, 149; John, 98,
  149; Robert, 28
LOVELACE, Francis, 142, 172;
  Governor, 167
LOWERY, William, 134
LOWLE, Andrew, 152; Jane, 152;
  Tacy, 152
LOWNDES, James, 19
LOWNES, George, 101, 191;
  James, 172
LOWNS, James, 19, 26, 45;
  Susannah, 26
LOWRY, William, 113, 160, 161
LOWTHER, Ann Sharlot, 105; Anne
  Sharlot, 144, 145, 152, 153,
  154; John, 144, 145, 152, 153,
  154; Margaret, 144, 152, 153;
  Margot, 105; Margret, 105;
  William, 105, 144, 152, 153
LOYD, David, 162

-M-
MCCALL, Ann, 35; George, 35, 36
MCCAMISH, Ann, 194; Patrick,
  194
MCCHIN, Thomas, 7

MCCLENAGON, John, 135
MCCONACHEY, Robert, 22
MCCULLOUGH, James, 115, 116
MCDOWELL, Robert, 187; William, 126
MCFARREN, John, 163
MCGAUGHY, William, 126
MCKAIN, Thomas, 46
MCKEE, Robert, 135, 134
MACKEY, Robert, 142
MCKIN, William, 98
MCNEILE, Archibald, 123, 145; Elizabeth, 123, 145
MADDOCK, Benjamin, 140; Elizabeth, 140; Henry, 79, 80, 94, 95; John, 80, 94, 95; Mordecai, 79, 80, 82, 84, 94, 95, 130
MADDOX, Joshua, 33, 114; Mary, 114
MAFFIT, William, 183
MAGEE, Anne, 131; Richard, 131
MAGEES, Richard, 64
MALIN, Isaac, 74, 75, 76, 77, 150; Randal, 179
MAN, Richard, 184
MARCELLUS, Mathew, 135
MARCKUS, Mathew, 182
MARDON, Richard, 24
MARIN, Walter, 99
MARIS, Elizabeth, 62, 66, 140; George, 61, 62, 66, 67, 78, 79; Hannah, 129; Jonathon, 191; Richard, 53, 100, 140
MARK, James, 97, 110
MARKE, Thomas, 53
MARSDEN, Richard, 37
MARSH, Richard, 2, 12, 72; William, 158, 184
MARSHALL, Abraham, 67; John, 91, 139, 140, 150; Samuel, 85, 86; Sarah, 85; Thomas, 136, 137
MARTI, John, 57////can't find on page
MARTIN, George, 144, 145; John, 39, 66, 83, 145, 158, 185; Joseph, 186; Mary, 185; Thomas, 57, 58, 61, 62, 82, 84, 106, 107, 132, 185; Walter, 41, 73; William, 108
MARTINS, Walter, 180
MARTYN, Mathias, 183; Samuel, 145
MARY, Christian, 129, 130
MASON, Richard, 63
MASSEY, James, 106, 107; Mordecai, 53; Phobe Coppeck, 72; Thomas, 53, 106, 107, 124
MASSY, Thomas, 72
MASTERS, Thomas, 62

MATHER, J., 18; James, 24, 37, 42, 49, 51, 52, 58, 59, 63, 64, 67, 69, 82, 143, 144; John, 24, 36, 37, 45, 46, 52, 64, 122, 124, 160; Mary, 45, 46, 122, 124, 160; William, 18, 43
MATHERS, John, 32; Mary, 32
MATHEWS, John, 176; Robert, 54
MATHIAS, David, 154; Edward, 91
MATLIN, Randle, 115; William, 115
MATSON, Neal, 172; Neals, 173
MAYTEEN, Barbara, 114; Martin, 114
MEAD, John, 11, 34, 81
MECHUM, Francis, 73
MEGHEE, Richard, 26
MELIN, Isaac, 74, 75
MENDENHALL, Aaron, 55, 56, 60, 61, 62, 67, 68, 119, 120; Benjamin, 2, 12; Elizabeth, 62, 66; Esther, 61, 67; George, 61, 67, 119, 120; John, 6, 7, 61, 62, 66, 67, 100, 188; Rose, 119, 120; Susanna, 100; Susannah, 6, 7, 61, 62, 67
MERCER, Thomas, 67, 73, 74
MEREDITH, John, 135; Rees, 104, 169; Simon, 153
MERRY, Thomas, 105
MESSAR, John, 44
MICKLE, Samuel, 36, 47, 98, 156, 178, 179
MICKLES, Samuel, 48
MIDFORD, John, 54, 105
MIDWINTER, Robert, 18
MILES, William, 175
MILL, Ann, 73
MILLER, Andrew, 63; Ann, 86; Gawen, 11; Gayen, 120, 125; Henry, 16; James, 13, 45, 86; John, 16; Margaret, 120; Robert, 120, 123; Salem, 127; Sarah, 63; William, 27, 70, 86, 120, 172, 186
MILLERS, William, 126
MILLISON, John, 73
MILLS, James, 41; Robert, 58
MINCENT, Mathias, 19
MINSHALL, Hannah, 23; Isaac, 110; Jacob, 21, 39, 69, 72; John, 23, 24; Rebecca, 141; Sarah, 21; Thomas, 16
MINSSORMAN, Jan, 4
MODLE, Ann, 121; John, 121
MOLYN, Isaac, 32, 136
MONTGOMERY, Alexander, 151
MOOR, Andrew, 63; Nicholas, 84, 98

MOORE, Andrew, 174; Elizabeth, 179, 180, 181; Hannah, 174; James, 155, 156, 174; John, 113, 139, 158, 163, 174, 179, 181; Mary, 104, 112; Nicholas, 27, 66, 188, 193; Ruth, 53; Thomas, 18, 100, 104, 112, 113; William, 105, 145, 152, 154, 155, 156, 183, 186, 187
MORGAN, Evan, 26, 29, 31, 43, 186; John, 3, 67, 86, 103, 108, 123, 135, 142, 195; Thomas, 24, 25, 26, 29, 31, 33, 43
MORRIS, Anthony, 41, 73, 74, 122, 172; James, 175; Jonathon, 100; Mordecai, 100; Phebe, 73, 74; Samuel, 43; Thomas, 139
MORTENS, Morton, 3
MORTIN, David, 3; Eleanor, 3
MORTON, Andrew, 3, 4, 5, 101, 119, 120, 121, 126, 127, 128, 135; Anne, 127, 128; David, 3, 4, 30, 82, 135; Eleanor, 3, 4; Elizabeth, 126; Ellin, 5, 30, 126, 135; John, 119, 127; Jonas, 101, 180; Katherine, 5, 126; Latitia, 126; Lawrence, 135; Letitia, 5; Lydia, 5, 126, 127; Margaret, 82; Margret, 3, 4; Mary, 121; Mathias, 121, 135; Morton, 4, 5, 127, 128; Rebecca, 5, 126; Timothy, 36
MORTONSON, David, 29, 30, 190; Ellin, 29, 30; Morton, 29, 30, 190
MOSES, Alexander, 14; William, 194
MOULDER, Benjamin, 8, 169; Robert, 99, 111, 168, 169, 180
MUGLESTON, Thomas, 30
MULLIN, Harper, 158; James, 25; William, 49
MUSGRAVE, Abraham, 6; Hannah, 6, 7; Moses, 54; Thomas, 6
MUSGROVE, Abraham, 120, 144; Hannah, 119; John, 148; Thomas, 7, 119, 120; William, 72

—N—

NATSSOILLES, Mathias, 4
NATZEILLES, Otto, 185
NAYLE, Henry, 37, 112
NAYLES, Henry, 19
NAYLOR, Richard, 120
NEALS, John, 27
NEALS (FRIEND), Widow, 173
NEALSON, Anthony, 173

NEASE, Sam, 152
NECELIUS, Mathias, 190
NEEDERMARDT, Conrad, 135
NEILSON, Olle, 104; Woole, 191
NELSON, Olle, 102
NESELINS, Mathias, 30
NETHERMARK, Cunrad, 111
NETHERMARKE, Conrad, 28, 30
NETSELLIES, Mathias, 4
NEVEN, William, 151
NEWCOMB, Richard, 1
NEWCOMBE, Richard, 2
NEWLIN, Edith, 98, 99; Elizabeth, 188; Hannah, 133; Jane, 84; Jemima, 6, 7, 188; John, 6, 7, 27, 28, 66, 67, 84, 188, 189, 193; Keria, 6, 7; Kezia, 27, 28, 188; Mary, 6, 7, 28, 188, 193; Nathan, 67; Nathaniel, 6, 7, 27, 28, 50, 58, 67, 84, 99, 125, 133, 139, 174, 188, 189, 193; Nicholas, 6, 7, 27, 28, 66, 67, 98, 99, 188, 189
NICE, Cornelius, 56
NICHOLAS, Edward, 128; Richard, 3
NICHOLS, Amos, 119; John, 105; Margot, 105; Richard, 111, 135
NICKINSON, John, 130
NICKLIN, Joseph, 133
NICOL, John, 144, 152, 153; Margaret, 144, 152, 153
NOBLETT, Mary, 159; William, 159
NOHR, Lawrence Christopher, 113
NOOK, William, 39
NOOKES, Ruth, 12; William, 12
NOOKS, Ruth, 100, 101; William, 39, 100, 101
NORRIS, Charles, 43, 130; Deborah, 162; Isaac, 33, 42, 43, 79, 95, 114, 130, 131, 149, 158, 162, 191; Mary, 42, 43, 130; Samuel, 130, 162
NOSELINS, Mathias, 29
NOSSETER, Sarah, 178
NULSON, Olle, 140, 177, 178
NUTER, John, 130

—O—

OAKLEY, John, 171
OBORN, Hannah, 102
OBOURN, Henry, 133; William, 133
OGDEN, David, 26, 38, 148; Jonathon, 38, 39, 42, 68, 80, 116, 148; Martha, 38; Nehemiah, 80; Samuel, 191; Stephen, 90
OLDFIELD, George, 18, 19

OLDHAM, Thomas, 149
OLLESON, Hans, 140, 177, 178, 191; Hanson, 139
OLLISON, Hance, 104; Haunce, 102
ORA, John, 103
ORCHARD, John, 135
ORD, John, 107, 115
ORIAN, William, 167
ORMO, Mary, 3; Richard, 3
OSBORN, Henry, 99
OSBORNE, Charles, 14, 87
OSBURN, Samuel, 81
OTLEY, Phillip, 39, 69
OTTLEY, Jonathon, 180
OWEN, Ann, 100; Evan, 15, 66, 84, 96, 99; George, 194; Griffith, 10, 11, 124, 125, 126; Hannah, 27; John, 4, 8, 17, 24, 27, 28, 31, 33, 42, 48, 49, 59, 78, 79, 80, 87, 92, 103, 109, 115, 117, 174, 187, 194, 195; Owen, 32, 136; Richard, 32, 106, 136; Thomas, 182; William, 100, 191, 195
OWENS, John, 26, 29, 33, 43

-P-

PACKER, John, 123
PAGE, John, 11
PAINTER, Samuel, 48
PALMER, George, 1, 2; John, 1, 2, 108, 133, 136, 137; Thomas, 1, 2, 108; William, 2
PARK, Nathaniel, 133; Robert, 23, 26
PARKE, Abel, 59, 60, 68, 93, 171; Deborah, 93, 171; Hugh, 170; Rebecca, 59, 60, 68, 93, 171; Robert, 29, 32, 37, 42, 46, 47, 51, 52, 59, 63, 64, 68, 69, 78, 80, 82, 93, 96, 171; Thomas, 55, 56, 60, 68, 93, 120, 142, 171
PARKER, Abraham, 76, 150, 151; Eleanor, 150, 151; John, 190; Joseph, 2, 8, 9, 18, 19, 23, 25, 27, 29, 30, 31, 32, 34, 35, 36, 41, 42, 44, 46, 51, 54, 60, 69, 71, 73, 80, 81, 92, 93, 94, 95, 96, 100, 101, 102, 103, 104, 108, 109, 112, 115, 117, 118, 119, 121, 122, 124, 126, 127, 128, 131, 133, 138, 139, 143, 144, 146, 150, 156, 157, 159, 160, 161, 162, 166, 174, 176, 177, 180, 181, 184, 188; Richard, 142, 190; Robert, 35; Thomas, 27, 60, 188, 193; William, 130

PARRY, David, 194; Hannah, 144; James, 106, 116; John, 33, 44, 98, 99, 106, 111, 144, 145, 153, 154, 162, 163, 164, 182
PARSON, Joseph, 87; Susanna, 87
PARSONS, Edward, 179; Elizabeth, 178; Esther, 178; Joseph, 87, 194; Susanna, 87; Thomas, 34, 178; William, 1, 32, 183
PASCHALL, John, 114; Jonathan, 185; Jonathon, 142; Mary, 185; Thomas, 91; William, 51, 74, 75, 76, 77, 150
PASCHALLS, John, 33
PATEW, William, 142
PATTEN, Anne, 192; John, 192
PATTERS, Samuel, 158
PATTISON, Thomas, 33
PATTON, John, 192, 193
PAVER, Edward, 115
PEACOCK, Edmund, 11, 81; Edward, 34
PEARCE, George, 2; Henry, 19
PEARCES, George, 12
PEARSE, John, 52
PEARSON, Benjamin, 70, 130; Enoch, 53; Isaac, 142, 185; John, 52; Katherine, 95, 96; Margery, 52, 53, 95; Robert, 52, 53, 95, 96, 141, 194; Thomas, 28, 52, 53, 69, 95
PEARSONS, Robert, 87
PECKOVER, Edmund, 145
PEIRCE, Caleb, 63; Edward, 84, 98
PEIRSON, Lawrence, 131, 132
PEMBERTON, Isreal, 130, 162, 176
PENN, John, 115, 122, 130, 134, 135, 149, 150, 153, 155, 158, 161, 162, 172, 183, 184, 186; Leitita, 9, 10; Richard, 115, 122, 130, 134, 135, 149, 150, 153, 155, 158, 161, 163, 172, 183, 184, 186; Springett, 172; Thomas, 115, 122, 129, 134, 135, 149, 150, 153, 155, 158, 161, 163, 172, 183, 184, 186; William, 1, 2, 3, 6, 7, 9, 10, 11, 12, 13, 15, 16, 19, 20, 22, 25, 27, 31, 34, 35, 36, 37, 38, 41, 43, 44, 52, 53, 54, 55, 58, 61, 62, 64, 66, 70, 72, 74, 75, 76, 77, 78, 80, 81, 84, 86, 87, 88, 89, 90, 91, 93, 95, 96, 97, 98, 105, 106, 107, 108, 112, 113, 115, 119, 120, 122, 124, 125, 126, 133, 138, 139, 141, 144, 147, 148, 150, 152, 154, 155,

209

158, 159, 161, 166, 167, 169, 171, 173, 174, 175, 176, 177, 179, 185, 187, 188, 193, 195
PENNEL, William, 60
PENNELL, John, 27, 132, 133; Joseph, 97; Joshua, 162; Mary, 132, 133; Thomas, 184; William, 16, 17, 179
PENNOCK, Christopher, 69; Joseph, 13, 69, 175; Mary, 175; Nathaniel, 175; Samuel, 86
PENROSE, Robert, 53
PENTLAND, Alexander, 10
PERKINS, Ann, 67; Caleb, 67, 164; John, 62, 158
PERRY, John, 105
PERSELS, Jeremiah, 141
PETER, John, 135
PETERS, Benjamin, 178; Richard, 134, 135, 149, 150, 158, 162, 163, 170, 183, 184, 185, 186; Sarah, 178; William, 135, 136, 149, 163, 185
PETERSON, Mounce, 3, 4, 111; Peter, 3, 4, 29, 111, 190; Reyner, 173
PHILLIP, Eleanor, 124; Phillip, 31
PHILLIPS, Eleanor, 138, 156, 184; Mary, 93; Phillip, 42; Thomas, 109; William, 84
PHIPPS, Joseph, 85, 96, 117
PICKERING, Charles, 172
PICKLE, William, 23, 138
PICKLES, Nathan, 79; William, 9
PICKRIN, Charles, 145, 152, 154
PIDGEON, Joseph, 15, 66, 84, 96, 99; Rebecca, 85; Stephen, 85
PIERCE, Caleb, 54, 67; Edward, 27, 66, 188, 193; George, 54, 107; Henry, 7, 28, 58, 67, 92, 118, 119, 189, 193; Joshua, 146
PIKE, Joseph, 119, 120; Richard, 145
PIKES, Joseph, 120
PIM, Thomas, 120; William, 7
PINDAR, John, 52
PLAIN, John, 129, 130; Mary, 129, 130
PLUMSTEAD, Clement, 50, 51, 102, 145, 181, 182, 190; William, 136
POPE, Nathaniel, 172
POUN, Edwar, 73
POWELL, Agnes, 155; Ann, 19, 20, 21; Anna, 20, 21; David, 116, 120, 146; Elizabeth, 19, 21; Evan, 27; John, 19, 20,

21, 134; Joseph, 20, 21, 120, 134; Mary, 19, 21, 27; Samuel, 44, 155; Sarah, 18, 20, 21, 27; Susannah, 20, 21; Thomas, 18, 19, 20, 21, 103, 115; William, 116
PRATT, Joseph, 147, 148
PREECOS, Thomas, 4
PRESTON, Samuel, 9, 44, 87, 180, 181, 182; William, 18, 119, 175, 176
PREW, Caleb, 194; Mary, 194; Sarah, 194; Susannah, 194
PRICE, Abigail, 175; Benjamin, 174; David, 6, 120; Hannah, 6, 7, 120; John, 175, 178; Leyson, 158; Rice, 165
PRITCHARD, Anna, 92; Edward, 173; Elizabeth, 173; Griffith, 116; Hannah, 92; Phillip, 173; Rees, 92, 183, 186
PRITCHET, Samuel, 28
PUGH, Henry, 17; John, 95; Thomas, 117
PULFORD, Thomas, 30, 33
PULLIN, Christian, 39, 40
PUMFREY, George, 149
PUMPHREY, Walter, 129
PUSSEY, Ann, 5, 6, 31, 78; Anne, 174; Caleb, 5, 6, 13, 14, 31, 38, 69, 72, 78, 82, 84, 114, 117, 132, 160, 174, 175, 179; William, 6, 114
PYKES, Joseph, 7
PYLE, Jacob, 171; John, 61; Joseph, 124, 131, 133, 150; Nicholas, 11, 37, 62, 122, 125, 158, 167; Ralph, 73; Robert, 6, 60, 61, 65, 66, 167, 168; Sarah, 133; Susannah, 16, 65, 66; William, 48, 54, 61, 65, 107, 176
PYLES, William, 150

—Q—

QUARE, D., 94; Daniel, 13, 93, 94, 139, 166, 169

—R—

RADLEY, William, 65, 66
RADLY, William, 112
RANKEN, David, 119, 124, 127, 128, 131, 139, 150, 156, 157, 159, 174, 176, 180, 181, 187, 195
RATTEW, William, 132
RAWLE, Francis, 85; Martha, 85
RAWSON, Andrew, 104, 179, 181; Charles, 179, 181; Elizabeth, 181; Gartrax, 104; Johannes, 157; John, 104; Mary, 104;

Olle, 102, 104, 139, 168, 169, 177, 178; William, 104; Woole, 191
RAYNERS, Joseph, 53; Mary, 53
READ, Charles, 15, 96, 102; James, 7; Mary, 7
REDMAN, Joseph, 25
REECE, George, 122; James, 8; John, 4, 144; Lewis, 49, 142
REED, Nicholas, 153
REENS, Jurian, 142
REES, David, 182; George, 172; Isaac, 17; John, 77, 108, 183; Margaret, 84; Michael, 108; Morris, 108; Thomas, 84
REESE, David, 157; Samuel, 168
REGESTER, David, 88, 89, 90, 112
REILEY, John, 99
REILY, Edward, 163; John, 185, 190
REMAX, Jonah, 149
RENTFRO, George, 183
REYNER, Joseph, 30, 35; Mary, 30
REYNERS, J., 69, 79
REYNOLDS, Francis, 156; Henry, 134, 166, 167; John, 166, 167; Joseph, 33; Prudence, 166, 167; William, 182, 187
RHOADS, James, 194
RHODES, Adam, 170; Catherine, 170; Hannah, 146, 147, 148; John, 146, 147, 148; Joseph, 87
RHYTHEY, Rees, 106, 108
RICHARD, Thomas, 32, 136
RICHARDS, Eleanor, 7; Elizabeth, 151; John, 3, 151; Joseph, 17, 117, 123; Lydia, 117; Margaret, 27; Martha, 151; Mary, 151; Nathan, 172; Nathaniel, 45; Samuel, 92
RICHARDSON, Ann, 17, 70; Anna, 174; Catherine, 150; Eleanor, 150; Elinor, 74, 75, 76, 77; Elizabeth, 74, 75, 77, 150; Isaac, 51, 74, 75, 76, 150; John, 77, 123, 150, 174; Joseph, 17; Katherine, 74, 75, 76, 77; Martha, 74, 75, 76, 77, 150; Mary, 74, 75, 76, 77, 150, 174; Richard, 50, 51, 70, 183, 186, 187; Samuel, 17
RICHMOND, John, 141
RIELY, John, 94, 111
RIGG, Elizabeth, 162; Robert, 162
RILEY, John, 60, 99, 101, 164, 168, 178, 180; Jonathon, 102;

Susannah, 162; William, 161, 162
RINEERS, Joseph, 109
RING, Elizabeth, 177; Nathaniel, 177
ROAD, Charles, 66, 84, 99
ROADS, Adam, 109, 117; Katherine, 117
ROBERTS, Aaron, 123; Aubrey, 96, 117; David, 8, 117; Edward, 181; Hugh, 157; Owen, 17; Ruth, 117; Susanna, 8; Thomas, 106
ROBERTSON, Peter, 36; Robert, 11
ROBINETT, Allen, 137, 182; Allin, 17; George, 183; James, 182; Joseph, 182; Mary, 183; Nathan, 182; Samuel, 86, 115, 182, 183; Stephen, 182
ROBINETTE, Mary, 17; Samuel, 17
ROBINSON, Eleanor, 155, 156; George, 116, 129; James, 156; Joseph, 116
ROBISON, William, 43
ROCKARDS, Joseph, 143
ROGERS, Francis, 175; George, 175; Nicholas, 49
ROLSON, Johannes, 41
ROMAN, Jacob, 35, 36, 71, 109, 131; John, 167; Jonah, 168; Phillip, 7, 47, 120, 167, 168; Ruth, 167, 168
ROMANS, Jacob, 35
ROSS, John, 46, 70, 174, 187; Jonathon, 118; Lawerence, 30
ROUTH, Francis, 176
ROWAN, Abraham, 192; Anne, 192; Cornelius, 192, 193; David, 192; John, 192, 193; William, 120
ROWE, William, 133
ROWENS, William, 126
ROWLAN, Thomas, 133
ROWLAND, Mary, 11, 27, 169; Rachel, 27; Samuel, 168, 169; Thomas, 27
ROYNER, Joseph, 9; Mary, 9
RUDDEL, John, 149
RUDYARD, Thomas, 84
RUSSEL, Edward, 78
RUSSELL, Dinah, 138; Edward, 84, 124, 138, 160, 187; James, 115, 116, 117; Michael, 13, 93, 139

-S-

SAGAR, Thomas, 54, 55, 56
SALKELD, Agnes, 18, 34, 81, 117, 118; John, 13, 18, 34, 68, 78, 79, 80, 81, 100, 109,

117, 118, 134, 149, 177, 186;
Joshua, 11; Joseph, 34;
Thomas, 109, 133, 134;
William, 117, 118
SANDELANDS, David, 51, 58, 131;
James, 9, 24, 25, 36, 37, 38,
42, 51, 52, 58, 72, 79, 124,
157, 158; Jonas, 8, 9, 18, 23,
24, 25, 26, 27, 28, 29, 30,
31, 32, 33, 36, 37, 42, 43,
51, 52, 58, 64, 79, 84, 92,
108, 111, 114, 121, 131, 143,
175; Mary, 9, 18, 23, 24, 26,
27, 29, 30, 31, 33, 37, 42,
51, 64, 79, 92, 108, 143;
Rebecca, 131
SANDERLANDS, James, 45
SANDERS, Paul, 41
SANDLANDS, Jonas, 78
SANDLEANDS, James, 24
SANGOR, John, 39, 40
SARSONS, W., 16
SAUNDERS, George, 165; Henry,
44; Paul, 9, 158; William,
181, 182
SCALL, William, 120
SCARLETT, Eleanor, 123, 124;
Humphrey, 123; John, 123, 124;
Nathaniel, 110; Shadrack, 110
SCOTHORN, R., 129
SCOTT, Samuel, 2, 80, 81, 86;
Thomas, 149
SEAL, Susannah, 65; William, 65
SEATON, Alexander, 101, 102,
103, 124; Michael, 121
SELBY, Joseph, 52
SELESON, Thomas, 151
SELLARS, Samuel, 85; Sarah, 85
SELLER, Hans, 141
SEWER, Francis, 36
SEYMOUR, William, 41
SHAGHNESSY, David, 160, 161
SHANNON, John, 104
SHARDLO, William, 164
SHARDLOW, William, 27, 129,
188, 193
SHARK, William, 84, 98
SHARLO, William, 66
SHARLOW, William, 129
SHARP, James, 78; John, 11;
Joseph, 10, 11, 111; Samuel,
165
SHARPLES, Abraham, 161;
Benjamin, 161; James, 177;
John, 21, 22, 23, 31, 42, 51,
64, 70, 78, 79; Jonas, 43;
Joseph, 161; Lydia, 161;
Nathan, 161
SHARPLESS, John, 79

SHAW, Anthony, 14, 133; Arthur,
38; John, 14; Rebecca, 14;
Samuel, 7
SHEEL, Arthur, 43; Mary, 43
SHEIL, Arthur, 25, 26, 27, 29,
43, 51, 58, 79, 92, 108, 175;
Mary, 25, 26, 27, 29, 43, 51,
58, 79, 92, 108, 175
SHELL, Arthur, 26, 27, 29, 51,
58, 59; Mary, 26, 29, 51, 58,
59
SHELLY, Rodger, 36; Roger, 35,
168
SHIEL, Arthur, 28, 30, 31, 59;
Mary, 28, 30, 31, 59
SHIMP, Christopher, 141
SHIPPEN, Edward, 10, 134, 170,
172; Joseph, 190
SHOEMAKER, Jacob, 110
SHURMOR, Ben, 16
SILL, Thomas, 22
SIMCOCK, Benjamin, 69;
Elizabeth, 12; George, 13, 14,
129; Jacob, 10, 69, 114, 127,
159; John, 2, 12, 16, 19, 27,
34, 66, 69, 82, 84, 98, 107,
114, 132, 159, 188, 193;
Martha, 34
SIMPSON, George, 9, 25, 85,
108, 117, 131, 137, 161; John,
25, 105, 144, 145, 152, 153,
154; Ruth, 25, 85, 137
SISSELL, William, 63
SKEAR, Albert, 120
SKETCHLEY, John, 59, 101
SKETTEL, Amos, 194; Robert, 194
SLOCUM, Susanna, 48
SMEDLEY, George, 12, 39, 101;
Thomas, 63, 97
SMITH, Ann, 6, 24; Daniel, 54,
55, 56, 113; David, 82;
Edward, 5; Eleanor, 122;
Elleanor, 123; Grace, 24, 25;
Jane, 82; John, 6, 13, 54, 55,
56, 96, 122, 135; Jonathon,
30; Mary, 16, 32, 52, 190;
Nicholas, 37; Nicolas, 1;
Ruth, 82; Sam, 150; Sarah, 23,
24; Thomas, 2, 24, 25, 82,
109; William, 4, 5, 16, 74,
76, 122, 123, 131, 151, 177,
194
SMOUT, Edward, 194
SPAKEMAN, Randle, 55, 56, 119,
120
SPEAKMAN, Randle, 187
STAMVIS, Joseph, 144, 153
STAMVIX, John, 152; Joseph,
144, 153
STANDFIELD, Deborah, 95;
Elizabeth, 95; Francis, 95;

Grace, 95; Hannah, 95; James, 95; Mary, 95; Sarah, 95
STANWIX, Joseph, 105
STARR, James, 13, 130, 179; Jeremy, 86; Moses, 13; Rachel, 130
STEEL, James, 116, 134, 135, 179; Samuel, 135
STEPHEN, David, 122, 153, 172
STEPHENSON, Gayen, 10
STEVENSON, Gaein, 13; Gaien, 114; Gayon, 160
STEWART, Martha, 49, 50; Robert, 49, 50
STINSON, John, 186
STOCKING, Francis, 50; John, 50, 51
STOCKLEY, Thomas, 169
STORY, Richard, 34; Thomas, 10
STREET, James, 9, 23, 25, 72, 158
STROUD, George, 167; John, 49
STRUTT, William, 87
STUART, Martha, 151; Robert, 150, 151
SULIVAN, Jeremy, 177
SURMAN, William, 72
SWAFER, James, 147; Joseph, 20
SWAFFER, Elizabeth, 47; Jacob, 22, 23; James, 47; Joseph, 21, 22, 23; Mary, 22, 23; William, 22, 47
SWAIN, William, 13
SWARFER, Ann, 35; James, 110; Joseph, 21
SWEETING, William, 170

-T-

TAGG, John, 134, 152
TALBOT, Hannah, 187; John, 187; Joseph, 187
TALKINTON, John, 37
TALLYWIELER, John Jacob, 113, 114
TANNER, William, 11
TATE, Magnus, 98, 99, 109
TATNALL, Thomas, 5, 180, 188, 190
TAYLOR, Abiah, 41, 128, 176, 187, 188; Abraham, 123; Ann, 40, 41; Anne, 40; Deborah, 187, 188; Elizabeth, 21, 23, 162; Grace, 40, 41; Isaac, 13, 18, 33, 38, 39, 40, 42, 54, 56, 109, 178, 187; Isreal, 135; J., 81; Jacob, 15, 37, 40, 41; James, 149; John, 7, 10, 12, 16, 21, 25, 28, 35, 37, 39, 41, 62, 63, 65, 67, 71, 73, 74, 86, 88, 90, 99, 109, 112, 113, 137, 158, 160, 161, 162, 189, 191; Jonathon, 49; Joseph, 20, 25; Josiah, 151; Martha, 39, 40, 41; Mary, 40, 41, 65, 67, 158; Mordecai, 93; Peter, 16, 21, 23, 115, 116; Philip, 112; Phillip, 40, 41, 67, 73, 74, 134; Samuel, 187, 188; Sarah, 33, 42; William, 67
TEMPLAR, Joseph, 49
TEST, John, 168
THOMAS, Ann, 3, 136; David, 163; Esther, 136; George, 185; Grace, 195; Humphrey, 44; Jacob, 106, 107; James, 38, 74, 76; Jenkin, 154; John, 70, 123, 139, 154, 193, 194; Joseph, 106, 107; Lewis, 184, 185; Martha, 38, 73, 74; Morgan, 115; Oliver, 42, 131; Owen, 32, 136; Peter, 106, 107; Reece, 10, 44; Rees, 73, 74, 168; Reese, 74; Richard, 74, 75, 76, 139, 195; Richard ap, 150; Sarah, 114, 131; Thomas, 155, 164, 170; William, 39, 40, 103, 114, 178
THOMPSON, Alex, 187; Edward, 147, 148; Joseph, 111; Joshua, 97, 99, 130, 131, 191; Margaret, 130, 131; Peter, 184; Ralph, 150; Rebecca, 132; Thomas, 132
THOMSON, Joshua, 140; Rebecca, 106; Richard, 19; Thomas, 106
THREHEARNE, William, 43
TIDMARSH, Hannah, 137; William, 87, 137
TIPPING, Robert, 161
TODD, James, 93, 94
TODHUNTER, John, 85
TOE, John, 126
TOMKINS, John, 24, 25
TOMLINSON, Mary, 23; Samuel, 8, 9, 23
TOMLINTIN, Samuel, 7
TOMPSON, Joshua, 100; Peter, 100
TOPHAM, Christopher, 169
TORTON, Andrew, 119; Hance, 3, 5, 126, 127, 128; Latitia, 126, 127, 128; Letitia, 5
TOVEY, John, 128
TOWNSEND, Joseph, 40, 41, 53
TRANTOR, Richard, 161
TRAVERS, Henry, 179
TREGO, James, 1, 2, 57; Peter, 93; William, 12, 39, 69, 101
TREGOE, Peter, 148
TREGOES, William, 141

TREHEARN, Catherine, 92, 176;
  William, 48, 79, 92, 175, 176
TREHERN, Adam, 170; Catherine,
  108, 118; William, 29, 108,
  118
TREHORN, William, 29
TREMBLE, Henry, 164
TRENER, Solomon, 43
TRENT, James, 44
TREVELLER, James, 175; Richard,
  120
TREVILLE, James, 139; Richard,
  138, 139, 174, 193
TREVILLER, James, 193
TRIMBLE, Margery, 133; William,
  133
TROKE, John, 37
TUNES, Anthony, 113, 114
TURNER, Charles, 48; Dorothy,
  21, 23; John, 39, 69, 148;
  Joseph, 105, 144, 145, 152,
  153, 154; Robert, 3, 148, 186;
  Samuel, 54, 105; William, 37,
  109, 133, 134
TYLER, Esther, 7, 8; John, 7, 8

-U-
UNDERWOOD, Samuel, 190
URIN, Andrew, 3, 82, 111; Hans,
  29, 30, 190
URINS, Hance, 3; Hans, 4, 190

-V-
VALEER, Bernhardns, 95
VANCULIN, George, 127
VANLEER, Barnard, 100;
  Bernhard, 165, 184
VAUGHAN, John, 117
VAUGHN, John, 108; William,
  157, 177, 178
VERNON, Abraham, 63; Ann, 62,
  148; Ellenor, 110; Hannah,
  113; Isaac, 112, 113; Jacob,
  2, 12, 62, 63, 107, 110, 148;
  Jonathon, 159; Joseph, 2, 21,
  22, 23, 78, 110, 159; Lydia,
  2, 22, 23; Moses, 177; Randel,
  82, 84; Randle, 133; Randolph,
  2, 12; Robert, 110, 112;
  Thomas, 6, 82, 84
VESTALL, William, 103, 133
VON, Margaret, 39, 40

-W-
WACE, John, 73, 74
WADE, Frances, 13, 53, 68;
  John, 13, 14, 37, 38, 53, 68,
  80, 81, 82, 117, 138; Joseph,
  68; Lydia, 30, 35, 36, 45;
  Robert, 35, 36, 45, 53, 92,
  117; Sarah, 117

WAINWRIGHT, Samuel, 125
WALDREN, Edward, 114
WALDRON, Edward, 130
WALER, Daniel, 152
WALKER, Abel, 91; Daniel, 153,
  154; Enoch, 182; Lewis, 91;
  Mary, 126, 153, 154
WALLACE, John, 28
WALLIS, Elston, 44; William, 44
WANTON, Edward, 53, 177, 187;
  John, 53; Joseph, 53; William,
  53
WARD, Thomas, 65; Timothy, 80
WARE, John, 107
WARNER, Isaac, 168; Joseph, 151
WATSON, Joseph, 46, 125;
  Thomas, 56
WAYNER, Francis, 195
WEAVER, Elizabeth, 101;
  Richard, 27, 101, 165
WEBB, Elizabeth, 106; John, 70,
  86; Joseph, 10, 112; Rebecca,
  129, 146; Richard, 14, 48, 56,
  65, 66, 105; William, 10, 14,
  58, 103, 123, 145, 146
WEBSTER, Samuel, 151; Thomas,
  187; William, 107
WELCH, Anne, 131, 132
WELDEN, John, 41
WELDON, Elizabeth, 157; John,
  111, 157, 159, 164; William,
  23
WEST, Edward, 55; Eleanor, 155,
  156; Elizabeth, 155; Joseph,
  155, 156; Rachel, 155, 156;
  Thomas, 155, 156; William, 155
WESTON, Thomas, 72
WHARLEY, Daniel, 160
WHARTON, John, 9, 17, 26, 29,
  31, 43, 79, 93, 135, 138, 160,
  161; Robert, 14
WHITACRE, Edward, 157, 165;
  James, 165, 166
WHITAKER, Charles, 8;
  Elizabeth, 65; Mary, 67;
  Peter, 67, 68; William, 65
WHITE, Catherine, 163; John,
  123; Thomas, 120, 186
WHITES, John, 149
WHITPAIN, Ann, 73; John, 73;
  Mary, 73; Richard, 73, 74;
  Sarah, 73; Zachariah, 73
WHITTAKER, James, 111
WHITTING, Richard, 92, 105,
  139, 148
WICKERSHAM, Thomas, 72;
  William, 84
WIDDALL, Samuel, 91
WIDDOWS, James, 39, 40
WIDLO, Francis, 6
WIKERSHAM, Thomas, 6

WILBOURNE, Edward, 109
WILCOCKSON, George, 117
WILCOX, Barnabas, 147; Esther, 147; Hannah, 147; Joseph, 147; Thomas, 133
WILDY, Elizabeth, 168; Obidiah, 168
WILEY, John, 179; Susannah, 194, 195; William, 194, 195
WILLARD, Elizabeth, 52; George, 52, 148; Joseph, 52
WILLES, William, 49
WILLIAM, David, 92; Edward, 114
WILLIAMS, Daniel, 153, 154; David, 92, 148; Edward, 33, 85, 117, 164; Hugh, 123, 155; John, 179, 183, 184; Joseph, 122, 152, 153, 154, 168, 172; Lewis, 116; Mary, 183; Robert, 162; William, 70
WILLIAMSON, Daniel, 52, 131, 132, 147; John, 131, 132; Mary, 52, 97
WILLIS, Bud, 65; Edward, 112; Esther, 64, 65, 80, 81, 112; John, 19, 64, 65, 80, 81, 112, 177; Thomas, 88, 89
WILLISON, John, 74
WILLS, Ann, 38, 39, 48; Thomas, 38, 39, 48
WILLSON, William, 192
WILMER, James, 76
WILSON, Hannah, 103; John, 102, 103, 170, 184; Thomas, 84
WILY, John, 125, 126; Martha, 125, 126; Rachel, 27; Thomas, 27
WINDLO, Francis, 5, 6, 72, 104
WINKERSHAM, Thomas, 104
WINN, James, 14
WINTON, Mary, 191; William, 191
WOGAN, John, 12
WOOD, George, 77, 78, 184, 185; Hannah, 77; John, 4, 5, 47, 77, 129; Joseph, 129, 176, 177, 190; Nathan, 176; Rebecca, 70, 77; William, 77, 78, 129
WOODIER, George, 25
WOODMANSEE, William, 41
WOODROW, Jane, 153; Simon, 153
WOODWARD, Alice, 131, 132; Deborah, 95; Edward, 48, 58, 84, 131, 159; George, 85; Henry, 187; Joseph, 85; Mary, 177; Richard, 40, 41, 92, 118, 119, 129, 177; Thomas, 177
WOOKIARS, George, 85
WORKMAN, Samuel, 54, 55, 56
WORLEY, Francis, 114, 160; Henry, 31, 35, 36, 78, 117, 118; Mary, 31, 35, 36, 78, 106, 114, 132, 160; Nathan, 67, 80, 82, 109, 138, 139
WORRAL, Benjamin, 191; Elizabeth, 191; John, 95; Jonathon, 191; Joseph, 95; Peter, 95, 100, 184, 191
WORRALL, Elizabeth, 191; Jacob, 178; John, 9, 12, 23, 47, 69, 115, 148, 187; Peter, 70; Thomas, 146
WORRALS, John, 39
WORRILAW, Ann, 71, 72, 96, 97, 110, 112; John, 36, 71, 72, 91, 96, 97, 109, 110, 112; Thomas, 71, 96, 97, 109, 110, 111, 112; Walter, 71, 72, 96, 97, 110, 158
WORSLEY, Daniel, 70
WORTH, Thomas, 70
WORTHINGTON, Daniel, 103
WRIGHT, Jacob, 75, 76, 77; John, 29, 34, 35, 37, 78; Mary, 75, 76, 77
WYNN, Jonathon, 116; Thomas, 116

-Y-

YARD, Benjamin, 1; Mary, 32, 33
YARNALL, Alice, 72, 96, 97; Dorothy, 36, 37, 96, 97, 111, 112; Francis, 106, 107; John, 63, 85, 90, 96, 97, 106, 107, 112; Moses, 106, 107; Nathan, 97, 109, 110; Peter, 71, 72, 96, 97; Phillip, 28, 36, 37, 71, 72, 96, 97, 110, 111, 112, 117; Rachel, 97, 109, 110; Sarah, 112
YEARSLEY, J., 81; John, 73, 74
YEATES, George, 19; Jasper, 19, 35, 36, 60, 104, 143; John, 35, 36
YEATS, Jasper, 143
YEION, Andrew, 30
YOUNG, John, 47; Mary, 47

www.ingramcontent.com/pod-product-compliance
Lightning Source LLC
Chambersburg PA
CBHW051050160426
43193CB00010B/1133

9781585490080